# WAYLON

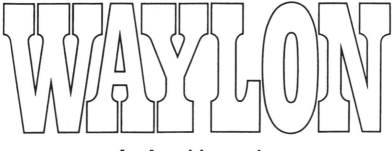

# WAYLON

## An Autobiography

By **Waylon Jennings**

with **Lenny Kaye**

**WARNER BOOKS**

A Time Warner Company

Warner Books, Inc., 1271 Avenue of the Americas, New York, NY 10020

A Time Warner Company

Printed in the United States of America
First Printing: September 1996
10  9  8  7  6  5  4  3  2  1

Library of Congress Cataloging-in-Publication Data

Jennings, Waylon.
    Waylon: an autobiography / Waylon Jennings with Lenny Kaye.
      p.   cm.
    ISBN 0-446-51865-4
    1. Jennings, Waylon. 2. Singers—United States—Biography.
I. Kaye, Lenny.  II. Title.
ML420.J476A3   1996
782.421642'092—dc20
[B]
                                       96-2587
                                        CIP
                                       MN

*Book design by Giorgetta Bell McRee*

# CONTENTS

*For Jessi*
*If you read this book you'll know*
*why I'm blessed to know her*

# ME

HERE'S TO MY LADY, SHE'S MORE THAN A WIFE
SHE'S BEEN MY BEST FRIEND THE BEST YEARS OF MY LIFE
THROUGH THE GOOD AND THE BAD TIMES, SHE'S
   MANAGED TO SEE
A LIGHT IN THE DISTANCE AND THE BEST SIDE OF ME

HERE'S TO MY CHILDREN AND THE LIFE YOU HAVE FOUND
I LEAVE A LOT TO LIVE UP TO AND A LOT TO LIVE DOWN
MY STRENGTH AND MY WEAKNESS—THE TRUTH AND THE
   LIES

HERE'S TO MY COMRADES THE WEAK AND THE STRONG
IT'S TIME WE STOPPED COUNTING THE RIGHTS TO BE
   WRONG
WE'RE EQUALLY GUILTY FOR THE TROUBLE WE'VE HAD
WE BRING OUT IN EACH OTHER THE GOOD AND THE BAD

I'M STILL A DREAMER AND DREAMERS SURVIVE
AND I'LL KEEP CHASING RAINBOWS EACH DAY I'M ALIVE
BELIEVING IN PEOPLE AND KEEPING A LIGHT
FOR WAYFARING STRANGERS AND SHIPS IN THE NIGHT

# WAYLON

# PROLOGUE

*N*ighttime. Highway. I've seen this unraveling dream many times before, endless distance flicking white stripes on a black top. Riding along.

I sit in the shotgun seat, arms folded across my chest like an old Native American, staring out at the exit signs. Norths and souths. Backs and forths. Crisses and crosses. A life in between.

It's like a screen, that big bus window, especially in the dark. You can watch any movie you want, mostly your own, as you roll past the side of the road. We're coming up on Big Daddy Don Garlits's hot rod museum, or the Club Risque, whose motto is "We Bare All." I-75. Must be somewhere outside Ocala, Florida. Could be anywhere.

Let me see that map. Jigger, you know of a Cracker Barrel near here? Maybe we should stop and grab some breakfast when it gets light.

I'm enjoying this. You know how to get it out of somebody. Every time I talk to you, I come up with something else I remember. Some of it's not that pretty, but I'm proud of most of it.

There's a lot to sort out. Put in perspective. I've been there, and here,

1

and wherever I'll be tomorrow. Sometimes I feel like I've gone around twice over. You're talking to a guy who never went to sleep. I've lived a couple of lifelines. Maybe that's why I don't feel tired tonight. We can stay up late. Watch the road. Count off the miles.

You want to get started?

CHAPTER

1

# WEST TEXAS RAIN

The storms boil up out of the west; a red-black cloud taking over the sky, streaming across the New Mexico border into Texas. You can stand there and watch them coming at you, nothing to stop them on the high open plains, seventy, eighty, ninety miles an hour, moving like a dark horse across the flatlands, bringing sand, and dust, and tumbleweeds. Always from the west.

I've seen chickens go to roost at noon, it'd be so dark. The wind howls through those old tar-paper houses, the sand sifting across the road till you can't see where the blacktop begins, and the grit gets in your teeth. Many a time I'd be going home, running down the street, trying to beat the storm, and I'd have to stop and grab hold of a pole to keep from getting blown over.

You look under your window, or beneath the door sill, and there's a pile of sand seeping in, and fine dirt. It covers everything. The sand drifts up against the fences as if it were snow. The wind that blows it circles town from the outside, driving back along Bula Highway, then around to Spade Highway, Littlefield rising out of the whirling dust like a mirage.

"Lonesome," Momma used to call the noise the wind made, and it haunts me to this day. It sounded like the end of time to me. Sometimes I think I make music to shut out the wind, to find a place where the sands can't touch, and the air smells sweet and clear on a spring morning after the rain.

It rained a lot that spring I was born. More than eight inches fell in the two weeks before I arrived, bringing with it hopes of a bumper cotton crop and the toil of replanting. The hail spared Lamb County, though it wreaked havoc north to Dimmitt, east to Plainview, south to Lubbock. There was a shortage of laying hens. We were on the fringes, seven or so miles northeast of Littlefield. On Tuesday morning, June 15, 1937, Momma went up to the main farm house, owned by a Mr. J. W. Bittner Sr., and birthed me. Daddy got to celebrate his first Father's Day that Sunday.

My coming wasn't recorded in the Lamb County *News* or *Leader*. Downtown, where Norma Shearer and Leslie Howard were starring in *Romeo and Juliet* and the society pages were all fussing about the Duchess of Windsor, they paid no notice to what was happening to us subsistence farmers working the fields. Dirt-poor (we had the floor to prove it), we shared a two-room house with my uncles and aunts and cousins. The bed was in the living room, and there was a kitchen. Twelve people; I don't know how we did it.

At least that was a step up from the half-dugout my Uncle Bud lived in, by Hart Camp: a roof over a cellar. Momma and Daddy first got married out there, maybe ten miles from Littlefield, a town that had a school house, a cotton gin, a grocery store, and not much else. Don't blink, or you might miss it.

They'd met at a dance, William Albert Jennings and Lorene Beatrice Shipley. He was a musician in a one-man band, just him playing harmonica and guitar. She couldn't have been more than fourteen, from Love County, Oklahoma. She danced every dance. Momma used to get mad because Daddy didn't know how to dance, and she'd have to hold the harmonica for him in his mouth—they had no holders in those days—and wouldn't get to dance every set.

They got together in 1935 and moved in with Grandpa Jennings. There were sixteen people living in their two rooms, up in a little house on a hill, though, if truth be known, it was more like a bump on the earth. Nobody had any money. They papered the walls with newspaper, pasting it up with flour and water. They did it to stay warm; for insulation, not for looks. It covered up the cracks in the wall.

My daddy was the hardest-working man you ever saw. He did everything at one time or another. He worked in the fields, he ran a creamery, he owned a gas station, he drove a fuel delivery truck. One time he broke his back; he'd been working over in Hobbs, New Mexico, and a piece of lumber fell on him. He got out of the hospital, in a back brace, and immediately went out and pulled cotton. It hurt so bad he had to do it on his knees, but he wanted to get us money for Christmas.

It was never easy for our family, even after Momma and Daddy moved over to the Bittner farm. One time I remember my dad setting in the chair and crying. His head was in his hands. I couldn't have been more than two years old because my brother Tommy was still a babe-in-arms. (I've always had a good memory, even that early, and I can go as far back in time as when I was bouncing in my jumper swing, reaching for my dad's guitar.) Daddy had worked sunup to sundown, and we still didn't have nothing to eat. A dollar a day was what he made.

Yet it wasn't a rare thing when he laughed. He laughed a lot. He'd tease us unmercifully and give us all nicknames. Daddy called me Towhead, because my hair was light colored, or Little Wart. When he smiled, the whole room lit up. Kids trusted him. My daddy could walk up to any child, and they might be bashful and shy and turning away. In a minute they'd be right over cuddling next to him. He was constantly joking.

Daddy finally got himself enough money to buy him a truck. He had a '41 Ford, short bed; a bobtail, they called them. Grandpa Jennings had traded in his span of mules for a tractor and moved out by Morton, west of Littlefield, near Enochs. He had eighty acres; that was about all you could handle in those days. We were doing all right, even if Momma still tells the story of how she had to put me up on the stove while she was cleaning the house to keep the rats from getting me. That's kind of country, isn't it?

Saturday night, we used to sit on the Bittner farm and see the lights of Littlefield off in the distance. We grew cotton and maize on the patch of land we worked. We were farm laborers, not even sharecroppers, and when Daddy got back from a day in the fields, he had to milk about twenty head of cattle. On hog-killing day, we'd get out the ice cream freezer and break open watermelons. Yellow meat watermelons. They'd weigh fifty or sixty pounds, and nothing tasted closer to heaven.

They were originally going to name me *Wayland*: "land by the highway." It's no wonder I've spent my life on the road. Momma wanted to call me *Galen*, and my grandmother had a boyfriend that she was going to marry who had died of some disease, and his name was Wade. Daddy thought I should have the initials W.A., which was traditional for the oldest through the Jennings. The first ones that ever migrated to Texas were William Albert and Miriam.

So it came down to Wayland Arnold. But when a Baptist preacher stopped by to visit Momma, he said, "Oh, I see you've named your son after our wonderful Wayland College in Plainview," so she immediately changed the spelling to Waylon. We were solidly Church of Christ, saved by baptism instead of faith. She never got around to switching it on the birth certificate. I still hate my middle name, and for a while I didn't like Waylon. It sounded so corny and hillbilly, but it's been good to me, and I'm pretty well at peace with it now.

Littlefield is on the cap rock, right at the foot of the Great Plains as they stretch through Denver all the way north to Canada. It's up about four thousand feet, but it's so flat your dog could run off and you could watch him go for three days. They say you can stand in Littlefield and count the people in Levelland, twenty miles away. There's nary a tree anywhere; and the sky surrounds you like a huge blue bowl. At night it's almost like you're being sucked up into the stars.

When you're born in Texas, you think that you are a little bit taller, a little bit smarter, and a little bit tougher than anybody else. It's a country unto itself, it really is. In fact, it was the only place that was a country before it was a state, and the people who live there still feel that way. My wife, Jessi, hit it right on the head when she said "They think the rest of the world is overseas." Of course, she's from Arizona. She knows what it's like being around cowboys.

We could just dream about being cowboys. For us, life on the farms was all we could look forward to. Littlefield is part of the cotton belt, and it sits astraddle the line between dry-land farming on the west side and wet irrigation to the east. We pulled cotton all around Littlefield, getting up at four in the morning to be in the fields before dawn. It would already be so hot and dry that the gnats would be swarming at your eyes, trying to get at the moisture. By the time the day was too hot for them, we'd be halfway down a row, hunched over, dodging the snakes, pulling the bolls and chopping at them, trying to get to the water jar we had waiting at the end of the row. We were able to stand up when the cotton was high, and virtually stooped in half to reach the low.

There's a saying, "He's in high cotton now," which means it's easier to pull. Or to pick it. You don't have to bend over. For low cotton, which is thicker on the bush, you haven't lived till you've bent over all the way down a row, which may be three quarters of a mile to a mile long, and then tried to stand and straighten your back. Or bent over to get that stuff, pulling a crying kid on a sack. My momma pulled bolls; we didn't pick it like they did in East Texas. You'd pull the boll and the cotton off the cotton stalk and then they'd have a cotton gin that would separate the boll and the seed. The boll was green, and when it dried out it would open and be real brittle. It would just cut the shit out of your hands if you didn't wear gloves.

In the late summer and fall, Littlefield would be full of transient laborers from Mexico. You couldn't walk down the street on Saturday afternoon, they'd be so packed. We were working right there alongside of them. They delayed school two weeks at the start of every year to chop cotton and gather in the harvest. In the summer we went barefoot, mostly because we couldn't afford shoes, but every fall till I was fifteen we went out there to get the money to buy our school clothes. I hated the cotton patch.

There's nothing I have ever heard in my life as mournful as the whistle of a steam freight train in the distance when you're kneeling down in a field. It sounds like death. I'd be out in the cotton patch, dragging a sack twelve foot long and half full, putting in dirt clods to bring up the weight, and that lonesome howl would just go plumb through me. That train was on its way out of town and I wasn't on it. I knew that there was a better way somewhere else. I didn't know where, but all I had to do was go looking for it.

The last time I was pulling cotton I was about sixteen. I said, "I didn't plant this shit, and I ain't never gonna pull it up no more." And I quit. I left that sack sitting right there. It may be there to this day, as far as I know.

The Shipleys and the Jennings were complete opposites. My grandpa Jennings wouldn't take a drink or say a cussword if he had to. My dad was that way, too. We couldn't keep dice or even mention the word "sex" in our house.

My grandpa Alfred Blevins Shipley was a hard-working man and could get drunker than ole Cooter Brown. It was not a sickness with him. It was just something he liked to do, but not until there was plenty of food in the house. He was a strong man, a good provider and protector of his clan. He was the boss 'til the day he died. In a lot of ways I'm like him. I wanted to be. He may have been where I learned to cuss—he was good at it—but I couldn't get into the snuff dipping. He was good at that too.

He drove a truck all his life, bringing fruits and vegetables back and forth from South Texas. I don't know how he ever made any money. He would go down to San Antonio, load up, bring it back to Littlefield, give half of it away, and sell the rest. Then he would repeat the whole process again. When he started home (four or five hundred miles away), if he had any money left, he would buy some whiskey and get drunk. I'm talking about *drunk*. Stone blind and weaving drunk. Trying to keep it between the lines. (In twenty years, the only accident he had, he went off the road into a ditch.)

There were two kinds of people Grandpa didn't trust, a preacher and a cop. He'd say "They both think they're sanctified in everything they do." It's no wonder he was always arguing with Grandma. Grandma, Dessie Bell Shipley, was a Jehovah's Witness, and I swear Grandpa would study the Bible just to tell her how wrong she was about it, and nothing made him madder than catching her on a street corner selling the *Watchtower*. They fought most of their lives and I never heard them say much good to each other. But that was between them, and no one else had better join in.

The Shipley line had come to Texas through my great-grandfather, who was a farmer and a lawman. He rode a horse all the way from Tennessee and had a handlebar mustache. He wound up in Hart Camp after being a constable in Leon, Oklahoma, and a sheriff in Marietta. Along the way, a lot of Indian blood mixed in. My grandmother Dessie Bell's maiden name was West, and her father had been a cotton farmer. He never worked a day in his life. His six boys did most of the hard labor. He was really a trader, and could make fifty dollars in an afternoon just sitting on a sack of beans. I heard he was part Comanche, and her mother was Cherokee. Full-blood.

She had traveled the Trail of Tears to Fort Smith, Arkansas, where she went to school till they burnt the fort down. My great-grandfather's name was Wily West. He was so skinny that he could go somewhere, sit down, cross his legs, and both feet would lie flat on the floor.

Let me get this right now. If I don't, I could get shot by some relatives. My great-grandfather West married a woman who already had a daughter about twelve years old. He had another child by this woman, whoever she was, which was my grandmother. Now my grandmother had a sister, right? We thought that my grandmother's mother had died, but we found out later that wasn't true. She had run off and left both kids with him. So he married the original daughter, which made my grandmother's sister her stepmother.

Nobody knew this until Grandma Shipley died. Then it came out. On the marriage certificate for Great-grandfather West and Grandma's stepsister, it said her mother was colored. That was the way they referred to Indians in those days. I guess that happened a lot back then, her half-sister becoming her stepmother. Being out in the middle of nowhere will do that to you.

It might've been even more complicated had not Wily West been such a rounder. Great-grandpa West, my grandmother's father, and my grandfather's mother, Delilah Shipley, had known each other when they were young. Supposedly they'd been in love. He called her Lila; she was some piece of work. She was beautiful and carried a gun. They might've been going to get married, but he went off on one of his tears and he took off. When he came back she was gone. She'd married the sheriff of Ardmore, Oklahoma. They never saw each other again until his daughter and her son met and were married.

Years later I took him up to see her in an old folks home in Lubbock. He stayed with her, and I went and did my business and then came and picked him up. On the way back, he was sitting real quiet, staring out the window. All of a sudden he blew his nose and you could see he'd been crying. "When Lila was young, there wasn't a handsomer woman alive," he said. "You never know how things are gonna turn out."

The Jennings were a different breed. Irish and Black Dutch, as far as I could tell, and as God-fearing as they come. They belonged to the Church of Christ; my Dad was as close to being a preacher as he could without being a preacher.

Daddy was truly my hero. He would never punish us kids—me and my three brothers—for something he himself did. Anyway, he could never hurt us. He'd sooner put a foot of quilts over us and beat the hell out of that cover with the belt. His motto was "I'll never whip one of 'em for what I do in front of them, what I do and they know that I do." Like smoking. Or cussing. He'd not even say "dang it." Instead of tobacco, Daddy chewed ice. We just watched what he did and knew we were expected to do the same. He had a quiet strength.

He was built stockily, like his dad. It came natural from his side of the family. All of them were heavy, and big boned. My grandpa Gus weighed close to three hundred pounds, and always wore his belt buckle to the side. I used to think he liked the look of it better over there, but my cousin Wendell Whitfield says it was probably because there was no room for it in front. He also wore a black hat.

The Shipleys were slim. When they gained weight, it went to the face and stomach, just like it does to me. When I gain weight, my face gets real wide even if my legs stay thin.

We had to ride in the back of the truck out to Grandpa Jennings's place, no end gate to it and just a tarp flapping. We'd ride in the back of that truck all day long; they didn't go that fast then. If you fell out of one it wouldn't hardly hurt. You could run and catch up with it, chasing down Route 54 straight as an arrow till it took a right-angle zigzag around Bula High School, near the spot where I first heard Johnny Cash sing "Cry, Cry, Cry," bouncing over a buffalo wallow that we thought deep as a canyon, and out to the Jennings farm.

Grandpa Jennings never let anything bother him. He thought no matter how bad it might look today, it'd probably be all right tomorrow. He'd set and twiddle his thumbs and look off in the distance; he was kind of a homebody. His cotton planting day was June 6, unless it fell on a Sunday. Everybody else had already planted twice; they'd be hailed out and have to go back. Grandpa just waited for his day.

As you'd expect, we ate good there. We'd get up in the morning, always before daylight, and fix big platters of eggs, frying or scrambling them. We'd just scrape off what we wanted. Then there would be bacon, pork chops, sausage, and butter. Homemade butter, that you would churn "frush." I used to do that myself.

Breakfast was the big meal. Lunch was called dinner, and we'd have fried chicken and eat the leftovers after five that night. Grandma Tempe would keep the butterbeans going for at least two days. There's one thing I could never understand about her. After church on Sunday we'd go back to the farm, and she'd put on her old feed-sack dress, grab some poor chicken by the neck, and wring its head off. Now I know it was Sunday dinner, and we all had to eat, but some transformation happened between the hymn and closing prayer and jerking that poor chicken's neck. Grandma Jennings was a stern woman. I can still hear her muttering "nasty nasty nasty" anytime she'd catch us talking about girls. In later years, after I'd have sex, it seemed like someone ought to come up and shake their finger at me, saying "nasty nasty nasty."

Supper wasn't that important, though it was probably the most fun. You'd dip corn bread into sweet milk, and Daddy was always taking peanut butter and putting it in karo syrup, stirring it up. You'd have a little bread with it. Our staples were coffee, bread, and sugar: We would take biscuits and open them up, butter the breads, pour sugar on them, and pour coffee over that. Momma used to make milk chocolate and pour it over crackers. We weren't so much poor as pour.

The depression sure bred some strange things. For greens, we'd eat lamb's-quarter. It was a wild weed that looked a lot like spinach. We used every part of the hog we could. We didn't waste anything. We even made tallow and soap out of the skin. Lye soap, like to take your flesh off.

If you had any left, that is, after they got finished with you in Sunday School. We were staunchly Church of Christ, especially my dad.

Of all the religions I've run into, the Church of Christ has probably got it wronger than anybody. They're self-righteous, narrow-minded, and truly believe they're the only ones going to Heaven. If you don't believe the way we do, they say, you're going to go straight to hellfire and damnation. With a side order of brimstone.

They don't allow women to speak in the church. They think it's a sin if you have music in the church. They say, bring your organ over here. Mr. Organ, would you lead us in prayer? If it leads us in prayer, then it'll be all right. Well, what's the whole building for—the pulpit, the pews, the carpet, the microphones—if not to lead you in prayer? It's people that do the singing.

Once I even gave preaching a shot. Momma wanted one of her boys to be a preacher. I was trying to please, but it was the scaredest I ever was in my life. On Wednesday nights they let you give talks. My mouth was so dry, I thought I was going to pass out. I thought, if I don't do it I'm going to hell, and if I do do it, I'm going to stunt my growth. I knew what I was saying was fear, was instilling terror in people, and when I got up to speak, I was living proof.

Their concept of God was of a Father who told His offspring, "I created you, but I'm not going to be there ever. You're not going to see me or hear my voice, and I'm going to give you a book that is not easy to read at all, it's hard to understand, but you are not to question it. It's a sin to question it. If you don't follow my words, and do everything that book says, even though you're my child and I love you, and I'm your Father, I will throw you into a lake of fire and you will burn eternally and I'll hear you scream for the rest of eternity."

That's what the Church of Christ teaches, and it's not my concept of believing. If God knows yesterday, today, and tomorrow, why would He cause us so much misery in this world? I don't think God would destroy the earth and let Satan live again. Or blame us for the Forbidden Fruit. That's our sacred knowledge, the emotion that we're able to give back to God. It's what makes us human.

I've read the Bible. There are thousands of religions derived from this book, and it seems to me that the inspiration of that book lies in what it says to you, individually and as a person. You should live your life, and your religion, according to that.

Love is one of the truest feelings in the world, and it's based on the attraction a man feels for a woman, not to mention vice versa. The Church of Christ called it lust and said it was a sin. You should only make love for the purposes of procreation. That's bullshit. I've never been able to believe that. I look at Jessi and have to watch myself. I want her every day of my life. And as for playing music . . .

I thought, man, I'm going to hell, 'cause everything they tell me is a big sin is something I like. A lot.

Of course, once outside of church, everybody pretty much went about their own business. Me and some of my friends would go over to where the Holy Rollers met and find the tobacco where they'd thrown it out the window when they'd get saved, and we'd get it and smoke it. A lot of times we'd be there the next morning and find they'd been out there looking for it themselves.

My dad was a good man, and he didn't need the Church of Christ to tell him to do right. He was solid as a rock. He just tried to live the best he could, the way a Christian should, and I never knew him to get really mad. He was a disciplinarian, but he was kindhearted. He'd sooner give you the back of his hand than grab a belt if you pushed the wrong button. I'd be in the back seat fussing with my younger brother Tommy, and he'd say "I'm going to slap the slobbers out of you, boy," and we knew to duck 'cause that hand would be swatting back at us. We'd hit the floor and keep quiet for the rest of the trip.

About the maddest I ever saw him get was one evening when I went to the movies on Sunday afternoon, and we were supposed to go to church that night. It was a double feature, and Wendell and I watched it twice. Walking home, my dad pulled alongside us in the car. "You shain't go to the movies anymore on Sunday" was all he said. Anytime he said "shain't" you could tell he was angry.

I always knew he would protect me. One time I saw something nobody ever gets to see out of their dad. This kid, Billy Stewart, was a little younger than my brother Tommy, and they'd gotten into it. Tommy was maybe ten, and Billy had run home crying. He was a little crybaby anyway. So here comes Strawberry, his older brother, who was about twenty-two years old and a Golden Gloves boxer, a big guy standing at least six foot two. He grabbed my little brother, and Tommy's screaming bloody murder, and Strawberry said he was going to give him a whipping.

My dad was chopping weeds in the garden, about two fences away, with an empty lot in between, and after that stretched the grass and wildflowers of the prairie. Daddy said, "What are you doing with him? You turn that boy loose."

"Well," answered Strawberry, "he hurt my little brother and I'm fixing to kick his little ass."

"No, you're not," Daddy replied in a low, even voice.

"Old man, stay out of this."

Daddy dropped the hoe down, didn't even take it with him, and he climbed over the first fence. He was pale as a sheet. "You touch that boy and I'll break your back."

Strawberry said, "Old man, I make my living fighting. I whip people twice the size of you every night. You better stay away. I'll hurt you if you come over here."

All Daddy would say is "You touch that boy and I'll break your back." He went over the next fence.

"You come here and I'm going to kill you," Strawberry shouted. My dad didn't even slow up. Finally Strawberry looked at him and turned Tommy loose. "Aw, old man, you're crazy," he said, and backed off.

I knew right there what my daddy was all about. I was twelve years old, and I knew he would shield me from harm, would walk through fire if he had to, and that he was a brave man. A hero. He wouldn't let anything stand in the way of him and his child. He never even stopped to think twice; he just kept on going, one foot after the other, telling Strawberry all the time he would break his back. And I believe he would've.

Momma was, and always will be, restless. She has a lot of energy, and like me, that's worked both for and against her in a lot of ways. I feed that urge for going by traveling on the road. Momma gets high-strung and flighty, and sometimes I think she doesn't allow herself to be happy.

I got my determination from her, and maybe my sense of perfection. Momma doesn't bend, and she would always know when I wasn't telling the truth. "You're lying and I can see it written all over your face," she'd say. My cheeks would be turning all sorts of colors.

When I was little, it seemed like we moved every three or four months. Momma had pneumonia once, and we relocated to the Rio Grande valley in South Texas, but Littlefield had a hold on us. We lived at the corner of Austin Avenue and Reed Street, a long shotgun house with no bathroom, and then settled across from the high school on North Lake. By the time I was in grammar school, we were back on Austin, at number 123, in the heart of town, in a twenty-four-by-twenty-four house that my daddy built.

It was the first house we ever owned, and our first inside bathroom. Previously, we had taken our baths in galvanized washtubs. The back bedroom was mine and Tommy's, Daddy and Momma had a room, and we had a living room and a kitchen. That was it, and when years later the family moved to Sixth Street, they just took the house with them and built onto it.

Momma worshipped her boys, and after Tommy and me—quite some time after—along came James D., who was eight years younger, and then Bo, who was born when I was sixteen. His name was Phillip Doyle, but Daddy started calling him Bimbo because of a song Jim Reeves had out at the time, and he was Bo forevermore.

Brothers do work at being as different from each other as possible, and I guess our family was no exception. Tommy's more outgoing than me, at least when we were growing up. He'd talk the wheels off a Volkswagen. He wanted to be an entertainer, and he's a pretty good songwriter; he played bass with me for a while in the sixties. James D. is a lot like my daddy, honest and upfront as the day is long, running a Conoco station diagonally across from where Daddy had his service station for a time; but he was the gripiest kid. Lord, he didn't let any of us off easy. I remember the first time I ever brought my first wife home. Daddy let me use the car, and James D. was just sitting there, pouting. It was a

Saturday night, and as I started out the door, he come right behind me hollering "Dadblame you, and that dadburned girl. It's
because of you we gotta stay home on dadblamed Saturday night
because you want to go somewhere with that dadburned girl." He
followed me all the way to the car, just chewing my ass out. What
a character.

There was a big gap between James and Bo. Me and Tommy
were practically all gone and grown when Bo grew up, so he was
really like an only child.

Littlefield can be a tough town, and I was a grown man before
I left. I guess if you went back with anybody and traced where
they came from, you'd figure out a whole lot about them. I spent
all my early life there, and there's a lot of me still walking those
streets.

Once only inhabited by buffalo herds and Indians, West Texas
was thought "unfit for cultivation" as late as the 1830s. What
would become the town of Littlefield grew from one of the largest
ranches in the world, the XIT, which covered over three million
acres across nine panhandle counties and had been given to the
Chicago financial syndicate that had built the state capitol in
Austin. Texas had more land than cash in those days.

When the XIT spread finally went under at the turn of the
century, the first tract—the southern Yellowhouse Division—was
sold to Major George Washington Littlefield, an Austin banker
and cattleman, who paid two dollars an acre in 1901. The town,
laid out by Arthur P. Duggan, officially opened on July 4, 1913,
and was given a commercial shot in the arm when the Panhandle
and Santa Fe Railroad made it an official station. Today it's the
seat of Lamb County, named after a Lieutenant George A. Lamb,
who was killed at the Battle of San Jacinto, and contains almost
eight thousand persons, about double that of when I was born.

It's never been easy to make a living in Littlefield, and we had
it harder than most. I don't think anybody had anything in reserve for a rainy day. Even the more well-to-do farmers lived from

one harvest to another. When we got up in the morning, all we had was the daily prospect of hitting the cotton patch, or getting in a truck, or going down to the warehouse.

You'd make fifty, sixty cents an hour. That's all the money you had to look forward to. You might be dreaming about going away to some far-off land of opportunity, but you also might be building hen houses for Buck Ross, or doing something for one of the local contractors, Carlisle Russell or Bob Jennings (no relation). You could be working down at the local service station, six weeks there, six weeks across town hauling trash. Next month you might not have anything to go to. You lived for that day, and that day only.

Saturday night was when you let it all out. Whatever little money we had, we put it in a box for groceries and rent, and then took a couple of dollars out for Saturday night. That was the entire life of Littlefield. There was none of this long-range planning, stock markets, investments, retirement benefits. We never put away money for vacations because there wouldn't be any vacations. You never even thought in those terms. My folks needed to get the house paid for, have a car that would run, and try to keep everybody healthy. They were just making it from one Saturday to another.

When you thought success, it was to show people in Littlefield. We didn't know any better. We'd go to the store on Saturday (Sunday was for church only) and put a pair of boots on layaway; buy a jacket or a belt buckle, put it on layaway. A dollar down, a dollar a week, and when you got it all paid off, you'd pick it up. That was the little rewards in life. Get a little carry-out barbecue, a stick of baloney, a few groceries. Next week there would hopefully be work that'd last until the weekend. Nothing beyond that.

We didn't know any better. There's a charm about Littlefield, and there's a lot of things we would laugh about when we were growing up. Most of the time we tried to be happy with what little we had. We never begrudged anyone anything. We had a good time, but we didn't know what was out there.

Home improvements? In those days, a house was just a place to keep you warm and dry. I remember the first time I ever saw linoleum. I thought it was the slickest stuff; we still lived in a place that had a dirt floor.

Sometimes I don't know how those houses would stand up to the changes in weather. It could get above a hundred in the summer and below zero in the winter. It might rain two inches in the morning, and then a sandstorm would blow in the afternoon, and sometimes last for days at a time. In the winter, the wind changed direction; we called them blue northers, and they'd carry blizzards.

In the late summer and fall, we'd have tornadoes. They're the weirdest storms imaginable. If a tornado struck a house, it would look like somebody had taken a fist and crushed it right on top. It always seemed like tornadoes had a thing for cotton gins and trailer parks. Once a tornado hit these caged chicken coops, and they found chickens for miles. The force of those things would put a straw through a telephone pole, all the way through, or an egg through a two-by-four. It would take a tractor and put it on top of a barn. You'd hear that it blew a baby out of a woman's arms, or a woman's arm off and left her standing there. We had six touch down one night, all around the county.

And yet, people loved living there. It's a rough place to be, if you want to know the truth, but if you can survive Littlefield, then you can pretty well handle the rest of the world. I have to go back every once in a while, just to see where I've been and who I am. I don't know why that is. Daddy never wanted to leave there, and Momma's never wanted to leave. People who live there bitch about it all the time, but they don't want to go anywhere else. Home is home no matter where it is.

Littlefield gets in your soul, in your blood, in the same way sand gets in your craw. I think that's part of my sound. All the damn sand I swallowed is in my singing.

Did you ever parch peanuts? I would sit around an old potbellied stove with my dad, putting peanuts in a pan and roasting them a little bit. We'd eat those peanuts listening to the Grand Ole Opry, and when Bill Monroe would sing, Daddy would look at me and grin.

He loved Bill Monroe. He was my dad's favorite singer; I think he liked that high voice. We would park the pickup outside the house and stick some booster cables through the window and attach one end to the truck's battery and the other to the radio. We were able to pull in the Louisiana Hayride, and on Saturday nights the Opry came through loud and clear over WSM.

Daddy never played out much after I was born, but since nobody had televisions or record players, the only entertainment was going over to people's houses and singing to each other. He'd sing "Sweet Betsy from Pike" and "Old Zebra Dunn," and a cowboy song about some old boy who had a girl he was going to wed. He took her out on a cattle drive with him and the Indians attacked and an arrow come and "dashed out her brains." Those were the actual lyrics.

He used a thumb-and-finger plucking style, and I later found out that Jimmie Rodgers and Mother Maybelle Carter did that a lot. My dad taught Momma a few songs, and when I learned to play, me and her would sing together, "Maple on the Hill" and "The Girl in the Blue Velvet Band." She put all her soul into her singing; she could be so moved by it. Whenever she heard Roy Acuff's "Wreck on the Highway," she had to go outside and cry.

I was fascinated with the guitar from when I had to stand on tiptoes to reach the strings. It was Momma who showed me how to shape my first chords. She was real patient, sitting on the couch and humming "Thirty Pieces of Silver," placing my fingers so I could change keys. She liked C and D. I was guitar crazy by then. They had a drive-in theater about a mile behind the house, and one week they had an Ernest Tubb movie. For the next month, I'd sit out with a broomstick behind the cafe my Grandpa Shipley had for a time, listening to the jukebox, trying to get my little squeaky voice down there low enough to sing like Ernest Tubb: "Yes I know I've been untrue / And I've hurt you through and through / Take me back and try me one more time . . ."

The first guitar I ever touched was my uncle Pat's. It was more like a bow and arrow than a guitar, and I tried my damnedest to play that. Next door to us were some boys that moved in from Arkansas: snuff-dipping, guitar-playing, way-back-in-the-hills Arkansawyers. They had a Gibson, and their real names were Rastus and Sambo. There wasn't anything black about them, and they let me bang on their guitar every once in a while. My uncle Jabbo also had one, a Kalamazoo with a hole in it. It had a good tone. That's where I learned to play "Kentucky."

Then Momma pulled cotton and bought me one for five dollars. I guess it was an old Stella. I don't know if it even had a name on it. She bought it from this guy named Weldon Tate. Then we ordered a guitar, a Harmony Patrician, and it came in time for Christmas. Tommy got a mandolin. I had that guitar for years. I even sanded it off one time and put a varnish on it, and ruined it of course. I painted it, and polished it, and put my name on there like Ernest Tubb had on his.

I tried to take a couple of lessons, but the guy I was taking them from spent more time trying to show me how to hold the neck than playing. I just got frustrated with it and wouldn't go back. But I wanted to play so badly I went ahead and learned myself. Daddy had a little song called "Spanish Fandango American Style," and that was the first thing I ever learned to pick. It was so pretty, but it wasn't really a tune. It was more of an exercise. Momma taught me another song I used to practice: "I had a cow / She had a hollow horn / Fed that cow / On green popcorn . . ."

By this time Daddy had set himself up a produce store at the corner of Xit and Third streets. It doubled as a creamery, and he bought and sold dairy products, eggs, and chickens. It was the job of us kids to test the cream for butterfat and candle the eggs. Daddy took cotton sacks and hung them in the back where we'd keep the chickens, and we'd go in there with a light and hold up the eggs. Sometimes you would see a bloody speck, and that was a number two; and number threes were cracked. Number ones didn't have anything wrong with them. All the bakeries in town bought the number twos or number threes, and I always thought of that every time I would eat a doughnut.

Daddy seemed prosperous in that time of our life. Not rich or anything, but he had a little money ahead in the bank. Farmers would pull up and I would go and get the cream out of the car, or grab buckets for the eggs, and while we tested them, the farmers would sit on the porch, or just inside the front door, chewing tobacco and whittling on a piece of wood; we called it the spit-and-whittle bench. Or the Dead Pecker bench.

I drove them old farmers nuts, trying to learn to play the guitar in the back room. I'd sit on an old feed sack, pounding away, and every once in a while one of them would come in the back, snuff rolling down his face, saying "If you're playing that ol' guitar in parts, well, leave my part out. 'Cause you ain't worth a shit. I know that ol' Bob Wills, and he ain't nothing but an old alky-holic. Anybody who plays that ol' guitar they won't never amount to a hill of beans, and you'll just be an old alky-holic."

Alcohol never seemed to be my problem. Daddy didn't drink; he had an ulcerated stomach and the most he would ever do was act like he was swigging out of the bottle. He just never liked the taste of it, and I never have either. It's probably saved my life on more than one occasion. Over on the Shipley side, it was another story. My momma's uncle O. C. West was drunk all the time. I don't ever remember seeing him sober. Once I saw him mixing up grapefruit juice and brake fluid, that's how bad he was. Finally they sent him off to a sanitarium. He came back when they said there was nothing they could do to help him. He wasn't an alcoholic; he was a drunkard, and there is a difference. He got drunk because he liked to, and that's all there was to it.

We kept the produce store till the early fifties, when the bottom fell out of the farmers' market and Daddy went broke. It almost put me off chickens; they really are nasty birds. They'll peck each other's eyes out, given the chance. I hated those damn things, but I hated more to watch Daddy out of work again, smoking Bull Durham and eating beans seven days a week.

When we moved to Austin Street, Momma covered mine and Tommy's room with cowboy wallpaper. We'd sit back with our BB guns and shoot at the cowboys, one by one.

You'd figure growing up in West Texas we'd practically be cowboys ourselves, but most of our six-gun lore came from the movies. I considered us farmers. Texas wasn't the West, and somehow, I didn't even consider New Mexico to be the West. Arizona was the West to me. You just never thought of Littlefield as cowboy country. Flat plains: there was nothing exotic about that.

We'd go down to the Palace Theatre on Saturday afternoons. I was eleven years old, and I had a quarter. One thing I always bought was a box of peanuts, a round box about four inches tall, and along with the peanuts it would also contain a nickel, or a penny, or sometimes even a dime or a quarter. It cost five cents, and I'd go to the movies and that would cost another ten. Later I'd buy a dime toy at Perry's or Ben Franklin's, a puzzle or a G.I. Joe, and that was my Saturday quarter.

When Rex Allen came along, I thought he was such a great singer. I was never real crazy about Roy Rogers's singing at all, but I loved his movies. Gene Autry and Roy were almost like enemies, fighting over who was going to be King of the Cowboys. Tim Holt was the one that always looked weird to me. And the Durango Kid usually had a guest spot featuring Bob Wills and the Texas Playboys. It always impressed me that Tommy Duncan never took the cigarette out of his mouth while he was singing.

In particular, Lash Larue was my favorite. He dressed all in black and carried a bullwhip. Like most of the heroes of the day, he had a horse, Black Diamond, and a sidekick, Fuzzy. His movies, like *Son of Billy the Kid* or *Mark of the Lash*, played downtown quite often, and we'd all go and pretend we were him fanning his revolver and cracking his whip. I even made a whip out of a conveyer belt, and put a shoestring on the end of it. Then you could pop it. I tried to wrap it around Tommy's or Wendell's legs, but they wouldn't let me trip them with it.

Lash came to our town on a guest appearance in the late forties, and I was right in the front row. He was going to do his act on-stage, and they were also going to show some of his movies. The Palace had a small stage, maybe twenty feet wide at most, and he was in the middle of his whip act, guns and all. He missed and whipped the screen, and ripped it.

When the lights came back on and the cartoons started, I went out to the lobby to get a drink of water. There stood Lash Larue. He was having it out with Bill Chesire, who owned the theater, and Truitt Benson, the manager. Lash still had his gun on, was carrying his whip, and had his hat cocked over.

"You're going to pay for the screen," they were telling him.

"I told you the stage was too short," he said. "I told you it was dangerous, even for my assistant. You should've had insurance."

They said, "You're going to pay for it."

Lash looked them straight in the eye. "I got a gun and a whip that says I won't."

I looked around and thought, I'm the only one that ever heard that. I bet God wasn't even listening. From then on, if I was playing cowboys out on the prairie, no matter who I was supposed to be, somewhere in my dialogue I had "I got a gun and a whip that says I won't."

The cowboy movies were in black and white, and so was their notion of good and evil. All my life I was told you were going to Heaven or you were going to hell. There was no middle ground, no in-between. The Church of Christ taught that "straight and narrow is the way and few will be that'll find it." I was getting lost more'n most.

Football, fighting, fucking—the three f's of West Texas, and probably a whole lot more places besides. I was on the football team at junior high, a pretty good kicker and playing in the back-field some. I could go up to the Catholic dances on Bula High-way if I needed to prove how tough I was. And I was also starting to discover girls.

Or maybe they were starting to discover me. These two little girls who lived down the street, the Griffin sisters, said they'd give me some pie if I took my clothes off. They told me to lay down on top of them. I couldn't have been more than five or six years old. From there, it was all downhill. I used to neck all the time with another girl from the neighborhood. We had this junk car and I had her in the back seat, and she had her panties off and everything, but her little brother wouldn't leave us alone.

Mostly we sat around in a clubhouse we had across the alley from my house, a shack in back of this old woman's house, telling dirty jokes and lying about women—the ones we had and the ones we were going to get. We'd make up ghost stories. Most of all, we'd smoke.

It sometimes seemed like we'd smoke anything. Old cigarette butts that we'd pick off the streets and blend together in roll-ups. Grape vines. Cedar bark. You inhale that and it's something you never get over. It'll take the hide off your tongue. We would've smoked a pickle if it wasn't so soggy and hard to light.

Where there's smoke, there usually follows fire. One morning, about seven-thirty, I was sitting around behind a granary with Tommy, smoking away. There was a board up against the wall that had some cotton caught on it. We'd touch it with the tip end of the cigarette and it would smolder. We did that for a while, amusing ourselves, and we thought it had gone out. I left and went up to Grandpa's house in Morton with Daddy. That night we came back and found the granary had burned down. Runny-nosed Johnny White told on us, and the police and fire department came knocking at the door. "Your boys burned the granary down," they said.

"What time did that happen?" asked Daddy.

"Well, it happened at eight o'clock this morning."

Daddy looked relieved. "Eight o'clock this morning those boys were in Morton at their grandpa's with us." Of course, nobody stopped to realize that cotton will smolder for an hour before it catches on fire.

We weren't so lucky with the Hilltop Dairy. It was up on the only high spot in town, more of an incline than a hill, really, on the fringe of the prairie. We set that on fire one time, watching as the brown grass around it charred and curled in wisps of smoke, feeling the heat on our faces.

It seemed like one thing led to another. We broke the lights in the school ballpark with slingshots; we cracked windows inside the school. We scraped teachers' cars with nails; mean kid stuff. Once we broke into this truck that the Curtis Candy Company was using as a storehouse and stole a bunch of candy. We took it back to the clubhouse and ate it. You've never lived till you've tried to chew a month-old marshmallow.

They finally caught up with us, and there was a real possibility they were fixing to send us to reform school. A guy named Skipper Smith was all set to pack us away. I think he was more concerned with us cussing than he was with any of the mischief we'd gotten into. But Houston Hoover, a scoutmaster, spoke up and he said that he'd like to have us down at the youth center one day a week. He knew we had just gotten off on the wrong foot, and that reform school would likely only make us worse.

It was Daddy who really let me off the hook. I might've escaped going to reform school, but I was still depressed. I thought I was the rottenest thing on earth, that I'd ruined their lives and they were never going to care anything more about me.

One day Daddy and I were in the produce store. He had his back to me, working testing cream. I was really down, thinking suicide and everything. I didn't want to live.

"Son," he finally said, not turning around. "I know you feel so bad 'bout what you did. All those things were wrong, but you can only feel bad for so long. You've got to forget it, and put it behind you. I want you to know one thing. You were wrong, but I've done worse."

That's all he said. What a way to let me up. Momma might never cut you any slack, but Daddy was all heart and forgiveness.

School and I were destined not to get along. I never could seem to get much work done during the year, and I think I probably had some learning and comprehending difficulties. I was a terrible student, even though at the end of the year I would work real hard and get the teacher on my side so they would pass me.

They still enjoyed giving me a hard time. I had a tough ol' redhead for a teacher in sixth grade at the primary school. One day I was wearing one of those crinkly shirts that you could see through; they came out about the time they first started dealing with synthetic materials. We didn't have money to eat in school, so we went home for lunch.

I came back late, starting to my seat. "Wait a minute, Waylon," I heard the teacher say. I turned around, and I realized she could see a pack of cigarettes in my pocket.

"What are you doing late?" she asked in a tone of voice that said she already had an inkling.

"I had to go to the store for my uncle," I said.

"And whose cigarettes are those in your pocket?"

"Them's my uncle's cigarettes."

She took the pack out. Four or five were missing. "If you just went to the store and got these for your uncle, how come they're opened?"

"I had to give some to these guys at the store."

"Tell your uncle I've got his cigarettes and come see me. In the meantime," she said, opening her desk drawer to get out a straight-edge paddle, "I'm going to give you about five licks for not getting them back to your uncle."

Hell, five licks wasn't bad. The schools had corporal punishment, and they'd hit you on the butt, right in front of the class, girls, boys, and all. Every teacher had a paddle. Most of them had two or three. Some would have little short skinny paddles, some would have big long ones; some used rulers. Mrs. Crosby, she'd open a drawer and show you all the paddles and say "pick out the one you want." You got to choose the one that beat your butt.

I lasted up to the tenth grade. One day I took a corner shortcut across the grass, when I wasn't supposed to. We had to keep to the sidewalks. The principal came at me with a paddle, and I took it away from him and told him I was going to whip his ass with it. It was a standoff for a couple of hours. Finally the football coach stepped in and talked me out of it.

I came down with yellow jaundice after that and was sick for a couple of weeks. When I was well enough to go back to school, the high school superintendent called me into his office. He was a big fat guy, with an overbearing attitude to match. "Are you going to play football?" he asked.

I shook my head no. He said, "Then why would you want to come back to school?"

There wasn't much thinking over to be done. I imagine he was tired of messing with me. "That's a pretty good question. Maybe you're right." And I quit.

I was sixteen years old.

My dad had one thing to say about my leaving Littlefield High. "If you're smart enough to quit school, you're smart enough to go to work."

In those days, you were either with the gang, or you're with the guy who runs from the gang, or you're a clown. I tried to be a hoodlum, walking around with my collar turned up. I could fight pretty good, which I'm not proud of, but just the same, sometimes you had to. Alvin Holmes used to be the biggest bully, and picked on me. I thought, look how big he is. Why mess with him? One time he came up behind me and made me mad, and I kicked his ass bad. I liked it so well I went and found him twice more that day and whipped him again.

When you drop out of school, you can't really hang out with kids who are going to school. Their parents won't allow that. So you have to hang out with other people who have quit, or people who are older than you, and you get into things you shouldn't even be thinking about.

One guy who quit when I did wound up six months later in reform school. I saw another one about six years ago who had spent thirty of his fifty years in prison. He's since been killed in a robbery attempt.

I had to work, and that probably saved my life. The rest of the guys who quit school usually got in a lot more trouble than I did. Down deep inside, I guess I regretted leaving almost immediately, because one of the first things I did after I got out was buy a dictionary. But Daddy made me work, and when you're tired, you slow down a bit.

He kept me off the streets. I helped out down at the Produce most of the time, and then seemed to get a job just about all over town. I didn't last too long anywhere, usually enough to know I wasn't good at any of them.

I was probably more like a mule than a horse. There was something about mules that I liked. They're strong—I could lift a hundred-pound sack of feed down at the Produce—and hard-working, but they're stubborn sonofabitches. If a job was too big or wrong for them, they'd know it. A horse would pull till it injured itself, but a mule wouldn't do that.

All my work had dead end written over it. I'd be standing on the back of a cotton stripper, which is the last thing they do before they plow the stalks under. You put a mask on, and goggles, and you use pitchforks to pitch it back, and the other guy would be trompin' the cotton. If that pitchfork slipped out of your hand, he's a goner. You can't breathe and those cotton fibers get up your nose, and the clods and rocks come shooting out of the chute and you have to watch it or else you get your ear chopped off. We'd do that all day long.

I stocked shelves at a dry goods store. I was a projectionist at the Mexican movie theater, and I'd always get the reels mixed up. I unloaded trucks at the Piggly Wiggly's. I ran an air hammer at a paint-and-body shop. Once I got a job at a service station. I went to work about six, and this guy came in and wanted his oil changed. I drained all the oil, and replaced it with transmission fluid. I looked around, realized what I'd done, and just went home. I did that a lot.

In truth, there wasn't much else to do. Littlefield didn't want kids congregating for fear they'd get into trouble. It had the opposite effect. With nothing to keep us busy, we just roamed the area, looking for ways to get our kicks.

We used to lean on car fenders in town, smoking cigarettes and talking. We'd wear white shirts with the sleeves rolled up, and we'd also roll the legs of our Levis, which we bought long, to show off our boots. We'd push our pants down real far, so they'd pop in the back when we walked. They'd hang so low it looked like eighteen families moved out of the ass end of them. We'd pull our cowboy hats over our eyes, click the metal taps on our boot heels to create sparks, and the most exciting thing was to walk across the street till some car would come by. You'd whack the side of it. Real hard. And then act like they hit you.

Oh, we were cutting up. When I was old enough to drive, we'd drag Main, cruisin' bumper to bumper, a set route moving from the railroad station up to the municipal building where we'd turn and head back the other way. Put two dollars in the tank and you could entertain yourself all night. I had a '47 Chevy with the high-torque engine and a vacuum shift. Anytime you mashed the gas the windshield wipers would stop. I lowered the back and put skirts on it, but I dropped it so bad the front main couldn't get any oil and it kept throwing rods. You worked on those cars more than you drove them.

Sometimes it got a little crazy. Out on 54 there'd be drag races, and every once in a while someone would miss the curve at Bula and get killed. With the cars we had, eighty miles an hour was unbelievable, out of control. We'd bait the cops, and they'd chase us through the back roads and cornfields. It was almost like a game.

A lot of people kept fighting roosters; that used to be a big sport. And violence never seemed to be far away from the front page of the newspaper. I remember once some guy thought his wife was fooling around on him, and he hid in the trunk of their car. She had a rendezvous outside of town, and he got out of the trunk and shot them both, her and her lover, five rounds worth. He got off.

I was too busy trying to hold down a job to get in more than your basic trouble. I was no stranger to work; I'd been working pretty regularly, after school and on weekends, from the time I was ten years old. In fact, it probably was easier for me to know how to work than to play. I had a hard time learning to have fun, and it only got worse as I got older. Sometimes it seemed like all I had ever done was work.

That was probably why I took to the guitar so single-mindedly when I had the chance. It was a way out. We couldn't afford lessons, but I wasn't about to let that stop me. I almost never let the instrument out of my hands. When I got home, I'd walk in the house, say hello, sit down, and start picking at the guitar. My brother James D. recalls that I could be looking right straight at him and never know he was in the room. I'd just be banging away, singing a song I might've heard on the radio, lost in my own world.

I was expelled from music class in high school for "lack of musical ability." If they wanted a B flat, they'd just hand me a B and I'd flatten it. I never learned to read music.

But I couldn't think of anything else other than to be a musician. I took my guitar everywhere I went, and hung onto it for dear life. I'd play with anybody I could. My dad was the only musician I knew on the Jennings side, though the Shipleys could boast my great-grandmother Nora West—grandma's half-sister—who played harmonica and a little piano and accordion. She liked to huff and puff "Freight Train" on the harmonica, complete with chugging train noises, and sing old folk hand-me-down ballads.

*Oh shut your mouth you little bird you*
*Don't you tell no tales on me*
*And your cage shall be lined in the finest of gold*
*Hung high in the green willow tree, oh tree*
*Hung high in the green willow tree*

When relatives would come to town, I showed up with my guitar and sang for as long as they'd listen to me. I had a good ear, and sometimes, even after hearing a song only once, I could give it a whirl.

Country music was looked down upon when I was growing up. It was the music of the "have-nots." We may have had patched clothes and we weren't invited to the right parties, but still, sitting around the potbellied stove listening to the Opry, we had a kinship with the performers. I felt chills all over me the first time I heard Hank Williams sing "Lost Highway." I would stay up late on Saturday night listening for him, happy if I could just hear him speak. I always wanted to be a singer, but he etched it in stone. I even had a premonition of him dying. I was in a drugstore downtown, and I put on "I'll Never Get Out of This World Alive." I thought, wouldn't it be weird if he died with that record out; and he did. It tore me up terribly when I heard the news. It was like my world had ended.

I played what I heard. We listened to Chet Atkins and Hank Snow; we took pride in the fact that Ernest Tubb came from Guthrie, Texas, down by Fort Worth, even though that seemed an eternity away. He was Texas through and through, and Momma took an especial shine to him. Daddy was a big Jimmie Rodgers fan; in fact, he loved all bluegrass. I idolized Carl Smith so much I even tried to comb my hair like his.

I had other influences, too. When I would deliver ice across town, in the Flats where the black people lived, I used to stand outside Jaybird's Dew Drop Inn and listen to the rhythm and blues. On Saturday night it was a jumping joint, with crap games, gambling, and bootleg whiskey. Albert "Jaybird" Johnson himself drove around in a baby-blue Cadillac with a continental kit.

Lamb County was dry, but you could head over to Jaybird's and they'd bring alcohol out to the car. Liquor wasn't cheap. A pint of Old Crow would cost you five bucks, and the beer came in a quart bottle for a dollar.

In terms of race, Littlefield was as typically southern as you could get. About the time I was born, you could still go down to the Palace and see a vaudeville show starring the Kentucky Coon Hunters and the South Plains Colored Amateurs with Bozo Bailey, Table Spoon Tommy, Hot Feet Harry, Hair Lipped Harry, Blossoms, and Liza. Less entertainingly, a drunken black man who allegedly killed the local sheriff had to be taken to an undisclosed location to save him from a white lynch mob.

I grew up with "them" in the balcony and "us" down below, the colored fountain and the white fountain. Dunbar School was over "there," literally across the Santa Fe tracks. I never went to an integrated school. Yet I pulled cotton with black people, and I played with the little black kids, and never thought anything about it.

We weren't perfect, and there did come a time when I realized some of the things I had been saying all my life were wrong. Tommy and I had been playing in these trees with our slingshots, only we didn't call them slingshots. Three or four black boys, bigger than we were, came up and asked us, "What you got there?"

Tommy said, "Niggershooters." So they made Tommy climb the biggest tree and made me shoot at him. At least they didn't kill us. But there was really nothing racial about it. It's just how we were taught. I was raised being told that if I don't quit crying, that nigger man over there is going to get you. We didn't know "nigger" was a bad word.

I was the only white boy that was allowed in the Dew Drop Inn. I'd listen to the black musicians play, and you could start to hear how the beat was spilling over into the first glimmerings of rock 'n' roll. There was a guy there who called himself Chuck Berry Jr. He could walk like a spider with his legs over his shoulders, balancing on his hands. He had two gold front teeth, with a four-leaf clover in each, and he was the first person who ever taught me to move all my guitar strings up and put a banjo string on the bottom where the high E is. Then I could push those slinky strings clear up the neck.

I was starting to take my guitar out in public. From family gatherings I'd progressed to the Youth Center. I not only got to perform for the Jaycees and the Lions Club—they didn't pay me, though they'd say "Think of the experience you'll get"—but they taught me how to eat with a fork. I used a spoon at home till I was twelve or thirteen.

It was about then that I won my first talent show. Momma drove me over to Muleshoe thirty miles west. From there, I made the rounds. When I sang "Hey Joe" over Channel 13 television from Lubbock, my whole family trooped out to my aunt Frieda's to catch me. I won a watch, and I was so excited that it wasn't until I brought it home that I realized it wasn't working. It was empty inside, like those dummy watches they put in a shop window. I had to take it all the way back and get the real one.

Without dances to play for, since kids might be tempted to have fun, most of my appearing was done at the Palace Theatre at their Tuesday local talent night. You could win a twenty-five-dollar war bond, and I'd do three or four songs on my own, and then maybe back up a couple of the other performers. Sometimes I played with James Jolley, who was three or four years older than me and actually wrote his own songs. I thought that was pretty unusual. Before I heard his "Apple Blossom Time," I never thought about writing a song.

It didn't matter whether you could carry a tune or not, but folks came from all over the region to show what they could do. I can remember a little girl from Sudan named Terry Sue Lewis, and Terry Vance, a guy from Lubbock that jumped around like we heard Elvis Presley did.

I was also fixing to get married. Maxine Carroll Lawrence lived out by Spade, had won a local beauty contest and was a senior at the high school there. She was a cheerleader, with black hair and blue eyes, and I'd wait for her after the team bus got back from the football game. Or I'd pick her up after I'd spent an afternoon pushing back cotton for Curtis Dyer, all covered with lint, dirt, grass, mud, everything.

You had to drive by the sewer to get to Spade. Ask one of the spit-and-whittle crew how to find it, they'd say "You just go out the Lubbock Highway till you smell shit and turn left." Maxine lived a lot farther out than that, in a little house with her mom, and if you were quiet, you could see the jack rabbits and coyotes passing by. She was a natural beauty, and I loved her black hair, just the opposite color of cotton, and her long eyelashes.

It was a typical West Texas courtship. I didn't have very much money. I'd usually pick her up late, so I wouldn't have to buy her a hamburger. Sometimes we'd go out and get a Coke; she loved Cokes. We'd sit out there at the Chat 'n' Chew, or the Dairy Queen, or the Tastee-Freez, and maybe spring for one of their foot-long hot dogs. "Goin' with," as we used to say. Steady.

Most Saturday nights we'd drive over to a jamboree in the little town of Whiteface, named after the cattle. There used to be a theater there, and they paid me enough for gas. Maxine and I would park on the way back, trying to get out of the way of the steering wheel, off some back road near the county line separating Lamb and Hockley, while the flatlands of Texas receded all around us.

Or we'd go to Ed Taylor's drive-in. It didn't matter what was showing. We were always in the back seat, necking. You just knew this was the night. This had to be the one. I'd try to get her to give-it-up at the drive-in, and we'd usually stop on the way back home, where I'd give-it-another try.

For the first year, all Maxine really gave me was the stone-aches, bad. After I'd drop her off at the house, I'd be doubled over, having to walk spraggle-legged from where I'd kissed her good-night. I couldn't wait to get out of sight. The only way I could relieve myself after one of our hot dates was to jump out of the car, go around the front and grab the bumper, spread out my legs, and strain real hard to lift it off the ground.

We were just kids. We had no idea what we were doing, both Before and After. Even though I'd had plenty of girlfriends, I was dumber about women than anything in the world. My daddy had taught us boys to put our mother on a pedestal, and that she could do no wrong. There was none of this smarting off or talking rough to Momma. Daddy wouldn't put up with it. Consequently, even though my momma may not have been perfect, we thought she was, and every girl in the world was going to be like her.

On Christmas Eve, 1955, I went with Maxine, our moms, and Tommy to the home of the Church of Christ's pastor in Clovis, New Mexico, and got hitched. It was a Saturday night, and it wasn't really considered a wedding. It was more like going to get married.

Maxine thought she was pregnant. I didn't tell Momma, and I don't think she told her mother, but they probably suspected. You could get married without a blood test in New Mexico.

We didn't know anything about birth control. Rubbers and rumors, that was about it. Even if I had a clue, I never had the nerve to go in the drugstore and get them. In Littlefield? Are you kidding me? They kept them behind the counter, so rather than risk embarrassing yourself, you took the chance of ruining everybody's life, including your own. No reflection on Maxine, but I didn't want to get married right then.

I was so young. You can't have a clue at that age about marriage and trying to make a go of it, especially when you're a country boy right off the turnip truck, uneducated and still searching for your place in the world. You start realizing you have to make a living, and worry about raising children. I couldn't figure out how I was going to take care of a wife and baby.

I couldn't even figure out how late she was. I never thought about abandoning her. Hell, I'd already committed the ultimate sin from the way I was raised. We went ahead and got married, and on our wedding night she started her period. That's old country boy luck for you.

Still, there we were, already married, so I was going to make the best of it. The women gathered around and gave her a shower at the home of a Mrs. R. C. Blevins on January 5, and we moved to a small house opposite the high school on North Lake. It was the same place I'd lived as a kid.

We had no idea how to even get along. As far as being helpmates to one another, we'd get in a fight over the stupidest things. I'd think we were going to have Mexican food, and she'd make a hamburger casserole, and it'd hurt both our feelings. For spite, we'd wind up throwing it out and going hungry.

As it was, we could hardly make ends meet. I was working for the Thomas Land Lumber Company, earning forty-five dollars a week. Verle Roberts at the Roberts Lumber Company thought I was a good worker and wanted to hire me. I told him I wouldn't change jobs for less than $48.50 a week take-home, and after some wrangling, he finally gave it to me.

That slavedriver made me earn every bit of it. He was a taskmaster, having me come in early and stay late, picking at me with his high voice, working me to death. One day I was driving the cement truck and I took a corner too damn fast. If you turn quick in a cement truck, it'll *slarsh*, all go to one side, and you're a goner. It rolled over on me, spilling across these people's lawns. That was the last day I worked at the lumber company. I got out of the truck, shut the door, and went home. Once again.

## WEST TEXAS RAIN

*Hello, this is Waylon Jennings coming over the Voice of Lamb County, KVOW, 1490 on your radio dial in Littlefield, bringing you twenty-three reguley, uh, regularily, uh, regularlee scheduled newscasts a day. . . .*

I was on the radio. I might not have been able to pronounce "regularly," but for six hours, from four in the afternoon to ten at night, the airwaves were mine. I had a two-hour country show, and then another two hours of the classics, where I had some more pronunciation problems, and then another two of whatever was left over: Waltz Time, Today's Symphonies, Mantovani.

KVOW specialized in block programming, which meant they played all kinds of music. The whole station was held together with barbed wire and spit, and I'd been working there since I was barely a teenager. By the time 1956 was underway, I was almost an old pro. I'd play the records, announce the ads, and sing songs over the air. A man named Ed Taylor loaned me an old Martin guitar, and I used to take requests from the listeners, even if it sometimes meant I would sing one song to the tune of another.

I couldn't afford to buy a guitar of my own. I'd had an electric guitar, with one pickup and an Alamo amplifier. I hit a big E chord and that thing jumped a foot off the floor. The speakers just busted immediately. I ordered a Kay out of a catalogue, and I thought it would never arrive. I had to sell it after I got married. Keeping a guitar and a wife was way out of my range.

I knew I would be leaving Littlefield soon. It was just a matter of time. I always figured in the back of my mind that people divide themselves in two: the ones who don't know it's out there and those who know there's something somewhere else.

When you live in Littlefield, you're at the center of the world as you're aware of it. You might hear about things, but there's really no way of being sure they exist. You can catch a glimpse in the movies, or listen real hard and hear it on the radio, or sniff it out of the air. The ones who know something's out there and don't go looking for it are the ones who grow old fast. The ones who don't care, well, they're happy staying where they are.

I couldn't be like that. I had to get out. From the time I was a kid, I never considered doing anything but playing music. Everything else was a stepping-stone. I was stubborn enough not to lose sight of what I wanted, and dumb enough not to realize just how long and hard the road was going to stretch for me, and how much I would have to fight for what I believed.

Jimmy Stewart, who still runs his tractor along Hall Avenue when he's not pitching horseshoes, likes to tell me that I never gave up and I never gave in. I didn't have a choice. All I could do was dream, sitting under that big Texas sky. It was like I saw a black cat running across my path and I pulled my handkerchief out and chewed the corner off of it to kill the bad luck. That cat was my lifeline if I stayed in Littlefield, and the handkerchief was my guitar. My singing did the chewing.

I used to love going to the carnival when I was little, especially to see the carousel horses. It wasn't so much riding them around and around, grabbing at the brass ring, that got to me. Rather, it was their look. They were all wild, they were all free, they were all running. Not controlled by anyone or anything. That was what I was drawn to. The motion of freedom.

If I'd stayed in Littlefield, I might have wound up like one of those coyotes they tie to the fence post and let rot, as a warning. Or maybe I would've ended like Ol' Pat, sick and crippled and no teeth. We kids would go to the store for him, or visit him in his little one-room shack; he was real lonely. He let us smoke, and we'd sit and talk to him and keep him company. Ol' Pat didn't want us messing up his bed, so he hammered nails through a board and put it under the bedspread. One day, when I was about nine, I came in and found him. He was the first dead person I'd ever seen.

The empty shells of wooden windmills surround Littlefield like sentinels watching and waiting for a war that's already passed. There was a time they pumped water and caught the wind. Sometimes the taller they stood, the more precarious their hold on the earth, and the more they had to battle that which they were designed to catch. The world's highest windmill was built on the XIT ranch in 1887. Its 132 feet was toppled by the winds in 1926. Only a replica now stands at the corner of Delano and Phelps.

The higher I tried to rise, the more chance I might've had to be blown over.

My hometown hasn't changed much since I was a little boy. Whenever I'm back, I get in the car and start driving around. I'm searching for my youth. Looking for my past. The trees I planted with Tommy are still there; they're grown now, and so am I. Sometimes, if I squint a bit, I think maybe the folks I'm expecting to see are still there too. Around the bend, turning the next corner, about to open the door.

Tater Gilbreath lives over yonder. He and his family can pull a bale and a half of cotton a day. He's my best friend, and in the summer our feet get so tough from running barefoot that grass spurs, goat's heads, and devil's claws can't break our stride. Not a day goes by that we aren't fighting. Tater's momma comes running out of the house with a belt or a switch and starts whipping on us. She wears thick glasses and can't see nothing but two pairs of overalls. If I'm on top and beating Tater, I'll get the worst of it.

Marge Veach, the war bride, she's going to make some cakes and fudge for us after I get back from Brawley's grocery store. Look at Fred Harrell's two Cadillacs, both bedstead green, a '39 with a wheel in the running board and a '47 convertible. Maybe get me one like that someday.

We can stop for a bite at Two Gun's restaurant. He's cross-eyed; one eye goes to Dallas and the other to Fort Worth. Hey, there's Cleve up in the tree, singing for all the world like Roy Rogers. Let's play cowboys and take a pretend shot at him. I know that crazy idiot'll fall plumb to the ground. If he gets hurt we could take him over to Doc Simmons. He's not really a doctor, but hell, Cleve's head is too hard to hurt much anyway.

# WAYLON

You hear about the murders over on Seventh? Killed the man and his wife, left the kids tied up in the bedroom. Or the wedding party where the best man tore down the back roads after the happy couple off on their honeymoon. The newlyweds made a left as the road swerved. The best man didn't. They're still picking up his pieces in the cornfield.

Maybe I'll go see Rae, prancing like a thoroughbred racehorse, or Georgeanne. Try to get them to take a ride up to Blueberry Hill lover's lane. Nasty nasty nasty.

Here comes Wendell and Tommy cutting me off as I'm driving out of town, running over the field and through the alley, trying to catch me. I can't stop now. I'm on my way.

CHAPTER

2

# BUDDYS

"What if," I asked my dad one day somewhere in the early 1950s, "they mixed black music with the white music? Country music and blues?"

"That might be something," Daddy replied, and went back to pulling transmissions.

On a fall morning in 1954, listening to KVOW's *Hillbilly Hit Parade*, I heard that something. I was taking my brother to school. It was about 8:20, and the reason I remember is that the program was only on for fifteen minutes each day, from 8:15 to 8:30 A.M.

Elvis Presley was singing "That's Alright Mama" and "Blue Moon of Kentucky."

The sound went straight up your spine. The way he sang, the singer sounded black, but something about the songs was really country. Maybe it was the flapping of that big doghouse bass, all wood thump, and the slapback echo of the guitars wailin' and

43

frailin' away. It just climbed right through you. I had grown up hearing Bill Monroe sing "Blue Moon of Kentucky," but this was something entirely different.

I thought, what a wild, strange sound. Up at the station, I looked at the yellow Sun label from Memphis as if it were from Mars. I started listening for it. They didn't know what to call Elvis yet on the radio, though they thought of him as a country artist. "That's one of our boys there," they'd say, just to let their listeners know. But nobody was sure of what he was going to mean.

One thing was for certain. When he came to Lubbock in January of 1955, he was billed as the King of Hillbilly Bop. Dave Stone of KDAV had first booked him for an ungodly little amount, a hundred and fifty dollars or something. Fifty dollars apiece for the three of them.

Bill Black, Elvis's bass player, called Dave to set up some details of the date. He was kind of acting as manager then. Now Bill Black sounded black; he had that Memphis drawl, and we hadn't heard many Memphis people. Dave didn't know what he had gotten himself into; he was talking around it, through it, and finally came out with it. "Bill, are you black?"

"Hell, no, we're white," said Bill. That was how it was then, back when black people could write the songs but nobody wanted them to sing them. Which is how Pat Boone got to cover Little Richard's "Tutti Frutti," if you can believe that. In Lubbock, audiences might have been legally integrated, but blacks still sat in the balcony while whites sat in the orchestra.

I didn't get to see Elvis the first time he came through town. I heard about it up in Littlefield, how he performed at the Fair Park Coliseum with Hank Snow and Martha Carson and stole the show in his red britches, orange sport coat, and white buck shoes. How he played the Cotton Club out on Slayton Highway southeast of town and got in a little scrap or something there.

The second time Elvis hit Lubbock, they paid him four thousand dollars. He was part of a package tour that also featured Billy

Walker, Jimmy and Johnny (though Johnny had already been kicked out of the group and was replaced by Wayne Walker), and Tillman Franks, who played bass and managed Jimmy and Johnny. He later worked with the *Louisiana Hayride* and as Johnny Horton's and David Houston's manager.

Usually up-and-coming performers would spread out when they hit a region, trying to earn a little extra traveling expenses and a few additional fans. I booked a show for Billy Walker and Jimmy and Johnny at the Littlefield high school auditorium. They asked me to put up the posters, and they'd give me a percentage. My then-girlfriend Maxine took the tickets. I'd also get to sing on the show.

I had heard there was a talent scout there. Jimmy, of Jimmy and Johnny, was making eyes at Maxine, singing "If you don't want to love me, honey, somebody else will," and trying to make out with her. I never realized that was part of being a singer. Finding the girls. I hated him.

Billy told the longest joke I ever heard in my life. I'm laughing. I'm sitting there with my eyes like dollars. I'm thinking Tillman Franks might be the Mercury Records talent scout.

Right in the middle of my spot, I was singing a Faron Young song, "If You Ain't Lovin' You Ain't Livin'," when my voice went. In the back of my palate, I have a long thing that hangs down like a match stem. Sometimes, if I'm anxious or nervous, it'll touch down to the back of my tongue, or hit my vocal cords, and that'll just take my voice away.

All of a sudden I stopped singing. I thought my life was ruined. I couldn't believe that there was my big chance and I blew it.

I did make thirty-five dollars at the door. And I got to meet Elvis in Lubbock. Even then, he was about the hottest thing to hit West Texas. They invited me backstage, gave me free tickets, and the whole show was there. He and Scotty were standing over by the stage, and Elvis was just jumping around everywhere, bouncing and bubbling over with enthusiasm, full of more energy than anybody I ever saw. He was talking to me like he'd known me a thousand years.

"I'll sing you my next thing I'm going to record," he said. It was "Tweedle Dee," the LaVern Baker song. "My next single," though I don't think he ever recorded it. He did it on the show that night.

I was crazy about Elvis. I loved that churning rhythm on the bottom. He didn't even have drums yet, but the rock 'n' roll part was unmistakable. You'd think it was overnight, but he'd been plugging away a long time. He had a hard way to go, because they were fighting him from every corner in the South, calling him names—white trash bebop nigger stuff; though he could pretty well handle himself. I think he popped a couple of guys on his way up.

On my radio show we'd do some of the rock 'n' roll things: Chuck Berry, Ray Charles, Little Richard. Every time I played a Little Richard record the owner would come all the way back to the station from home. He wouldn't even call. He'd just cuss me, until one night I played two of them in a row and he fired me.

My hero then was Sonny Curtis. He was so far advanced to what I was as a guitar player that I seemed struggling compared to him. His uncles were the Mayfield Brothers, a bluegrass group, and Ed Mayfield had actually been in Bill Monroe's band. Sonny couldn't remember a time when he didn't know how to play guitar. We had met when he used to come to Littlefield to perform at the Palace. I'd do a few songs, he'd do a couple more, and then we'd sing "It's Been a Blue, Blue Day" and collect our ten dollars.

We were all coming out of the woodwork. We'd seen most of us at the small-town talent contests and country music shows in the area, and when KDAV in Lubbock started hosting *Sunday Party*, as early as August 1953, we got to meet each other on a regulee, regularily, uh, regularlee scheduled basis.

KDAV was located in a small shack outside of town, with a big tower rising beside it and 580 KC. painted on the side. On Sunday afternoons at about two all the local teenagers would drive out and park around the station, radios tuned to KDAV, sitting on their cars and watching us play through the station's glass windows. It was kind of a free-for-all.

Everybody had bands, and whoever booked the gigs would mix and match musicians. I had a band with a steel guitar player, Bill Clark. I didn't get as much into the Elvis thing as I did Bill Haley's sound, because of the steel. There was Hope Griffith, who was about fourteen and dressed like a cowgirl, and had appeared on a local television show in Lubbock; I played rhythm guitar in Hope's band, alongside steel guitarist Weldon Myrick, who became one of the best pedal players in Nashville. Later on a singer from Wink, Texas, named Roy Orbison would turn up. Nobody thought Roy had a chance with his high voice.

One night I was in a restaurant in Lubbock over on Avenue Q, with Sonny Curtis and Weldon. We didn't have any money, and I had hitchhiked to Lubbock. Sonny took the only nickel that was among us and put it in the jukebox and pressed Chet Atkins's "Poor People of Paris." Sonny could play in that finger-picking style. I admired him so much, I wanted to change my name to Sonny. I even tried to stand like him.

There was one other musician with us at the restaurant. His name was Charles "Buddy" Holly. He was only a year older than me, but he seemed to have a lot more experience. He had been born in Lubbock, and was half of a group called Buddy and Bob, later expanded to include Larry, and I'd seen him every now and again. He sang mostly country songs with Bob Montgomery, in classic Delmore/Louvin Brothers fashion; but after Elvis came through like a whirlwind, he added Larry Welborn on bass, so he had his Scotty and Bill. Sonny Curtis sometimes joined them on fiddle.

He was a highlight of the *Sunday Party*. He didn't look like the type of guy you'd expect to turn on the crowds, but I always enjoyed him as a performer. He wasn't as impressive a singer in country music. But man, the minute he hit that rock and roll, he was something else.

Buddy called it Western and Bop, which could include everything from the "Annie Had a Baby" rhythm and blues he heard coming out of *Stan's Record Rack* on KWKH in Shreveport, Louisiana, to the country and western that sprouted from the same town on the *Louisiana Hayride*. Much like the western swing of Bob Wills, when rural string band music started colliding with the big band jazz of the early thirties and the Hot Club sound of Django Reinhardt and Stéphane Grappelli, this new breed of country crossed all boundaries. It was called rockabilly, bay-buh.

KDAV was the first full-time country music station in the country, and Pappy Dave Stone, the Man with a Smile in His Voice, ran it along with disc jockey Hi Pockets Duncan. They were kind of a team. Dave was the businessman. He knew how to make money out of these things. Hi Pockets was the guy who came up with ideas. He was a tall, walking encyclopedia of country music, kind of a ladies' man, and his favorite food was chocolate cake with cream gravy. Is that rich enough for you? He had a winning smile, and a brash, self-confident look about him. In those days, disc jockeys were stars. If a singing star came to town, the disc jockey was probably the bigger of the two.

Hi Pockets would do voices on the air, real slapstick country stuff. He'd be Herkimer, or speak high and scratchy like an old woman. His theme song was the "I.H. Boogie," a guitar shuffle that he said stood for "Introducing Hi Pockets." He was a natural-born emcee. For the live shows he would dress up and do comedy. Later, when Buddy, Bob, and Larry got to be so popular that they had their own scheduled slot on the *House Party*, he became their business manager. He was always good for a glad hand and some discreet advice. Hi Pockets would always talk to you where Dave might have been talking down to you.

There was some question whether this new rockabilly was country, but that's a question they're always asking. Though they gave him a hard time at the Grand Ole Opry, KDAV came down on the side of Elvis being country, and even instituted a *Rock 'n' Roll Hit Parade* for a time. For Dave Stone, it was rockabilly with an emphasis on the *billy*. Buddy not only appeared with Elvis at the opening of a Pontiac dealership when he was just starting out in early 1955, but supported him on a package show with Ferlin Husky headlining later that year. Buddy's big break came at a Bill Haley concert in October 1955, at the Fair Park Coliseum, when "Lubbock's own Buddy, Bob, and Larry" were discovered by Eddie Crandall of Decca Records. Rather, Buddy was. Decca was probably looking for their own version of Elvis, who had just been signed by RCA Victor, and Buddy was it, even though they clearly didn't understand rock and roll judging from Buddy's experiences in Nashville. I thought about that in years to come when I made my first records there.

He went to Nashville with Sonny Curtis and a new rhythm section, drummer Jerry Allison and bassist Don Guess; the rest is his story.

In the meantime, I was busier than a three-peckered goat. People have always said that I "attack" work, and I guess I can't help it. I was always doing something. I'd play at a parade or the community center and then go do my radio program before trying to win a trophy in a talent contest. After I got fired from KVOW I went over to KLVT in Levelland, where I had a country show. I'd start making up these little songs about the radio station—jingles set to the tunes of the day. I'd do imitations of Hank Snow, which sounded like Waylon trying to imitate Hank Snow, or John Cash, or George Jones. It was attention-grabbing, and I was noticed by the Corbin family, whose dad, A.G., and two of his sons, Slim and Sky, were about to buy a station in Lubbock, atop the highest, most prestigious building in town: the Great Plains Life. They were pretty tall themselves; each Corbin brother stretched about six feet five inches, and their mom wasn't far behind.

Lubbock was the biggest city in the south plains, the Hub of

the Plains, as they liked to say. KLLL, the station started up by
the Corbins, hit that town like a truckload of geese. They bought
it, hired me, and there we were, shit-on-the-boot cowboys ready
to take on the competition. KDAV had already staked out their
claim; they were country, and we were country. There was nothing left but to go to war.

We started using the station's studio as a production center. I
taught them how to do jingles, and we prided ourselves in being
airtight. In those days, KDAV would be very loose and sloppy.
"Here's Hank Williams," they'd say, and there'd be some dead
space and then the record would start. We'd cue that record right
up to the groove and let it go when we finished talking. KDAV
read all their commercials; we produced them.

We didn't make fun as much as cut up about being country.
We used it as humor. Instead of "Friends and neighbors, y'all,"
we'd say "Hi there, all you friends and neighbors out in radio-
lint."

We did remotes from local grocery stores and meat markets. I'd
sing a little, and talk to the owners, Morris Fruit and Vegetables
at 704 East Broadway, or his competitor, George Sewall. Ten
pounds of flour for forty-nine cents, twenty-five pounds of potatoes for just seventy-nine cents, sausage at three pounds for a dollar, mustard greens at ten cents a bunch; where you can save
yourself a bushel of money, friend, on good vittles. One time I
said, "Come on down to George's Fruit and Vegetables. You can't
beat George's meat." The phones lit up pretty bright after that
one, and those cards and letters kept comin' in.

Nobody knew what to make of us. People went crazy because
of all these "hillbillies" up at the station. The secretaries in the
Great Plains Life Building would walk past on their way to the
restaurant at the end of the hall and they'd stare through the glass
at us. I think they liked what they saw, and we'd be looking back
at them, especially Ray "Slim" Corbin, who was my best friend
for many years. We were wilder than guineas.

Hi Pockets joined us from KDAV, and he became one of the

four main K-triple-L disc jockeys. It was a daytime station, though we used to have a guy who was a holdover with the station, named Mr. Sunshine. An old hypocrite was what he was. He'd be talking sweet to these old ladies and shut-in women on the phone, trying to put the make on them while he was playing some gospel music on the air, and we'd be fixin' to get his ass. He had a disc of "Give the World a Smile Each Day," and it was Mr. Sunshine's theme. We duplicated the sticker and put Jerry Lee Lewis's "Great Balls of Fire" on it. "It's time now for the Sunshine Hour," he said, and turned it loose. *You shake my nerves and you rattle my brain . . ."* He sat there and watched it go around until it played completely through, acting like nothing happened.

I usually was on the radio in the afternoons. They tried me on the morning shift, but that didn't work out too well. I was still living in Littlefield, and I'd oversleep. I'd have to listen to the *sshhhh* of dead air for thirty-three miles as I raced down 84, late again. Once I was coming along and there was a tornado watch out. I was driving a '56 DeSoto convertible, and I had the flap down. Suddenly it got real calm, and I thought, well, I'm out of it. I kicked into gear and was up to seventy miles an hour when all of a sudden the tail end of the tornado whipped that car right off the highway into the grader ditch alongside. The suction just pulled me over and off the road.

No matter how successful I was on the air, being a disc jockey for me was still a stepping-stone. All I ever wanted to be was a singer. I was pretty funny on the air, but I kept writing songs. We had an eight-by-five-foot studio in the station, with a tape machine that could run fifteen ips. That's where I learned to overdub and sing harmony with myself. It was a really good experience for me to get used to recording.

The Cotton Club helped hone my live skills, not to mention my ability to take care of myself. It was a rough joint and earned its reputation as the Bloody Bucket. On a typical Saturday night it was like an orchestrated fistfight, and they used to have to put chicken wire up to protect the band. I don't suppose it was very civilized. Somebody in the crowd would want to hear "Temptation," and if you didn't play it that song or the next, you'd be liable to see a beer bottle sailing through the air. It was a good place to get your chops right, though. You learned to dodge and sing, and never miss a note.

Artists would usually play the Coliseum, and later that night they'd play a dance at the Cotton Club. It could get really drunk and mean. One night Hi Pockets Duncan was promoting a show there, and he saw a guy start beating up his wife. Hi Pockets, being the gentleman that he was, pulled the guy off and hit him, and then the guy and the woman both turned on him. It was that kind of place. Buddy Holly played there a lot before he signed with Decca, and then after, when he started recording the demos that would make him a legend.

Buddy's success gave us all hope. He had traveled the world with his music, appeared at the New York Paramount with Alan Freed and a "Caravan" of teen idols, and was one of the first rock and rollers to write his own songs. Though he may have been inspired by Elvis, he knew that there was an Elvis already. Buddy sounded like himself. His experiences in Nashville, where they tried to change his unique style, had helped to mature him, make him more sure of what he was doing as an artist, and when he took the Crickets, J.I. and Joe B. Mauldin, over to Norman Petty's studio in Clovis, New Mexico, he knew pretty much what he wanted from his music. He was ready for international stardom.

Buddy wrote "That'll Be the Day" after seeing John Wayne use the phrase all the time in *The Searchers*, and he and Jerry had "Peggy Sue" as "Cindy Lou" for a year or two before he recorded it. Guitarist Niki Sullivan, who was the fourth Cricket, never really fit in the group, though during the recording of "Peggy Sue," his essential mission was to flick Buddy's electric guitar pickup switch from the bass to the bright spot for the solo and back again for the rhythm. Buddy couldn't break stride long enough to do it himself.

Mr. Holley, Buddy's dad—Buddy had dropped the "e" for his stage name—was the dearest man, and he was so proud of his son. One day, he came up to the station with Buddy, and we got to renew our acquaintance. I was surprised to see how good Buddy looked. It was like he'd had himself redone; the way I remembered him, he had acne and bad teeth, but now his skin was smooth and he had a gleaming smile. He wore heavy black-rimmed glasses that gave his face a certain weight. He hadn't changed as a personality, though. Buddy was an upper, just a happy person. He would laugh and cut up all the time.

That was probably why he enjoyed being with us. We were a bunch of funny guys, Sky Corbin, Slim Corbin, his old friend Hi Pockets, and me. We laughed all the time, and he laughed all the time, and we were country. He liked that.

Every time he'd come to town, he'd head up to see us at K-triple-L. That was his hangout. We'd lay back in the studio and play guitars, and Buddy would tell us stories. Our eyes would bug out of our heads because he'd been all over the world. He would talk about people like the Everly Brothers and Jerry Lee and Elvis. After, we'd usually stop at the Night Owl, a drive-in hamburger joint on Broadway, looking for girls, cruising around town aimlessly. Actually, we didn't know what we were looking for, and I don't guess we found it. But it was a way for him to unwind from the things he was going through at the time with the Crickets and Norman.

They were falling apart, and it had gotten worse after he married Maria Elena on August 15, 1958. Petty could see Buddy slipping away, and Maria knew that Norman was ripping Buddy off. After all, she worked in the publishing business. On a song like "Oh Boy," the original writers were Bill Tilghman and Sonny West. Buddy cut the song, and after he left, Norman took the singing group he used for backing vocals, had them go "dum diddy dum dum, oh boy," and took a piece of the writing credit. He was really good at that. He took a part of all of Buddy's songs and hardly paid him any performance royalties. He kept a tight control on the Crickets' money.

Buddy had recently moved to New York, which kind of left the Crickets high and dry. Experimenting with strings and newer arrangements, like he did on "I Guess It Doesn't Matter Anymore," didn't help. There's a big distance between Texas and New York, and Buddy wanted to be close to his publishing company and record company. J.I. and Joe B. also didn't like the fact that Buddy was talking about starting a label of his own, and they didn't have a share in it. They were used to getting a third of everything. The new company was to be called Taupe, after the reddish-brown color of the Cadillac that Buddy drove. Its first artist was going to be Waylon Jennings.

"Help me finish this song," Buddy said when he visited the station in December of 1958. Slim and I were back in the station's studio doing jingles—Buddy had cut a few takeoffs on "Peggy Sue" and "Everyday" for K-triple-L promotions—but this was the first time we'd worked on any of his music. We didn't do much, maybe added a line here or there, and we clapped along while Buddy sang "You're the One." It didn't take more than an hour and a half from start to finish. I'm the one double-timing in straight eights.

Buddy had decided he wanted to record me that past summer. He could see how much music meant to me, and maybe he related my yearning desire to himself, growing up in a sun-baked West Texas town with music as an only outlet. On September 10, he'd taken me out to Clovis to do my first session. It was an unnerving experience. Norman made me feel the most unwelcome I've ever felt in my life. He didn't like me to start with, and he didn't want Buddy to get involved in a record company.

"Volare" had been a big hit during the summer for Domenico Modugno, an Italian-language song on top of the American Hit Parade, and that sparked Buddy thinking. He was having King Curtis, the famous R&B sax player who was on the Coasters'

"Yakety Yak," fly down to Clovis to play on a couple of his songs, and he thought it might be a nice idea to use him on the classic "Jole Blon," with me singing in Cajun-French.

We didn't know the lyrics, so I tried to learn them off the Harry Choates original. By the time we finished, you couldn't understand a word. I just sang gibberish, really. Buddy strummed rhythm guitar, and King Curtis called-and-responded around my fractured French. George Atwood and Bo Clark stepped in on bass and drums, playing a syncopated waltz beat. The Crickets didn't want to do it; they were still mad at Buddy. That was the straw that broke the camel's back. Buddy and Norman got into it the night that I was there. They were in another room, and they were arguing bad.

As a producer, Buddy was easy in the studio. He knew what he was doing. He was hardly twenty-two years old, but he sat there and directed the whole thing. I'm not saying he didn't need Petty, especially when he was starting out, though Norman himself has admitted that you can't manufacture talent. Norman could be a genius, and had the time and patience to allow Buddy to follow his own vision. He cut some great records, like Buddy Knox's "Party Doll." That's what convinced Buddy to travel one hundred miles to see him in the first place. If you weren't in a hurry to get married, there was no other reason to be in Clovis except for Petty's studio.

I didn't like Norman, either. Can you imagine a kid scared to death, cutting his first real record? He wouldn't even talk to me. Buddy couldn't be there when it came time to put my vocals and the background harmonies of the Roses on the B side, "When Sin Stops Love Begins," so Norman was the engineer. He treated me like I wasn't alive. I was so insecure and alone. He was real curt. He just didn't want to be doing it. He was still mad about Buddy, and he had me sing the song an octave lower than I needed to. He said it sounded sexier; I could barely get to the notes. It was his way of making Buddy see I wasn't worth shit.

I was musically naive. I had no earthly idea how things were done. I thought you cut a record and you were automatically a hit. I didn't know that studios and producers had that much to do with it. All I knew was that Buddy Holly had befriended me and taken me under his wing.

Still, I couldn't have been more surprised when Buddy walked into the station one day, pitched me an electric bass guitar, and told me "You have two weeks to learn to play that thing." He had taken a three-week tour starting in January 1959, because Norman had his money all tied up, close to a hundred thousand dollars worth that he'd put in some church trust fund. Petty had talked the Crickets into staying with him, and they had officially called it quits, though I think both sides felt kind of bad about it. Buddy was hurt, and mad, but he needed a band. He chose me, guitarist Tommy Allsup, who had come down from Tulsa with western swing influences he'd learned while playing with Bob Wills, and Odessa drummer Carl "Goose" Bunch.

I had never played bass before. I didn't even know till about a week after I was on tour that it was the same as the top four strings of a guitar, only an octave lower. It ruined my whole style of playing when I realized. I had memorized everything from the records.

We got off the plane at Idlewild. I could see Buddy's shadow behind the tinted glass of the terminal. We'd flown all night, and it was just starting to be daylight. He was waiting for us, and I was about to head into New York for the first time. As dawn broke, Buddy drove us to the city in his car.

It took my breath away. The sight of New York as we drove through Brooklyn along the East River was like nothing I'd ever glimpsed before. I'd been as far as Houston, but the tallest building I had ever seen was maybe fifteen stories high. I couldn't believe there was anything so big, or that there was so much of it.

We arrived around the fifteenth of January. The tour wasn't scheduled to start until the twenty-third, so there was time for rehearsal and getting acclimated. Buddy put Tommy and Goose at the Edison Hotel in Times Square, and I stayed at his apartment with him and Maria Elena. I slept on the couch.

He lived right down by Washington Square Park in Greenwich Village. The apartment building was at 11 Fifth Avenue, and it cost him four hundred dollars a month. That was a lot of money in those days.

Maria Elena was a sweet girl, and you could see that Buddy was very much in love with her. On the first night I was there she cooked us beans, and burned them. He whispered, "Don't say a word, just eat 'em." She was a terrible cook. She couldn't boil water, and I'd have to go out and get me something to eat later.

Buddy must have told her all about me. One time she was listening to one of my tapes that was in the apartment, and she said, "Waylons"—that's what she called me—"you could be a pop singer." She didn't speak very good English. "Every time I listen to you sing, it gives me goose bumples." Buddy would crack up laughing when he heard that.

Buddy was the first guy who had confidence in me. Hell, I had as much star quality as an old shoe. But he really liked me and believed in me. He said, "There's no doubt you're going to be a star. I know. The way you sing, there's no limit. You can sing pop, you can sing rock, and you can sing country."

New York looked just like the movies to me. The Reg Owen song "Manhattan Spiritual" was big when I was there, and I could hear it as I walked around those crowded streets, so different than Lubbock's broad, empty avenues. I thought there was nothing but gangsters lurking around, and strange looking people that would as soon jump on you as ignore you if you'd stepped too close to them. Me and Goose walked around for two days in a row looking for the Empire State Building, and we were standing right under it. I'd never looked up. And I remember girls that were so beautiful they'd take your breath away.

Buddy liked to make me marvel. We'd be walking down the street, and I'd see a pretty girl, and I'd say "Goddamn, there goes a good-lookin' woman," and he'd say "That ain't a woman; that's a man dressed up like one." He had me to where I almost bought some blinders because I was afraid to look at any girl, scared she was a boy and I didn't know it.

I couldn't figure how to take the New York attitude. In West Texas, people are always asking "How you doing?" when you go into a store. They seem like they genuinely care about the answer. But New York had me up a tree. I'd go in and buy something, and they wouldn't even say thank you. One time Tommy and I bought some shoes, and I'd had a couple of beers. That's all it took to get me half-loaded. As we started leaving, I asked the clerk, "Ain't you gonna tell us to come back?"

"Come back?" he said. "Hillbilly, there's eight million people in this city, and if I never see you again, it'll be too soon."

Buddy didn't think anything of it. He'd learned the ways of the city. About the second day I was there, we were looking for a cab on Seventh Avenue and it was raining. Buddy said, "Stand over here," and he flagged a cab down. He turned around to say something to me, and this woman who had been hiding between the cars tried to get into his cab. "Get your ass out of there," he told her. "That's not your cab." I started pouting on him, but he said, "You don't understand how to get along in New York."

Eating the food was like being in a foreign country. Buddy, Tommy, and I went into a delicatessen. I had never been in a delicatessen in my life. I'd never seen so many different sandwich meats. Baloney was all I was used to, and they didn't have any, nor ham and cheese. Tommy ordered liverwurst, and I said "I'll have one too." The waitress brought our sandwiches over and I took a bite. It tasted awful. It sat there with one bite out of it.

The waitress came back. She was real gruff. "All right, I know you don't like that. I'm going to give you another sandwich, and I'll just charge you for half." Buddy suggested I get some corned beef. I had never had corned beef either. "Now there," she said, "eat that."

I took a bite and it was worse than the liverwurst. I thought she'd kill me if I left it over, so like any good, red-blooded, macho, bigger-than-life Texas hombre, I did the manly thing. I put it in my pocket.

I was starving to death. The steaks weren't any better. I was a beans-and-potato boy, and in Texas we cook our beef till it stops wriggling on the plate. In Manhattan, you'd order it well done and they'd tell you you were ruining a perfectly good piece of meat. You'd get a hamburger, and half of it was raw. To a Southern boy, that's a sacrilege. I think maybe if those New York people ever saw a side of beef being butchered, they'd never order rare again.

We didn't stay in New York too long, enough for maybe a rehearsal and to buy some clothes. Buddy bought me a jacket and an ascot, along with two or three shirts. Goose and I bought long trenchcoats and hats, just like the gangsters.

We were so friendly, it was easy to forget how big a star Buddy was. But one afternoon we went up to where Irving Feld, who booked the tour, had his General Artists Corporation (GAC) office. Everybody on the tour was supposed to meet there, and Buddy said he'd be back in a minute. He went into the office. I waited out in the lobby.

Dion came in. The secretary introduced me. "Where's Buddy?" he asked, and went looking for him.

The Big Bopper slid through the door. "Where's Buddy? Is Buddy here yet?" I don't think Ritchie Valens was due in for another day. Everybody was looking to find Buddy.

Buddy never asked if they were there at all. That's when I knew how big a star he was. He was the one that everybody wanted to be around.

Right before we left, Buddy recorded a bunch of songs in his apartment. He'd just gotten a new Gibson guitar, and Petty had sold him the tape machine he recorded his biggest hits on. He was always thinking music and trying new ideas. He was musical all the time.

He sang "Peggy Sue Got Married" and "Love Is Strange." He thought the world of Mickey and Sylvia. One of the things he did was a version of Little Richard's "Slippin' and Slidin'." That was supposed to be a Chipmunks-type song. They had just had a hit over Christmas, and Buddy thought those high, squeaky voices were the coolest thing. So he performed it real slow, figuring he could speed it up when he was done. Later on they released that, him singing half-time. They just didn't get it.

*Flash!* We're in a photo booth at Grand Central Station, Buddy and I, smoking cigarettes. He has his glasses on; I'm in my sunglasses and trenchcoat.

I smoked Salems. Buddy was trying to quit smoking, but he liked to bum them off me. "Waylum, you gotta Salem?" he'd ask, and I'd flip him one over.

The Winter Dance Party was about to head out of town. "Stars in Person" read the ads: Buddy Holly and the Crickets (though that upset Buddy, since the Crickets were back in Lubbock), the Big Bopper, Dion and the Belmonts, Ritchie Valens, and Frankie Sardo. In that order.

Opening night was at George Devine's Ballroom in Milwaukee, Wisconsin, on January 23, and the tour would run for twenty-five straight shows to wind up in Springfield, Illinois, on February 15. There wasn't a night off to be had, crisscrossing the upper midwest in a bus in the middle of winter. I know Buddy wouldn't have taken that tour if Norman hadn't tied up his money, but he had to work, and besides, "I Guess It Doesn't Matter Anymore" had stalled in the charts. Maybe it was the plucked strings, or maybe his career needed a quick boost in the here today, gone tomorrow world of Top Forty music. And he was used to playing live; he'd come off an eighty-date Alan Freed tour the year before, as well as traveling overseas. Buddy loved to perform. He'd even done a remote with K-triple-L at Morris Fruit and Vegetable when he'd been home in December! I think he was ready to hit the trail.

We were taking the train at Grand Central to Chicago to meet up with the rest of the troupe, stopping in the photo booth to document the moment. There's one picture where Buddy is giving the finger in front of my face. Looking at the shades-and-cigarette shots, grinning and foreheads touching, even today you can tell that we were happy to be with each other. He was watching over me. We were Buddys.

' All the other musicians but one were hot at that time, having hit records and representing their geographic area of the country. Dion and the Belmonts were from New York, a doo-wop group made good. They were little Bronx neighborhood street toughs, Dion DiMucci and Carlo Mastrangelo and Freddy Milano. The fourth Belmont, Angelo, was in the army. Dion introduced me to pizza and chocolate milk. I still think of Dion every time I smell parmesan cheese.

Ritchie Valens was the youngest, not even eighteen, and he'd come out of the Barrio in East Los Angeles with a Spanish-language rock 'n' roll. I could relate to that, since there was a lot of Mexican music in Buddy's strumming rhythms. The Big Bopper, J. P. Richardson, was a good ol' boy disc jockey from Beaumont, Texas, taking time off from his radio job to go on tour. I could relate to that too.

The "but one" was Frankie Sardo. It was rumored his family had, uh, connections, and he was the worst singer you ever heard in your life. His dad came to see us in Chicago with two big goons on each side of him. Frankie was Italian all the way. He had Tommy Sands-looking hair and wiggle, but it was all movements and no rhythm. He wouldn't have been able to cut a record. He'd sing so far off the beat that it might've been a different song; still, he was the funniest human being you ever heard.

Frankie missed his calling. He could make us roll in the aisles of the bus that carted us around from town to town. He was always on, always going. The night we froze up, stuck by the side of the road, he did a whole routine that had us in tears, talking about Mary and Joseph and Little Jesus, who he kept referring to as the Little Bastard. I always wondered if that had anything to do with the heat on the bus quitting.

The jokes helped take our mind off the wretched conditions we were traveling in. The musicians would be telling stories about other tours they'd been on, about LaVern Baker, who they said was wild as all get out; and Jack Scott, who was supposed to be really jealous of his wife, and when they'd start ribbing him he'd get to thinking about it and stop the bus and catch a plane home. They'd imitate the guy from the Coasters whose lips would flop when he talked: "Hey Bwuuudddy, Bwuuudddy," sounding like an outboard motor.

Fred of the Belmonts was another wild man. He bought a gun along the way. He was so happy with it. We had a black driver and he was always pointing it toward the front. Finally, the driver stopped and came back toward him. "Either you put that gun up or I'm getting off this bus right now. Never point that at me."

"But I love my gun," Freddy protested. "I can't wait till I get home and shoot one of my friends." That was Freddy.

I was just all ears, taking it in, listening to stories until late at night when we'd fall asleep in our seats. It was so cold on the bus that we'd have to wear all our clothes, coats and everything. My feet were constantly frozen.

I couldn't believe how cold it was. I wasn't used to that. When we got to a show, I'd run off the bus, holding my breath because it would freeze my lungs. We'd change in the dressing room, go on, get all sweated up, and then run back to the bus. We tried to hang our wrinkled suits in the aisle, and after a while, it got kind of ripe in there. We smelled like goats.

I didn't mind, though. It was just like the movies to me. When we got to Milwaukee to start the tour, I looked out at the snow, and those houses with the short lawns in front, and it was like the movie "The Best Years of Our Lives." For me, it was. I couldn't believe that I was on a rock-and-roll tour. Not only did we back up Buddy, but we played behind the Big Bopper, Ritchie, and Dion. There were other guys who worked with us, a piano player who kept talking about this girl who was a "bull dagger," maybe a horn player; but we were the house band, and when Buddy was on, we were the only ones accompanying him.

It was a fast-paced show, a dollar in advance or a buck and a quarter at the door. I've seen a series of photos taken at the KWMT *Teen Hop* in the Laramar Ballroom in Fort Dodge, Iowa, on January 30, which shows a clock in the background. By 9:30 Frankie would be on stage; fifteen minutes later, J.P., dressed in a full-length leopard-skin coat that stretched to his knees, hit the spotlight. The Big Bopper had a country show more than anything, which you might expect of someone who wrote "White Lightning" for George Jones. The Belmonts were grouped trio-style around an old Shure microphone when the clock struck four minutes of ten, and they were still there at three minutes past. Ritchie came on next, doing his "Donna" and "La Bamba" hits: 10:10. Buddy would close the show, and we'd play close to an hour, including all his biggest songs and some others, like "Salty Dog Blues" and "Gotta Travel On." That night he had on a red ascot with white polka dots. He's looking over at me. I had a gold one, flashing a big smile.

He held a definite charisma on that stage. The audiences might start off dancing, but by the end they'd be all jammed in front, shouting his name, rockin' and screaming their heads off. It would pump up the adrenaline. You couldn't help but think a part of it was for you. Sometimes I couldn't even hear him. I had the damn bass so loud, he'd keep turning around and saying something and I couldn't make out a word. Finally he'd grab the microphone and yell: "Turn that damn bass down!" I busted both speakers right out of that piggyback amp.

The Goose was the funniest drummer to watch. He had owl glasses just like Buddy, and on the paradiddles in "Peggy Sue," he'd be playing and reaching to push the glasses up his nose, and they'd start sliding down and he'd reach and push them back again and turn the beat around. It would stay around till they'd start sliding, and he'd push them back and we'd be in the pocket once more.

The shows drew great crowds, a thousand or more at each stopover. We'd pull up in the bus and there would be a line for two blocks, waiting in the cold to get in. We wandered back and forth between Wisconsin and Minnesota, Kenosha to Kankato to Eau Claire to Montevideo to St. Paul. Frankie Yankovic's polka band was either just before or after us at the stops; he must have had a similar booking agent. On January 29 and 30, we played two shows in Iowa, in Davenport and Fort Dodge, before heading back to Duluth on the shores of Lake Superior on the last day of January.

It was forty below that night. Making our way through northern Wisconsin, the old Flex bus we were traveling in just quit by the side of the road. Goose's feet froze, and we had to leave him in Hurley at a hospital to thaw out. Ritchie Valens stepped in, playing drums for us that night.

The tour was starting to get to Buddy. He was having trouble with Norman. We stopped somewhere once and he went to a pay phone. That's the one time I saw him really mad. He got back on the bus and was cussing. And I think he was missing Maria. He was really dedicated to her. There was some wildness going on; Dion lost his contact lens in the back of the bus with a girl one morning. Buddy had almost had enough of being true blue. He was about to start looking for a girl. I remember one morning we were both bitching about the local sheriff closing down the whorehouses and gambling places in a wide open town the night before we got there.

We didn't really have time to do much of anything. We'd sit on the bus and sing old bluegrass songs. Dion would just go crazy; he'd almost be crying. We taught him "Be Careful of Stones That You Throw." Mostly they treated us like animals. They sent a road manager out on the road with us, but his job was to make sure GAC got their money. After the original bus froze up, they got us a converted school bus to travel in. They really didn't care.

One morning, Buddy shook me awake. "Do you want to go to England?" he wondered while I got ready for breakfast.

Did I? From West Texas to New York was more than I could imagine, but England?

Buddy started walking around. "Don't tell Tommy," he said, " 'cause he's not going. And don't tell Goose, 'cause he won't be going either. Don't say anything to either one of them.

"I'm going to ask J.I. and Joe B. We're all going to get back together."

I thought, well, what am I going to do? I'm the bass player, and if Joe B. comes back, I'll be out of a job. "We can have some fun," added Buddy, as if he knew what I was thinking. "We'll go over there, and I'm going to have you open the shows." As usual, he was looking out for me; I was his protégé. He told me he would be calling the Crickets in the next couple of days to let them know the good news and work out the details.

That would have been a relief to J.I. and Joe B. Relations between the Crickets, who now included Sonny Curtis, and Norman Petty were wearing thin. As far as Norman was concerned, Sonny was sort of a bastard child. By the beginning of February, the Crickets were trying to reach Buddy on the road by phone, hoping to make peace.

I've often wondered what Buddy saw in me. He really liked me, I could tell. Toward the end I was probably closer to him than anybody. I was green as a gourd. I hadn't been anywhere. As a bass player, I must've been terrible. I was a good harmony singer, but people didn't come to see Buddy for the backing vocals.

He talked to me all the time about music, and I think maybe it was like he was looking in a mirror, reminding himself of the things he had learned along the way. Maybe he could see how hungry I was, and how much I cared about being a singer. "Waylon," he'd say, "you don't ever have to be restricted as a country artist, 'cause you can cut rock records and pop records if you ever want to." He'd tell me about not getting locked in, and developing a style. I learned so damn much from him, about rhythms, and not overstaying your welcome, and not compromising.

Don't ever let them tell you what to do, he'd emphasize. If people ask, say you're pop. That gives you room to move; don't say rock 'n' roll, don't say country. He'd had a dose of Nashville, where they wouldn't let him sing it the way he heard it and wouldn't let him play his own guitar parts. Can't do this, can't do that. Don't ever let people tell you you can't do something, he'd say, and never put limits on yourself. Don't back up.

It was all in the singer and the song. That was it. Buddy would talk about getting a groove and keeping it going. If the music was right, the song will take care of itself. The whole thing is getting the rhythm to where you can feel it. That was the difference between rock 'n' roll, country, and pop.

Years later, I'd be in the studio, and the track would really get in the pocket and feel good, and I'd hear those Nashville producers saying scornfully, "Man, that sounds like a pop hit." And I'd remember Buddy talking to me, telling me they thought he was crazy, as that freezing bus moved down the highway from Green Bay, Wisconsin, to Clear Lake, Iowa.

The Surf Ballroom was packed, fifteen hundred strong. Even though that February 3 was a Monday night, it seemed like half the town's teenagers had turned out to "Rock Around with Ollie Vee."

We opened with "Gotta Travel On," Billy Grammer's Top Ten smash of the past month, and then blazed through "our" hits: "That'll Be the Day," "Maybe Baby," "Rave On." The show had been scheduled to start at eight, and we didn't get off the bus until six that evening. We were so cramped it was almost a relief to get on stage and shake our bodies loose.

The next night we were due in Moorhead, Minnesota, over four hundred miles northwest. We'd be "traveling on" through the night. If we were lucky, and the bus didn't break down again, we might get there by tomorrow afternoon. Buddy was exhausted, and we didn't have a clean shirt among us. He asked me and Tommy if we would like to go with him on a charter flight to fly ahead of the troupe to Minnesota, so we could hopefully get some sleep and do laundry before the next night's show at the Moorhead Armory.

We agreed, and the dance hall manager made the arrangements with Dwyer's Flying Service at the Mason City airport, to fly to Fargo, North Dakota, across the Red River from Moorhead. A young pilot named Roger Peterson signed on for the flight, with take-off time set for after the show, at 12:30 A.M.

In between acts, the Big Bopper came up to me. He was a large man, at least two hundred and fifty pounds, and he could hardly fit, much less sleep, on the seats of the bus. He had been sick with the flu. "Buddy's chartered a plane for you," he told me. "Waylon, would you mind letting me have your seat?"

Heck, I was skinnier'n a rail and could sleep anywhere. I was excited to be on the bus with the other performers. I said sure, "but you have to talk with Buddy. If it's okay with Buddy, it's okay with me."

Across the room, about the same time, Ritchie Valens and Tommy Allsup were flipping a coin to see whether Ritchie might take Tommy's seat on the plane. Tommy called tails and lost.

The next thing I know, Buddy sends me over to get a couple of hot dogs. He's sitting there in a cane-bottomed chair, and he's leaned back against the wall. And he's laughing.

"Ah," he said. "You're not going with me tonight, huh? Did you chicken out?"

I said no, I wasn't scared. The Big Bopper just wanted to go.

"Well," he said, grinning, "I hope your damned bus freezes up again."

I said, "Well, I hope your ol' plane crashes."

That took me a lot of years to get over. I was just a kid, barely twenty-one. I was about halfway superstitious, like all Southern people, scared of the devil and scared of God equally.

I was afraid somebody was going to find out I said that, and blame me. I knew I said that. I remember Buddy laughing and then heading out for the airport after the show. I was certain I caused it.

The next morning was sunshine, and kind of warm. It was a little after ten when we pulled into Moorhead. I had been in the back of the bus sleeping all night long. We were parked in front of the hotel. The tour manager went in and hurried back out. He said, "Waylon, come here. I've got to talk to you."

I knew something was wrong. I didn't know what, except that it was likely to be bad. You could hear it in his voice. I said no; that's just what I said. No.

I turned around to Tommy. "You go."

Tommy went outside and came back a moment later. "Boys," he said, "the guys didn't make it. Their plane crashed."

I was just numb.

Back in Littlefield, my mother thought I was dead. Over the radio they'd announced that "Buddy Holly and his band" had been killed. They had found a bunch of our clothes and Tommy's billfold in the wreckage, and that's what caused all the confusion.

I didn't think to call home. I could see the newspaper headlines across the lobby, something about rock and roll stars, and the word "killed." I wouldn't go over and look at the pictures. I was thinking of Mr. and Mrs. Holley, of how much they loved their son. That's when I thought to ring my folks, and that was the first time they found out I was alive. My brother Tommy had heard the news down at the cafe and had just come through the door all bent over when the phone rang and Maxine answered.

It was just chaos. Buddy hadn't a chance in that plane. They were flying into a front, a blizzard, and the pilot hadn't been checked out on instruments. There were some rumors that the altimeter on the plane was reversed from what they were used to. They thought they were going up when they were going down. They knocked snow off the top of a roof about a mile back. Maybe if they hadn't hit a fence post, they might've landed.

I've often wondered if Buddy wasn't flying that plane. Every time we'd go in a plane in West Texas, the minute we got off the ground, he'd say "Let me take the wheel." That young pilot— who's going to say no to Buddy Holly?

I don't know if it makes any difference. Even with the bad

weather, Buddy wouldn't have hesitated taking that flight. Even if they said it wasn't safe to fly, he might've given the pilot more money to do it. He wasn't afraid.

They found a gun in the wreckage that probably belonged to Ritchie Valens. Years later, they found Buddy's glasses. He could hardly see. If I'd go in his room in the morning and wake him up, he didn't know who it was. He couldn't see that far, to the foot of the bed. And he couldn't see into the future.

I just wanted to go home, but they wouldn't stop the tour. Irving Feld from GAC called us and promised to fly us to Lubbock first-class for the funeral if we would just play that night. He begged me. I said I didn't want to do anything. "Just stay with us until the day before the funeral when we fly you home, and then make up your mind."

That night we played the show in Moorhead. I was trying to get drunk, but I couldn't. The boy that imitated Buddy, Bobby Vee, was on the bill. He'd won a talent show for local performers that afternoon, when they needed artists to fill out the program. The promoters had told us when we got to the Armory that they were grateful we were letting the show go on, thanking us, saying "we know this is so hard for you" and telling us they'd have lost everything if we'd cancelled the night. Then they tried to dock us because Buddy and Ritchie and the Big Bopper hadn't shown up. They tried not to pay us.

The tour manager came out to the bus and told us they were holding up our money. I said, "If they don't give us our money, we'll tear that damn place up to where it will cost them more to fix it than to pay us." He went back and got paid.

The money to fly us home for the funeral never came in, despite all the promises. They just screwed us around, not giving us a dime until after the tour was over, making sure we stayed out there, finishing up the dates. Everybody pointed the finger at everybody else. It's not us, it's GAC. It's not GAC, it's Irving Feld. I couldn't believe people would act so unfeeling. If that was the way things were, I didn't want any part of the business. I thought, I don't ever want to go out in the world when there's people like that.

We stumbled through the rest of the tour. We got lots of telegrams from other performers, like the Teddy Bears and Jimmy Bowen. Frankie Avalon and Jimmy Clanton came in to substitute for the three stars. I thought Clanton was trying to walk off with Buddy's guitar, and I got it back. I was about to whip his ass but Tommy came between us. I was so torn up I would have whipped anyone's ass.

Dion took care of me as best he could. I was out there all alone, lost and scared to death. I had no clue. It seemed to take forever, crawling through Ohio and Iowa and Illinois. In Chicago, we played the Aragon Ballroom, and a girl named Penny took me under her wing. She was the wife of a Chicago disc jockey, and when we got to Springfield, she took me out to see Lincoln's house. She looked so much like JoAnne Campbell, and tried to act like her. Years later, I was out in California, playing at the John Wayne Theatre, and there was a picture of JoAnne on the wall. It got me thinking of Penny. That night we stopped on Santa Monica Boulevard for coffee. This girl across the room was looking at me, and finally she got up and came over.

"You don't remember me, do you?" she asked.

"Yes, I do. I was talking about you this afternoon." It was Penny, and when I looked over at a calendar on the wall, I saw it was February 3.

One of the strangest things that happened was when "Bill Parsons" came on that tour. He had a song out called "All American Boy," which was kind of a takeoff on the Elvis theme—"Get yourself a gui-tar, put it in tune / You'll be a-rockin' and a-rollin' soon"—that ended with the singer going into the army. I was trying to drink a little then; I was all messed up. He was rehearsing, and I was watching him. Finally I said, "That ain't you doing that record." He sounded more like Ernest Tubb.

"No, he's in the army now," replied "Bill." "His name is really

Bobby Bare." Later, Bobby played such a big part in my life, and still does, and that was the first time I'd ever heard of him.

Tommy and I never got along after Buddy died. I think he was jealous of the friendship Buddy and I shared. Dion said, "Waylon should sing," but Tommy immediately sent for this hotshot Elvis-looking guy named Ronnie Smith to take Buddy's place. Buddy hadn't been that crazy about Tommy himself, and I guess Tommy didn't think I had very much to give to the world.

He slipped me the first pill I ever took. We were going home, on our way back to New York. After the last show, I had a beer, and for a joke, Tommy put a couple of Benzedrines in when I wasn't looking. I was awake all the way from Chicago to New York, my mind racing, thinking all these horrible things. The bed started moving and shaking. I didn't know what was wrong with myself or the world. Everything I'd hoped for was gone.

I had no intention of ever playing another note. When we got back to the train station, I put the bass and amplifier in a locker at Grand Central Station, mailed the key to Maria Elena, and walked away.

I'd known very few people who had died, and I was heartsick about missing Buddy's funeral, especially since they'd promised to fly us down and back, and give us what Buddy would have normally gotten if we'd just finish the tour for them. They never gave us half of our money, and screwed us around besides.

It just broke me up. It seemed like, of all the people on the tour, me included, fate picked the best ones and killed them. As I look back, we were the only ones who cared. At GAC, they didn't give a shit. They just wanted somebody out there.

After the tour they called a meeting in Irving Feld's office to see who would continue as the Crickets. Sonny, J.I., Joe B., and their new singer, Earl Sinks—or Earl Henry or Snake Richards; he had several names—had been scheduled to record on February 14 at Bell Sound Studios on West Fifty-fourth Street as the Crickets for Brunswick, and had driven up from Texas. They met the tour as we came in from Chicago.

Irving Feld said "Now, Waylon," and offered the singing job to me, and of course J.I. and Joe B. "We can't have two groups of Crickets."

Maybe he thought I was going to play guitar. I said no. "All I want is my money and to go home. I'm not a Cricket."

He said, "You can be a part of it if you like," and I said, "I don't want to be."

Tommy stayed on, because he was a lead player, and J.I. and Joe B. got Earl to stand in front. They had already cut the record with him. Sonny and Goose were left out in the cold. I guess Goose was used to that. I don't think his feet had unfrozen yet.

Sonny didn't want to do it, either. Everybody had always thought Sonny was the one that would make it, and here Buddy had torn up the world. We used J.I.'s '58 Chevrolet Impala to come home in; Sonny and I, the kid—Ronnie—who Tommy had brought up there, and Goose. It was about sundown when we left town, the last twilight of day shining off the Empire State Building, and as we went out the Lincoln Tunnel toward the New Jersey Turnpike, I looked back at New York and thought, well, I'll never be here again. That's all over. But I was here once.

Sonny and I didn't trust the other two to drive, so we took turns at the wheel. Goose couldn't see, and we didn't know about Ronnie. That boy finally OD'd on glue. He was into drugs really strong, even then.

It was cold, and we were hungry. I think I had about ninety dollars rat-holed, and they gave us enough gas money to get home. We bought popcorn and Cokes and tried to drive as far as we could without stopping.

As we passed through Ohio along Route 22, we looked up and saw what I thought was a town on fire. There was a hotel burning, sitting on a hill. We stopped and stared at it awhile. Things going up in smoke; there was a moral there somewhere.

# BUDDYS

I slept for a while, and then woke as we topped a rise over-
looking Cambridge, Ohio. The antifreeze in the car was only
good to five below, and it must have been at least minus fifteen.
It was so cold we blew a freeze plug, and we coasted into the
town, silent as ghosts. We didn't have enough money between us
to fix the car. The airbags had gone out as well.

We waited until morning and pushed the car to a Chevy dealership. We didn't know what else to do. Finally Sonny walked over
to the manager and asked, "Is anybody a Mason here?" The guy said
he was, and though Sonny had only gotten to the second degree, he
agreed to fix the car for the thirty-five dollars that we could scrape
together. "You're on your way, boys," he said, and we took off.

It was Saturday night. A truck driver gave us some pills to help
us keep going. We were listening to the Grand Ole Opry on the
radio, riding right over the top of it. We were so tired, but we
wouldn't let the other boys drive. To stay awake we got to playing a game. If you could sell yourself right now, how much would
you ask for yourself? I said ninety thousand dollars, because I had
ninety dollars that I was hiding in my pocket. Sonny always
wishes he'd had enough money to buy me then. I sure wasn't feeling I was worth too much at the time.

We finally had to sleep by the time we hit Texas. We told Ronnie we were going to let him drive, but if we looked up and saw
he was going over fifty miles an hour, we'd take him out of the
car and beat the crap out of him. We climbed in the back and
passed out. We were all over each other, flopping around. I woke
up one time and my head was behind his back, and I'd done fallen
down in the seat. When we finally got to Amarillo, we broke out
some of the money and bought Mexican food.

Sonny took me by my mother's house in Littlefield, and he continued on to Lubbock. I got out of the car and went in the door. It
was like somebody who had been through a hurricane and survived it. I had no earthly idea what I was, or what it was all about,
or what had happened. I just knew I was back where I'd started.

CHAPTER
3

## PHOENIX, ARIZE

**M**y whole world was destroyed.

I didn't know what I was going to do. I thought it was all over for me, even though I was the center of attention. Everybody wanted to talk about the crash, and why I gave my seat to the Big Bopper, and what Buddy was like in his final hours; but I didn't have anything to say.

How could I? He was the first person to believe in me. He was my friend. All I could think about was what a good soul he was, and what a happy man. He loved living. He was in love with his wife and in love with his music. He was so young. To this day it doesn't seem fair.

He had all these plans. Instruments don't make music, Buddy liked to say; it's what you do with them. He thought Ray Charles was the greatest, and wanted to use his arranging style, only move the licks over to guitars. It was like the strings on "I Guess It Doesn't Matter Anymore" and "Raining in My Heart." "That guy

74

who put his name on as arranger, all he did is what I do on the guitar," Buddy told me. He made me see that music was personal, and it didn't have anything to do with what people called it. All through my life, there isn't a couple of days that go by that I don't think about him.

Buddy was the biggest thing to ever come out of Lubbock. His folks never got over his loss. It just broke them in two. You'd visit Mr. and Mrs. Holley's house, and it was always 1959, until the day they died. His pictures were on the wall, and everywhere you'd look, there'd be something of Buddy's. They were such sweet people. I'd go over to the house, and they'd show me his shoes, and things they had in the closet. They gave me his guitars one time, but people would try to steal that Stratocaster, so I took them back. Mr. Holley wanted to promote me, because he said Buddy believed in me, but I had enough sense to know that wouldn't be right. He bought me clothes and things like Buddy would. I wrote a song called "Buddy's Song," using all of his titles, and I gave that to them. I also signed over any royalties I might receive from "You're the One." I said, we didn't write any of that; we just finished the one line and Buddy took it and straightened it out.

I went back to work at K-triple-L, but I was useless. All the sparkle had gone out of me. I was supposed to be a wildman disc jockey, though I couldn't turn it on the way I used to. Even if I'd play Buddy's records, I wouldn't say much. I had lost my center of gravity. I wasn't worth shooting.

I didn't want to sing; I didn't want to play guitar. I had no interest in anything. I left my guitar at Momma's house and couldn't even pick it up. I was empty, drained of hope. Maybe I felt a little like my dream had slipped through my fingers. I didn't know that hard work and paying your dues was how you got ahead. I thought people like Buddy could just make it happen, and now I'd blown it.

At the station, Sky and Slim Corbin tried to help me along, but the only one who made any sense was Hi Pockets. He knew what was wrong. He was an older guy, and he understood what I was going through. Hi Pockets could see I was messed up, and that I was feeling guilty, because I was the one who survived.

One day he sat down and talked to me. He spoke for over an hour, saying it wasn't my fault and that I didn't have anything to do with what happened. "What makes you think you're so powerful that you could cause something like that?" he asked. "If you could bring them back here, and make them alive and standing in this room, would you do that?" I said yeah.

He said, "Can you do that?" I shook my head no.

"You couldn't kill them either. You couldn't will them to die. You don't have that ability. Unless you take a gun and shoot them, you can't make them die. And you weren't anywhere near them."

Hi Pockets had to get it down to that level for me to understand. I had to admit he was right. He was kind of an old country philosopher, though he liked playing the fool. Every once in a while he'd hit on something that would just raise the top of my head off, speaking with the simple honesty and wisdom of a man who home-spun records and jockeyed discs, and made me feel that maybe my life could begin again.

I came home. I'd been out working, and I was probably late. Maxine was standing on a chair with a necktie around her neck, tied to a light bulb. As I walked through the door, she jumped.

Of course, the light bulb broke. She collapsed to the floor. Still alive. I don't know what she was trying to prove; I knew she couldn't have been serious. It seemed more like a sick joke. She had a strange temper, and by this time, we both knew we'd never get along.

Maxine and I shouldn't have been married. I hardly knew her, and we were just kids; pretty soon we started having them. I was nineteen when Terry, our oldest, was born on January 21, 1957, and Julie Rae followed a year and a half later on August 12, 1958. Buddy came along on March 21, 1960.

Terry had Maxine's eyes on my face, and he was pure energy, a buzzsaw. If you let him, he'd stay up two or three nights running, always on the move, a bullet tearing from here to there. He was a peacemaker. He needed to be, around Julie. She was the first girl in the Jennings family in generations, and she showed a lot of my temperament, as in Bad Temper. Nobody could tell her what to do. She learned to cuss from her Grandpa Shipley and me when she was about two years old. She was never afraid of anything, and even then she showed she could switch immediately from mad to glad and back again. We used to call her Froggy because she used to swell up when she got angry. Buddy was laid-back and easygoing, and we were worried when he didn't talk for years. He'd jabber, and his brothers and sisters would tell us what he said. Then we realized he didn't have to talk, since they were doing it for him; and he still doesn't unless he has something to say. That's why I always ask him for advice.

We both loved the children, but they were all we had in common. I felt trapped. Each time we thought we were going to get out of the marriage, that we'd had enough of driving each other up a wall, we'd have another child. I didn't see any way out, and it wasn't all her. I was doing my share of messing around, a hotshot disc jockey with a lot of leftover guilt.

I wanted to do the right thing. I was determined to see the family through, even though I was on a downhill slide that kept getting steeper. Things were going from bad to worse. I thought, that was a good try, but it just wasn't meant to be. My hopes had been in one little basket, and even though I went back to life as it had been before Buddy, it wasn't the same. Especially since he was my friend. What if he were my brother? I don't see how you can get blindsided by some of these things fate hands you, and come back from them. It was too sudden. It got to where I just didn't give a shit.

There was a little irresponsibility in me, and I needed more money. They were kind of struggling at K-triple-L. I didn't think they were, though they were. They offered me more money at KDAV. Quite a bit more. I got mad and quit, and went over to the other side. But that didn't work out at all; I didn't fit in over there. I could never be on time, and it was a whole different thing. *Friends and Neighbors* . . .

They were from the old school, and I was a foreigner, in their eyes. And in my own, probably, as well. One in the middle of the night, I left for Arizona.

Maxine's dad got real sick, and we went out there to see him. He lived in Scottsdale, and her sister lived in Coolidge. It was the first time I'd been that far west, and it took hold of me.

You look at the mountains, and you don't know if they're Indian or cowboy. The desert is still and strong. You ain't got a chance. You can't push it back. You just surrender to the surroundings. When I got there, it was like I stopped pushing toward something and just let myself go, floating where the winds would carry me. I felt lonesome.

You gain strength from the environment; you don't try to destroy it. It was like I passed through myself, and all of a sudden I came out of the desert into Phoenix, nestled in the Valley of the Sun, all palm trees and shadows. It was beautiful.

We moved back and forth. I couldn't find a job in Texas. They'd hire me some at K-triple-L every once in a while to work holidays and things like that. I tried Dallas. I couldn't find anything, and went over to Odessa and found a job at KOYL. I had an old '51 Dodge with no left window; I had to put pasteboard over it, like in *The Grapes of Wrath*.

I went to work for a little bit of nothing. Whenever I sent money home, I could choose between breakfast and supper, but I could only eat lunch twice a week. Maxine and the kids were living back in Littlefield. I was trying to get enough money to bring them down and rent a house. As it was, we were having to move every time the rent came due.

I don't doubt Maxine cared about me in those days; but she could turn on the tears when she wanted to. That used to be one of her things when her parents came by, to show them how Maxine could cry. I never knew for sure why. She could just stand there and look at you and start crying. She didn't know what to think when I went off on the road. I'd been there all the time and now I was gone.

I still don't manage money well, but I was worse then. I had to watch every nickel and dime. I was so broke I couldn't buy cigarettes. My old farmer friend Jimmy Stewart had to loan me a quarter once when we were sitting at the Chat 'n' Chew in Littlefield, drinking coffee. I'd spent all my money buying gas to get to Odessa. When I got there, I'd call home person-to-person to let them know I'd arrived okay. We had a code: If I asked for my dad, I'd made it; otherwise, I'd ask for Momma if I needed to talk.

I was having a little better luck in Coolidge, Arizona, where Maxine and I stayed with her sister. There was a guy named Earl Perrin that was buying a bunch of radio stations and tying together what amounted to an Arizona network out of them. In 1960, that was ahead of its time. I was playing at a place called the Galloping Goose with a pair of local boys, Billy Joe Stevens and Claude Henry. I was big-time when they found out I had been with Buddy Holly. I probably made as much as they did, which was fifteen dollars a night.

Radio was the only thing I knew, besides pulling cotton. Earl offered me a job; the station was called KCKY. That's where I met Jim Garshow, who is still one of my dearest and best friends, and a guy I can always depend on. Our big saying was "I'll do the thinking around here," because we remembered all those Western movies where the villain tells that to his henchmen. That's me and Jim, only we can never decide which is who.

He was working at the radio station in Coolidge, and we didn't like each other at all when I went there. Another guy was stirring it up, telling Jim I was out to grab their jobs, get them fired, and take over. Jim finally walked up to me and said, "I just don't like you."

I said, "Well, I couldn't care less. Now how about that. I really don't like your ass either." So we set there and faced off, and seeing that we weren't afraid of each other, after a while we started enjoying being together.

He was hooked up with Tom Haley, who had hired Jim to make a short radio-type show, complete with commercials, to play in the fifteen to twenty minutes between feature movies at drive-in theaters. *Hello, everyone, this is Jim Garshow and welcome to intermission time at the Dove Creek, Colorado, Drive-In Theater: enjoy the stars, out under the stars. Intermission time is brought to you by Singin' Sam's Diner, where you get beans with everything.* Dove Creek was the pinto bean capital of the world, and Sam always seemed to own some business somewhere. Sam's Cleaners. Sam's Hardware.

When Tom was sober, he was one of the dearest, most giving people. But he was awful when he was drunk. He was mean to everybody. He was like a Jekyll and Hyde. If he got drunk, and you didn't do what he liked, he'd call you a star-acting sonofabitch. He was the guy who made me hate the word "star."

Despite this, Tom was wanting to make a star out of me. My record of "Jole Blon" had come out on Brunswick in March of 1959, but nothing happened with it. I think I heard it one time on a car radio, over some distant station. If Buddy had been alive, it might probably have had a chance, but that was over and done.

Right before I left Lubbock, I had recorded four songs for a company named Trend. They released only one single, "My Baby Walks All Over Me," backed with a song written with Bill Tilghman—a recitation, actually—called "The Stage," which I had started writing on February 3, 1961, not realizing that was the date till the song was done. It was originally titled "Stars in Heaven" and described a "show" up there: "The angels stand in silence as Buddy sings / His voice is clear, his guitar rings . . ." Pretty corny. It didn't help that they took the tape and speeded it up to where I would sound younger.

In those days, you needed a teenage sound. I never cared for that. I had no desire to be a teen idol. Frankie Avalon or Fabian— I couldn't understand their appeal. I liked clever writing, like

Chuck Berry's "Sweet Sixteen," but "Venus" or "Turn Me Loose" never moved me. I was more into "C.C. Rider"; the blues thing.

I listened to rockabilly, the country-edged Sun Records of Carl Perkins, Roy Orbison, Bill Justis, Johnny Cash. Jerry Lee Lewis singing "It'll Be Me" and "Whole Lot of Shaking Going On." I thought "Whole Lot" was the Judgment Day coming when I first heard it. Jack Clement, the producer, is still a genius, and I never dreamed in all my dreams that he would produce me someday. Much less be my brother-in-law.

If I'd tried to be a rock and roll singer, it would never have worked. I was married, for a start, with three kids. I never felt young. And though I thought it was awful cool for girls to be screaming at us on the stage like that, it also frustrated me. Even back then, I wanted people to listen to me.

Make no mistake, they were getting their chance now, here in Dove Creek. I'm atop the snack bar, dressed in a blazer with some kind of emblem on it. Billy Joe is playing lead guitar, I'm strumming rhythm, and behind us is a drummer we've hired for the night from a local strip joint. There we are singing "White Lightning" and I feel like taking my clothes off.

Tom Haley had decided to combine all his schemes into one, booking me and having Jim emcee. *Remember, on July 22, on the top of the snack bar during intermission, you can see Waylon Jennings and his band.* Tom would visit the drive-ins, say "Hi, I'm from the Grand Ole Opry," though he'd never been to the Opry, and book a show for intermission. Then he'd tell us to wait in the motel. "I'll be back in a little bit."

He'd go into town and come back with five thousand dollars, selling the night's advertising. They'd pay him in advance. Tom was a good salesman; you believed every word he said. He was always driving around in a Cadillac. He'd tell the salesman he wanted to "try one out for a day or two." He'd drive to Colorado from Arizona and back again and say "Well, I'm not too sure about that one."

Jim and I would cut the program for the drive-ins in a garage. They say there's a hundred days of a hundred degrees in Arizona, especially in the summer. In July it would get up to 120. It was so hot in there, we'd have to take off our shirts, socks, shoes, everything. All we had on was our pants. Sweat would be rolling off us, but Jim, in his great radio voice, would be saying "Hi, this is a wonderful evening under the stars tonight."

Tom had loaned us his car. It was an old Chrysler, and it wouldn't turn right. If it was a one-way street in front of the house where we were headed, you had to go one block past and turn left, go another block and turn left, and go still another block and turn left again to get where you were going.

I did that for a whole summer, round and round and round. Increasingly, whenever Tom got drunk, he and I would get into it. At one point he pulled a gun on me. Finally, in Blackfoot, Idaho, I said the hell with this and headed south to Salt Lake City. Billy Joe went with me. We got a job in a place called the Esquire Lounge. Billy Joe and I walked in and asked to play there, and the manager hired us, though it was a Dixieland joint. That is, she hired me. Her name was Lynne Mitchell, and she was to be my second wife.

Maxine didn't like living in Coolidge. She wanted to go back to Texas. She didn't want to clean house. I think the only thing she liked was fighting with me.

Terry had to be about three years old, and I was fixing to go to work at the radio station. As I headed out the door, she told him "Go with your dad. He wants you to go with him to work."

I couldn't take a little kid to the station. Terry knew he couldn't come, but Maxine kept egging him on. "If he don't take you, that means he don't love you." Terry thought it was a game, but she kept at me. "You don't love your son? He wants to go with you." I can't help but guess she might have been drinking then, and I didn't know it.

I stayed up in Salt Lake City for a couple of months. Lynne was eight years older than me, and I'd never met anybody quite like her. She had a look of royalty about her, a pretty thing, though she had a nasty mouth. You didn't expect it out of her. She could tell you the dirtiest joke in the world, with a preacher standing there, and laugh like there was no tomorrow.

Lynne was married to a guy named Ivan Mitchell, and we didn't have anything to do with each other for a long time. But soon the summer was over, and it came time to leave. I moved back to Coolidge and got a job in a place called the Sand and Sage Bar, until a better gig came along in Phoenix at a steak house named Wild Bill's. I'd drive back and forth every two or three nights. The next thing I know, along comes Lynne. She left her husband and followed me down to Arizona.

There was a sensuality about her that I found irresistible. Lynne was thin and dark and very sexy, with medium-length auburn hair that she wore up, every strand in place. She stood straight and tall, confident, and she carried herself like I imagined Sophia Loren would, sure of herself and her effect on men. She was great in bed and would be completely into it. Lynne had gotten past all the complexes, to where she was the one who taught me what to do, if you want to know the truth. She had me by the yin-yang on a downhill pull.

In my mind, I thought that was love. Maybe it was. She had a spirit to her that I couldn't see in Maxine. They were night and day. Lynne liked to mix it up with the boys, outgoing and gone. She'd worked in bars, was older than me by almost a decade, and gave as good as she got.

I knew that the first time I met her. I went into the club, looking for a job, and after a while my mind went from getting work to getting her. "What's your name?" I asked. "What's your whole name?"

"Pussy," she said.

She'll do fine, I thought.

Maxine had had her fill of life in Coolidge. She was going to force my hand: "I don't like it here, I'm leaving, and I'm taking the kids and going to Texas." By then, baby Deana was on the way. She knew I loved them even if I couldn't stand her. We were nothing alike. Finally, she moved back to Texas and took the kids and that was the end of it. And her.

Her going just pushed me and Lynne together. Maxine had done pretty much what I wanted her to do, though I hated the kids to leave. I knew I hadn't been a good husband to her at all. I can't tell you in one way we were compatible. We never belonged together.

Lynne started working at Wild Bill's, and soon enough I had moved into her apartment. Somehow Maxine got the number from the club where I was playing and called there. Lynne answered the phone. Now there was no going back to Maxine. It was all over.

I was back to playing music. "Wild Bill" Byrd fired me—he was notorious for giving bands the heave-ho—and I moved over to Frankie's, an old bar that could hold about ninety people, over on Thomas Road in the center of town. Billy Joe didn't seem to have the drive for it, and I was going broke in Phoenix. I got a starter Fender guitar and a little amplifier and started performing on my own.

There wasn't more than twenty people in Frankie's every show when I began. One night, a guy came up to my corner of the riser that served as a stage and asked to sit in. He was heavyset and held his guitar left-handed. He wanted so bad to play, though he worked in a shoe store during the daytime and would be so tired that he'd almost go to sleep on stage, leaning against the piano. We played four hours, from nine to one.

I didn't pay Jerry Gropp anything for a time, and then got to paying him fifteen dollars a week. I taught him to do what we called the rickety rack, a fast rhythm with straight eights. He was good, and pretty soon he got better than me.

His cousin, Ed Metzendorf, was also left-handed. He had a Danelectro bass, and I think I taught him how to play that as well. Now I had these two guys, each with their guitars pointing the wrong way so it looked like I was the one out of place, and I'd taught them both to play in my style. We were a band, or at least the start of one.

Playing every night was good for me, too. We did everything, from rock 'n' roll to country to pop ballads, and the late-night bar crowd started to grow each week. As a singer, I have a wide range, even though I don't have a falsetto. I could sing as high as Roy Orbison, but he couldn't go as low as I could.

Pretty soon we were back at Wild Bill's, which probably held a hundred people. It had high ceilings, sawdust on the floor, and a western-type atmosphere that brought out the cowboys. Lynne worked there. She'd always have to go to work early and set up, and I'd be eating a baloney sandwich at home alone. They served dinner till nine, and then I'd go on. They had a huge dance floor, and I couldn't play "The Race Is On" enough. It had been written by a guy from Phoenix named Don Rawlins, and Jimmy Gray, an Indian kid who later played guitar for me, had made the first record of that song on a local label. When they hollered out for it too much, I'd finally tell them "If you want to hear that damn song so bad, why don't you go out and hear Jimmy Gray sing it?"

Wild Bill fired us again, and we got picked up by the Cross Keys, which had been a jazz club, out at the corner of Scottsdale Road and Camelback. It was a strange place to have a nightclub, a retail area in "exclusive" Fashion Square right across the street from Goldwater's Department Store. It was one of a string the family built into a fortune that launched Barry's political career. The Cross Keys was smaller and not as well known as Wild Bill's, but the owner was able to give me a better deal. My crowd was starting to follow me. I kept the bar-hoppers and the cowboys, and added the up-and-coming professionals, among whom were baseball players spring-training in the Cactus League, like Tony Conigliaro.

Two building contractors dropped in one Saturday, saw the

place was wall-to-wall people, and started coming around. They liked my music a lot. They were about to build a club for a man named Jimmy D. Musiel, who had a part ownership in another place crosstown called Magoo's. He'd had a business falling out, and his ex-partner, Bob Sikora, kept Magoo's. J.D. hired these old boys to build him a double-decker club on Rural Road, just over the Tempe line, down by the River Bottom district. There was to be music both upstairs and downstairs; downstairs capacity would be about three hundred, but upstairs they could fit more than four times that many. J.D. said if I signed a contract to play regulararlee, regularily, uh, regulee, then he'd design the club around me.

I chose to play upstairs. I helped design the stage and get the sound system together, though then if you had one microphone for singing and another for background vocals, you had more than most. There was a beautiful dance floor in front of the bandstand, and a long bar running the length of the opposite wall, ninety feet from one end to the other. Downstairs, the River Bottom Room, was rock 'n' roll, booked by J.D.'s son, Jimmy Jr., and everyone from the Grass Roots to Bill Haley and the Comets played there, accompanied by shimmying go-go girls.

J.D.'s was automatically a smash. People were trying to get in that club every night of the week. I was the honcho, and it put me on the map. We were closed on Sunday and had half a house on Monday; but from Tuesday it was packed through the weekend. J.D.'s gamble paid off like a slot machine.

That's where I saw I needed drums. I had met Richie Albright through Tom Grasel, who hung out in a bar on Whiskey Row in Prescott called Matt's. It would get really hot in Phoenix in the summertime, and Prescott was a lot cooler, being almost a mile high in the pines. Tom had brought Richie to Frankie's one night, and when I came to Prescott to play the annual Fourth of July Frontier Days up there—Prescott was the original site of the first competition rodeo—we played at Matt's, alternating with Richie's band. He stayed put on the drums. There wasn't much other room to sit; it was so crowded in that little bar, you weren't able to start a fight because you couldn't draw your hand back.

I didn't want a drummer at first. I liked the *boom-chicka-boom* of Johnny Cash and the Tennessee Two, bare and basic. But Richie had a kind of infectious smile, and you couldn't not like him. The way he played reminded me of Sandy Nelson. Because we didn't have a regular drummer, our sense of beat wasn't definite. It snaked around. Richie didn't keep a straight time or anything, but he was a sinuous drummer; he could keep that rolling rhythm going.

I took him back to the bass drum and the snare. I hadn't been used to drums, so I said, "Just hit the foot and the snare; don't put anything else in there until I tell you." Gradually we kept adding the other pieces of the kit: the toms, the high hat, the cymbals. But we made sure the rhythm kept pumping. Richie played a lot of the up kicks, the "ands" of the beat, and gradually we found our own style.

The music started coming together at J.D.'s. On the weekends, we played afternoons as well as afterhours. At night we played four sets. In the first, I wouldn't do dance music, and people would come out and sit for the opening hour and watch. By the second set they'd start dancing, and I'd be talking to them, having some fun, just like I'd been used to on the radio. It wasn't that hard. Being funny is my second nature. Of course, being sexy is my first one.

We were right by Arizona State University, and the students started coming around. All the other bands in town were western swing. We played all kinds of songs; I didn't just sing country music. We did rock 'n' roll and some folk music and some blues. We played things the cowboys liked as well as the students, the professors, the baseball players, and the rock 'n' rollers. Everybody got along, which is how I started to realize that music can be a common denominator that draws people together. If they let it.

At J.D.'s was where I learned the value of a band. I can't imagine working without a regular group, getting up there every night with strangers. It's hard enough to get used to another guitar. For a singer, a band is a crucial instrument, and I've never been without one.

Richie was my right hand. Wiry and sharp-featured, he had been born in Bradley, Oklahoma, and grew up in Bagdad, Arizona. Bagdad is an open pit mine, is what it amounts to. His brothers are old roughhouse boys, and he was the baby of them. When I tracked him down on his Coors beer delivery route and asked him to come to Phoenix, the band truly became the Waylors, named after yours truly. He was always loyal; he would've killed somebody for me. We would be together for more than twenty years, and it took us that long to run it through the wall. We're still as close as kin. I'm godfather to his son, and I named my son after him, and he named his daughter after me.

Gropp was fun-loving, with a grin at the ready, and we were always winding each other up. You could say anything you wanted to him, and it would just run off his back. He'd laugh and come back with some comment. I always knew he was going to screw up somewhere, and he'd be the first to let you know if you made a mistake. He'd be on my left side, with that guitar pointing into my ribs, and if I hit a bum note or sang something flat, he'd lean over and mutter "Wrong." That's how that song came about.

I'd be on stage and he'd be talking to me all the time. If I went "Oh, I love her so," I'd hear him ask "What's her 'so'?" He drove me nuts. He was an excellent guitar player and had a good voice, but he never understood singing. He could scream as good as any rock 'n' roller, though. He called me all kinds of nicknames, playing off my own: Penrod Jenkins was one. Gropp started calling me Waymore, after Waymore Svenson, the Swedish yodeler. That one stuck, and pretty soon it was how the Waylors referred to me.

Ed Metzendorf quit right before J.D.'s, and Paul Foster came in on bass. He was about to get married and settle down, but he played with us while we made a name in Phoenix. Pretty soon the crowds were lined out the door to get into J.D.'s every night, stretching over the hill and practically into Scottsdale. We'd kick off the Cajun beat and that place would be romping to where the whole floor would be shaking. Then I'd turn around and do a ballad like Roy Orbison's "Crying," and you could hear a pin drop. When I went for the high note at the end, the crowd would come unglued. They just screamed. I was living and breathing and sleeping the life I loved; I ate it up.

The club put a grill cloth with WAYLON and J.D.'S on it in front of the amp line. My reputation was spreading throughout Arizona. I was the hottest thing in town. I was making decent money for the first time, and paying the band. The crowds were listening to me, and I was getting to them. I could tell the girls liked me and the cowboys thought I was a good ol' boy. But most important, in the middle of a set, I'd turn around and look at Richie and we'd be going off on this tangent, jamming, letting the song carry us along, and a smile of satisfaction would spread across our faces. I just knew musically that we fit.

Most of the material we did at J.D.'s was covers ("He makes others' hits his own" was the way they put it), but I still thought that writing a good song was one of the most satisfying things you could do. If a song says what you want it to say at the end, and draws a mental picture, there's few things in life that can make you feel more creative.

You can't write a great song very often, but you can sure try. I filled up boxes with lyrics, and tried to put them on the rhythms I was playing. When I was at K-triple-L, I had written a song with Sky Corbin called "Young Widow Brown," which Frankie Miller made a semi–pop hit out of in 1958. Both Sky and Slim encouraged me to write, but I hadn't found what I wanted to say yet. We got into writing soap operas; I think one was called "Portia Faces Life."

We got a kick out of writing those songs, but I wasn't sure I had any gift for it. The songs I was listening to in my head weren't like the ones I was hearing on the radio. When Don Bowman, a San Diego disc jockey who had once worked at K-triple-L, called to ask if I might want to help him work on some tunes, I figured I may as well give it a chance.

I'd never thought of him as a songwriter, but he had gone to California and made a name for himself, writing for, among others, Homer and Jethro. I knew he could be funny. Don and I had always gotten in trouble at K-triple-L. One of the ways the station paid for their lease was that every thirty minutes we had to announce "Studios atop the beautiful Great Plains Life Building in downtown Lubbock, Texas." Well, one day it sounded awfully funny for us to say "Studios in the basement of the ol' courthouse and it's been condemned." We didn't have to say that more than three times and they had him on the carpet.

We were a little out of control. We'd put on a long-play record and go out and bowl a few frames. Finally, they got to where they put up a sign saying "Waylon Jennings and Don Bowman are not allowed in the control room at the same time while on the air" and posted it right next to the FCC regulations.

I remembered all this when he called me. We had gone our separate ways, and I was impressed at how far he'd traveled. He had just signed with RCA and had put out an album composed of mostly novelty songs, including the prophetic "Chet Atkins, Make Me a Star." He heard I was playing around Phoenix and was curious to know if I wanted to collaborate. About the first thing he brought over was "Just to Satisfy You." He had a verse and no melody, and we went ahead and finished that. It happened so quick, I thought that can't be any good.

We wrote several things together, and I learned so much from working with Don. He taught me that you have to have humor, whether or not the song itself is funny. If you get too damn serious, it becomes work. Every once in a while we'd get hung up on a phrase, and I'd go to the bathroom and take a piss, and while I was in there I'd think of a line. We called it a bathroom line.

Don was friendly with Jerry Moss out in Los Angeles, and he

took some of my demos over to him. Jerry was just starting A&M Records with Herb Alpert, a trumpet player who had struck gold the year before with "The Lonely Bull." Jerry and Herb decided they'd like to try something with me.

On July 9, 1963, a contract arrived at 2022 North Thirty-sixth Street, apartment B1, in Phoenix, giving me a 5 percent royalty rate for two sides of a single: "Love Denied" and "Rave On." The flip was the Buddy Holly song, while Bill Tilghman wrote "Love Denied." It had a real high ending, almost like Roy Orbison. I think that was one of the things Herb and Jerry were impressed with, my range.

Herb didn't like country music, though as a singer, he felt there was a something about me that he didn't feel was country. I think he was hoping I was more of an Al Martino, while I was leaning toward Flatt and Scruggs. There was a girl on the label at the time, Lucille Starr, who'd originally been in a group from Alberta called the Canadian Sweethearts. She'd had some success in the country market, and maybe they figured I could hit both.

Folk music was also starting to be popular then. I loved Bob Dylan and Joan Baez, and songs like "Don't Think Twice" and "Silver Dagger." I found *The Freewheelin' Bob Dylan*, the "Blowin' in the Wind" album, in a dollar bin, and though I thought Dylan was the weirdest singer, there was something about his voice that pulled me in.

Herb and Jerry brought me out to Los Angeles and did something in that vein, a version of Ian Tyson's "Four Strong Winds." We backed it with "Just to Satisfy You"; I think Jerry lead-whistled on it, and Herb played the horns on "Four Strong Winds."

Herb kept looking for something in me he couldn't find. It just wasn't there, really. He truly liked my singing, and he wanted me to make it, but even if you get a bigger hammer, you can't fit a round peg into a square hole. One night we tried "Unchained Melody" countless times. I never understood, though I do now, what he was talking about. It was too far over my head. The only word that matters in that song is "hunger"; if you get that right, the song is yours. I never got it.

I wasn't comfortable in the studio. I was just too green. In L.A., I talked myself into a sinus infection and a cold. I thought, if I do this wrong, they won't want to work with me anymore and it'll be all over. Herb made me very nervous, because I respected him and wanted to please him so bad, more than anything he did at the recording. There was a greatness about him, and Herb and Jerry are two of the most caring, honest people I've ever met in the record business. They were wonderful to me.

But it wasn't right. We cut "The Twelfth of Never," "Kisses Sweeter Than Wine," and "Don't Think Twice," and for a third single, "Sing the Girls a Song, Bill," backed with "The Race Is On." A&M released my three 45s during 1964, one every couple of months from April through October, which helped my popularity at J.D.'s but didn't make much of an impact anywhere else. "Sing the Girls" was a radio hit in Nashville and gave me some credibility; though if I could've used any encouragement, I had only to look out at J.D.'s nightly throngs to know I was doing something right. I just needed to figure out a way to capture it on a record.

In the fall of 1964, I went into Audio Recorders in Phoenix, a studio owned by Floyd Ramsey, where Duane Eddy had done his earliest singles. Floyd owned a record label, Ramco, that had leased my Trend masters, and he had built a new, larger studio across the street. Richie, Paul, Jerry, and myself spent four or five hours one night cutting some of the most popular "screamers" we did in our live show.

It was a varied bunch of material, an album to be sold at the club as a souvenir. We covered everything from rock 'n' roll to folk and country; Mel Tillis's "Burning Memories" and Buck Owens's "Love's Gonna Live Here" to Bob Dylan's "Don't Think Twice" and Buddy's "It's So Easy." On Harlan Howard's "Sally Was a Good Old Girl," there's a lot of howling and growling as the song faded into the desert air. We went a little wild with the echoplex on "Dream Baby," one of two Roy Orbison songs. I still thought he wouldn't be big because of that high voice. And yes, I hit the note true at the end of "Crying," and drained it to the last drop of reverb.

I was living on North Thirty-sixth Street in Phoenix when Kennedy was assassinated. I was there the first time I ever heard the Beatles over the radio. It was the first nice place I'd ever had.

Lynne knew how to take care of money, and we were getting ahead. She had come from Pike County, Kentucky, where her dad had been a moonshiner. He had to move the family out to Idaho when Lynne was little, and he hadn't been there too long when he was hit by a car going across the street in the little town of Chubbock. The feds came and dug up his body to make sure it was him. He must've done something pretty wrong back in Kentucky for them to go to all that trouble.

Her mother chewed tobacco, just a little pinch where you couldn't tell, in her lip; and she loved me from the word go. Lynne wasn't so sure. She never had respect for me as a man as far as intelligence went. She was older than me by almost a decade and couldn't forget that. She had strong opinions on everything and thought she was so smart. She was smart, but she was never smarter than me. That's where our problems started.

Lynne did not trust men. She was married twice before, and I think she had a complex about not being educated. She liked to be in control, and that was always a hard call with me. At the beginning, the age difference was in her favor. It gave her an edge; she was more streetwise, tougher than I was, though I later realized a lot of it was based on sheer bravado. Then it turned around the other way, where she worried that I was going to run off with a younger woman.

More problems in marriage are brought about by insecurity than anything else. If I said something about loving my mother in front of Maxine, she thought it took away from my love for her. For Lynne, the more popular I got, the more she suspicioned it was turning my head around. I'm sure there were moments she could feel me slipping away.

We had some good times. Every Monday night we'd visit a restaurant in Scottsdale named Monte's, where they had a great steak and salad with Roquefort dressing. We'd cook out in the backyard. We'd play cards. Working in bars, we didn't go out much.

Whenever we had too much time out of bed, we'd get in a fight. It must be a law of nature that the very things that turn you on about each other make you insecure later. We quarreled as many minutes as we were cuddling up, and the fighting may have been part of the lovemaking. One usually seemed to follow the other.

I think you feel guilty when you're married and start seeing somebody else. It was wrong, we both knew that. After my divorce came through from Maxine, we needed to justify our behavior, because it was all too easy to throw it up in each other's faces when we got mad. "Oh, you were easy to get," I'd tell Lynne, and she'd answer, "I didn't have to do anything to get you in bed." Neither of us could cast the first stone. In an odd way, I think we got married to see if we could get along better. After all we'd been through, went the reasoning, at least we ought to give it a try.

I brought out what I called the marine sergeant in her. She was one of those people who could get mad and stay angry for two weeks, never speaking to you, even though you were in the same house. She had strength and weakness mixed up, always unsure of herself and her grip on me. Things were starting to roll my way, and there were more demands on my time. It couldn't have been easy, but her way of holding on was to dig in and ridicule me. She was afraid of seeming vulnerable. It got worse when Maxine sent my kids to live with us. I was trying to do the best I could; still, I couldn't get any cooperation from Lynne. She would not accept children by another wife in the house.

Lynne had a miscarriage before we were married. She had

nephritis, which is a kidney disease, and when she got pregnant we had to have an abortion to save her life. It was our most tender moment together; I felt so bad for her. She wanted a baby more than anything, and the loss really affected her. I don't think she felt she was a full woman, and maybe she hoped that it would cement our relationship, to have a child that was truly ours.

We brought Tomi Lynne home to our apartment when she was three days old. Through friends, Jo and Jan, we found a young girl who was going to have a baby; Lynne and I both knew the mother. She had become pregnant by a married man, and financially or circumstantially she could get no support from the father. We arranged the adoption through a lawyer, and we chose Jo as her godmother. A couple of years later, I would return the favor by introducing Jo as my sister to "Ballad of Paladin" singer Johnny Western when he came to spell me at J.D.'s. When he left Phoenix, he took her with him, and they've spent the rest of the years since happily married.

Our new daughter arrived on our doorstep in a bassinet that had "no information" written on it. Her underarms and her little feet were cracked and bleeding. No one had thought to put oil on her or anything. Tomi Lynne lay there in my lap that night; she was so tender and beautiful. People say babies can't see, but she looked at me and she'd go to sleep, and then she'd wake up and look at me. I guess she felt secure.

We were doing quite well. At J.D.'s I was taking home over a thousand dollars a week, and I was able to buy the first brand-new car I had ever owned, a '64 Chevrolet. As a family, we moved over to Pierce Street, and then got a house in Scottsdale, on East Amelia right off Indian School Road. We needed the room because my kids from Maxine had arrived. They were a little confused by the new situation, though they tried not to show it. I'm sure my separation from their birth mother hurt them, dividing their tiny loyalties, but they seemed resilient enough. Like most kids from broken homes, I think they always hoped that it might miraculously change back. There wasn't much chance of that, but they were happy to see me, running up the walk and throwing their arms around me, while Lynne watched from the side, giving me the cold shoulder, inwardly fuming.

Lynne would show all the love in the world to Tomi Lynne, and none to my other children. She'd make them stay outside all day, and only let them come in to play in the family room and their bedroom, and eat in the kitchen.

She hated that they were there. All of her attention went to her little girl. Lynne would cuddle with her and kiss on her and never pay any attention to the others except to correct them, holler at them, or tell them to go to bed. She could never speak kind to them.

This went on for a year and a half, two years. One night they were all there, and she was playing with the baby, and the baby was squealing, and Lynne was laughing and tickling her. The other kids were in the room. Buddy was about four years old, and he walked up to her and put his hand on her arm. "Wynne," he said in his little voice, "do you wike me?"

That broke my heart. "Sure," she said. "I like you. Go set down," and she went back to playing with the little girl, hugging her. She never kissed one of the other kids in her life. There was no affection there.

I kept thinking things would change, but it was never for the better. We could go for a week and not say a word to each other. One time she made me so mad I grabbed the metal closet doors and pulled them off, and cut my hands to keep from hitting her. She hated that my kids were around. They wanted Lynne to love them, and I saw them trying to win her approval. But she was cold to them, and consequently me. All she did was scold.

I thought, This can't go on. So I called Maxine and told her I was going to send the kids back. I bought her a brick house, filled it with furniture, and packed up the kids' clothes and toys in a trailer. I kissed Terry, Julie, and Buddy, and the baby Deana good-bye, for how long I couldn't know. My brother took them back to

Texas, and the night they left I sat up crying. I didn't go to bed at all.

The next morning Lynne came over to me. I was still sitting in the chair, red-eyed. We hadn't even spoken for two weeks. "Hon', don't be sad," she said. "Everything is going to be all right. Don't you worry, we'll make it fine."

I looked at her. "If you'd called me a rotten sonofabitch, or told me to fuck off or something like that, you might've been able to hold on to me. But you ain't got a chance. I'll never live with you." And I got up and left. She tried everything she could to get me to come back. I couldn't forgive her for making me send my kids away, though she was the first woman I ever thought I loved.

I had met Barbara at the Cross Keys: long blond hair, pretty blue eyes, built like you wouldn't believe. Richie was the only unmarried man in the group and she became friendly with him so she could always be around. But he was just the excuse. Barbara Rood had her eye on me, even though I was still with Lynne, and I wasn't exactly blind either.

I remember the night she showed up at the Cross Keys. Everybody did. It was like something out of a movie; she was the star. It was summertime and she was wearing a sundress. She pulled up in a red convertible outside the club with her girlfriend and walked in, the center of attention, tall and tan. Statuesque. Even in the glamor town of Phoenix, she stood out like a lighthouse in the fog.

We stayed away from each other as long as we could. We'd talk some, but we never did anything. Finally I went to Houston to have some talks with a record label there, and she came down. It was the first time we were together. She was never comfortable with what we were doing, and I wasn't either. Still, it was hard to keep away, and we started seeing each other on the sly. I'd have to go over to her house in the daytime.

Barbara was a golden girl and a dear heart. Her dad had invented a cotton machine that picked up cotton between the rows that the boll puller would miss. He was worth about thirty million dollars, and she had a lot of money. She even bought a car the same color as mine. She was definitely more of a party girl than Lynne.

I wrote "Anita, You're Dreaming" about her when we first got together. I had most of it done and Don Bowman helped me finish it. She was "Anita . . . dreaming of a world that just don't exist." I was telling her that it didn't look like I was ever going to get loose from Lynne, and she was young and deserved a better deal than I could offer. She was dreaming if she thought it could happen.

But dreams have a way of revealing truths, and when I left Lynne, I went right to Barbara.

That wasn't the only fantasy crossing the line into reality. Don had become friends with Bobby Bare, who had gotten out of the army and, rather than coasting on his Bill Parsons persona, had scored hits with "500 Miles Away from Home" and "Detroit City" under his own name. Bowman was always telling him about me, and he got to find out for himself when he was driving through Phoenix one time and heard "Just to Satisfy You" on the radio.

He brought the record to his producer in Nashville, Chet Atkins, and said he wanted to record it. Chet was familiar with "Just to Satisfy You" because Bowman had brought him a copy of the record, but he turned it over and said "Hell, this is the one I want to do." So they wound up doing them both. "Four Strong Winds" turned out to be a big hit for Bobby.

Chet had also heard of me because he'd done one of my songs with Don, "Help Keep Ol' John Out of Town." It was a novelty song about this guy who's fooling around with the wife of a country star who's on the road, wearing his clothes and smoking his cigars. The punch line was "So buy all his records / And go see his shows / And help keep ol' John out of town." Chet thought it was clever.

The next time Bobby came through Phoenix, in November of

1964, he headed over after his gig to J.D.'s and we did a duet on "Just to Satisfy You." He had the next day off so he came to see me and the band play. Somewhere between Phoenix and Las Vegas, he got to thinking about it, and stopped at a pay phone.

"Chet," he said. "I've just seen Waylon. He's the best thing since Elvis. I know he and I are doing the same kind of songs, the same kind of material for the same kind of audience. But I dug everything about him: his voice, the way the band stays out of his way so you can hear him sing, his hold on the audience. He is so good, he deserves to be on a major label."

Chet had heard similar praise from Skeeter Davis, who called him at home to tell him he should sign me, and Duane Eddy. It wasn't like an agent or a manager coming in and hyping someone; that doesn't mean anything. But coming from Bobby, who liked country and folk and had been a part of rock 'n' roll, the recommendation meant something. We loved the same songs.

Bobby gave Chet my phone number.

To be on RCA and have Chet Atkins produce me. To have him call me and tell me he would like to sign me, having never even seen me. I'll never forget that day. I was sitting at home, and I could hear this real gentle, kind voice on the other end of the phone, saying "We'd sure like for you to record for RCA. Would you be interested?"

Would I be interested?

It was impossible to say no. That was the ultimate. RCA—or Victor, as I'd seen on so many Jimmie Rodgers and Carter Family 78s—was recorded country music from almost the very beginning, dating back to the Bristol, Tennessee, sessions organized by Ralph Peer in 1928; and Chet was a legend. Not only was he a well-regarded artist and repertoire executive who could put a gold seal on your career, but he was a musician's musician, an originator who had his own Gretsch guitar named after him: the Country Gentleman. He was Sonny Curtis's idol!

You could book on the road without hit records, because you

were on RCA and Chet Atkins produced you. God's right hand, they called him. "Are you signed to a label?" Chet asked me.

A&M was just a little independent then, built around the Tijuana Brass. They hadn't yet signed Captain Beefheart or Procol Harum or Cat Stevens or the Carpenters. From such acorns oak trees might grow, but at that time there wasn't much more than a seedling sprouting. I had gotten the call that every country boy dreams of. I asked Herb and Jerry if I could get loose to go with RCA, though if they wanted me to stay, I said I would. "Sure, Waylon," Jerry agreed. He knew they'd be unduly pressured to have a big hit with me if I turned down Chet's offer. "We don't want to stand in your way. We understand what Chet would mean to you."

Herb understood as well, but he countered RCA's bid with something more personal. "I hate to give up," he said. "I really think I could do it with you. I believe I can." He offered me a percentage of the company, eight or ten percent, if I would stay. It was the hardest thing in the world to say "No, I really want to try this." They were the best people for giving me my release, and still are. They taught me how to truly sing "Unchained Melody."

When I look down today at my guitar, caught in the spotlights of whatever town is giving me a place on their stage, it's essentially similar to the instrument I played at J.D.'s. It's a Fender Telecaster; solid body, maple neck. It ain't got but two knobs on it. You turn it on and you have the same sound all the way through.

You can put a guitar against you and feel it vibrating as you play it. They're never really in tune, especially the B string. I hate the B string. What you learn to do is pull 'em into place with your finger. For me, they're a lot like women. You can touch one of them in the dark and know she ain't yours; or you're with the right one.

My original Telecaster was covered in leather tooling by a cleanup man at Wild Bill's named Howard Turner. He customized a 1953 model, a gift to me from the Waylors. Barbara was in on it. I think she bought the matching Fender amplifier, a black-face Super Reverb, and the band put a fifteen-inch "Living" Lansing speaker in it. We all had identical guitar straps with our names inscribed—Waylon, Jerry, and Paul—and we wore short Mexican tuxedo jackets and matching pants with a stripe down the side.

I was still playing "White Lightning." Only instead of standing on top of a concession stand in a drive-in, I was looking out over a sea of bobbing heads, swaying bodies, packed together too tightly to dance, all moving to the ricketty racket we were setting in motion from the J.D.'s stage. Buddy had always said to leave them wanting more, to quit while you were on top. Then they'd exaggerate to the good. I was aiming to leave.

In the desert, a few inches of rain can turn into several feet of raging water. That dry river bottom, located right next to J.D.'s, had been a rushing torrent in 1964, when the club had gone under in a flash flood, and they'd had to muck it out. I felt like the same flood had caught me in its current, swept me away on the river of music, giving me hope and possibility and the challenge of staying afloat. I didn't want to drown in the next overflow, or have them find me years later in the River Bottom district.

There was another couple of sets to go on this night, and the next, and the next. At least now it looked as if I might be given the chance to keep on playing. Maybe for the rest of my life. It's all I ever wanted to do.

CHAPTER

4

# FROM NASHVILLE BUM . . .

I started out for Nashville with a yellow Cadillac and a yellow-haired woman. The band loaded an old Chevy flower car from a funeral home with our equipment, and I went to pick up Barbara.

We left late at night. I put her big red trunk with the brass fittings in the trailer behind the Cadillac and we drove off. I was getting a divorce from Lynne, and it wasn't exactly clear in the whole world's mind what mine and Barbara's relationship was going to be. We weren't about to risk any chances of getting stopped at the border.

The journey seemed to take forever. When we got to Tennessee, it was daytime. It might have been my anticipation, but all I remember are the winding roads before I got to the freeway, twisting and turning back and forth, like I was continually glancing back over my shoulder at my past life before heading into the future. We climbed over one hill after another, Memphis aiming east toward Nashville, until finally Music City stuck its head over the horizon like a rising sun. I could hardly believe this was going to be my new home.

It was a big step for me, a chance I was taking, and I was anxious to get started. I'd thought long and hard about leaving Phoenix, even asking another RCA artist passing through town what he thought of moving. His name was Willie Nelson, and he'd been having success as a songwriter. "Crazy" and "Funny How Time Slips Away," for Patsy Cline, were already standards, and Faron Young's "Hello Walls" was well on its way to becoming a classic. He was a fellow Texan, appearing across town at the Riverside Ballroom. We had never met before, but my first album was about to come out, and he'd also just gotten his start recording as an artist in his own right. He liked my singing and I liked his.

Willie came to town and sent word he wanted to meet me. I went over to the Adams Hotel and spent the afternoon finding out how much we had in common, asking him about Nashville and what I might expect. He had just moved there. I told him I had a good deal at J.D.'s. By then, I was up to maybe fifteen hundred dollars a week, clear. Not bad for a "sit down" job, as we called gigs that you didn't have to go on the road for.

"Don't move," he told me. "And if you do, let me have that job!"

As usual, I followed the opposite course. I'd been in Nashville a couple of times during the previous year, 1965, looking around, cutting songs with Chet, and getting a feel for the city. I'd been there once before Bobby saw me, and tried to see if I couldn't get something going. I found the doors closed. I didn't know anybody then, and nobody knew me.

Eight months later, Chet's blessing had made all the difference. I was the talk of the town. When I arrived, it was at Nashville's invitation, and all along the grapevine the word was out. Sometimes you don't need a hit record: If you go somewhere and set down and make enough noise, they'll know it's you that they want. They came to me. There was a buzz, and I was the buzzard.

Bobby Bare put me up when I went to record officially for the first time as an RCA artist. I spent three days in mid-March—for the record, it was the sixteenth, eighteenth, and nineteenth—cutting most of what would become my first album, *Folk-Country*. In those sessions we recorded twelve songs, including my first single, "That's the Chance I'll Have to Take," as well as a couple of B sides.

Chet let me bring my band in the studio: Gropp on guitar and Richie on drums. We'd been playing "Stop the World (and Let Me Off)" in the clubs, and had it all worked out. Chet did a wild thing. He liked the way Jerry dubbed his strings, muting them when he played, so he put a microphone next to his pick hand on the electric guitar. It was like a percussive drone.

I started playing the break. I looked over in the control room and realized "I'm playing guitar in front of Chet Atkins!" So I just grabbed me a string and held on for dear life. It made a good middle eight, though.

Folk-Country was Nashville's scheme to snare some of the hootenanny folk audience, which was then starting to cross over to rock. Along with me, it was hoped that John D. Loudermilk, John Hartford, and George Hamilton IV might win a few extra converts to country. I didn't mind the label; to me, folk music was the original country music, sung by folks, plain and simple.

I stayed over a couple of extra days and did one of Bare's sessions, playing guitar and singing harmony on "Streets of Baltimore" and "Memphis," making a little expense money.

We went back to performing in Phoenix. Though it wasn't the megalopolis it is today, I was a big frog in a not-much-bigger puddle. The entertainment columnist at the local paper kept referring to me as "That Guy down at the River Bottom": He couldn't bring himself to say my name. People knew I was going to leave, and that only filled up J.D.'s even more.

My first single came out in May, and Chet called me back to Nashville on July 28 to cut a few more songs for the album. Among the newer things I did was "Anita, You're Dreaming." By the time I came back for a third time in the middle of February, 1966, cutting a variety of material that ranged from "(That's What You Get) for Lovin' Me" to the Beatles' "Norwegian Wood," "Stop the World" had gotten into the Top Fifteen, and "Anita" was riding midway in the country charts. *Folk-Country* was coming out the next month. Chet had declared March "Male Singer Month" at RCA, and the company was riding high with ten entries in the Top Twenty-five. Included along with me was Porter Wagoner, Eddy Arnold, Hank Locklin, Jim Reeves, Archie Campbell, and Staff Sergeant Barry Sadler with "Ballad of the Green Berets." It was time to move.

First I had to let Phoenix know what they would be missing. If you leave on top, Buddy said, it'll make it appear even bigger than it really is. Still, we couldn't have gotten any larger unless we'd moved the show over to the Coliseum. On the first weekend in April, and my last weekend as a local performer at J.D.'s, it was monstrous. The word was out that this was going to be my fare-thee-well stand, and they packed close to two thousand people upstairs. Johnny Western warmed up the crowd, playing the appropriate theme from *Have Gun Will Travel*, while I waited backstage at my coffee pot, having another cup. Substitute the word *guitar* for *gun* and you had me. The Telecaster Cowboy.

Gotta travel on. Stage, that is. It was unreal, the crowd screaming their heads off, hanging on every word. I showed out. You can't do it any other way. When they go that crazy, you can't give them any less than your best, a hundred and twenty percent instead of a hundred and ten. It was a hell of a three days. People were happy for me; but there were a lot of folks crying in their beer because I wasn't going to be theirs anymore. I kind of missed that part myself. Wish me luck; and this one's a ladies choice.

*Waitin' for my big break to come*
*Livin' on catsup soup, home-made crackers and Kool-Aid*
*I'll be a star tomorrow but today*
*I'm a Nashville Bum*

\*　　\*　　\*

We like to have starved when we got to Nashville. We were jumping in with the big boys and girls; performers we'd heard on the radio all our life, and the thousands of hopeful newcomers that come each year to the hub of country music looking for a quick spin. We were giving up a steady job. Richie had a Thunderbird and a playboy apartment and all the women he could ask for. He knew it was only a matter of time, but he hated to leave Phoenix.

The Nashville we arrived in had Roger Miller's name written all over it. He had just gotten nine Grammy nominations, with "England Swings," "Husbands and Wives," and "I've Been a Long Time Leavin' " all on the Top Fifty charts at the same time. Not bad for a guy who used to bellhop and run the elevator at the Hermitage Hotel while he was trying to get someone to listen to his songs.

Red Sovine was driving "Giddyup Go" while the Statler Brothers talked about smoking cigarettes and watching Captain Kangaroo. Buck Owens was "Waitin' in Your Welfare Line" listening to *Cute 'n' Country* Connie Smith crooning "Nobody but a Fool." And hovering in the teens on the country charts was a newcomer named Waylon Jennings, whose "Anita, You're Dreaming" sat between Little Jimmy Dickens's "When the Ship Hits the Sand" and Roy Drusky's "Rainbows and Roses" one week, and Kitty Wells's "A Woman Half My Age" and Tommy Collins's "If You Can't Bite, Don't Growl" another.

Over on Sixteenth Avenue South, they were breaking ground for the Country Music Hall of Fame and Museum. Win or lose, I was now part of it, a tiny patch in country music's rich quilt.

I still needed a place to live and a way to feed the band. The second priority was probably more urgent. Until my records started selling, I was not going to be a big money man, and even then, a hit country album could only be counted on to sell twenty or thirty thousand copies. W. E. "Lucky" Moeller, a booking agent, had promised to keep me working, which in Lucky's terms meant I wouldn't be home that much.

Lucky sold volume. His principle was "Keep the 'billies on the road." You might play three or four times a year at the Flame in Minneapolis or the Horseshoe in Toronto, crisscrossing the country with hardly any rhyme or reason. To keep the band busy, he would discount them at lower prices. I'd be on the road all the time, generating Lucky's ten percent by the week or fifteen percent for one nighters, and it would get me a lot of public exposure.

Lucky was like a father figure to me. He wore black-framed glasses and had a thin mustache. An old-timer in the booking business, he was a match for Harry "Hap" Peebles in Wichita, or Smokey Smith in Des Moines. Over the years he booked anybody and everybody. He'd run his own clubs and dance halls in Texas and Oklahoma, and had managed Bob Wills and Webb Pierce, so he knew the business from both sides of the fence. He knew what he needed, and how to get it. He'd not only paid talent, he'd sold talent. He was like an actor who directs.

That sword could cut two ways. The clubs and carnivals and state fairs might be assured of shows, and your date sheet might be filled, but he didn't fight for big money. Lucky would rather sell more dates at the same price, even into the next year, than hold out getting you the extra five hundred dollars that could spell the difference between subsistence and pleasure. And by booking you so far in the future, it might backfire, as Little Jimmy Dickens found out when he scored a major pop hit with "May the Bird of Paradise Fly Up Your Nose." He couldn't break out of the low-ball contracts he had signed a year in advance. By the time he was able to book new shows at a bigger figure, the Bird of Paradise had flown up his ass.

Lucky paid it no mind. Even though you were scraping by, he'd say "At least you're still on the road!"

\*     \*     \*

Living out of a suitcase, I stayed in hotels with Barbara. We started at the Anchor Motel and worked our way around to the Noel, the Andrew Jackson, the Downtowner.

Before I'd left Phoenix, I'd talked with John Cash about sharing an apartment when I got to Nashville. But the closer I got to calling him up when I arrived, the worse an idea it seemed. I was hanging out with Barbara, and even though I'd gotten to know John a bit, there was still something of the starstruck teenager in me who had heard "Cry, Cry, Cry" over the car radio, making the only left turn heading west on Highway 54: "Everybody knows where you go when the sun goes down."

I had met John through June Carter, who had crossed my path years before when I was still a disc jockey in Lubbock. I was a little in awe of the Carter family, as you might expect. When I'd gone to record in Nashville that last year, Mother Maybelle invited me to dinner. It was an even bigger thrill than having my records cut. It was like being given the Holy Grail.

My relationship with June had nowhere to go but up. The first time I met her was the first and worst time I ever got drunk. She was on a package tour that came to Lubbock to play the state fair. Ray Price was headlining, and Skeeter Davis was also on the bill. I was going to play bass for Ray.

When you played a fair tour, it was customary to visit about five or six towns around the fair's location to publicize it. That was part of the deal. We'd perform two or three songs, setting up one little microphone, and finish by telling the audience to "come see us tonight" at the fairground. We did the circuit all day once, and June was riding with me. She and Carl Smith had already split up; she was just the sweetest thing you ever saw.

We were in Spur, Texas; it's the desert. They've got rattlesnakes seven feet long and more, and coyotes. Where the cap rock starts heading down, that's Spur.

The promoters told us we were going to have a hamburger fry at a nearby ranch. When we got out there and looked around, they'd pulled up the rug, put a microphone in the corner with some amplifiers, and had a little bitty table plumb full of booze. They were intending on us playing the music while they danced. There wasn't no food nowhere.

I was starving to death. We hadn't eaten all day. It pissed me off, so I just joined the party. I decided to drink the liquor, and had a little bit of everything on the table. I got so drunk, I stumbled outside and passed out. They left me there and put a pillow under my head, right in the middle of nowhere.

When I woke up it was getting dark. I opened my eyes, unsticking them one at a time, and looked right into the snout of a black and white spotted hog that had come up and was snorting at my face. I must've let out a bloodcurdling scream. He took off and hit the side of the house at full tilt, squealing and squalling.

June got me and walked me to the car and put me in the back of the station wagon. The next thing I knew they were letting me out at K-triple-L. I had to work that day.

She came back through Lubbock a couple of times before I left for Arizona, cute as a bug's ear and funny as she could be. The next time I saw June was at J.D.'s around 1964, and she had John in tow. We hit it off. He liked me immediately. Beyond what we saw in each other as performers, we had a mutual respect, centered around the songs we knew as kids. Our backgrounds were so similar, sharing the poor cottonfields and a love of music back as long as we could remember. "You ever hear this one?" was where our conversation started, and it didn't stop until we challenged each other back all the way to Vernon Dalhart and Carson Robison in the twenties. We shared the music more than anything else. We felt like old friends from the first time we sat down together.

Later I went to see him in Albuquerque, with Tex Ritter opening. John told me he was thinking of moving to Nashville. He was having some "trouble at home" trying to get June to marry him, and he needed a place to flop when he was there. "Why don't we get us an apartment together?" he asked.

I didn't know if he'd still be into it when I got to town, but when I called around Mother Maybelle's looking for him, she told me "John's really hurt." I phoned him up and said, "If you're serious, we'll have no problem."

It was just a regular one-bedroom, on the first floor of the Fontaine Royale Apartments in Madison, right off Gallatin Road. Barbara moved down the hall, about four or five doors away, which made it real convenient. We were trying to keep our relationship a secret until I got a divorce. Lynne wasn't making it easy.

Mother Maybelle thought John and I would be "good for each other." I'm not sure that's the way I would describe our housekeeping style. It was like a sitcom; we were the original Odd Couple. I was supposed to clean up, and John was the one doing the cooking. If I'd be in one room polishing, he'd be in the other room making a mess. Making himself a mess. He'd be stirring biscuits and gravy, dressed in one of his thin black gabardine suits, and the flour would be rising in clouds of white dust all over him.

June and Momma Maybelle would come over about once a week to scrape the place down, and Maybelle would feed us whenever she thought it was getting out of hand. She'd fix hush puppies, because she knew I loved them. After a meal there, we knew it was her way of telling us to straighten up. She played a good game of poker, and she'd even have a beer once in a while. Maybelle demanded respect, and John and I were only too happy to give it to her.

Both of us never slept. We put two king-size beds in one room, and there wasn't space to walk around them. I don't know why we got such a small apartment. He'd have to jump over my bed to get to his if I was there. We hardly used them, though. We were both always gone, and we usually only slept there as a last resort. I'd come in and find he was crashed, and he'd get up when I'd stagger in from the road.

We were so much alike in many ways, it was scary. We both dressed in black, like Lash Larue. Later, when we met Lash on the set of the *Stagecoach* movie, we were worried he was going to bust us for taking his style. Looking at John was like catching a reflection of myself; driven, restless, searching for acceptance. We liked to get wild, but we were funny, and we didn't get mean. We used to egg each other on. It's a worn-out word, but we were soulmates, and our lives would continue to run parallel through all the changes the years would bring. There was a connection between us we didn't understand then, and may never still. It's kind of like knowing what someone's going to say before they say it.

We flipped over each other from the moment we met, though at first we stood back. It was so sudden we were kind of afraid of each other. John and I were both manly men, and we liked to walk macho and talk macho; but after a while we learned we could be ourselves.

He had a defense when I first met him. I could break it down in minutes, just like we periodically kicked in the door. We were always locking ourselves out. John would get home crashing and put the night latch on, or I'd do the same thing. Whoever was stuck outside would have to batter his way into the apartment. We weren't so much harmless as helpless. The landlord finally turned the door around, opening it out instead of in, to keep us from doing further damage.

We'd just get giddy and silly around each other, and laugh a lot. That would be when I'd be calling him John. Or Maynard. He had a lot of names. "Johnny Cash" was formal, as in "Mr. Cash." There was Johnny when he was just lounging around. And then there was Cash. Sometimes you couldn't tease John or he would become Cash. He was very seldom Cash with me. Cash was usually when he was mean, or when he was on drugs.

Me and John were the world champions at pill-taking, but we each didn't let on to the other that we knew it. We never shared drugs. I can laugh about it now, saying, hell, I knew he couldn't handle it; but he couldn't. I guess he felt the same way about me.

I had a problem, and he had a problem, but we never made it a mutual problem.

I hid my stash in the back of the air conditioner, while John kept his behind the television. He'd tear the place apart if he ran out. If we had started combining supplies and sources, we probably would've bottomed out and killed ourselves, feeding each other's habits. We had enough mutual respect for each other, as human beings and as men, that we didn't want to help destroy what we had between us. He could get so messed up it was unbelievable; it didn't matter if he had ten pills or a hundred. He took them all. I wasn't far behind.

I'd started popping pills back in Salt Lake City. Sheryl Millet, a guy who played guitar with me, was into them. When you're young, you're bullet-proof, and I thought nothing of staying up all night, singing and trying to write songs. John and I could never do that together. Two guys on amphetamines—we were too scattered. We worked at cross-purposes, trying to find a common axis. Strung out, lying to each other about what we were doing, it's a wonder we got along as well as we did.

I never liked downers. I was hyper as hell and taking uppers on top of that. I never hit the ground for twenty-one years. I had incredible stamina; I prided myself on the fact that I could take more pills, stay up longer, sing more songs, and screw more women than most anybody you ever met in your life. I didn't know when to stop, or see any need to.

I didn't know till later that they were addictive. I thought they were medicine. Playing six nights a week in Phoenix, I'd use the pills as an energy boost. You'd be tired, but you wouldn't know it. Later, when I got out on the road, and would have to drive eight or nine hundred miles to the next show, and the next one after that, arriving just in time to put my clothes on and hit the stage, they seemed the only solution to get where you were going. I was just trying to make it through the night, the day, and the following week.

Almost everybody in Nashville took pills. When Roger Miller

and I got to be close, it seemed like washing down a handful of pills was a natural part of life. He was the cleverest and craziest man I ever met. He never quit being funny. He could think faster than anyone and forget it quicker. I'd say a cliché, and he'd write a whole song around it. If I'd ask him to repeat it, he'd shake his head and shrug. "Damned if I know what I just sang."

If you listen to the songs he wrote, they're like children's rhymes. "You Can't Rollerskate in a Buffalo Herd" or "Dang Me." Even "King of the Road." They were just novelty things that he thought were funny when he wrote them down. "England swings like a pendulum do." It was like he decided to sing them as an afterthought. Kids love Roger's music.

No matter how wasted he was, Roger always looked fresh. He might've been up for a week, but you'd never know it. Where we would stay in the same clothes for days, he carried a portable iron and always rinsed his shirts in the sink and pressed his pants.

He had briefcases full of pills, and we had as many names for them as they had colors. Roger took these things called Simcos, so we called him Roger Simco. They were what was known as an over-and-under: one side was a tranquilizer and the other would be an amphetamine, and they had a vitamin in them. There were Johnny White Crosses and Waylon's Phoenix Flashes. L.A. Turnarounds were the best. We liked to say that you could take one and drive to Los Angeles, turn around, and come straight back.

Speckled Birds. Little bitty Desoxyns. Desbutol pancakes. Somebody would want to trade a couple of "Footballs" for some real "M&M's." Pills were the artificial energy on which Nashville ran around the clock and then some. They were the drug of choice; and for a while, it seemed like eighty percent of the people in that town were comparing notes on who was taking which ones and what they were doing to them. Pill talk.

In a way, they were a great leveler. "You got any pills?" was a query that drew Nashville's elite and aspiring together, the haves and have-nots, and after the bars closed, we'd congregate at Sue Brewer's to share uppers and downers and guitars and songs.

She called the place the Boar's Nest. It wasn't a club, but her apartment. The best music ever to come out of Nashville was written right on her floor. Sue had come to Nashville in the fifties with a country music star, who got her pregnant and kicked her out. Sue told him she'd screw every Opry star there ever was, the minute they hit town, and she'd make sure he knew about it.

She had a wall of fame that went plumb up to the slanted ceiling, filled with men's pictures that each had numbers on them, in the order that she'd met them. I never got a number. We were too good as friends. She was the greatest country music fan on earth, all big eyes and dark hair. One of her favorite sayings was "The only time I ever said no was if somebody asked me if I had enough."

Sue worked in a place called the Derby Bar until three in the morning, when she'd come home and set out the welcome sign. She'd stock the refrigerator, and every once in a while one of us would come in and give her a little money for beer and food. We'd sit on the couch and deal poker, talk about the new things we were working on, or maybe finish a song. Struggling songwriters would stop by, like Kris Kristofferson and Dallas Frazier, and though it was an unwritten law that you couldn't bug anybody, if you had a good song you could sing it for Faron Young or George Jones, Mack Vickery, or Merle Kilgore. It was like a jungle telegraph: If I came in early in the morning and sang a song, somebody might be talking about it in the afternoon to so-and-so, and maybe they would think to give it a listen. A lot of songs got cut that way. The Boar's Nest was open well into the daylight, and sometimes, if she was taken with you, it could become a bed and breakfast. Finally she would grab three or four hours sleep, get little Mikey off to school, and head back to work.

She was like a sister to us. She'd cook in the evening if somebody was hungry, or watch as we passed the guitar and sang. Her heart was open to pickers and songwriters. When you'd play her a song, I don't care if it was terrible, she'd go "Oh my *Goood*; that is so wonderful, you oughta show that to Webb Pierce." I played her some bad songs, and it was the same reaction. She saw me through some rough times.

Sue's place was located in a triplex apartment building at 911 B Eighteenth Avenue South. The building is still there; there were two apartments downstairs, but you'd take the middle door and head upstairs to the Boar's Nest. To the right was a bedroom and left was the living room with the wall of fame. You could run into anybody and everybody there. People would park on the street or, if it was too crowded, just pull their car into the front yard.

One night Richie was coming up the steps and ran into Jack Clement. He knew Jack had produced Johnny Cash's records, and thought this might be a good time to meet him. He said "Hi, Jack, I'm Richie Albright," and stuck his hand out. Jack took it and promptly got sick in the bushes, hanging onto Richie's hand and shaking it and throwing up.

I was married to Barbara by now. After I got my formal divorce from Lynne, it was either get hitched or go our ways. I wasn't ready for that. I loved her, and she did me. We thought marriage was the missing ingredient, and we added it to our already-spicy relationship on October 22, 1967. She was shaking like a leaf as she walked down the aisle at her parents' house. I thought she might be scared, but when she got next to me, she said "God-damn, I've got to go to the bathroom."

Consequently, I didn't get out and around a lot. But Richie moved into an apartment behind Sue's, and I would drop over and see him. I got to be friendly with little Mikey. I'd take him to buy a toy and pick something out. "How 'bout that?" I'd ask him.

"Well," he'd say, all of four years old, "that's a little high-priced." I think Mikey kind of looked at me as his second dad for a long time. His real dad always ignored him. One time he came by when Mikey was playing downstairs. He started walking up to Sue's. "You better not go inside," Mikey warned him. "Waylon Jennings is up there and he'll knock you right back down them stairs."

Sue talked about sex till the day she died. She had cancer, several times, but she never let it stop her laughter. They kept operating, but it was a losing battle. I leased her a house, and took care of her for the last few years of her life, but there came a time when she just couldn't stand the pain any longer. Even then, she could let loose that Sue Brewer smile whenever I walked in the room.

We still give out two music scholarships a year in her name, and in 1984 I helped put together a television special in her memory. We called it *The Door Is Always Open*, because that's the way it was at Sue's house. Roger, Faron Young, Hank Williams Jr., Willie Nelson, Harlan Howard, Mickey Newbury, and me sat around in a circle and had an old-fashioned guitar pull, singing songs and telling tales about Sue. It was the best kind of tribute we could make to her.

You could go to a lot of other good-time places to drink and hit on people—and that's not to say you couldn't do that at Sue's—but the Boar's Nest was where the music was. Sing her a song, and you had the key to the front door.

Downtown, it was closing time at Tootsie's Orchid Lounge. Tootsie Bess herself might give you a big chubby welcoming hug when you came in, but she didn't care for anybody when the night was over. She'd blow that police whistle, and if you didn't move fast enough for her liking, Tootsie would stick you right in the ass with a hat pin. We'd spill out on the sidewalks and cross the street to Linebaugh's.

Broadway. On the shores of the Cumberland. Nashville, U.S.A. Beneath the long shadow cast by the Ryman Auditorium, home of the Grand Ole Opry, everything was happening, played out in a block or two that became a country music mecca for anyone who'd ever crossed a fiddle with a steel guitar.

There was no Opryland or TNN. No Branson. Nothing had moved away. Nashville was a big small town down there, a place to hang out, with Ernest Tubb's Record Shop and Roy Acuff's museum to watering holes like Tootsie's and the Wagon Wheel.

Linebaugh's served as the local cafe. It was the greasy spoon of the world. Their specialty was hot dogs split down the middle and served on a hamburger bun. There was a big plate-glass window all the way across the front, and you could look in to see who was there. It was just a square room, with some booths against the wall and tables in the middle. They had lights across the ceiling, as bright as a power station. It looked like it was daytime, all the time. They probably sold about fifty gallons of coffee over the course of an evening. Everybody was wired to the gills, staying up, looking for somebody to talk to. People clustered. You sat wherever you could find a seat.

Once inside, you'd keep an eye peeled on the front door. Besides the folks already in there, one minute Roger Miller might come strolling through, or the Louvin Brothers, or songwriters like Hank Cochran and Harlan Howard. A big music publisher would have three people in tow. Marty Robbins was a day sleeper and spent the dark hours at Linebaugh's. One night, about three-thirty in the morning, I was sitting there trying to write a song called "The Last Time I Saw Phoenix." Tom T. Hall came by; I'd never met him. He was sobering up and pulled over a chair. He ordered a cup of coffee to get him home. I was about to crash myself.

"What're you doing?" he asked.

"I'm writing on this song," I said, and showed him what I had.

"Can I help you?" He came up with a great verse, and part of another verse, and I finished that off. That's all we said to each other. We wrote the song and didn't even ask "How you been?" I didn't see him again for another ten years.

When it came time to lift a few, if it wasn't past her curfew, you'd walk across the street to Tootsie's. The backroom was where the hillbillies hung out, and it was as close to an extra dressing room as the Opry had. On weekend nights it was always packed with the stars appearing at the Ryman. Hank Williams, Patsy Cline, Cowboy Copas—they all raised a glass there. Their signatures covered the walls. I wrote my name top to bottom when I had the chance. It's still there, just like Tootsie's.

Printer's Alley, a small string of clubs and strip joints off the main drag of Nashville, was where you went when you wanted to do it up right (or was it wrong?). It was really an alley, originally home to a big newspaper print shop, and there were probably eight or nine clubs in a row, mostly pop-oriented cocktail lounges. The Black Poodle alternated between a strip joint and a country club; Skull's was run by an old carny; and then there was the Carousel, which Boots Randolph eventually bought.

The Rainbow Room was where a lot of Nashville musicians who worked sessions during the day gathered. Buddy Harman, one of the greatest Nashville studio drummers, used to play drums for strippers every night at the Rainbow, big names from that era like Candy Barr and Tempest Storm. When Boots took over the Carousel, he'd run jam sessions, and it wasn't unusual to see Chet Atkins on guitar, Floyd Cramer at the keyboard, and Gary Burton on vibes.

I high-tailed a lot with Johnny Darrell when I came to town. He was a fishing buddy of Bare's, and a runaround buddy of mine, with a real rich baritone. He could smell a good song from twenty miles away, though he got to be very bitter, because he would find these great tunes and record them, and along would come a bigger artist and cover them and have the hit. It was like he was making demos for the stars. Johnny wasn't on a major label. His first record was "Green, Green Grass of Home," but I used to love to hear him sing "My Elusive Dreams," "Hickory Holler's Tramp," and "With Pen in Hand." He found "Ruby, Don't Take Your Love to Town" and gave it to me. Billy Reynolds was another friend. I knew Kris Kristofferson, but he was too bashful when I was around. He was so shy he never wanted to play me his songs. He would hang out with Richie more than he would me. He loved me and John, and one time when I got mad at "Cash" during a recording session and moved out, Kris thought that was the most awful thing that could happen.

There was Leon Ashley, the frustrated preacher. Whenever he'd get drunk he'd start feeling guilty that he'd quit preaching. The next thing you knew he'd be singing hymns at the top of his lungs. Mack—Basil MacDavid, who worked with me and the Waylors—was around. So was Richie. With his long Beatle haircut, he had a girl in every bar. They were forever crying on my shoulder. I'd have to tell them he hated the thought of marriage. He'd been married one time, for about three or four months, and was really bitter about it. A whole three months; how could it get that bad? "She was terrible," he used to say. "I ain't never doing that no more." Like me, it took him a long time to get it right. But he liked the ladies, and for their part, the girls had it made. Everybody would hit the road, and then somebody else would come to town. Those gals had a fresh batch every week.

The whole town went into overdrive at the end of October when the country music disc jockeys held their annual convention. It had started when a dozen of the most influential country disc jockeys in America—Smokey Smith from Des Moines, Cracker Jim Brooker from down at WMIE in Miami, Nelson King at WCKY in Cincinnati, Dal Stallard from Kansas City, Joe Allison from WMAK in Nashville—held a meeting to exchange ideas. Like the apostles, they founded a church: the Country Music Disc Jockey Association, which later became the roots of the Country Music Association as we know it today.

These weren't just radio announcers. All the disc jockeys promoted shows in their area, and there wasn't one country artist in Nashville who could have his or her records played without working for the affiliated stations that played their records. It was a very cozy, inbred system.

Soon, with four or five thousand disc jockeys gathering under one roof, the record companies discovered it was a perfect way to showcase their artists. They'd host suites with free booze and food, open all day and all night. It just kept getting wilder. They made sure the disc jockeys went home remembering what a great time they'd had in Nashville, in the hopes they'd play their records for the rest of the year.

Nobody went to bed for a week. We'd terrorize the town.

Everybody was drunk, everybody was high, everybody was everything. In the hotels, all the rooms had their doors open, and each had a little guitar pull going. People wandered the halls. You never knew who you would run into around the next corner.

I performed there as a new RCA artist. Lynne came up with me from Phoenix, and I was on the same show as Willie. Hank Locklin was the older, more established artist headlining. Hank was sitting right beside me and across from Lynne, talking about that beautiful red-headed woman over there. "Look at her," he kept saying. "She is so goddamn fine. I wonder who that is."

I allowed him to go on for a while, but finally I had to let him in on the secret. "Well, she's my wife."

Hank didn't bat an eye. "She reminds me so much of my daughter," he said, real quick.

I was walking with Barbara along the hall from the apartment I shared with John to the apartment I shared with her. We were having it out, for a change. The more she yelled, the quieter I got.

Barbara's hair was down that day. It was long, almost three feet down the small of her back, and I caught it from the corner of my eye, swinging in an arc. She had her hand back and cocked. She went plumb to Fort Worth to get that punch. I turned around just in time for her to hit me right in the chin.

You do see stars. I felt my knees go. My first instinct was to fight back. She covered up her face like I was going to pop her one in return. But I got tickled when I thought of her stretched out, hair flying, eyes squinting, five foot ten inches of long tall girl taking aim at me. I just cracked up laughing.

Really, it was Barbara who never knew what hit her. I'd taken her out of Phoenix, in the West where she felt at home, and brought her to Nashville. Transplanted, her desert flower couldn't blossom; she just sat in the apartment all day. She hated Music City: what I was, what I was doing. She had a lot of innocence about her, and the music business brought out all her insecurities. She just knew that any minute someone was going to come along and I was going to run off. She thought I was going to be a big star and want to leave her.

She didn't stand a chance. Barbara was a good woman, but she got me at a point where I didn't trust women. She deserved a better shot than she got. We fought like cats and dogs. When she got hysterical, I didn't know what else to do but clam up. I wouldn't argue. It was something I'd learned from Lynne.

Barbara and I never got along on the road, and my drug use didn't help. She didn't use drugs; none of my wives did. I'd be up all night, roaming around, and she'd get disgusted and storm home. Then she'd get all torn apart not knowing what I was doing, and suspecting what I was up to. She didn't want to be in hotels; she couldn't take me on the stage, with the girls at my feet, throwing themselves at me. Everywhere we went, there was a town full of females. That just drove her up a tree.

Yet she had a tender heart. If she saw a bird with a broken wing, she'd take it home and try to feed it and nurse it back to health. When it died, it was a traumatic experience for her. She couldn't even step on an ant accidentally. Maybe she hoped that deep down inside I was some sort of stray cat that needed taking care of, looking for a home to be content. Love is like a mirror sometimes; we only see our own reflection.

She wanted me to settle down and be a husband. Barbara was the only daughter of a very rich man, and her father once offered me anything I wanted if I would just make his daughter happy. He wanted to give me enough money so I wouldn't have to travel, or even work. "I'm buying blue sky" was the way he put it. I don't blame him, though. That's what she had in mind, getting me away from the music business. The very thing that drew her to me she wanted to change. She couldn't separate me from my image. She couldn't separate the music from the man.

She never understood what made me keep going after the sound I heard in my head, and why I wanted to perform so bad. Which meant she never understood me.

\*     \*     \*

The first place I landed when I got to town was Harlan Howard's Wilderness Music. If the nights were when the wild ones hung out and roared, the daytime trips took care of most of Music Row's business. I would carry my guitar and visit the music publishers, like Tree, where Roger was based, and go from there to Acuff-Rose, or Cedarwood, or Central. We'd play each other songs and sit in on each other's recordings. Session-hopping, we called it. You wound up in the corner of a lot of strange records that way.

Don Bowman was "West Coast starvation buddies" with Harlan, and so was Bobby Bare. Harlan was everybody's friend. His childhood hero had been Ernest Tubb, and he hadn't grown up much since then. In fact, he thought that if you were really into country songs, Ernest probably had more influence than Hank Williams. Depending on how close you lived to Texas, he may just have been right.

He had become Nashville's leading songwriter in the early sixties and had a catalogue of Harlan songs a mile long: "Heartaches by the Number," "I Fall to Pieces," "Busted." I've covered over seventy of them myself and even did a whole album called *Waylon Sings Ol' Harlan*.

He loved fishing, and there's a shot of us in a boat together on that record. Despite the photographic evidence, and it might be noted that I'm sitting there with a guitar while Harlan is holding his pole, I didn't care much for relaxing in a boat with a line dangling over the edge waiting for a bite. I didn't have that much patience.

I also remember the time when Barbara and I had come out to Center Hill with Bobby Bare. We were fishing with live spring lizards, and he told me to bait my hook. I said, "I can't stand to touch them things."

They had a head like a snake. "Well, don't think snake, think bait," he told me. I tried to reach in the bucket. They were all squirmy. I'd get my hand only halfway in before I'd grab a lizard, panic, and sling it out. Finally I just gave up and sat back while

Bobby snared three wiggling springers on a single hook. He reared back and cast it over yonder. Barbara was in the front of the boat with her hair pinned down and wearing a wiglet. He hooked her hair and threw the wiglet way off in the water, much like he once hooked a guy's earlobe, before piercing for men became socially acceptable. "Let's go in" was about all I could say.

I was writing more and more, and Harlan talked to me continually about the craft, giving me advice. He used Jim Reeves as an example of "smart" singers who knew how to "snoop out a song," to pick material. He even figured out a way to pitch songs to me. He'd say, "Here's a song I wrote, and it's a great song, but I wrote it for somebody else, and you can't do it, but I sure would like for you to hear it." He nailed me every time.

Probably because he liked fishing, he taught me about hook lines. You can write a great song, but if you want an added guarantee, you've got to bait that hook. A title is important, but a hook line is what people remember; and singers can't resist a good hook line and sinker. Sometimes he'd confuse me about my writing. "You can't say the same word," he'd emphasize, or "If you take time, you can find another word." Harlan didn't like near-rhymes. He was a craftsman, and I respected that. He was particularly into titles. Harlan thought if you heard a song on the radio and the disc jockey didn't tell you who it was, you should be able to guess the title and head immediately to the nearest record store.

He wrote every morning, till it was time to hang out. I've never been able to be that kind of productive writer. I've got to have something that really turns me on to the idea, which is why so many of my songs are autobiographical. I'll take things that happen to me and try to understand them, sometimes making them sadder or happier to encompass more of an audience; a writer's prerogative. Harlan was different. He wouldn't write if he was troubled or upset. In his mind, that was frivolous, though he'd remember the feeling and tap into it when he needed the emotion. An exception was "Yours Love," which was a hit for me in 1968. He had written a poem to his to-be wife as a wedding present, and then, as he said, "writers are such sluts." He put a melody to it and thought of it as his best, most positive love song.

He found ways to get his creative juices flowing through the music, not through the use of diet pills. Paradoxically, Harlan saved them for his fishing trips, when he wanted to stay up all night under the stars and cast for bass. He didn't like to write on speed; he thought it would get him past the point of sensible. He was usually right, me included.

Harlan used to write without a guitar, just holding a legal pad. More than most, the strength of country music is its lyrics. I filled up pages and pages. I'd write about every notion that came to mind. When I ran out of paper, I'd scribble words on anything: napkins, matchbooks, dollar bills. I didn't worry how to sing the songs. Melodies form a marriage with the words. They'll tell you where they want to go, and you can always change them. Harlan's first hit was "Pick Me Up on Your Way Down," and when he sang it for you, his voice would rise on the first three words and fall on the last four. It wouldn't make sense otherwise. Your melody goes where the words take you. I depend on a lyric to give me a melody, and a good lyric will pull the melody out of you.

You never knew who you'd see when you walked into his office in the 800 block of Seventeenth Avenue. Roger or Willie or Mel Tillis, back when he was first getting started as a singer, would be sitting around. Hank Cochran might be leaned up against the wall. Conway Twitty pulled up a chair when he stopped by, or Lefty Frizzell. Even Tex Ritter. Sometimes we'd have unplanned parties. It was like Grand Central Station.

That's where I first met Don Davis. Don had been a steel player for Hank Williams, and was married to Anita Carter when I came to town. The greatest practical joker on earth, he was running Wilderness at the time for Harlan. Lefty Frizzell and Dallas Frazier were notorious for throwing up when they got drunk. They'd make loud moaning crying noises. So Don got them in the back seat of a car, took them over the roughest stretch of road he could find, and had them drink warm beer. When they started hollering "Pull over, I'm getting sick," he recorded it. That tape made the rounds of many a Nashville session.

You could reach up and touch the stars in Nashville then, or at least get ribbed by them. Though some were a little aloof, most of the bigger names made me feel welcome. They kind of laughed at the "star" thing. I liked that. Carl Smith could make me real nervous. I tried my damnedest to look like him and sing like him; I even combed my hair like his, and I didn't want him to notice. I knew he liked me a lot; he'd insist on me being on his tours. I wanted to tell him he was my hero, but if I said anything complimentary, he'd be real hard on me. "You little pipsqueak. Don't be trying to suck up to me." He let me know I was really all right by giving me a rough time.

Porter Wagoner was another one who was encouraging. He was already a big star, all bright suits and television lights. There wasn't a hair out of place on his head, but when he sang "Satisfied Mind," you knew he wasn't just a flashy dresser. He was perhaps the most even guy I've ever met in my life. I can't imagine what he thought of me, looking like a tramp. In this crowd, I was the ugly duckling. Faron Young used to call me a greasy sonofabitch. They'd all tease me a lot; you can tell when somebody accepts you. I had all that hair, and Faron was losing his. He always told me, "You laugh, but yours'll be goin' one of these days, too." Now, every time I see him, I point at my head, as if to say "It ain't started yet."

You'd sit around and talk Nashville shop till maybe it was past eleven, and then you could head over to an illegal afterhours bar that someone had set up in a house down the Row. The Professional Club: You knocked at the door and they looked through a peephole, and if they knew you, they let you in. There was a pool table and blackout drapes over the windows. They'd be open all night, or until everybody left, and then, just as they locked the entrance, along would come John Cash with Glen Douglas Tubb, Ernest's nephew, to break down the door.

One night, Faron got hit with a cue ball there. He had to have his head shaved on one side, which didn't help his hair. Another time I dropped some cigarette ashes down the pocket of my new deerskin jacket. I'm on fire! It flared up and burnt the sleeves right from my body. I kept patting at the flames, sitting there, too high to think of taking it off.

We were swarming everywhere. Sleep was a waste of time. It was so exciting, all that stuff happening around you, that you were afraid to take a nap, scared you'd miss something. Napoleon only slept three hours a night; that was my big excuse to stay up. The cops would never bother you. They knew we were taking pills and getting high, but they'd just come by and wave, say hi, because we didn't hurt anybody. The only people we were screwing up was ourselves, and we didn't seem to care. They didn't mess with us at all.

Music Row was a neighborhood of houses, along tree-lined streets that made it seem more friendly. You didn't have to have appointments. You could stop by to see Owen Bradley and Chet Atkins, and ask if they were busy. You were welcome everywhere, if you were welcome anywhere, though if they wanted to ignore you, they sure could.

I had brought the Waylors with me. I needed a band for road-work, and they were my friends; in Tommy's case, my brother. He was playing bass for me. But "sidemen" were not welcome on Music Row. We were in some big shot's (don't forget to dot the *i*) office one time, and whenever Richie or Jerry would make a comment or ask a question, the guy behind the desk would look at me and answer it. After a couple rounds of this, I could see the hurt in the band's eyes.

The next day I was going back to the same office. "C'mon guys, let's go," I said. "Nah," they answered. "We're going to hang around the hotel."

They had been with me through thick and thin. I tried to let the powers that be know how I felt. We've been hungry together, I told them. My band is here for the long run.

"You don't bring your own cliques to Nashville," they told me, and "you don't bring sidemen down on Music Row." I took it all in.

"Those guys are with me," I said. "They've been everywhere with me. If they can't be here, then I won't be here. If they're not welcome, I'm not welcome either." I walked out.

It was the same closed society at sessions. They didn't understand the concept of a band. They let me use Richie, or they let me use Jerry Gropp, and then treated them like aliens. It was like you either played the road or sessions. They actually got mad when I wanted to use my band on my recordings. "Well, road musicians can't play in the studio."

I'd say, "Why not?"

"Well, they're just not smooth enough."

I always wanted a live sound in the studio. Wonderful, I thought. Now we're getting somewhere. I liked things that weren't perfect. It was okay if the microphones leaked into each other, like a stage performance. I wanted to hear Richie's foot drum, loud and clear. I wanted to feel some excitement.

I could never play with a band that moves on the beat, or under the beat. I couldn't get into it. It has to be on the edge. My music is built on edge; that's the rock and roller in me. When I'd hear it on the beat, it felt like it was dragging. I needed it to push. The Waylors may not have been great musicians, but neither was I. Neither was all that slick shit I was hearing. That about wore me out. I couldn't even find a place to come in.

Guys like Roy Acuff, Bill Monroe, Ernest Tubb and the Texas Troubadours—they had a style. You knew it was one of their records from the first intro. There was a certain weight in the guitars, a kick to the rhythm, an authority in the singing. They didn't sound like everybody else.

I had to figure Chet out. When I first got there, whether we worked together or just sat around and talked, he was real quiet. It didn't take me long to understand how he responded to things, to read him, to see what reaction I could get out of him and know that I had him.

For Chet, a smile meant "that sounds pretty good." A grin was wonderful out of him in the studio. If he said "Man, I liked that," it was probably going to be a number-one record. I often fantasized about being out in the studio recording, and Chet getting up in the control room, standing on top of the console, jumping through the plate-glass window, rising up, wiping the blood off and yelling "Goddamn, that is a smash!"

And I'd say, "Chet, I'd like to try it once more. I think I can do it a little better."

It thrilled me to see his name on a record next to mine. If he thought you were good, something had to be there. Everybody knew that. Chet wasn't overly demonstrative, but he was always listening. He had a kindness about him. He may have been shy, yet he knew when it was the right time to not say anything. He made me work at arranging the songs. He'd say, "You do it. You're doing good." If he saw me at a wall, he'd step in with a suggestion, but otherwise he let me find my way within the framework he set up.

That was part of the problem. It was his framework, part of a Nashville sound that had been engraved in stone. They had a system. It was like an assembly line, and they rolled off records like clockwork, working more for efficiency than emotion, a song per hour and maybe a fourth if there was ten minutes till the three-hour session was scheduled to end.

Chet wanted me to be myself, but he wanted me to be myself with musicians he knew were great, that he'd been relying on. Chet had his comfort zone: a drummer that never wavered, a piano solo that tickled the same ivories, a smooth backing vocal from the Jordanaires or the Browns or the Anita Kerr singers.

Chet wasn't wrong. You wait all of your life to be able to go to Nashville and record with the likes of Chet Atkins. He'd hire the best musicians, guys like Jerry Reed on lead guitar, Fred Carter Jr. on dobro, Ray Eddington on rhythm guitar, Charlie McCoy on harp, or piano players like Floyd Cramer or Hargus "Pig" Robbins. I always thought you could've had a piano player that owned the world if he'd have Pig's left hand and Floyd's right. Ray Stevens would play keyboards and do harmony. Sometimes it made it harder to get my point across. Bobby Bare had told Chet when he went to record for him that he didn't want any well-known musicians to play on his sessions. "Who am I to go up to Grady Martin and say 'Don't play it like that, play it like this,'" Bobby would tell me. It wasn't his place, nor was it mine.

Bobby had told Chet that the best way to record me was with my band, but after the first session or two, Chet got nervous and called in the studio pickers. In his view, he probably had a point. Bands that work in clubs with the artist aren't very fast about learning new arrangements, or changing things on the spot.

Chet called it the Shotgun Method, and it had been around in country music since the twenties. It was partly an offshoot of recording in radio stations, like WSM, with one microphone in the middle of the room and ten people grouped around it, and the need to get four songs in three hours. Part of it was convenience, because the hits kept coming. Part of it was because there wasn't a lot of competition, and part of it was that country records didn't sell all that much in the sixties unless you went "pop," which was considered a dirty word.

Chet would get together with me and discuss who to hire in the studio, and we would wait to get to the session to work out the arrangement. At first I was a little hesitant about suggesting things, but Chet appreciated ideas. He believed that, in the record business, you sell an awful lot of records by not following trends; instead, the idea was to start a trend of your own. We both had the same idea, but we were coming at it from different directions. The important thing was to find somebody who was different, and unusual and appealing, and he thought I had an individual manner. "I found myself a star" was about the way he put it.

You sang the song as it went down. You had about one overdub, and I could do my own harmony, but most of the time it was live in the studio. On one side would be the musicians; on the other would be the background singers. I'd be in a little booth. Chet usually stayed in the control room, head down, concentrating. He didn't like to play on his own sessions, preferring instead to keep his attention on getting a good sound and the balance he wanted.

One time he did pick his guitar on a session of mine. When he was done, I laid back and shrugged my shoulders. "Chet, that sounds pretty good. . . ."

We'd gather around the piano before we started and sing the song over and over, structuring the arrangement. Chet and I talked over which particular effects or licks we wanted to use. He was a more open producer than someone like Owen Bradley. Owen made very clean, precise records, mostly telling people what to play. Chet was too modest for that. It was always easier for him to let the musicians express themselves. They all liked and admired him, and they wanted to help him get a hit. To the musicians, Chet was an equal, and they appreciated the fact that he could probably execute anything he wanted to as well if not better than they could.

Chet listened to the musicians; he would watch their expressions to see what was going on. He listened to everybody, which is probably why he was a great producer. He was making so damn many records, though, juggling twenty or thirty acts, that he could hardly concentrate on each one. Still, despite his many artists, as well as his executive duties at RCA, he would always look to get something different in each record, trying to spot something in the rhythm section he could feature, to make the record sound distinctive.

One of the ways we did that was with the twelve-string guitar. I like to think I helped introduce the instrument to the Nashville Sound. After I finished *Folk-Country*, I gave Chet a twelve-string, and he gave me the guitar that's on the front of that album. They weren't the luckiest of instruments: His was stolen, and mine met an undeserved fate at Barbara's hands, smashed against the wall during an argument. Chet also got the idea of using a Spanish dobro on records from me. When he heard "Four Strong Winds," he picked up on a guitar lick of mine that sounded a lot like a dobro. When he did Bobby's version, he put Jerry Reed on the instrument, having him fret it with his fingers instead of playing it with a bar. He was sure that helped make it a hit.

I had most of my second album, *Leavin' Town*, recorded in the February before I left Phoenix. On the last session of the three in which we cut things like "(That's What You Get) For Lovin' Me" and "Taos, New Mexico," Chet came up with the left-field idea of doing a version of the Beatles' "Norwegian Wood." It was this kind of unpredictability that endeared Chet to me. He loved those Beatles tunes, and I did too. After all, the Beatles were indirectly named after Buddy Holly's Crickets. I think I had probably done the song a few times at J.D.'s. John Cash remembers me singing it there.

Chet did the arrangement on "Anita, You're Dreaming" because I was too close to that song. He loved that song better than anything, and he usually agreed with my choice of material. It takes a big load off an A&R man's mind when you come in ready to cut. A couple of times Chet would find a song and play it for me. He picked material by what he liked. If he heard a song and thought, boy, that's clever, he went with the gut feeling and never second-guessed himself. He always followed his first impression, and he could surprise you.

Being a musician, Chet had to learn about caring for lyrics. He'd always listened to the music instead of the words, but as a producer, he saw how important it was to understand what the singer was singing. Words are so important to country music, you need to hear every one. He always tried to get artists to enunciate clearly, and I agreed with him. There are at least three different ways of saying the words "beautiful" and "darling," and each has a different meaning.

Hank Thompson, the western swing bandleader from Waco,

Texas, was the first one I noticed who pronounced his phrases perfectly. In fact, he might have overdone it a little. Though he started out on WACO as Hank the Hired Hand, he was well-educated and would use big words in his songs; big for our neck of the woods, anyway. I think his Brazos Valley Boys were the greatest swing band ever, and he was a superb showman. Hank's "Wild Side of Life" was hitting number one in 1952, just about when I was digging deep into my guitar; and though I never sounded like him, I always respected his perspicacity. What'd I say?

The first proper album that I recorded after I was living in Nashville was a tribute to Harlan Howard's songwriting. In two sessions spaced a week apart, on May 24 and June 1, 1966, the Waylors and I did twelve of Harlan's numbers, one right after the other. We rehearsed the album the night before each recording session, setting the band up in Harlan's office with a small two-track tape recorder. Don Davis helped on the arrangements. Some had been big hits and some hadn't. One of my favorites was "Beautiful Annabel Lee," which Harlan wrote after the Edgar Allan Poe poem. And I'm not sure we ever beat the office version of "She Called Me Baby," despite all the leakage and phones ringing and general mayhem.

All of our recording was done in RCA Studios. This was strict company policy, etched in magnetic tape. Chet thought there was nothing wrong with that. "Studios are all alike," he told me. "Same equipment, everything." But even at RCA, there were differences. Studio B was an older studio, with a reputation for warmth, a long room with a control room where the speakers had room to pump. Studio A was narrower and bigger, with high ceilings and a brighter sound. I cut more in Studio A, as a rule.

If truth be told, Chet and I respected each other's intelligence. I always had ideas, and he liked watching me make them happen. He wanted to see where I was going. I didn't know how much room he gave me until he used me on some other sessions, playing twelve-string. I watched these other artists who didn't bring anything to the table. They just went in there and Chet had to do all the work, arranging and everything. They were just standing there, waiting for their chance to sing.

Gradually, though, I think I made Chet nervous. It was drugs, more than anything.

He hated that, period. The first thing Bobby Bare had warned me was "Don't tell Chet you do drugs. If he asks if you take pills, tell him no." So, of course, about the third time I visited with Chet, he asked me if I did drugs. I thought, well, I'm not going to start this out wrong. I said yeah. Godomighty, he was mad. From then on, he was watching me. He didn't know how to deal with that, and he couldn't stand to see somebody throw their life away.

He did not understand drugs, and he didn't understand people on them. Chet didn't want to understand them. He'd been through Don Gibson, and then Roger, and then here I come. Chet was from East Tennessee, where they drink moonshine all the time. When he thought high, he thought whiskey. He never took a pill in his life. "I think you got so many beats in your heart," he'd say. "Why shorten them?"

Don Gibson had pretty much run Chet around the block. A notable songwriter and performer with such songs as "Oh Lonesome Me" and "Sweet Dreams," the latter of which he wrote for Patsy Cline, you could often find him flat on his back in Studio B, trying to do a vocal by singing up at the microphone. Chet even had an agreement that if Don couldn't perform in the studio, they'd call the session off.

One night, Don was having "trouble singing," and Chet came out to ask if they might not be better off postponing the session. "We'll get together another time," he said, and on the way back to the control room, he mentioned to Don's girlfriend at the time that "Don's not straight tonight, and we can't record." She slapped him in the face, right across the mouth. Upholding her honor, Don threw his guitar on the floor and took up a karate pose. "I'll kill you," he said. Chet didn't know what to do. He couldn't run. He just stood there. After they faced off for a moment, Don untensed and decided not to hit him. The night wound up with the Browns chasing the girl down the hall, yelling "You bitch, you can't hit Chet Atkins!"

It was that kind of manic pressure that started driving Chet crazy. He was a musician; he didn't like being an executive—the paperwork, the bottom-line pressure. He found it very difficult to go out and tell a singer "You're flat on this note," or that he would have to drop them from the label because they weren't selling. It tore his insides out. He was an artist himself, and he empathized with their fears, hopes, and desires. He took it all too much to heart.

Some of the performers had trouble with their husbands and wives, and would come to him to talk about it. When Skeeter Davis and Ralph weren't getting along, she spent more time asking Chet advice about her troubles than being in the studio.

I was no different. When I'd get high, I would want to go and see him, knowing full well that he hated talking to people who were on pills. Mary, his secretary, would try to intercede and head me off in another direction. She later married Felton Jarvis; but at the time I knew her, she had the sexiest, prettiest voice. She answered the phone, and that "hello" would melt you. Sometimes I think I went to the office just to catch a glimpse of her. In the beginning, Mary saved my ass so many times. She maneuvered me away from Chet, got my attention diverted somewhere else, and kept us both protected.

The pills built up my courage. When I was normal, I guess I felt a little worshipful of Chet. If I was comfortable with him in the studio, I was equally uncomfortable in his office, and maybe the drugs were a way I could tell him some of the things that were on my mind. Music meant so much to me, and I'd get high to have enough nerve to talk. I might've been seeking approval. I might've been tempting fate. I knew I was wrong, and he knew I knew, and when I knew he knew, we started to like each other a little bit less.

Visiting Chet was like sticking my head into the jaws of the lion. I have to give him credit for patience. He could've said, Hey, I'm not going to mess with you. You're out of here. Anytime.

But he stayed with me, because he knew when to let things take their natural course and when to let me find my way. His sensitivity was such that he cared, and always let somebody try what was on their mind. When we cut "The Chokin' Kind," in April of 1967, Harlan Howard had just written it. We listened to the demo, which was simply Harlan and his guitar, and when we headed into the studio, Jerry Reed got excited over the song. Him and Harlan got to running the session, and when they finished, it hadn't turned out the way I heard it at all. They'd just taken the song away from me.

I was so depressed. I loved that song, because it was really where I was at in my life at that time: "Well, I'd only meant to love you, don't you know it babe." Mary heard that I was feeling bad, drowning my sorrows in some downtown club, and she called and asked me what was wrong. "That session," I told her. "They just did it and it's done with and I didn't even get a chance to make my feelings known. They ruined my song."

She called Chet and he tracked me down. He said, "Don't ever leave the studio like that again. I will stay all night long with you, but don't let that happen. You come tell me that it's not right." He knew what music was meant to be, and how much I cared, no matter what shape I was in.

The next morning I came back to the studio; we were scheduled for another session. "What are we going to do?" the band asked.

" 'The Chokin' Kind.' "

"We did that yesterday."

"No, you did that yesterday," I said. "I'm doing it today."

Chet cut the best records of my early years. He may have told me once or twice to straighten up, and looked with disapproval on my drug use, but like Don Gibson, I think he thought of me as a good renegade.

He encouraged my strange harmony singing, even if I would combine tenor and baritone parts in the same overdubbed voice, with some odd notes besides. He picked up on the fact that I emphasized the 1 and 3 beat of a 4/4 measure. Most musicians will kick the 2 and 4, but the 1 and 3 is the way the public thinks if you get them clapping in an auditorium. And he liked that I didn't sound like anyone else when I sang. He always says he can tell in two notes if it's me singing.

If anything, Chet was too nice. He would internalize so much that he grew a tumor, and suffered cancer of the intestines. The business literally made him sick. The stress was too much.

I couldn't have helped, trying to communicate ideas that I was still trying to explain to myself. There just wasn't enough happening musically for me. I would be right at the edge of things, and the way the music unfolded didn't seem to be pushing it over the top. They were good, smooth records, and there I was, rougher than a goddamn cob. He'd let me use some of my band, and then put other people in there, and sometimes those things that he put in there were just enough to keep it from what it really was supposed to sound like in my imagination. If I wrote those songs and honed them on stage with my band, I had an idea what they should be. And they weren't.

Chet was at a point where he was just tired, and he was wanting out of it. He needed to go back and play his guitar. I can't fault that. He *is* the Country Gentleman.

We had some great times together, and we cut some wonderful songs. On February 15, 1967, nearing the end of surviving my first year in Nashville, we did a John Hurley/Ronnie Wilkins composition called "Love of the Common People." It had it all— the horn stabs that I loved so much, an insistent piano figure that lodged in your brain, and four (count 'em) key modulations upward, so that the song never stopped getting you higher. The lyrics were especially meaningful, for a poor country boy who had worked his way up from "a dream you could cling to" to a spot in the working world of country music.

A song is where it starts. Chet believed that, too. If you don't have a song, you don't have anything.

Where it finishes is late some night in Studio A. The musicians have gone home. The track is done. They've moved the microphone from the vocal booth to the floor, so I can have more room to move, though I don't move much. We're working on "Only Daddy That'll Walk the Line." I'm going to sing harmony with myself, the moaning *Oh* of "Only." If you slide into the control room, maybe with Bare or Johnny Darrell, you might catch Chet and the engineer bent over the board, listening to me in solo with the track shut off, trying to get a fix on the frequency where my voice is wandering.

I'm out in the studio. I've got the headphones turned up high. I'm walkin' the line and talkin' the line, doing a little dance to Wayne Moss's stuttering Tex-Mex guitar solo as it comes blazing through. Chicken-pickin'. Singing along to the chorus. *Oooooohh-nly Daddy*. . . .

Bobby turns to Chet. "Damn, I believe he's got something treed."

*Ooooooohh*. . . .

Howling at the moon.

# CHAPTER

# 5

# . . . TO NASHVILLE REBEL

EXTERIOR. FRONT PORCH. NIGHT.
ARLIN GROVE sits on the porch swing, strumming a guitar.
He wears a white T-shirt; there is a close-up of his face, the
light glistening off his slicked-back hair.
MOLLY MORGAN comes out to join him. She is wearing a
white shirt, knotted at the waist; her hair is in a flip, held by
a white band.

> MOLLY
> You sure do take good care of that guitar.

> ARLIN
> It's all I got. . . . That and about five zillion songs in
> there.

He points to the guitar case. She comes over and sits by him.

> MOLLY
> Don't you want anything else?

ARLIN

Yeah. I'd like to make my mark in life with music. You know, anything can be said with a song. I've got things I'd like to say in my own way.

MOLLY

Don't you want a home?

ARLIN

I've got a home. But it's a long way from here.

He sings a verse of "I'm a Long Way from Home." She gazes at him with growing affection. He puts his arm around her. They kiss.

Poor Boy comes to town. Poor Boy meets Pretty Girl. Poor Boy makes good, marries Pretty Girl. Treats her wrong. Poor Boy goes off the deep end. He comes back. Everything's okay.

There wasn't anything about a Nashville Rebel in the movie, as far as I was concerned. They cast the characters after they had the title, and I never thought it was about me. It was more like a Nashville travelogue, where you could see the inside of Tootsie's, the Grand Ole Opry, the Black Poodle, be entertained by stars like Porter Wagoner, Faron Young, Tex Ritter, Sonny James, and get yourself introduced to newcomer Waylon Jennings, as Arlin Grove, in an American-International motion picture, *Nashville Rebel*.

I had heard about the auditions, but I hadn't planned to do anything about them. John Cash was out of town, however, and I was floating around. I went past the building where they were holding the screen tests and decided on the spur of the moment to give it a shot. I was hours past any appointment. I read for the part, and was terrible. I promptly forgot about it. I was higher'n a kite.

Chet may have been behind it, but the next day I came to find out they chose me from about twenty other guys. I'm no actor. I started out filming near 170 pounds, and lost thirty of them before the three weeks of shooting schedule was over. I was up the whole time, never eating, fighting with Barbara, me on pills and roaring. By the time the movie started reaching its climax, with a scene where my wife is supposed to tell me she's pregnant by leaving some baby shoes on my anniversary-dinner plate, I looked like a gutted snowbird.

"Molly," my wife in the movie, was played by Mary Frann, later to star in *The Bob Newhart Show*. It was corny shit from the start. Arlin, my character, on his way home out of the army, is beaten up by a gang of toughs and left by the side of the road. He wakes, staring into her eyes. She works at Morgan Corners, "a one-pump gas station and grocery store."

Arlin heads down to the local "hootenanny" (I was folk-country, remember?) to play a number. Before he goes on, Uncle Ed Morgan (played by Cousin Jody from the Grand Ole Opry) shows off a hokum lap steel guitar instrumental, working out "Mockingbird" on "the old biscuit board," as he puts it, a routine that probably hearkens back to vaudeville, complete with bar swipes and flapping tongue. It gives you an idea where country started. I sing "Nashville Rebel," picking the opening guitar lick; then I'm back with my own tongue flapping, kissing Mary Frann some more. She shows me her naked back. She drops her towel. The camera focuses discreetly on a nearby clock, while her dad sends out shotgun-wedding invitations.

Using my best Roy Orbison voice for "Green River," Arlin is discovered by a Mr. Wesley Lang, played by Gordon Oas-Heim, the character actor. He's an attorney who wants to manage this hot new singer. Cue the lawyer jokes. He comes complete with cigarette holder, a sure sign of distrust, and we visit him on his estate the next day to watch him mistreat his horses. Good, meet Evil. He thinks I'm a "walking talking gold mine," his property to do with as he wishes. For my part, I ask incredulously, "You mean, all I have to do is sing and my manager will take care of it?" Sign here, thank you. Lang then presents Arlin to Margo

Powell (Ce Ce Whitney), who is instructed to get a suitable image together, teaching him "the facts of life."

The action heads to Music City. While I explore the city with Molly, interspersed with crowds and performances at the Parthenon in Centennial Park and the Opry, the movie becomes a souvenir time machine of the Nashville I knew then. Chet makes a cameo appearance. "Sounds pretty good to me," he says, and puts in a plug for the Nashville Sound, an "in-built feature of our musicians and singers."

Lang looks at him over his cigarette holder. "Just make sure he's got that Nashville Sound." There's even a brief shot of me recording in Studio B with the Waylors. You can make out Jerry's left-handed guitar, Tommy's bass, and guitarist Sheryl Millet, who was playing with us at the time. Richie is hard to spot, back behind the drums.

The live performances by Tex, Sonny, Porter, Faron, Loretta Lynn, and the Wilburn Brothers are like windows into the past, home movies of Nashville as it looked in the summer of '66, when the music was just a little bit younger and more isolated from the mainstream. When Faron sings Don Gibson's "Sweet Dreams," it peels back the years to a moment of star-crossed talents at the heart of why we sing, and the traditions we hear every time we move from one chord to another.

Both Tex Ritter and the Wilburn Brothers, with help from Loretta Lynn, tip their cowboy hats to the country artists that came before. Tex invokes the spirits of Hank Williams, Patsy Cline, Texas Ruby, Karl Farr of the Sons of the Pioneers, and many others in his visit to "Hillbilly Heaven"; while the Wilburns, Teddy and Doyle, present a similar salute, helped by Loretta Lynn, on "Christmas at the Opry." Both mention country clown Rod Brasfield, and I'd bet there aren't ten people out of a hundred who would even know who he is today. *Nashville Rebel* has kept his name alive, and I like that.

Back at the ranch, Tex is giving Arlin some good advice from the inner sanctum of Tootsie's. "We could use some new blood in this business," he says to "me." "Don't drive too fast on the road, and don't go wild." The camera pans around the walls, showing some of the signatures. You can glimpse Hank Cochran, Roger Miller, Leo Jackson, "Tubb," and a huge scrawled Ben Dorsey III. I should've known then Arlin was heading for a fall.

"I'll make him and I'll break him," says Lang, after he catches me rubbing down Margo's back. I enjoyed the scenes with Margo the best. At least I was closest to being myself. My character was such a goody two-shoes, I could hardly recognize who I was supposed to be. There's one point where I pour Molly some champagne. It takes me a while to get the cork out; it was the first bottle of champagne I'd ever opened in my life. I wasn't your biggest drinker. Finally I manage to pop it. "We're in business," I ad-lib. Looking at it some thirty years later, it's the real me. I still say it the same way.

Wesley sends Arlin to a society club in Chicago, where he predictably bombs. To add insult to injury, he has Henny Youngman come on after me, zinging Arlin's act with some of the oldest jokes in the universe. "If that's harmony, I'll take grits." "He has a lot of talent, only it's in Elvis Presley's name." Take my life, please.

This throws our hero into a fit of depression. "You're finished," Lang tells him. "You don't have what it takes." Distraught, Arlin wanders a nighttime Chicago filled with neon signs flashing dance halls and pancake houses. He swigs from a bottle.

Margo finds Arlin sacked out at a fleabag hotel. She bangs on the door. I run my fingers through my hair. "What's happening?" I ask dazedly. The line between Arlin and myself was getting less clear, the more pills I took while I was doing the part. At least I got some sleep in the movie.

She tells me to "be a man" and brings me to a country-western club where I sing "Tennessee," the camera dollying so close up it seems to be aiming through the gap between my front teeth. The crowd loves me. I go back to the Opry. Wesley tries to destroy me one final time by telling me Molly is pregnant and dying before

I go on; I speak to her over the radio, arriving at the hospital to greet Arlin Grove Jr. and renew our love.

*Nashville Rebel* was one of those movies that go straight to the drive-in. Depending on how you looked at it, I'd either come a very long or a very short distance from the top of the snack bar.

Barbara could not bear me kissing another girl on the screen. *Molly, if you can hear me . . . I love you.* She'd listen to me whispering words of romance to Mary Frann and think I was being untrue. She couldn't believe I was playing a role.

She didn't want me to do the movie, and when I went ahead and took the part, we started to split up, even though we were yet to be officially married. I think Barbara was just as loyal and true to me as she could be, and though she never believed it, knowing all those women were out there on the road, not knowing what I was doing, suspecting me of the worst crimes, I tried to be good by her. Because we'd had such misery through Lynne, I felt that I owed her a straight chance.

I had gotten a Nudie suit one time; he was *the* tailor to the country-and-western stars, and while I didn't want to be a flashy dresser, Merle Kilgore talked me into getting outfitted when we were on a Hank Williams Jr. tour. I had a white one made, with just a little sparkle. I should've known better. The first night I wore it was also the first night I'd taken uppers and downers together. Mix those white crosses and red devils and you're crazy. Loretta Lynn walked me all over the dressing room trying to sober me up enough to get out there and sing.

That night, when I left the show, I went back to the hotel with a woman detective Barbara had put on me. I kept falling asleep. When Barbara found out, she ripped the Nudie suit to shreds with a straight-edge razor. I found pieces of white sparkle for weeks. Then she took a Martin guitar Chet gave me out of the case and smashed it against the wall. It looked like ten thousand boxes of matches all over the floor. She just wanted to get back at me; that's how knock-down drag-out she could be.

Barbara helped me out of a lot of jams, and I tried to forgive and forget. Maybe I thought I deserved whatever she put me through. One time, working the Golden Nugget in Las Vegas, I went on a gambling jag and lost my whole week's paycheck. I didn't even have money to pay the band, or enough cash to get out of town. Barbara wound up calling her millionaire daddy, and he wired us a bunch of money so we could get to the next show.

It was just a constant battle. We'd fight on the phone; we'd fight on and off the road. All of my ex-wives hated what I did. They were so jealous of the music. It was like another woman. They kept hoping I would give it up for them. And they were right to be concerned; I wasn't about to stop playing guitar to keep my home life together. I remember Duane Eddy talking to Lynne, telling her she would have to grow with me in order for it to ever work. She had flat out told him she did not want me to be a star. Lynne, or Maxine, and now Barbara, knew that music, the real Other Woman, was taking me away. It had to hurt.

I don't blame them. I guess I left all my ex-wives, when you come down to it. They didn't leave me. What I'd say to the lawyer is "give it all to 'em"; I'll make it somewhere else. I just wanted out. I don't know why I just didn't find some good-looking woman, buy her a new house and a new car, and shack up for a little while and then go about my business.

Barbara is still a dear friend, along with her mom and brothers, and is still beautiful to this day. Even after we split up, she'd come to my apartment to sleep over. I'd wake up in the morning and she'd be in bed with me, snuggling up. But she might've died living with me. At the least, she would've killed a lot more guitars.

Sometimes, especially in a relationship with someone you love, you bring out different qualities. I brought out a meanness in Barbara that I couldn't believe. After a time, I knew that it was never going to work anymore, and I'd never be back. I took her home, for the last time.

Then I went wild.

\*     \*     \*

I was everywhere, all in a day that became night that became day again. I would never just go into a room. I went all over it.

Curtis Buck was a crazy sonofabitch, and he ran around with me. While I was singing, he'd go find the girls, and if we needed drugs, he'd find the dope.

I had two secretaries that didn't know how to secretary. One—I called her Squirrely—was my driver. She couldn't see as far as the hood. She'd be up in the front seat with Curtis, wearing the cutest little chauffeur's cap, and I'd be laying out in the back seat with the other. Suddenly there'd be this bloodcurdling scream. "Look out!" Curtis would be hollering and waving his arms. We'd be going around a truck on a curve with another truck aiming right at us! I thought, There ain't much I can do here. I'd just lay right back down, close my eyes, and pray for the best.

We'd pull up at a show. They'd get out of the car, all low-cut blouses, plenty of boobs, up-to-the-point miniskirts and black hose, and the hillbillies would come running for miles around to get a glimpse of these girls. I'd tumble out of the back seat, and they'd escort me to the stage. I had given up hope of ever being able to keep a marriage together.

If you saw the movie *Payday*, you'll know where they got the idea. Me, the limousine, and the women, driving up and down the road, shooting at signs with a .22 Magnum buntline. That's what I do for a living.

One night I even outdid myself, talking this guy out of his wife in Cincinnati, Ohio. We were on a bill with Wynn Stewart and Buck Owens. Wynn came running backstage saying "Goddammit, you're not going to believe this girl about three rows back."

Sure enough, I got out there and spotted her immediately. She was blonde-headed and beautiful and stuck out like an angel. All the time I'm up there, she's just going nuts when I'm singing, looking at me, giving me the eye. Sitting beside her is some old boy who doesn't understand what's going on, or maybe he does.

After the show I went up to the promoter. "If you want me for nothing tonight," I said, "you get that girl in here. It won't cost you a dime." Sure enough, two minutes later she comes around the corner, with that guy right behind.

"I want to talk to you," she says, all smiles, "but he won't leave me alone."

The guy she's with is fit to be tied. "I know what she wants to do," he hollers. "She don't want to talk to you. She wants to fuck you."

I'm thinking ninety miles an hour. I said to him, "Why, what makes you think that?"

"We're separated. We're getting a divorce. I know that the only reason she came with me tonight was to see you and get to meet you."

I said, "Wait a minute, son. Girl, you go over there and wait." I pulled him aside, put my arm around his shoulder. "Let me tell you something. You got your blonde, and I have my blonde. I was fixing to get a divorce from my wife. She did me the same way." I made up a story about how she was always running off and everything. "And then, one day, I took her back home to her momma and it all changed."

"What do you mean?" he asked. He was dumber than a rock.

"She calls me begging to come back every day, and do you know why? Because one time I dropped her off and said that's it. You better let her do the walking when you leave. A woman can't stand it when a man makes the first move."

He considered that for a moment. You could almost see steam rising from his ears he was thinking so hard. Finally, he said, "What do you think I ought to do?"

I closed the trap. I said, "Well, tell her to go to hell."

"But we're eighty miles from home."

"That's even better. Root hog or die, she'll never forget it. She'll be pounding your door down. She'll have to hitch home or find her own way. If I was you, I'd tell her to get fucked and walk out of here."

The Jennings Clan, pre-me. That's Grandpa Gus on the far right.

The Shipleys at the turn of the 1940s. I'm standing hand on head,
posing on the left in the second row.

Mom, Dad, Tommy, and I
in McAllen, Texas.

First grade.

Daddy and his boys. By now James D. is the littlest (Bo was still a couple of years away), and I've learned how to roll up my jeans.

July 1958

My first signature model guitar.

One of my first "Big Time" appearances, with Ray Corbin, George Atwood, and Kilmer Key. (*courtesy Corbin family/KLLL collection*)

Disc jockeys at K-Triple-L radio: Hi-Pockets, Don Bowman, and Sky and Ray Corbin. (*courtesy Corbin family/KLLL collection*)

Got a light? A photo booth at Grand Central Station in January 1959.

Three-part harmony: myself, Buddy, Tommy Allsup. (*courtesy William F. Griggs*)

How the audience saw my first taste of the rock and roll road.

Buddy Holly onstage
at the Teen Hop in the
Laramar Ballroom,
Fort Dodge, Indiana;
January 30, 10:31 P.M.
(*courtesy Don Larson*)

I believe they call this a grin . . .

Back on the radio in Coolidge, Arizona.

A formal portrait from the height of our J.D.'s rise to fame.

The original Waylors: Jerry Gropp, Richie Albright, and Paul Foster.
Dig those matching guitar straps.

That's why I'm a country singer: I've always loved the sound of a twelve-string guitar.

Showin' out with my brother Tommy on bass.

Afterhours in the late 1960s.

Backstage with Dottie West at Beloit High School, Wisconsin. Which shines more, her hair or my suit?

The look of love.

An early snapshot of Jessi, Jennifer, and myself. (*courtesy Martha Garrison*)

You sure look sharp wearin' sunglasses after dark.
(*courtesy* The Courier-Journal)

My girls: Momma and Jessi.

He stormed back to where the girl was standing, gave her the finger and a piece of his mind, and strode out of the room. As soon as he turned that corner, I said, "Girl, let's get out of here," and we took off.

The music, the pills, and the women—that was our life on the road. Sometimes I'd screw two or three a night. Richie remembers me reserving extra rooms in hotels, running up and down the emergency staircase to get from one to the other. Once, in Louisville, I had girls stashed on three floors. I had been awake for a few days and was determined to visit them all. "Waylon," he said to me, "you're going to kill yourself." I never knew when enough was enough. Too much was never enough.

I took pills by the fistful. I'd start with a Desoxyn or two, and some little White Crosses, and wash the whole mess down with an Alka-Seltzer to kick it in the ass. It would come on like gangbusters. Then I'd drink coffee, and every once in a while I'd pop another to keep going. A doctor once told me that if I took one Desoxyn every day for a month, I'd be a dead man. I had to laugh. I knew they would kill some people, but they didn't kill me.

I thought I was invincible. Twenty amphetamines a day was normal, and thirty wasn't unusual. I'd hit the ground running; I never had a hangover because I never gave myself a chance. If I would manage to go to sleep at night, I'd put a glass of water by the bed and about three pills right by the phone. When that wake-up call came, I'd take the pills, lay back down until they kicked in, and then get up and go. Got to go.

My dad came to the premiere of *Nashville Rebel* in February of 1967. He was real shy, though you could tell he was proud as all get out of me. His neck was so thick, he found it uncomfortable to wear a tie, but he put one on because it was such an important occasion.

After the movie was over, they had a reception out in the lobby. I caught him as he was trying to slip out the back door of the theater. He wasn't used to such crowds in Littlefield. We were stand-

ing there talking, and the first person that looked over and saw
him was Tex Ritter. Tex went right up to him. He said, "You're
Waylon's dad," and stayed chatting with him all night. Everybody came over and introduced themselves to him. He was just
in glory. I was glad he got to experience that.

Every time I saw Tex do "Hillybilly Heaven" in the movie, I
thought of Daddy. When he's reading from "the big tally book,"
as Will Rogers called it, he moves from greats that have passed
on to those whose roll call is yet to come. I couldn't help but
think my daddy's name was inscribed in there.

On June 3, 1968, he slipped away, dead of a heart condition. If
it was today, there are operations that could've given him another
quarter century of being with his family; he was only fifty-three
when he passed on. He hadn't even been sick.

Tommy called me from Nashville. I was in Toronto. "Big
brother," he said. "I got some bad news."

I knew what it was going to be before he told me. "It's Daddy,
ain't it?"

I refused to go down to the funeral home and see him. I wanted
to remember him as he was. I kind of passed out at the funeral,
and I got a taste of something I'd never seen before, which was
people standing around watching other folks' misery. At the
gravesite, strangers were coming up and wanting autographs. I
didn't know or care who they were.

It took a long time for Daddy's death to sink in. I thought he'd
always be there. When he was alive, I knew I was secure, that he
was the one person who would care for and about me, no questions asked, no matter what. I thought there wasn't any trouble
he couldn't help me out of, and after he died, I've never felt safe
since. It was like he passed over the reins of the family to me, and
I had to take over. "You're the man of the house now," I could
hear him saying, as if he was going away for a couple of days leaving me in charge. I kept remembering that day he took on Strawberry Stewart. Even though he had a hoe in his hand, he dropped

it on the ground when he started after him. He only needed himself to be strong.

I've never stopped missing him, in all these years, and I like to
think I've taken his best qualities and passed them along in my
music and life.

Lucky Moeller stepped right in as a surrogate dad for me. He'd
had a lot to do with me moving to Nashville in the first place,
even traveling to Phoenix to tell me he could keep me working.
He settled me. I'd spend a couple, three nights swarming all over
town, and then I'd pull up at his office. I'd park the Cadillac
about four times and almost put it through the front door. He'd
turn off the phone, close the office, and talk to me, about when
he used to drive an asphalt truck and when I pulled cotton.

He had come a long way, from being vice president of a bank
in Oklahoma to the head of Moeller Talent, Inc., which he ran
with his son, Larry. Lucky had come to town in the mid-fifties as
a personal manager, and with Jim Denny, who ran Cedarwood
Publishing, developed the bulk of offices along Sixteenth Avenue
called Music Row. His first love was booking, and with some
thirty artists on his roster, he slotted over thirty-five hundred
shows a year.

He booked north and he booked south, west over east, usually
in the same week. Moeller Talent had a circuit, locked down and
tight, and once you started, you kept going. They had their
White Horses, the top-line acts like Webb Pierce or Kitty Wells
(who once did an incredible 265 one-nighters in 1963); and they
might get up to twenty-five hundred dollars a night. But you had
to take all these other people as part of the bargain. If you didn't
pay the big white horse, Lucky still might not cut you out of the
picture.

They would book me into this place, and the owner would stiff
me. I wouldn't get the money, but they could call up Lucky and
get another horse from the stable. Saddle 'em up. You needed to
work. Some nights I would only get four hundred dollars. John

Cash took me with him on a couple of tours, but most of it was really rough.

You could only go so far and that was all. The farther I traveled, the farther in the hole I went. I was having to get advances from RCA to get me transportation. I needed to have something to drive to the shows. I was wearing out cars on a monthly basis.

It was a form of control, to keep us in debt and in their debt. Most of the time we didn't mind. We were all excited, wide-eyed and bushy-tailed to be going everywhere, though if we stopped to notice, it was always the same places, the same people, for the same money. To the Cow Town in San Francisco, down Route 5 through Fresno and Bakersfield to the Palomino Club in L.A. out in the Valley, then across to Phoenix and J.D.'s, where I was still the biggest thing to hit that town. Around the horn of Texas where it seemed like I played San Antonio twice a month: the Stallion Club . . . the Mustang Club . . . something like that. They had those big Bob Wills dance floors. That's what "Bob Wills Is Still the King" is about. I'd get up on the long bandstand, built for a twelve-piece cowboy orchestra, and I'd be telling my four guys to start spreading out. We're playing calypso beats, straight eights, double-timing, and the audience would start looking at me weird. They liked the songs, but they couldn't dance to them.

Up to Canada, through the upper Midwest, along the south Atlantic coast, the Virginias and the Carolinas. Every winter we played a cowboy bar in Jackson Hole, Wyoming. It was twenty-seven below. Then it would be the Gulf Coast in the summer. Or you'd drive from Minneapolis to Atlanta overnight. I always accused the booking agents of having a dart board with a map on it.

The band traveled in an old Dodge motorhome. It wasn't a bus; it had belonged to Red Sovine and had been sitting in his backyard. Every hose and tire was ready to give up the ghost. One time, going across the Rockies up in Canada, Calgary to Vancouver, the brakes went out. And I'll never forget that night in Red Deer, sleet and ice and snow and us under that damn motorhome, trying to unfuse the push-button transmission, get it in drive so we could keep going forward. But we were still in show business.

They'd load me in the back and I'd sleep all the way to wherever we went. Usually I'd been up for days, taking over-and-unders, and when I'd crash, there wasn't anything that could wake me up. Richie would come in the back periodically and listen for my heart to see if I was still alive. I wouldn't move, all the way from Nashville to Syracuse.

We had a horse trailer cut down to carry all our equipment in, and when it hit a bump everything in it bounced nine feet in the air. I could never figure out why my amplifier sounded different every night. Usually I'd look in the back and the speaker was hanging on by one screw.

The sound in the clubs was terrible, because there were no p.a. systems. You never even thought about a monitor. The difference between having a good sound and a bad sound was whether you could hear anything coming off the back wall. Like a beer bottle.

The honky-tonk circuit. It was inbred and in bed. Some of the business people in town were partners with guys out there buying the acts. This one over here was poker buddies with that guy who runs the record company. Another books the record company's acts and together they own a building. A music publisher controls a radio station; the disc jockey writes songs and wants a record deal. Nobody was in competition with anybody; everybody stayed out of everybody's way.

It was a family thing, which would have been nice if they didn't try to keep it all in the family. It was like the Grand Ole Opry, bless its heart.

I'd played at the original Ryman Auditorium with Bare the first time. I sang harmony with Bobby on "Come on Home" and "Sing the Blues to Daddy." It's a moment every singer dreams of, and I wasn't any different. That was one of the few things that ever scared me. I didn't get nervous till I got out there, and then I looked down and I knew that Hank Williams, Red Foley, Ernest

Tubb, and all those immortals had just stood there in that one place, and I wondered what the hell I was doing there.

They offered me a spot on the Opry. There's even a scene in *Nashville Rebel* where I pay my respects to Ott Devine, who ran the Opry in the sixties. At that time, you had to be on there twenty shows a year, and since it was broadcast on Saturday night, that's usually the night that you make the most money out on the road. I needed that night to make the rest of the week come out right. I had to turn them down. They wanted to give me ninety dollars, union scale.

At least I said no peaceably. John Cash had come to the Opry when he got his first record in the Top Ten country charts in *Billboard*. He'd sat out in the Opry manager's office for three hours, dressed in his black shirt and pants, sideburns, and rockabilly shoes, until they finally relented and let him on the show.

He encored seven times, and only had four songs out on the market. He sang "Hey Porter," "Cry, Cry, Cry," "So Doggone Lonesome," and "Folsom Prison Blues" over and over. Hank Snow and Minnie Pearl made him welcome, which pleased John no end, because Hank Snow was his hero. He was so proud he had torn the Opry up.

He joined the Opry but couldn't make most of the Saturdays because he'd be out working tours with Jerry Lee Lewis or Carl Perkins or Roy Orbison. John would do one Saturday and miss three. Finally, they called him in and said that if he was intending "to be a member of the Grand Ole Opry," he'd have to start showing up more.

Ultimatums are not the best way to get on John's good side. So he said, "Well, this'll be my last night." At the end of his final song, he dragged the microphone stand across the lights at the edge of the stage, breaking them all, one by one. "I was just having fun," he told me, "watching 'em pop."

The manager of the Opry was less than pleased. "You don't have to come back anymore."

"I don't plan to," said John, but when he got in the car with

June, he started crying. Someday, he thought, they'll want me back. In time, he did make his peace with the Opry. There's nothing John liked better in those days than sitting in a dressing room listening to the Jordanaires sing gospel, or trading bluegrass verses with Bill Monroe or Flatt and Scruggs. He even wound up doing his network television show from the Ryman Auditorium.

One of the phrases I always heard was "I wish New York and L.A. would leave us alone."

The Nashville Sound folks never realized that they actually did, to our detriment. If you were a country artist signed to Nashville, the record company treated you like an uninvited guest at a dinner party. They didn't set a place for you at the table. They didn't take you seriously. Their corporate base was in New York or L.A., and we were out of the power structure. No matter how many records you sold, all their promotion went to the big pop acts signed to both coasts. You had to fight and scratch for any attention at all from the record company.

Country music reacted to that by drawing in the wagons, getting defensive, building a wall around Nashville that kept country artists in rather than outsiders out. I went west to Los Angeles and cut Kris Kristofferson's "Lovin' Her Was Easier (Than Anything I'll Ever Do Again)" with Ricky Nelson's band. At the time, he had a good bunch of guys with him, including Sonny Curtis. It was a great record, uptempo, with a guitar riff that was like a clarion call to arms every chorus. They wouldn't release it because I recorded it in L.A. They didn't want to start a precedent. They wanted all the hit records to be cut in Nashville.

The closest I got to the top of the charts, as the sixties started running out of months, was "Only Daddy That'll Walk the Line." I waited a damn year to cut that song; Charlie Louvin's bass player had the original version for Capitol. I didn't want to cover him. I thought I'll wait awhile, and if it doesn't hit, I'll go for it. I think he outsang me on it, but I had the best track. I knew it had the potential to go all the way, and it might had not "Harper Valley P.T.A." kept it out of the number-one slot.

I like to say that I was a legend before I was ever a hit in country music. I was kind of a fair-haired boy when I arrived in Nashville. Everybody loved everything I did, but I was not cutting consistent chart records.

I never did feel at home. I didn't know it yet, but the minute I got there, I was in trouble. I found myself trying to fit in, and having people wedging me in places where I didn't work. I was being told, over and over, You just don't do this, or You can't do that. There's a certain way we do things here in Nashville. We know what's best for you. All you are allowed to sound like is the Nashville Sound.

I would think of ideas, and before I would get a chance to put them down, or even hear how they worked out, they'd tell me I was wrong. What the fuck do you mean, it's wrong? Well, it'll make the record skip if we put a big drum beat in it. We don't understand that rhythm. We have to smooth it out or we'll never get played on the radio. And the best one of all: That's not country.

I always hated labels, and they kept trying to stick them on me. They didn't know who I was or what I was about, and I tried my best to keep them in the dark. I remembered what Buddy had told me about not pinning yourself down. The things that weren't country about me scared them, even though they tried to call me everything but straight country. They always needed a marketing plan—folk-country, Nashville rebel—to understand me, to try and put my feelings in a frame, and even then they didn't get it. Music is just music. People who put labels on music are those who have to merchandise it. It makes their job easier for them.

I wanted to cut my records a whole different way. I wanted to build the song in the studio, not the control room. I wanted the dynamics to happen out there, alive, with the band.

I gave the Nashville Sound an honest chance, at first. I went along with what Chet, and later Danny Davis and Ronny Light, would suggest. I would use their bands and their pickers. Some of the musicians who played on my early records were great guys, but they were trapped by the number system. I'd go in, cut the tracks, come back the next day, and I wouldn't even recognize that it was the same tune.

When I first hear a song and it knocks me out, I can tell you what it's going to sound like when I get through with it. It's like a painter, a sculptor, and a poet rolled up in one; you should be able to see a picture, feel its shape, as well as hear the song's emotion.

I just did what felt good to me. It was like Grady Martin said when they asked him if he read music. "Not enough to hurt my playing," he replied. The truth is I never understood that much about the mechanics of music. I'd come in wrong, and I'd turn the beat sideways. I was the only guy in the world who could hum out of meter. My guitar playing came from inspiration only. I did it out of self-preservation. I could never stand to practice. Everything I know I learned in front of an audience. Whenever I'd pick up a guitar, I'd start to play a song.

Chet and I may have had our differences, but I think he liked the fact that I didn't back up, and never have backed up. I don't have a reverse gear when it comes to what I believe in.

There's more than one way to do things. There's at least two ways, and one of them is your way. You damn well have a right to try it, at least once.

I went through my marriages like Grant went through Richmond. I finally gave up. I said, hell, I'm not going to be able to be married. And just when I thought it was all over, when I quit looking, that's when I found the right one.

I started with Jessi on level ground. I was seeing Barbara before I left Lynne, and Lynne before I split with Maxine. Jessi, on the other hand, had just gotten unhitched from Duane Eddy. We were both free.

It wasn't like that the first time we met. I was in Phoenix working on "Norwegian Wood" in a studio there, and Duane brought her by. She was making her mark as a songwriter—Dottie West and Don Gibson had both done things by her—and she'd written a duet called "Living Proof." Duane asked if I would help out with the demo and I said yeah. So they set her up beside me, on a box because she's so little, and we sang into one mike. I thought, Man, she ain't bigger than a nickel.

A cute little ol' sweetheart was what she was. We had to move the box back because she had more volume than me, and we were all laughing about that. She was very respectful and everything. Not a bit flirty at all. I was married at the time, and she was too.

It was funny, though. We got through, made a copy of the tape, and I saw them to the door. We said our good-byes, and as they walked away, she turned around and looked back at me again. I've thought about that ever since, because I stood there waiting for her to do just that. It was as if I knew she was going to.

There was something there. The next time we crossed paths, she had separated from Duane, but they weren't divorced yet. Her sister, Sharon, brought her to a show, and I got her up on stage to sing with me. I was apart from Barbara by then. I looked at her and said, "Hey, little girl . . . want to run off with me?"

She gave me the eye back. "Call me in six months" was all she said.

I didn't see her again, but she caught me on a Buck Owens television special. I had on a gray Nehru suit that somebody had talked me into wearing, and weighed about 140 pounds soaking wet. I was gaunt and miserable. Skin and bones. "He needs me" was all she could think. She sent me a telegram saying she'd be home for Christmas, and if I could give her a call, she'd like to get together.

She hocked one of Duane's guns to get a new dress, a silver-gray wraparound number, and she came to J.D.'s to see me work. Her brother escorted her over to the hotel before the show. Lord knows what she thought. It was a whole other world from what she was used to, despite her marriage to Duane. The band was hanging out, four of us sitting around a table playing poker, me with no shirt on, a couple more sprawled across the bed, smoke curling around a room that looked as if it had been turned upside down. But Jessi wasn't scared by it. She found it "different" and fascinating, and that was the way I thought of her, too.

I was a perfect gentleman. We were honest with each other. I told her about my life, about my first wife and children, though she recalls I didn't go much into my second wife. She listened and didn't say much. Somehow she knew that I was in a place of hurt, and that I'd reached a point of trying to please my former wives and feeling like I failed. I was nowhere near over it, at a point where someone would have to take me as I was and who I was, raw and all. Right or wrong, I hadn't been understood. Jessi had no idea how long it would be before I would open up to trust another woman, and it was a good thing she didn't.

One of our first dates was out to the Navajo Indian Reservation in Tuba City, Arizona. There's nothing there, only the painted desert and two or three roads in the whole northeast corner of the state, each following an endless straight line that goes like an arrow until it hits the vanishing point.

We left Phoenix about noon, and I drove and drove. It was getting late. I was supposed to play in a gymnasium for the Indians up there, and I didn't know it was going to be that far. Along about dusk I almost hit the biggest horse I'd ever seen. It came out of nowhere, and when I hit the brakes, that horse looked at me as if to say "you stupid asshole." I started laughing, thinking about the expression on the horse's face, and she probably thought I was a crazy man.

After the show, we stopped at a motel in Cameron. We walked over to a canyon, hand in hand, the desert surrounding us like a watchful eye. Suddenly an old man sidled in beside us, hobbling along with a cane. "Where you from?" I asked him.

"I come from back east," he told us. "I've been a traveling salesman all these years. My health isn't too good, and my sons and daughters don't really want me. Me and my wife lived out here, but she died about five years ago, and now I don't have anything to live for."

I said, "That's too bad."

Jessi said, "Oh well, there's always the bottle."

I guess it was that spunkiness that attracted me to her. She never let me off the hook, and loved to pick at me and make me mad. She called it "getting my temper up." Finally, I told her that she gave me "more shit than anybody," and I was starting not to enjoy her very much.

"I like to see the fire," she said, pouring a little gasoline on the flames.

Like a fire can hurt you, we both knew right off it was something that could be dangerous. And like a fire can warm you, she started drawing me closer, bringing me in out of the cold. She lit that fire under me, kept adding fuel, and pretty soon we began traveling together.

Her momma was an ordained Pentecostal preacher, though she wasn't judgmental about our relationship. Jessi had been playing the piano in church and revival meetings since she'd been a little girl, and it gave her an inner strength, even though when I met her she thought she was in the cavern of her life, where she'd thrown off all that she'd known and gone seeking her own answers. Jessi had come back to a point where she realized that she needed something more than she could ever know; and on that rock, she built her faith.

For me, it was the music. For Mirriam Rebecca Joan Johnson Eddy, soon to be Jessi Colter, faith was expressed through the music. Together, we started learning the eternal melodies and infinite harmonies that has become our song of songs.

Meanwhile, back at the ranch . . .

Chet had decided finally to leave producing and return to playing music, and he put me with Danny Davis. He couldn't have made a worse choice. We were oil and water. I've always had a tendency to treat people right, with respect and honor. But I came pretty close to putting my hands around Danny's throat on more than one occasion, and I suspect he didn't like me much either.

Danny was the leader of the Nashville Brass, a big-band approach to country that was opening up new doors leading to crossover acceptance. He had known Chet since the 1950s, a former sideman who joined RCA's A&R staff in 1965. Danny had grown up in Massachusetts where he'd gotten a classical education, and he brought an "orchestral" feel to country with his *Nashville Sounds* records in 1968 and 1969. Which was fine by me. I loved horns, as I always told Herb Alpert, and was certainly in favor of going beyond the boundaries of country; but as far as our musical tastes were concerned, we couldn't have been further apart.

I would go into the studio and do the tracks, and when I came back I wouldn't recognize it as the same song. He'd overdub arrangements without asking me, and turn songs down without even playing them for me. He rejected "Abraham, Martin, and John" when I specifically picked it out. He wanted me to have my parts written out, and I liked to learn the arrangement on the spot. Danny would get bored, or make fun of me if I was trying to work out a chord change I wanted to hear. One time he was putting me down while I was overdubbing a guitar on a track, feeling paranoid because I knew he wasn't on my side, trying to get comfortable out in the studio. Jessi and Johnny Darrell walked into the control room and overheard him. Jessi gave him one of her meanest looks. "If I told him what you said, he'd kill you."

I almost did. Him and all the musicians. I hate pickup notes. Always have. A note or two used to introduce a phrase, I think it's like stompin' your way into a song, announcing that you're going to knock on the door before you actually do. It's something that irritates me no end, and one day I decided to put a stop to it. Merle Haggard had borrowed a gun of mine and brought it back to Studio A. It was a .22 Magnum pistol, a buntline; a long thing. I walked into the studio and said, "The first sonofabitch that hits a pickup note, I'm going to blow his fingers off. And as for anybody still looking at his chart after the third take, your ass is dead.

"And Danny." I turned to him. "I don't want to hear any shit out of you."

It was all over between us from then on. Maybe I was a little hard on him, but the last thing he should have been doing in this world is producing a country record on me, telling me what I can and can't do musically. I don't think Chet foresaw that. With my independent streak, he probably thought that all I needed was somebody to take down the titles and help me hire the musicians. Danny was the wrong choice, seeing as he'd just become a successful artist himself with the Nashville Brass, and had his own reputation to think of. He couldn't be as self-effacing as producers sometimes have to be.

Chet knew I wanted to make my own records. He opposed that mainly because RCA had several producers, and if he started letting artists like myself and Bobby Bare produce themselves, he'd lose some people he was very fond of, like Bob Ferguson and Ray Pennington. He told me in later years that, among other things, he was trying to protect their jobs.

Ironically, I'm a firm believer in producers. I can give someone a hard time when I'm not hearing it the way I think it should be, but I don't think any of us knows everything. You need someone to help you do your listening, and I love to see what people hear out of me. If it doesn't work, I'll tell them, but usually, you shouldn't have to even talk about it. The speakers will let you know when a song feels right.

I like to see what a producer has in mind; and between me not being able to do what they think I can, and trying to do what they want me to, a lot of times you come up with something that neither of you might have thought of in the first place. You have to be prepared to take advantage of the unexpected.

Danny didn't care what I was about; in his eyes, the producer was there to control the artist. He did want the best for me, but that was a value judgment he wasn't allowing me to make. "This guy could be the biggest star in the world," he told Johnny Western, who wrote the liner notes for *Waylon*, released in January of 1970, "but he's his own worst enemy." That can never work. You have to trust the instincts of the artists you're helping to record. I may not know that much about music, but I know what gets me.

One of the stranger things to grab my attention was a song by Richard Harris written by Jimmy Webb. I wore out the eight-track of "MacArthur Park," playing it in the limousine traveling between shows. It was one of the first times I ever realized that performance was the key to music, because here was an actor who could hardly sing, and his vocal mesmerized me. It was a wonderful song, and there was something country about it, especially that line about the "old men playing checkers in the park."

I broached the idea of doing it to Chet in early 1969, and I guess that's when he thought I was too far gone and turned me over to Danny. But it wasn't until I met the Kimberlys out in Las Vegas that the concept for the song started coming together.

They were two pairs of siblings married to each other, girl twins hooked up with two brothers, and a cousin playing bass. It kind of reminded me of my family back in Littlefield. They performed "MacArthur Park" as part of their show, and it got me thinking. I liked the song's range and its epic feel, and I liked Verna Gay Kimberly. We had a thing going; she was unhappy and so was I. It was before I had re-met Jessi. Her and her husband were splitting up, and she and her twin sister didn't get along. I didn't want to see the group dissolve as well, because they were really good.

I helped get them a deal with RCA, though they weren't really country-oriented, and in the spring of 1969, we recorded an album together called *Country-Folk*. "MacArthur Park" was the lead-off track, and Danny and I got into it a couple of times over the arrangement. I knew exactly what I wanted the strings to do; I had to hum the parts. He probably had his own ideas. But the single got into the country Top Twenty-five that fall, and when the Grammys came around, it won for Best Country Performance by a Duo or Group. By then, everybody was more than happy to claim it was their idea.

Years later Robert Duvall introduced me to Richard Harris. "You *bastid*," Richard said, throwing his napkin playfully on the floor and his arms around me. "Fuck you. You're the one who stole my Grammy."

\*     \*     \*

I woke up freezing to death. Where was I? Somewhere in the middle of nowhere, I guessed.

I got up and turned the air conditioner off. It was on high. The feeling was mutual. I went to the bathroom, then lit a cigarette and sat on the side of the bed, trying to think how I got there. In more ways than one.

I had taken Barbara home for the last time, and went from Phoenix to Las Vegas. We were booked in a casino for two weeks, and I stayed up for nine un-straight days and nights, gambling and taking pills. Going a little out of my mind. I knew it was over between her and me, and I was still crazy about her.

The last night we played there, before the show, I suddenly felt as if I couldn't get my breath. I felt like I had an anvil on my chest. I was weak and dehydrated so bad, running on empty. I went upstairs and started drinking milk and ordering steaks. It was the afternoon. Verna Gay came over with one of her little girls and tried to get me to rest. I finally got to sleep, woke up for the show, and then got in a car and took off toward Minnesota somewhere. My next stop.

I was a wreck. I caught some shut-eye by the side of the road, lying down in the car. Somewhere along in there, we pulled into a motel. It was a tourist court, a bunch of little cabins by the side of Any Road, U.S.A. I ate supper, then went to sleep again. I knew I might not wake up. I could hardly catch my breath. I was hyperventilating, sweat pouring off me. It was the last days of summer, 1968. That's when I turned the air-conditioning on.

Daddy hadn't been dead very long when me and Barbara split. We went to the funeral together, and maybe two or three weeks later we'd gone through our final days. When you're mourning, you reconsider your life. How many more things can you stack on to make it any worse? I could probably have stopped myself from going off the deep end if I had just lost one of them; but I was truly adrift in my own misery now.

I put the cigarette out and laid back. As I settled in, I looked up and saw my dad standing at the end of the bed. I know it was him, and I'll tell you why. My dad could not wear a necktie, or bear to have his shirt buttoned at the collar. His neck was real thick. He had a lot of gray hair on his chest, right up to his shoulders. He never had a shirt that fit him.

He had on a pinstriped suit, brown, with little gray stripes in it. That's how vivid the vision was. I noticed his neck. He had a Windsor knot in his tie; he was neat and dressed up.

But he had the saddest expression on his face. He never said a word. He just gazed at me, with eyes that said "Don't do this to yourself." Daddy was worried about me. He was really hurt that I would do myself such harm.

I guess I blinked, and suddenly he was gone. Daddy only had to look at me, and I knew.

On the road, we thought we were bullet-proof. We loved the music, but music was secondary to what we were doing. All we did was party.

We seemed to be in motion all the time. We'd be out there three hundred dates a year. We didn't work all of them, but we couldn't afford to go back. We weren't making any money.

The only thing left to do was have a good time. We were probably making terrible music, as I look back, but the edge was there. The edge kept it alive. It may not have been good, but it was rockin'.

The only problem was that we were teetering and toppling ever closer to the precipice. You can only break the law of gravity for so long. Like Humpty Dumpty, we were overdue for a great fall.

On February 9, 1969, the band was heading to Peoria, Illinois, riding in a pickup that had a sleeper stacked on top of it. You could rest in the back, and one person could fit crosswise over the top of the truck cab in a specially made bunk. I had ordered a Bluebird bus from down in Georgia, but it hadn't been delivered yet. It was to be my first new bus.

Richie was in the front and had just let Jimmy Gray start driving. Outside of Bloomington, along I-150 on the way to Peoria, they came to an old steel bridge over Kickapoo Creek. It was icy and snowy, and they had to make a sharp right turn. As they slipped on the black ice, the truck shimmied over and leaned a little bit to the side. Walter "Chuck" Conway, a bass player who had joined me just eleven days before, was asleep in the back compartment, over the truck cab.

The poor guy never knew what hit him. The pickup made the turn untouched and kept going, but the bridge clipped the sleeper, shattering it and shearing off the alcove. Chuck fell plumb in the river. Richie ran and jumped in after him, but he was too late. They said there wasn't a bone in his head that wasn't broken, and he died at the scene. Stew "Allen" Punsky, a keyboard player, was also badly hurt.

I was traveling behind them in the Cadillac, an hour or two after, and when I came on the scene, it scared me to death. The police found pot in the pickup, but when I went down to the hospital, those cops showed me the bag of marijuana and said "Waylon, you've got enough problems. We're throwing this away."

It scared me, made me feel responsible, even though there was nothing I could've done. We played the date, using Hank Snow's bass player, and I was just wobbling around, on pills and drunk. Merle Haggard and his manager, Fuzzy Owens, got me in a poker game and cleaned me out. I had four or five thousand dollars on me, and they won everything. They were there to get my money. That was it. I think Merle is a great singer and songwriter, and probably he was in as bad a shape as I was, but we've never been close since that night. I can still remember their faces. When I was broke, they said their good-byes and left. I never forgot that.

Richie and Jimmy were in for some more trouble on June 10, when they were arrested for marijuana possession at the Rainbow Bridge border separating the United States and Canada.

It had been a pretty tumultuous trip to Toronto. We were playing a week at Jack Starr's Horseshoe Lounge, and one night, after the show, we went over to Aunt Bea's afterhours club to have a little jam. Richie brought a trap case with him, and just as he slid it in the corner, he was coldcocked from behind by a big Newfie, which is what they call guys from Newfoundland in Maple Leaf country. "You hippie-looking sonofabitch," he snarled at Richie, and belted him right in the nose.

Richie's long hair always attracted trouble, but we were used to it. A little redneck hootin' and hollerin' was always good for a show; it gave us something to prove. But up in Canada that week, the taunts were meaner, less good-natured. The war between "hippies" and "straights" was getting more intense, and songs like "Okie from Muskogee" weren't helping, even if Merle insists his intent to be satiric was misinterpreted as flag waving.

Richie was mad as hell. He came back to me, and I said, "Let's go get him." We all tore down the stairs. A Mountie already had him in custody, but that didn't stop Richie. I don't think he even saw the policeman. The Newfie was huge, about twice his size, and Richie had to jump up to hit him. That started everything going wild. Pretty soon somebody's wrestling with the Mountie, the Newfie and Richie are rolling around on the floor, and we're all bouncing around. I kicked that Newfie right in the nuts, as hard as I could, and all he did was growl like a damn bear or something.

A cop swung a nightstick. I felt it go whistling past my head, just barely missing me. Sonny Ray, who was playing bass with us, yelled "You almost hit the chief!" and he took off after the cop, nearly knocking him out.

That Newfie took on all of us. I grabbed him from the back and he kicked me off, ramming me into a corner. I turned to Curtis Buck and said, "He's gonna whip all our asses." Curtis said "No, he ain't" and took a shotglass and hit that big guy right in the mouth. That took him out of the picture, and when the dust had cleared, Richie, Curtis, and Sonny were on their way to jail. It took us all night to get them sprung.

We still weren't home free. Heading back across the border to Nashville, our two-vehicle convoy—my Cadillac and the Dodge pickup—got stopped at the Niagara Falls crossing. Longhairs in limos? The Cadillac got through, but the pickup was thoroughly searched. Jimmy Gray tried to toss the "evidence" out the window, and that alerted the cops, and pretty soon they found themselves in the slammer. It was Richie's second time in a week!

Boy, were they mad. At the cops and each other. I was laughing and calling them criminals, and then I really gave them a reaming. I said, if you hadn't messed with that shit, you wouldn't get in trouble. I was kind of upset with them. If they'd just taken pills, like me, they'd have been okay. I even fired Jimmy. I was an easy boss, except when it came to dictating how you took your drugs. Of course, I never considered pills as being against the law.

It was like a little game with us. We didn't know we could go to prison for pills. We weren't afraid of being busted because all you had to do was show your prescription bottle. Or get somebody to write a prescription. The big excuse was weight gain, though we were so skinny we could stand sideways and hide. We used to know a Dr. Snap out in east Nashville, in a rundown neighborhood, who would give us 'scripts. We could take them around the corner to the black drugstore and fill the prescription. We could get a hundred little yellow Simcos a week, or fifty Speckled Birds a month. I didn't think there was anything unusual about it. I had a big bottle hidden, and I'd put some extras in a small bottle, and if I was stopped, at the border or driving along, nobody would bother me. Hell, I carried handfuls of uppers. I'd pull my pockets inside out and white Bennies would scatter everywhere.

The thing was, I thought they were on drugs, and I was taking prescriptions. None of us realized that there was no difference. We'd gotten started on pills by getting them from doctors, or pharmacists, who gave us no warning. Booking agents slipped you the pills to help keep you going. That's no excuse, but we never even thought about them being addictive. We didn't know that they could kill you. Or make you kill yourself.

I didn't like anybody who drank. Never touched the stuff; that was my big boast. And cocaine, I thought that was terrible, at least then. As for pot, I didn't enjoy sitting there grinning.

Richie and I wouldn't socialize much. He was with the band more. The drugs divided us, and as things grew more out of control, Richie started thinking about taking a break. He was just running himself down living on amphetamines, and had been for two years and more. He needed to head home for a while and settle himself.

He came to see me on the bus. "I have to leave," Richie said. "I'm wore out."

I nodded. "Man, I wish I could go with you."

Jessi and I got married the next day after Richie left. I can't say one caused the other, but I was reaching out. Her hand took mine, and that was when I realized I couldn't be complete without her.

She wasn't surprised. Jessi knew the time was coming when I'd ask, and she had the dress. I didn't get down on my knees or anything. It was more like "You want to get married, don't you?" We were both a little distant from our families at the time. She'd already had a big wedding, and neither of us were interested in an ornate ceremony.

We went to a Las Vegas marriage mill on October 26, 1969. My bass player stood up as best man, and the justice of the peace started reciting the vows in a monotone. It was the forty-fourth wedding he'd performed that day.

It hit Jessi funny and she started giggling, then laughing hysterically. The more she howled, the more serious I got. There might have been a little underlying tension. Here we were at one of the most important crossroads of our life, and she was giddy and I was impatient. Neither of us could really believe it. She could hardly get hold of herself long enough to catch her breath and say "I do."

But we did. Forevermore.

CHAPTER

6

# "THERE'S ANOTHER WAY
# OF DOING THINGS
# AND THAT IS ROCK 'N' ROLL"

The Navajos call it the Long Walk. Forced into exile from their native land, marched to Fort Sumter in eastern New Mexico where the government attempted to turn them into farmers and traders; contrary to their hunting and shepherding ways, they endured five years of desolation before America admitted its failure and sent them home to the Wondrous Place.

I had come to the reservation as I had many times before. The Indians liked me, and I felt at home among the Indians. Sometimes I think if it hadn't been for them, I'd have to get something else to do. I could always draw a crowd there. They were among my most loyal fans.

The Indians had initially been won over by "Love of the Common People." In March of 1969, I had been booked to play Flagstaff, Arizona, by Johnna Yursic, a local boy; to promote the concert, he asked the area disc jockey, Mike McQuade at KGAK, to feature my current hit single, "Mental Revenge," from the album I had out at the time, *Jewels*. It was a Mel Tillis song, but they didn't like it at the station, so they started spinning the B side of "The Chokin' Kind," nearly two years old at this point. They couldn't believe the reaction. Suddenly they were getting requests to play it before the record had a chance to fade over the air. Even after McQuade repeated it six times in a row, the phone would ring and a Native American voice would be on the other end of the line, asking to please hear "Common People" again. The "Navajo National Anthem," as Mike said, was singing to them.

"Living on dreams ain't easy." "Family pride." "Faith is your foundation." "The Love of the Common People," if you think of "Common" as shared heritage, hopes, a tribe to cling to, and a warm conversation. Strong where you belong.

At seven-thirty the parking lot in the recreation center where I was scheduled to play would be empty. By eight, it would be filled with what they called Navajo Cadillacs, pickup trucks with eight or ten Indians jammed in the back. They'd come out of nowhere. I could hear the song beating through their hearts as they stood bunched in a crescent, waiting for me to come out from the wings. There would be a half-moon of empty space in front of the stage. When the band finished their warm-up, I'd walk to the microphone and they'd surge toward me in a wave. They trusted that I understood them. They understood me, which at that time took some doing.

When I first started playing the reservations, they didn't applaud at all. They didn't need to. I could feel their concentration, their respect, the riveting energy of their attention. They were shy people. I'd cut up with them, try to put them at ease. "Hey, where you goin'? Come over here and say hello"; and they'd make me feel easy too.

Once I was standing backstage and a Tonto Apache came over to me. I don't think he was a Mescalero. We were up in the reservation just north of Farmington, New Mexico. "Hey, Waylon," he said to me. "Would you take a picture with my wife?"

I said sure, but he'd have to bring her back to the dressing room. I couldn't go out front.

"Okay," he replied, and headed back to the door. He turned around. "Hey, Waylon. You gotta camera?"

*Hey, Waylon.* They took to me like kin, and I felt a bond with them that went beyond my great-grandmother. They had a basic credo of trust and honor, and they lived their religion all day, every day, in the shadow of the Great Spirit. We both handled liquor about the same way, only in their case, they couldn't just buy a drink. If the cops caught them with alcohol, they'd take it away and put them in jail. So what they did was buy a whole bottle and swallow it all. They weren't buying a drink; they were buying a drunk.

The same was true of me, only it was my pill intake that was purchasing oblivion. I had a sense of loss, of unfulfilled purpose. Even though it's hard to draw a comparison between the fate of a downtrodden, honorable people and one man's struggle to have his music heard, sometimes I felt that Nashville was fencing me in the same as these proud Indian tribes had been enclosed in their reservations.

I'd lost my way.

The more I worked, the more in debt I got. The more my records sold, the further they receded from what I had in mind, the sound I wanted to hear, the impact I wanted them to have. I kept trying it their way, and I saw I wasn't going to get it.

In the summer of 1972, I had dates booked in the reservations north of Gallup. I'd gotten an antibiotics shot in town for a tooth problem, and Father Dunstan Schmidlin, the priest who booked us for the show, told me that when I went up into the Indian settlements, I shouldn't eat or drink anything because there was an epidemic of hepatitis.

I remembered his warning right after I'd eaten some pie and drank some milk in a little cafe near the Colorado border of the Ute reservation. That night I witnessed the damnedest fight I ever saw in my life. A cop whose hobby was beating up Indians put on his gloves and waded into a crowd at a bar. There he was with his burr haircut, in his glory, pushing and punching them toward the door, and outside they were beating his car all to hell; there wasn't one place that wasn't dented.

When we got back to town, I felt like that car, sick and battered. We headed on to Buck Lake Ranch and played our show. I had on a gold shirt, and after we finished, exhausted, I went back to the bus and laid down. I couldn't get up. My back was killing me; my kidneys hurt. Jessi came in and told me I was looking yellow. "Nah," I said, real upset. "It's the reflection of this shirt."

They took me home. I didn't even wake up during the ride. The next thing I knew was the doctor looming over me. I was saying "Bullshit, I ain't going in no hospital," and he came and stood by the bed, looking seven feet tall. I said, "Goddamn, you run a giant in on my ass."

I didn't even know what hepatitis was. I didn't want to quit. I was ready to keep going. Give me some pills. I'll get right up from here again.

I got to feeling worse. Jessi was just like a little chihuahua, nervous, not knowing whether I was going to live or die. Finally she talked me into getting treated at a hospital. It was the first time I'd pulled to a halt in years.

Stop and start over. It's been the pattern of my life whenever things get beyond my control.

Lying there, I started thinking about what I'd won after ten years of banging around the honky-tonk circuit. My health was shot. I was nearly close to a quarter of a million dollars in debt, and getting deeper in the hole whether I played shows or not. The IRS was on my tail. I was paying alimony to three wives. If I went on the road I lost money. If I stayed home, I lost more.

As for record sales, I never got ahead of the five percent of ninety percent and the packaging fees and the overseas split and the studio costs and the multitrack accounting books. Whenever they gave you a piece of the royalties up here, they took it away down there. You couldn't figure who owed what and why I wasn't getting any with a team of lawyers and accountants, and besides, we were supposed to be aw-shucks country boys. They thought we were stupid, that we were so thankful to be able to play guitar and sing, so grateful that they gave us our start, and were happy they were there when we needed them, as long as we didn't ask for any real power or look too closely behind the scenes. If you don't make waves, RCA and Decca and Epic and Capitol were telling us, we'll let you keep making records. Thanks, boss.

"Next year is your year." That's what they promised; but they were just stroking me. My year always seemed to be the next year, the one over the horizon, after the next single, the next album, the next tour, not the one in which I was struggling to keep my band and my music afloat.

Chet would've turned the world over to keep me going. He had all the faith possible in me. He took over the reins to the Nashville operations after Steve Sholes died in 1968, but though he could sign talent and spend some money, he didn't have the kind of promotional power that he needed. He was a guitar player, not a company man. Sholes, who had been Chet's mentor at RCA since the mid-1950s, had usually stood between him and the label's executive offices in New York. Now it was Chet's turn to call New York to get approvals, and they held him, and us hillbillies, at arm's length. They still ran everything from both coasts, and we were caught in the middle.

I was tired of getting ripped off. Lucky Moeller was my manager as well as my booking agent, and I couldn't understand, even after being on the road more than two-thirds of the year, every year, how I still owed him thirty thousand dollars.

I found it hard to grasp how I could write a song for my own publishing company, Baron, and get screwed. Baron was administered by Harlan Howard's Wilderness Music. He sold half of his company to Tree Music, which meant they owned a piece of my company, too. I was finishing a song called "Yellow Haired Woman," about Barbara, when Red Lane walked in. I was fixing to record it that day, and I asked him to help me finish it. I said I'd give him half of the song. In fifteen minutes we had it, and it wasn't any big deal.

Red was a writer for Tree, and Jack Stapp, who ran Tree, said that they couldn't share the publishing because Red was an exclusive writer for them. But you administer my company, I said, which is part of your company. Tree still refused to give me a share of the song. I said, "Fucker, that's my song first."

I went to Harlan and told him I thought that was wrong. He said he couldn't help me. "They're my friends," he said. They weren't any friends of mine; it was just greed on their part. They acted like I didn't exist.

RCA celebrated my hospitalization by releasing *Ladies Love Outlaws* in September. It was a pretty good album, all things considered, especially with that sweet cover of me in full gunslinger regalia staring down at my five-year-old niece, Ladonna.

The only problem was that it wasn't finished.

Most of the tracks on there had only scratch vocals, which is the way you sing when you're concentrating on the band getting a good track. Sometimes they come out sounding all right, but more often you need to do them over, so you can concentrate on your performance. But they didn't ask me anything about what I thought. They just put it out. I still cringe whenever I hear myself singing Hoyt Axton's "Never Been to Spain." It sounded like I'd never even been to Cleveland.

After Danny Davis, Chet placed me with Ronny Light. Ronny was young, one of the nicest people in the world, and didn't deserve the misery I put him through. I got more freedom with him as a producer, although I was still using musicians who didn't know what I was about. By then I was probably so peeved at the system, I gave Ronny trouble just for being around. When we cut "Good Hearted Woman," I point-blank told him to stay in the control room and let me get on with doing it in the studio. I wanted him to make sure it got to the tape machine, and that he stayed out of my way. I was starting to realize it wasn't the individual producer that made the difference.

Nashville had a definite, set formula for what a country record should sound like. There's more than one kind of country music though—a wide range that takes in everything from bluegrass to western swing. Their country was smooth and pop, one road that led to a Nashville Sound. Well, I couldn't do that. I didn't want to do that.

I had an energy, and it made them afraid. In response, they tried to control me, make me a cog in their machine, and it didn't stop with record production. Everybody got in on it: the marketing departments, the promoters, the talent bookers. "I didn't like his last album; he had some songs on there that sounded like rock and roll to me." Maybe there was a heavier bottom, a rock and roll beat driving a country song, but if there's no edge in the music, there's no edge in me.

"Why don't you just do what you're supposed to? What everybody else does?" After a while, I didn't see the point. I never was a part of their world. They'd have on their rhinestone suits, or real fine-looking golf clothes, and here I am in my damn Levis and leather jacket, hair slicked back, all cigarettes and drugs. They "loved" my music, but they wouldn't allow me to make it. They were afraid of me because I wouldn't kiss their ass. They thought I was a troublemaker. I would ask for something and they'd tell me a dozen reasons why I couldn't have it, over and over and over.

All I was trying to do was survive.

Richie had come back in early 1972. One of the conditions of his return was that he could have his own stash—meaning pot. I guess it worked for him. The first thing he'd done after leaving me was head back to Phoenix, buy a pound of grass, and lock himself in his room for a month, sleeping and eating and getting off pills. Eddie Fox, who had been with Marty Robbins, had drummed in his place over the couple years he'd been gone, but Richie and I were close enough to know that it was only temporary.

Having been away, he was a little shocked at the changes in me. He wasn't the only one. I was lying in bed, getting more and more depressed over my prospects, wondering why I was sliding deeper into Nowheresville. I'd finally said to myself, I'm never going to have hit records. I'm never going to be a success in this business. I might just go back to a nightclub somewhere and play my music. It's all over.

Richie listened while I told him all this. He'd thought I was at a real low when he left; now he saw that not much had changed, except for the worse. "You're fixin' to quit, aren't you," he said.

I thought, Yeah, I am. And figure out what I was going to do with the rest of my life. "Probably head back to Phoenix, maybe work in radio. . . ."

"Wait a minute," he said. "Before you pack it in, I think we can give it one more shot. Just try it. There's another way of doing things, and that is rock and roll."

Why not? It made a lot of sense. I was mentally rockin' and rollin'. It was an attitude as much as a music, and we were rock and roll in everything but our allegiance to country. Even then, there was a lot of rock in that. We were proud to be country, but that didn't mean we had to be trapped by country music's conventions, or the way artists were treated. Maybe if I stopped trying to fit in, and started saying "fuck it," I was going to get a chance to do it my way. If it didn't work out, I'd be the only one to blame.

Rock and roll was no stranger to my world. Every time I would go to Los Angeles, rockers would flock to the shows, helped along by Kris Kristofferson telling everyone about me. Gram Parsons, who joined country and rock at the hip with the Byrds and the Flying Burrito Brothers in the late sixties, was among those who came to see me; he may have been the only guy that did more drugs than I could. "What I did was take your music one step further," he told me. Even Dylan came down to the Palomino.

But Richie was talking about rock in a broader sense, from on-stage production values, like carrying sound and lights, to such luxuries as roadies. "What's a roadie?" I remember asking him. We were still humping our own equipment into the shows. Each band member would tote his gear into the gig, and one of the guys in the band would tune my guitar, and that was it.

Richie was especially referring to how rock music was regarded by the big companies. Jessi had seen Duane Eddy treated with respect and admiration when he came to Nashville to record the *Twangy Country* album. I knew that rock acts on RCA, like the Jefferson Airplane, got huge budgets to record, with promotion to match, while we were expected to make our albums in a few days. The Airplane had spent fifty thousand dollars on an album and then scrapped it and started over. Maybe that's why Grace Slick was raising hell about America when I was on a television show with her. I was getting mad, telling her that I'm the first to agree there's a lot wrong with our system, but it's still the best out there, and she's talking about communism and striking karate poses. "There ain't a chance in the world me being afraid of you," I said, and that turned her on. She was all set to send her German boyfriend off; I didn't see her sharing her recording budget, though.

Nashville was just too insular, too caught up in itself. I needed somebody from outside the loop, who could speak the forked tongue. Someone who knew where the bodies were buried.

"I want you to meet Neil Reshen," continued Richie. "You're not going to like him at all. He's not like anything you're used to. You're not going to trust him, but he's what you need now. He's your man. I just want you to talk to him."

While he was back in Phoenix, Richie had done some road managing for Goose Creek Symphony, a country-rock band managed by a man named George Lappe. Neil had handled some of their business affairs, and Richie was impressed with his connections and cutthroat determination. "He can tell you things about this music business," Richie told me, "what's been holding you down and why, and what can be done about it."

I had asked RCA for an advance on royalties, twenty-five thousand dollars, so I could get by while I was recuperating. At first the New York office agreed, and then Jerry Bradley came by my house. He was Owen Bradley's son and had taken over most of Chet's executive duties at the record company.

Richie had brought Neil around that day, and he was sitting quietly in the room when Jerry showed up. I was flat on my back. He didn't know who Neil was, and I wasn't about to tell him.

Jerry said to me, "If you will sign again for five percent, we'll let you have five thousand dollars." The royalty was the same rate I'd gotten as a newcomer. He went on about how bad he felt coming out there while I was sick and telling me that, and he even brought out my record royalty statements, to show me that this was all they could give me, though they wanted to help me in any way they could, and really, they loved me and thought of me as part of the RCA family. I thanked him and told him I would think about it.

After Jerry left, I sat down and went over the statements with Neil. He had a black beard that made him look like Abe Lincoln's unsavory twin, and he was a New York lawyer, a carpetbagger, to boot. Reshen was about as un-Nashville as you could get. His company, Media Consulting, specialized in audits, and he had worked with Miles Davis and Frank Zappa. He was used to difficult clients.

Neil ran his eyes over the figures. "They're a bunch of whooers," was all he said. He didn't need to add, or subtract, anymore.

When Bradley came back, I told him I wouldn't honor the new contract. "Before I sign that, I'll quit. I won't be recording anymore." Jerry later confided to me he was never so glad when anyone said no, that he felt like a snake trying to take advantage of me when I was down.

He also knew that Neil was no innocent bystander.

Driving back to the airport, Richie introduced Neil to Willie Nelson. Willie had retreated to Texas by that time and, like a lizard in his lair, hardly ever came out of Austin. "He's going to be Waylon's manager," Richie said.

"Well, let him manage me, too," said Willie. Typical.

There was a time when Neil fed me and Willie, and if it hadn't been for him, I don't know what we would have done. He helped us immeasurably. He got things for us that no country singer had ever gotten before. If we were going to become Outlaws, though we didn't know that yet, we needed an Outlaw Lawyer, as Willie called him.

Neil was perfect for the part. He was like a mad dog on a leash. When he got his teeth into something, he never let go. He placed himself between us and the business-as-usual; and he wasn't about to be distracted by somebody throwing us a bone. We knew it wasn't going to be a forever thing. I told Willie, "Someday we're going to have to run him off. But we can have a good ride."

We never went to the trouble of working out a contract between us. Why bother? Neil was a genius at negotiation, and Willie and I had no chance of coming out ahead. He'd figure ways of beating people, or make people beat themselves. He would get these ugly looks. He must've practiced for hours on end making faces in the mirror, working out his responses.

He could sit silent endlessly. It would just drive you crazy. The first one that spoke gave in, that was the way they did things.

We were in Chet's office, with all these executives from New York, negotiating my new record deal. Frank Manceine was there; so was Joe Galante. New York could tell Nashville what to do, but Nashville couldn't tell New York: The power of attorney only flowed one way. Neil wanted me to see how it was done. He was making these faces; I wanted to slap him. But he knew what he was doing. If you peeve somebody to the point of anger, you jar them from their train of thought, and he wanted RCA off balance.

It was down to a twenty-five-thousand-dollar sum, and they were not going to give it to me. He wanted it. We were setting there, not a word spoken, and the silence got unbearable. After a while, I couldn't take it anymore. "Chet," I said, reaching over to a bowl on his desk, "where'd you get these peanuts?"

Neil glared at me. "Shut up, Waylon."

You could hear a clock tick in the room. It got even quieter. Minutes passed. I rose up, never said a word, walked out. I went to the bathroom to take a leak. When I came back, Neil greeted me in the hall. "You're a fuckin' genius," he said.

"What?"

"Walking out like that. That sewed it up." He was positively gleeful. "Where'd you go?"

"I had to take a piss."

"That's a twenty-five-thousand-dollar piss," said Neil. "They asked me where you went and I told them I didn't know. 'Waylon's mad, I'm sure. He's crazy. He's liable to do anything.' 'Will he be back?' they wanted to know, and I shrugged. 'I guess he's gone, so we may as well call this to a close.' And that's when they gave us the money."

It took Neil almost a year to get the contract sorted. RCA hadn't officially picked up my option for 1972, addressing it in care of Chet instead of me, though I'd accepted an advance and been in their studios recording, which might have signified approval on my part. Still, without a formal agreement, it was a gray area whether I was officially still on the label. It probably served them right for sending me mail with "Dear Artist" inscribed as the salutation.

Neil chose to ignore the questionable option and immediately opened talks with other labels. It was probably the best time to apply pressure to RCA. There was something coming to the surface in my career. They saw that I was fixing to happen, with or without their help. Willie had been given a career boost with his shift to Atlantic, and that was one of the labels bidding for my services. RCA didn't know when, or how, but they knew they would regret losing me.

It didn't help that we caught them with their pants down. They were stealing me blind. One day I got the idea to find out what they were paying the songwriter, as far as mechanical royalties are concerned. If I'd been the only one to record that song, and I found out what the publisher received, I could compare it with my own sales statement.

Red Lane was the sole writer on "Walk on Out of My Mind," and I was the only artist to record the song. From experience, I knew Tree Music, his publisher, wouldn't stand for getting shortchanged, so I called him to find out how much money in mechanicals he'd made on that. I discovered they'd only paid me half of what they owed me, holding the rest "in reserve" for returns. The reserve amounted to one hundred fifty thousand dollars once we got through inspecting their books.

I had to sue to get the money, and finally we settled for half of that, seventy-five thousand, because I couldn't afford to keep fighting them. I needed cash for taxes and a bus. Even though it was mine, RCA wouldn't give me the entire amount. But when Neil went up to their offices on Avenue of the Americas in New York, the computer kicked out two checks by mistake, each for seventy-five grand.

He called me up as soon as he got back to his office. "You won't believe this," he said, "and I know you're going to make me take them back." I was always honest as the day is long, and wanted everything to be upfront. Neil used to poke fun at me because I always paid my bills on time. "Send 'em a damn dollar a month," was his advice, "but you hillbilly boys always want that credit rating, don't you?" He laughed. "You could not pay for something today and buy it from the same people tomorrow."

I surprised him this time, though. "Don't you dare return those checks. You're going to cash them both."

He said, "You know they're going to find out about it and they're going to raise hell, and they're going to want their money."

"And when they do," I said, "we'll settle."

\*　　\*　　\*

WGJ Productions. It had a nice ring to it. Waylon Goddamn Jennings Productions.

Free at last.

When the smoke had cleared, I had gotten a recording contract I could live with. My percentage was up close to eight. Chet was amazed; it was a better deal than he had. "I didn't know they gave out big contracts like that." He told Neil they had him "till 1999 at five percent!"

I also received seventy thousand dollars up front. When they handed me over the check, they asked what I was planning to do with the money. "I'm going to start a record label," I answered. They couldn't tell if I was serious or not.

"I told you he was crazy," said Frank Manceine.

The best part was getting my own production company, which meant I could make records on my own and hand the completed masters to RCA. I finally had control over my music, how it was to be advertised and promoted, "sweetened" (in my case "soured") and mixed. Chet always worried that I was out to destroy something; he thought I was determined to ruin country music, that there would no longer be a reason for people like himself or Owen Bradley to produce records. That was never my intention. There are always people who need ideas, but I'm not someone who can be told what to do musically. If you stop and think about it, it's not because I'm such a genius. It might be that I'm not smart enough to follow instructions. I have to do what I feel.

What I was fighting for was the right to try it my way. Just let me have mine.

Win or lose, I was now able to use my band. Choose my own songs. Turn the bass drum up.

In theory, that is. Though I agreed to record in their studios, with their engineers, I found soon enough it wasn't going to work. They were on the phone half the time calling Jerry Bradley upstairs at RCA and telling him what I was doing. I was still screwed.

"This Time" was a song I had written four years previously.

RCA had said it wasn't any good, but with my newfound freedom, it became the centerpiece of one of my first albums under the WGJ logo. Recorded in October of 1973, Willie played guitar on it and helped me put it together along with a couple of his songs: "Heaven or Hell" and one of my personal favorites, "It's Not Supposed to Be That Way." As we worked, it became apparent that I was destined to go through the same runarounds every time I stepped outside Nashville's musical city limits.

Finally, I'd had enough. I moved the sessions to Tompall Glaser's studios at 916 Nineteenth Avenue South, nicknamed Hillbilly Central. RCA protested mightily, but I told them this was the way it was going to be from now on.

"That's all you got," was about the way I put it. Lash Larue would've been proud of me.

RCA had no choice. "We can't release this," they told me. They had a contract with the engineer's union that all their recording was to be done in-house, that RCA records could not release any record that wasn't cut with an RCA engineer, and that RCA artists had to use RCA studios whenever they were within a two-hundred-mile radius of Nashville. Jerry Bradley even went to Washington to get a waiver for one album, but the union wouldn't go for it. In the face of my stubborn refusal, RCA bit the bullet. They shipped the record and violated their contract with the union. That broke the whole system's back.

"This Time" went number one in June of 1974. It was my first chart-topping smash.

True to their fears, RCA lost the deal with the engineers in Nashville when they released *This Time*. More, I set a precedent for other artists on the label. Since all had been contractually obligated to work at RCA, and recording expenses were charged against their royalties, when they found out that I could work in an independent studio, everybody split. Porter Wagoner said, hell, I've got a studio of my own and I'm going to record there. Pretty soon, RCA was only getting transit business; without a monopoly, they eventually had to sell their studios. I tried to buy one of them. I was up on the executive floors at RCA, and had my eye on Studio B, but they wanted to turn it into a museum, so I put in a bid for Studio A.

Chet was standing there, lighting a cigar. "Why don't you let me buy that?" I asked him.

"You've got the nerve of Hitler," he said. "You're the reason we're having to sell it." He started laughing, but they still wouldn't let me have the studio.

Tompall Glaser and I were best friends. We'd met about the time that he broke up with his brothers, and I kind of took their place in his life. He had been in town a lot longer than I had, and I think I was a little in awe of him.

I loved his singing so much, but when he started airing his opinions, and he had an opinion on everything, you couldn't shut him up. One of my favorite Glaser Brothers songs was called "Words Come Easy." In Tompall's case, it couldn't have been more accurate. He'd rather argue than care whether he was right or wrong. Tompall will dispute with God when he gets there; or the Devil, whichever one grabs him first. We had a good time tearing up Nashville, and there'll always be a place in my heart for him.

The Glasers stood outside the Music City hierarchy, fiercely independent. They had that Nebraska farm sensibility about money—you put some away and don't touch it—and were good businessmen. They had started out as Marty Robbins's backup vocal group, opening their own publishing company; their biggest songs to date were John Hartford's "Gentle on My Mind" and Tompall's own "Streets of Baltimore." They used the proceeds to build their studio and offices over on Nineteenth.

Both his brothers, Chuck and Jim, were a lot more reserved than Tompall, and I never got to know them that well. Among his brothers, he was the black sheep. I was the black sheep of Nashville. Together, we had the makings of a flock. We each needed somebody to tell us that if we weren't exactly right, we weren't all wrong. That was the foundation our friendship was built on.

I hooked up with Tompall over a pinball machine. Probably we'd been introduced when the Glasers tried to pitch me songs, but mesmerized by the flashing lights and endless dramas of silver balls falling as they may, hanging at the Burger Boy, or J.J.'s Market on Broadway, me on pills and Tompall on whiskey, we would talk for hours about what we thought. Mental masturbation. We'd go play pinballs and get it all figured out.

We could spend a thousand dollars a night, a quarter at a time. Tompall could stay up as long as I could. Bobby Bare had three machines in his office, and when they were filled, or he closed for the day, we'd go all over town looking for pinballs, out Route 65 to a truck stop south of Nashville, down Dixon Road, then a grocery store a couple blocks from Tompall's offices. When we found one we liked, we practically moved in. One night at the Burger Boy, Tompall was playing a certain machine he liked up front, but he wanted to be by me in the back room, so he dragged his pinballs up the steps and planted it next to mine. The owner just watched open-mouthed, though he didn't say anything because we were probably paying his rent and more. Even after J.J.'s officially shut for the night, the clerk would sleep on the counter, waking up every now and then to change a hundred-dollar bill for quarters.

They weren't the kind of machines where you try to keep the ball going and rack up scores. You've got six squares and five balls, and you try to get your numbers to line up. It's a little like bingo: three in a row and you get four free games; four in a row another twenty games; five and you win anywhere from twenty-five to seventy-five dollars.

It took more luck than skill, because if you shook the machine too hard, it would tilt on you. There must have been some technique involved, however, because one afternoon these two hoods came into the Burger Boy and hit the machine just so, taking home a hundred dollars in about three hours. For us, once we put in a couple of rolls of quarters, there was no way we were going to win our money back. Pinballs required just enough attention to take your mind off whatever else was going on. A lot of time Tompall and I would talk business as we played. We shot the breeze and made decisions, one ball at a time, winning and losing hundreds of games as the hours passed.

It was like a marathon. You could stand there, pumping quarters in, and get lost in your own thoughts, idling in neutral. You'd unwind so much that it was hard to stop and do something else. Sometimes we'd be at the machines for two or three days, waiting for the six card to fall into place. Tompall once kept track of our spending, thinking he could take it off his income tax. At the end of the year, he'd spent thirty-five thousand dollars on pinballs.

One Sunday evening I had a date down in Columbus, Georgia. We were in the south part of town at a little grocery store. Captain Midnight, our sidekick, was with us. We couldn't leave the machines. Every time we'd get close to finishing, we'd win a bunch of free games and have to run them off, which would start the cycle all over again. Finally, about three in the afternoon, we pulled ourselves away, got in the car, and started driving toward Georgia. A record came on the radio. It sounded familiar. "Is that me?" I asked the Captain.

"I don't know," he answered. "Did you record it?" I honestly couldn't remember. It was actually an early Charlie Daniels song. It shows what state we were in.

We drove to the show and got there late. They'd had to shuffle the order, waiting for me. The band was all set up. I went and did the show while the Captain slept in the car, and then we turned around and drove another four hours back to Nashville and the pinball machines.

You could hypnotize yourself, the lights bursting, bells ringing, pulling the pin, flicking the silver ball, overhead fluorescent beams on the glass dazzling, *get the three, get the five,* bounce, rebound, ricochet romance. Those damned lights. I can look off to the side and they're still blinking. I might really hit it, whacking the machine, getting it over to where it pays the highest odds. Pinball fever. *Man, I'm really hot.* Let me have another roll of quarters.

The Captain could sleep anywhere. He didn't have a home. Shuttling between my house and Tompall's office, he kept us in balance, which was no mean feat considering that Tompall and I could go from talking to arguing, then back to friendship, all in the span of an evening. We were like kids about twelve years old. We'd each get mad and know why the other was mad, butting heads like two strong-minded and redneck ol' boys. Captain could soften that.

He was on the radio when I first got to town, a rock-and-roll disc jockey named Roger Schutt over WKDA, a two-hundred-and-fifty-watt station that was the tops in town despite its small size. 1240 on the dial, and every midnight, the Captain would come on. Roger gained some notoriety once when a guy who shot somebody called him, and he talked him into surrendering. Most of the people in town knew him as Midnight. Very few of his listeners could tell you his real name.

Midnight gave up his career to be our friend. He just hung out with us. The Captain was a good listening post. He'd ride around with Tompall or me, and we'd get a chance to say out loud a lot of things we had been thinking. He'd been friends with Tompall since 1959, and probably had a lot to do with keeping Glaser and me together. He always said, "Tompall and Waylon are doing all the robbing, raping, and pillaging, and they've got me holding the horses."

Sometimes he'd relay messages from one to the other, usually because each of us thought the other one was crazy. It was quite a match-up. Everybody in town was holding their breath, thinking this can't be.

It was love of the music that brought Tompall and me together—that and a sense of our own independence. We were a little suspicious of each other when we first met, but as outsiders, our defenses were continually up, and being crazed didn't help. If you gave Tompall a compliment, he'd say "Aw, don't be bullshittin' me." He thought you were trying to cheat him.

You could see more of the real Tompall as he'd drive around Nashville, steering his Lincoln Continental with his knees, strumming the ukulele. He and Captain Midnight would play a game. The Captain would call out songs from the thirties and forties, trying to stump him. Tompall could play at least a verse or a chorus from each one; he must've known every song recorded.

Even if he didn't trust anybody, Tompall was a smart entrepreneur. He knew the incomes and outgos of publishing, and how the totals were supposed to make sense in his favor. Me, I didn't even have a personal checking account then. I'd just go to my road manager and ask him to give me some money. I'd get a wad of eight or nine hundred dollars and stick it in my pocket. Midnight used to follow me around when I would change my britches before a show, picking up a trail of dollar bills and pills. Tompall once asked me, "Why don't you write a check?" I told him I didn't have a checkbook. He took me to the bank and set up a checking account. Then anytime I needed to buy a hundred dollars worth of quarters, I could write a check. Pinball operators across the mid-South cracked open a case of champagne when that happened.

Tompall also showed me how easy it was to make the studio your own. We were playing pinballs one night, talking about "Lovin' Her Was Easier." The next thing I know, Tompall's making a phone call, setting up a session for him and his brothers at their studio. It was the first time I ever had my finger on the "red button," as Tompall called it. I produced the song for them; it never did come out or anything, but I saw how much simpler it would be to do it for myself.

Simpler. That was it. That's what I wanted. Bringing it back to bass and drums and guitar. You've got to make them feel it before they hear it.

\*　　\*　　\*

"What are you doing to my song?" Billy Joe Shaver asked me.

"Billy Joe," I told him. "You have the last word, but you have to leave me alone to figure this out."

"I just want to know what you're doing to my song."

"I'm fixin' to sing it, if you'll let me." We were working on "Honky Tonk Heroes." He had originally written it slow, but in the middle of running it down, I stopped the take and started it cooking. Double-time. Though I'd "done did everything that needs done," he didn't understand what I was doing.

Billy Joe was all up in the air. I was "messin' with the melodies," he told me, "screwin' around the tune." Anybody else wouldn't have said anything to me, because they would've been scared I wouldn't cut the song, but Billy Joe just did whatever he took a notion to do. He never had anything like this happen to him, somebody performing a whole album of his songs and showcasing him as a writer. He was so unusual, and the songs were great; but he just couldn't calm down.

I was probably a little nervous as well. It was very nearly the first time I was in RCA without a producer, and everybody was on edge. The engineers would call upstairs every half-hour to Jerry Bradley, who'd ask what I was doing. "He's high," they'd say. Hell, yes, I was high. Loving every minute of my newfound freedom.

When people you know are not wanting you to succeed, and you're in the middle of it, that's an impossible situation. If it wasn't enough that the engineers were telling me what I could and couldn't do, Billy Joe kept hounding me. "I will be a-watching," he warned.

"Let me tell you something," I finally said to him in exasperation. "You are going to get your ass out of here and stop bugging me. I love your songs, but I'm starting not to like you worth a damn. Stand outside the studio, go for a walk, watch some television. I don't care what you do. When I get through, you can come back in. If you don't like it, I'll change it and do it another way, but now get the hell on the other side of that door." I was gruff, but I could understand why he might be feeling nervous. Songs can be like little babies, and you don't want to think that someone's abusing your child. Especially when you're first starting out. I'd been through enough of that myself.

They thought Billy Joe was from outer space when he first hit Nashville. He was so shy when I met him that he hardly looked up from the floor. Bobby Bare, who has one of the best noses for songs and writers in the business, brought him over for me to hear him sing. I didn't even have a home at that time. Jessi and I were living in the Holiday Inn over on West End and Eighteenth.

He asked if he could play me a song. All I could make out was mumbling. I couldn't tell anything but that I liked the melody, and I understood no more than a third of the lyrics. Soon enough, Bobby got him in a studio and played me "Ride Me Down Easy." It just killed me; I loved that song. I called Bobby and said, "Has he got enough material that I could do an album of his stuff? I think that guy can change the whole face of the music."

Billy Joe had gone through a lot even before he started writing songs. He didn't begin in "the business" (though he always called it a hobby) until he was nearly thirty. His daddy had left his momma before he was born in Corsicana, Texas, and he'd grown up around the honky-tonks of Waco. He'd had to drop out of school to work for a living, and had joined the navy when he was seventeen. He might've continued scuffling had not a sawmill accident clipped four fingers of his right hand and turned him into a songwriter. Billy always had a sense of humor about it, though. He was sitting on a bed one time playing guitar, and a guy who worked for me came in and said "Billy Joe, if you don't mind me asking, what happened to your fingers?" Billy started glancing around and digging in his pocket. "Damn," he said. "They were here just a while ago."

He slept in Bobby's office while he struggled in Nashville, and eventually Kris took a liking to him, covering "Good Christian Soldier" on his *Silver Tongued Devil* album in 1971. I heard him singing in a backstage trailer at the Dripping Springs Reunion in Texas the next year, though Billy remembers it better than me. As he tells it, I heard him play "Willie the Wandering Gypsy" while they were passing guitars around. I came running in from the back and said "Hey, man, I've got to have that song." Billy Joe agreed.

He tried to call me when I got back to Nashville, but I was always in a meeting or on another call or "not in." This went on for months. Even after Bobby brought him by, we had trouble getting together. He caught up with me one night at RCA recording. By then, Kris had produced an album of Billy Joe's for Monument, called *Old Five and Dimers Like Me*, and he was feeling a little more cocksure.

"I got these songs," he said, "and if you don't listen to them, I'm going to kick your ass right here in front of everybody."

He could've been killed there and then by some of my friends lining the walls, but I took Billy Joe in a back room and said "Hoss, you don't do things like that. I'm going to listen to one song, and if it ain't no good, I'm telling you goodbye. We ain't never going to talk again."

Billy played me "Old Five and Dimers," and then kept on going. He had a whole sackful of songs, and by the time he ran out of breath, I wanted to record all of them.

His songs were of a piece, and the only way you could ever understand Billy Joe was to hear his whole body of work. That was how the concept for *Honky Tonk Heroes* came about. Billy Joe talked the way a modern cowboy would speak, if he stepped out of the West and lived today. He had a command of Texas lingo, his world as down to earth and real as the day is long, and he wore his Lone Star birthright like a badge. We all did.

The music reflected this. It was so ragged, with mistakes and bad notes, that it hardly sounded finished; but it was as simple and to the point as I could make it. There was no mistaking what the songs were about. On "Ain't No God in Mexico," there wasn't more than three instruments. You didn't need a twenty-piece orchestra. It was all there. The song was true to itself. You could feel what was happening inside it.

"Honky Tonk Heroes" had come directly out of Billy Joe's experiences growing up. His momma and a girl named Blanche had run a honky-tonk called the Green Gables in Waco. She was a good-looking woman, red-headed and tough, and it was a classic dive, a dance hall with sawdust on the floor, spittoons, and a piano in the corner. The bar had a rail along the bottom, where you could stick your boot up and feel like somebody. Little eleven-year-old Billy Joe went there on summer afternoons, and the soldier boys from Fort Hood would give him nickels and throw him up in the air. That's where he started singing, tapping his bare feet and making up songs.

He wrote all this down years later, standing by the bar as a young man, hooking his boot heel on the rail and chicken-hawking tables, looking across to see who he wanted to dance with next. Seems like it was just the other day: the world of "lovable losers, no-account boozers, and honky-tonk heroes."

Like me.

CHAPTER

7

# COUNTRY MODERN

We're on a motorcycle, me and Willie, riding past five miles of backed-up traffic, people hollering, car doors opening in front of us, flags waving, girls leaning off pickup trucks, frisbees flying, a different song from each radio as we zip along the shoulder, covered with Colichee dirt and shouting ourselves hoarse, heading for the Dripping Springs Picnic.

Independence Day, 1973.

Willie has called a gathering of the tribes to this dusty patch of ranch twenty miles west of Austin. He's roped in Sammi Smith, who's just had a big hit with Kris's "Help Me Make It Through the Night," and myself to help him bring it off.

Naturally it's pure chaos. We've got Ernest Tubb, Hank Cochran, Charlie Rich, Kris Kristofferson and Rita Coolidge, Ray Price, Loretta Lynn, Johnny Bush, the whole Austin scene with Jerry Jeff Walker and Doug Sahm, and yours trulys milling backstage, along with seventy thousand of their most fervent fans out front. Rednecks and longhairs, rolling around together in the heat and the dust.

Nobody has a clue about what they're doing, when they're going on, who's in charge. Nobody can figure how to control it. Nobody wants to. Somebody steals the money and we don't get paid.

But there, right as rain, is Willie, beaming up at me. He knows it is the beginning of something.

"We hot, ain't we?" he says.

We hot.

If there ever was a free spirit on Earth, it's Willie Nelson. He'll tell you it's because his philosophy of life is "follow your intuition."

It's just that we go about it in different ways. Willie does not want to break the natural flow of things. He does not want confrontation. Whatever's bound to happen, he figures, go ahead and let it. Willie would sooner bend than break, leaning backward until he throws you off balance and gets his way.

With me, there's no gray area. It's all black and white. I'm in my element when I'm fighting for something. I'll stand right out there in the dirt and take on everybody in town for his and my right to believe in whatever we think is worth caring about. And if a truck is coming and I've got my back turned, you better holler and not let it run over me, natural flow be damned.

When Nashville started giving us both a hard time, Willie up and left for Texas. He didn't go back. I stayed in Nashville. I guess in the end we both survived as best we knew how, and came out on the other side with our pride and music intact.

He'll never change, and I don't think he should. He'll give you everything, say yes to anybody, trust that events will turn out fine in the end. He'll never be rich. He loves to be a gypsy on the road, playing that beat-up ol' guitar, wearing that silly-ass headband, singing through the side of his nose and signing autographs after the show, which is where his concept of karma comes in. He thinks you should be thankful if Miss Fortune helps reimburse you for a deed from another life.

I say, "Willie, I believe that what goes around comes around in this life, but I wasn't with you in the other ones. You better leave me out of this."

He never does, though, and I've had to start my life over several times because of him. If he'd ask, I'd do it all over again. He's my personal Willie, and I'm his Waylon. Yin and yang. Where there's a Will, there's a Way.

Willie was like a god in Texas. People there think when they die they're going to Willie's house. He had been raised in Abbot and cruised through Waco as a door-to-door salesman before becoming a disc jockey in San Antonio. He gravitated to Nashville and Tootsie's in the early sixties, selling "Family Bible" for fifty dollars before earning a songwriter's living with hits for Patsy Cline and Faron Young, and penning Ray Price's theme song, "Night Lights." RCA made over a dozen records with him in the late sixties. Though he had some success, he was mostly known as a songwriter, and loving performing as much as he does, that eventually started to bother him.

I didn't see much of Willie when he lived in Tennessee. His home was out in Ridgetop, on the fringe of Nashville, and when he wasn't spending time with his family, he hung out with Hank Cochran's crowd at Pamper Music in Madison. I was probably closer to his drummer, Paul English. His first wife worked at the Wagon Wheel downtown on Broadway, and I'd hear tales of her throwing an ashtray at him, and hitting Hank, or beaning Ben Dorsey with a beer bottle. Mostly our only contact was knowing that we were both outcasts on the same label. We'd play some shows together, but the road usually took us in different directions.

In 1971, Willie's house in Ridgetop burned down, and he got a deal with Atlantic Records' new country division. Allowed to use his own band and do his songs the way he heard them, and intrigued by his popularity in Lone Star honky-tonks, he saw no need to stay in Nashville. He returned to Texas, settling in Austin, where he felt an affinity with the redneck hippie community centered around a converted armory named Armadillo World Headquarters. In those days, the combining of those two worlds was a big deal: long hair, pot smoking, and youth didn't set well with country music or its truck stop audience.

Willie helped bring all that together, or did all that bring Willie together? Pretty soon he was growing his hair long and playing in front of whooping crowds at the Armadillo Headquarters, calling me up and telling me I should come visit this little nightclub in Austin.

I'd never worked the Armadillo before. I thought it was a cowboy place. After I set up, I peeked through the curtains and saw that it was a rock and roll club. We'd played a festival in Dripping Springs—they called it a Reunion—the previous July Fourth, but there were so many different performers on the bill that you figured some of the audience had to be yours. The Armadillo crowd was all young kids, longhairs, sitting on the floor. The smell of reefer hung heavy in the room. I thought about my head in the mouth of a lion.

I was upset. "Somebody find that red-headed bastard and get him here," I said. When Willie arrived, all smiles, I tore into him. "What the hell have you got me into?"

"Just trust me," he said.

I said, "I know what that means in Hollywood, but it better not mean the same thing here."

I didn't have to worry. They went nuts when I hit the stage, and even crazier when Willie came out to join me.

It was a new way of thinking. We were going against the grain, and yet we weren't alone in how we felt. Willie saw there were two streams of country music, moving parallel, sometimes further apart, sometimes growing closer. Each was just a little afraid of the other, and he wanted to bring them together.

What better way than to have a Picnic? Though modeled on Woodstock, Dripping Springs took on a character all its own as it grew, the old and the new together. Willie invited Leon Russell to add his road show into the mix; Tom T. Hall, Ernest Tubb, and Charlie Rich blended a traditional spirit alongside relative newcomers like Kris and Billy Joe Shaver.

Billy Joe especially had a wild Picnic. He'd played the night before at the Armadillo, passed out in the back, and woke up the next day to realize he'd been bitten by a brown recluse spider. He went to Johnna Yursic's room, who by this time was road managing me, and Johnna put him in a cold shower to keep the fever down. It certainly didn't do the trick, because later on Billy Joe was running all around backstage, healing people and thinking he was Jesus. About three in the afternoon he decided he was going to go out into the desert to die. He gave his car keys and billfold to his wife and went off, until he heard Sammi singing "Take the ribbon from your hair" and knew he wasn't in heaven. Billy Joe came back, looking like a basted turkey, with the worst song you ever heard about dyin' in the desert. He had decided to live.

We'd never seen anything like it. Everything we did at Dripping Springs was wrong, and it didn't matter. Nobody paid to get in; the fences were torn down. I'm singing "Bob Wills Is Still the King" and women are throwing brassieres on stage. My band just went to pieces. Girls with no tops, no bottoms, up on boys' shoulders and taunting you. If you didn't look, people were going to wonder about you; if you did look, they were going to know about you. They caught you either way. One ol' gal took her clothes off and got up on a tall camera platform. She was just lying there squirming and some cowboy jumped up and mounted and went to work. It started a whole orgy over in that area. Debbie couldn't do Dallas like she did. I never quite got used to that.

Backstage it was pot, whiskey, pills. And some cocaine. Coke was just coming in, though I was still carrying pockets full of uppers. The whole audience was as twisted as we were: all day and all night drinking hot beer. I wanted to know when and where they went to the bathroom, since they weren't about to give up their places in the front row to take a leak. There were streakers and star-struckers. It was a wonder nobody got hurt.

We were having a time, that was for sure—one big ball. I don't recall anybody looking sideways.

Billy Joe put it best. "We were all melted into the same comet." All we could do was grab it by the tail and hang on for dear life.

Suddenly, we didn't need Nashville. They needed us.

Our vision of country music didn't have any shackles attached to it. We never said that we couldn't do something because it would sound like a pop record, or it would be too rock and roll. We weren't worried that country music would lose its identity, because we had faith in its future and character.

In trying to broaden its appeal, country music had gotten safe and conservative. Awash in strings, crooning and mooning and juneing, Countrypolitan may have been Nashville's way of broadening its pop horizons, but it was making for noncontroversial, watered-down, dull music that soothed rather than stirred the emotions. It had honey dripped all over it.

To be real. To sing the truth, regardless of whether we were walking contradictions or not. We wanted the freedom to use any instruments we wanted, or not use them, whichever the song itself demanded. Why limit yourself? Country music is the feeling between the singer and the song. The instruments are only there to help.

When Roy Acuff sings "Wabash Cannonball" backed up by the Smoky Mountain Boys, and you take the Smoky Mountain Boys off and put on Henry Mancini's strings, what have you got? Roy Acuff singing "Wabash Cannonball." I loved all kinds of music, and I didn't want to be limited in how I interpreted a song. I couldn't be afraid of trying new things. I couldn't accept the phrase "musically, that's wrong," because if I mixed a horn, a dobro, and a harmonica playing in unison and it worked, then that was like a whole orchestra in three pieces for me. You can't worry what is or isn't country. I had confidence in the intrinsic values of the music, and a belief in the varied styles it could encompass.

Country was much stronger, had more depth and soul, than it was given credit. In a bid to become respectable, country music had been shying away from its rural past, its birthright in the honky-tonks and "skull orchards." That's why Billy Joe's song was more than a celebration of colorful barflys; it was a return to roots that lay at the core of country music's appeal: its beating heart and original sin.

All of us had grown up and learned our craft in the honky-tonks. You can get out and dance and yell and scream and whoop and holler and nobody says a damn thing about it. Hit the biggest clunker in the world and it's okay. At least you tried it. The honky-tonk might be low-class and low-rent, but that means you have to get even lower *down* with your music, cut it to the bone, make sure you don't waste a note. You're honing everything.

I developed my whole style of performing in the honky-tonks. You have to learn a lot of songs, paying your dues six nights a week, four hours a night and two more afterhours on the weekends. I'd get bored, and start changing the tunes, moving the rhythms around, improvising the phrasing, stretching my boundaries. Putting the music out and having it come back. If it just goes out and lays in the audience, you haven't reached them. If you get it back, amplified, then you become one with the crowd. When I learned how to do that, I never forgot.

It's a state of mind. I'll never be a symphony picker, but I can turn any place into a honky-tonk. Years later, when I played the St. James Theatre on Broadway in New York, the manager was going on to me about how honored I should feel playing there. I knew I should've been more impressed, but frankly, I wasn't. Walking out to the stage, I checked out the audience. "Look around," I told them. "A honky is a honky and a joint's a joint. I don't give a damn if it is on Broadway."

Richie clicked his sticks together, cracked the snare, and we were off and honky-tonkin'.

Kris Kristofferson was hardly a hillbilly. A Rhodes Scholar and a helicopter pilot, he was like nothing Nashville had ever heard before. He brought a new maturity and sophistication to country lyrics, an explicitness to the verse-singalong chorus-verse-sing-along chorus-bridge-verse-two choruses-and-out that was the standard country fare. Spelled X-plicit, meaning Sex.

One time we counted up and Kris had used the word "body" a hundred and forty-four times in his various songs. Nasty nasty nasty. For a while Nashville was a little afraid of him; but his songs were undeniably poetry, and he taught us how to write great poems. He changed the way I thought about lyrics, and he said one time that I was the only one that really understood his songs.

They all had double meanings, something like Kris's life. His father was a two-star general, which must have been slightly con-flicting for a guy who went to Oxford and wrote an essay on the visions of William Blake. He wanted to pen great literature, but instead Kris joined the Army Rangers in the early sixties and learned to fly helicopters, which came in handy when he landed a chopper on Johnny Cash's tennis court by way of introduction. Presumably the hours of KP experience he picked up in the ser-vice also proved useful. When he first arrived in Nashville, he started at the bottom as a night janitor at Columbia Records. By day, he worked the bar at the Tally-Ho Tavern. That's kind of like putting the fox in charge of polishing glasses in a chicken coop.

I saw him a lot at Sue Brewer's, and was one of the first to do songs of his, like "Sunday Morning Coming Down" (though it was John Cash who had the hit) and "Lovin' Her Was Easier." Roger Miller broke the Nashville ice with "Me and Bobby McGee," and John especially encouraged Kris by having him on his television show in 1969. By 1970, with "Bobby McGee" a posthumous smash for Janis Joplin, and Sammi Smith scoring with "Help Me Make It Through the Night," Kris was Nashville's brightest—in more ways than one—hope. His debut album was eagerly awaited, especially by hungry artists looking to cover his songs.

Kris was a Texan, born in Brownsville, and in 1973 he brought that Western heritage to good use by starring as William Bonney in *Pat Garrett and Billy the Kid*. He became a Dripping Springs regular, and though movies increasingly claimed his time as the seventies progressed, not surprising when you think how long *Heaven's Gate* is, he had a lot to do with showing that country music wasn't some Hee-Haw backwoods character with a bottle of sourmash likker and a corncob pipe, and that roots don't have to trap you in the ground.


"This Time" was my time. I shifted my base of operations to Hillbilly Central, got Tompall to administer my publishing company, and started practically living in his upstairs studio. At least it seemed that way. We could work around the clock. There were no windows, so you didn't know whether the sun was going up or coming down, and how many times day and night had passed.

There was a freedom there that I didn't have any place else. Both of us could experiment. I would help him and he would help me. We'd record something that wasn't worth shit, some dumb little ol' idea, and pretty soon it would lead us to another dumb ol' idea, and then pretty soon we'd have a good idea. We recorded a lot.

Kyle Lehning, who became one of Nashville's great producers, was our engineer, and he runs whenever we see him now. We gave him a trial by fire, Tompall and I. We plumb wore his ass out. He'd be sitting there, nodding, falling over after two straight days in the studio, and we wouldn't let him go home. I even got him out there to play trumpet at six in the morning. One night, and Captain counted, Tompall worked on redoing a phrase eighty times. He wanted to get it just right.

It was the same way we played pinball (the "marble machines," as Willie saw them) incessantly. Willie's taste was more for golf: "Once you hit one, you're hooked." I guess it's the same with music.

Hillbilly Central was like that scene in *Blazing Saddles* when they're sitting around a campfire eating beans. We'd laugh so hard that sometimes we'd just lose it, go completely to pieces. Then we'd pick up those pieces and put them back together in an interesting shape, and that would be a song.

We liked being best friends, me and Tompall. Captain Midnight remembers we'd be sitting around autographing pictures to each other—"To my Best Friend, Waylon," "To my Best Friend, Tompall"—back and forth, passing them around. Shel Silverstein came in and said, "Aren't you spreading this best friend shit a little thin?"

Midnight would say, "What about me, boys?"

The truth was we were all running buddies, Shel and Midnight and Ron Halfkine, who produced the Dr. Hook records ("On the Cover of the *Rolling Stone*"); and Ray Sawyer, who was Dr. Hook; and Kinky Friedman and Jimmy Bowen and Lee Clayton and Billy Ray Reynolds and Guy Clark and Donnie Fritts.

It was a fraternity, and Nashville was our college town. I Felta Thi. The Elks, the Moose, the F.O.E. Eagles, and us. We had a clubhouse. Parties with music. Jack Daniels and speed.

We could roar the cars up to the metal back door, climb the back stairs and hang out. One night I rear-ended my Cadillac into Tompall's Lincoln Continental Mark IV. When I went in the office, I said, "Tompall, who's just given you a brand new Ovation guitar?"

"You did, Waylon," he answered.

"Tompall, who's the best friend you've got in the world?"

"You are, Waylon."

"Tompall, who stands behind you when nobody else will?"

"You do, Waylon."

"Tompall, who just backed into your Lincoln Continental?"

He chased me down the hall, through the space where the door that I sawed in half and nailed over Tompall's window used to be. Why'd I do it? It got in my way.

Neither of us could take a backward step, and we could argue about something or nothing, but we challenged each other. The studio gave us a great opportunity to experiment. There wasn't anybody keeping score. I could take it back down to the drums and build it up in a different direction, using the control board as another instrument. I even learned how to engineer my own things. Hillbilly Central was high-tech, and yet we used it like a demo studio. Tompall was proud of the fact that he had the quietest signal-to-noise ratio in Nashville; our playing was dirty enough.

It was a marathon, five or six days at a stretch. We didn't know what to expect when we walked out the door, dark or sunlight. Not that we wanted to go anywhere. Everybody who came to town headed for Hillbilly Central.

All we needed was Cowboy Jack Clement. My brother-in-law.

Bubba was what he took to calling me after he married Sharon, and he called Jessi Sissi. I didn't believe it either. The very same Jack who was part of the incredible vortex of energy that was Sun Records, who produced Jerry Lee Lewis and Johnny Cash and Billy Lee Riley, had recorded Charlie Pride, Don Williams, and Dickey Lee's "Patches," and who believed that music should be made because you liked making it, was actually related to me.

He has a certain kind of insanity that's incurable, and I told him that right to his face. There's parts of him that don't ever get near real life. Every once in a while I needed a dose of Jack Clement. He was a sheer-out genius, all soul. If you got around him at the right moment, he could put the world back on track.

"Sometimes you give a grand performance, just for the hell of it," Jack would say. "You waste it and throw it away. Around here, everybody gets to thinking that if you stand up and sing, you better break out all the microphones. By the time you do that, you spoil the whole effect. Sometimes you just have to let the music go, blow it off the walls."

Blow out the walls, was more like it. Jack liked to record musicians without earphones, trying to set up an environment that was live without sacrificing acoustics. He wanted everybody to be in the room, to be able to hear and see and interact with each other. Once the red recording light went on, he felt, it was hard to get people to stay creative. With earphones shutting off everyone into their own world, the music seemed to settle into familiarity. He pushed the music to get out in the open, living and breathing, and to that end he covered up the control-room windows with drapes, pushed his musicians to take chances, and turned off the clock so that everyone could feel free to follow their instincts. Designed by the theatrical designer for *Oh, Calcutta!*, his Studio B on Belmont Avenue, down the street from Jack's JMI Records headquarters, was nicknamed Nashville's Magic Studio.

All magic needs a magician, and as a producer, Jack did it with mirrors and more. He would always try to get as much of it live as he could, though he was riveted on the rhythm section. The main thing was to capture the drums and bass, and even if you got the bass just right, you could work from there. I liked his concentration on the bottom. We felt the impact of the music's heartbeat in the same way.

He never liked to do the same stuff he heard on the radio, and his ears were always open. One day back in Memphis, after eating country fried steak with Jerry Lee at Taylor's, the luncheonette next door to Sun, they had gone back to the session where "Whole Lot of Shakin' Goin' On" was cut. They ran the song down, a live favorite, in between takes of something else. They didn't even listen back to it at the time. It was only when Jack and Jerry Lee were going over what they'd done that day that they heard "Whole Lot of Shakin'" and kept returning to it, fascinated by its off-the-cuff energy.

Between takes. Jack understood that the best music at a session is usually heard when the musicians are reparteeing among themselves, trading riffs, fooling around. That was the personality he was looking to capture, all natural licks and inflections. He was out to harvest a crop. "It's their music, their art," he would say. "A producer can't sing it for you."

He tried to set a stage, approaching recording like putting on a show. In terms of tempo, balance, moods, he heard an album as a voyage from cut one all the way through the fade on the last chord. A trip. Jack danced for you, up on his toes, a shadow moving around in the corner, giving you something to watch, anything to get you to take your conscious mind off your playing, to let you feel it rather than think about it. "I used to be a dance instructor," he'd say when asked, "and when the band starts doing it good, I dance. Even if I'm hung over. No matter how bad I feel, if a guy starts entertaining me, I'm going to get up and let him know. If he sees me moving around, he knows that everything's okay."

And like any good producer, he knew when to butt out. A lot of times he would just leave. He'd get somebody going in a certain direction, and then the best thing he could do was duck out and go down to the kitchen and whip up a snack. Leave 'em have it for a while. Then he'd come back and dance.

Jack and I didn't talk over the album that became *Dreaming My Dreams*. He knew the Glasers very well, having produced and written many sides for the brothers, and liked the homey atmosphere of Glaser Sound Studios, which is what the upstairs was officially called. It was small and compact, with a Studer twenty-four-track tape machine linked to an MCI board. We went to Hillbilly Central in September of 1974 and started cutting anything we felt like. On the back of that album, there's a picture of me and Jack. He's hovering over the control board, literally in the air, like some bearded angel, his hands raised like a conductor, while I'm cracking up and admiring my cigarette. It was a party. You hadda be there.

It took about six months to record, working on and off, mostly in the daytime for once. The label was fighting us, more or less all the time, but we moved at our own deliberate pace. We used bassist Duke Goff and Richie from my band, along with Ralph Mooney, the great Texas pedal-steel legend who had come on board the Waylors in November of 1970, much to my eternal joy and amazement. He was, to say the least, a character. Chet Atkins likes to tell the story of when Mooney had been riding on a plane and found himself seated near Johnny Gimble. Johnny admired Ralph a lot and went up and said "Hello, I'm Johnny Gimble, the fiddler, and I want you to know that I really love your steel playing. I appreciate your work."

Mooney could drink a bit, and when he did, he usually turned mean. "Aw, fuck you," he said to Johnny. Gimble slunk back to his seat.

About a year later, he ran into Ralph on a session. They were having a good time, and Johnny said, "Hey, Ralph, you remember when we were on that plane a year or so ago, and I told you how much I loved your playing and you said 'fuck you'? What did you mean by that?"

Ralph said, "Don't you know what I meant by that?" Johnny shook his head no. Mooney looked at him. "I meant *fuck you!*"

I played guitar. Jack thought my voice and guitar were one and the same; they were a matched set. Coming from a guy who often said he was a sucker for good voices—"Somebody's got a voice and good rhythm, I like to produce them"—that was high praise for my guitar. We built our guitar tracks, layering, ringing the strings to form underlying drones, and when he got to mixing, Jack acted on the music, making it more theatrical, giving it a mystique. It sounded real strange to me when I first heard it back, but I liked it and went with it.

I was playing twelve-string dobro on a John Cash demo the first time I met Jack. I had the idea he didn't like me, because he'd keep walking by without saying anything, though he'd look at me as he danced past. Finally I told John the next time he came by I was going "to stick this dobro right up his ass." John assured me Jack loved my writing and singing.

That was an understatement. He said I was his favorite cowboy after hearing me do "That's the Chance I'll Have to Take," and if he had a million dollars, he'd give it to me and put me on a pedestal in his office and make me sing to him. He recorded that song with everybody he ever produced.

On Thursdays, Jack would close Studio B and have his particular house band come over, guys like drummer Kenny Malone, Joe Allen on bass, and Charles Cochran, the pianist. It was at one of these informal sessions that Allen Reynolds got to producing Don Williams. They cut six sides one Thursday, and they wound up being Don's first six released songs. I stopped over there one day and Allen was writing "I Recall a Gypsy Woman." I told him "Finish it, and let me cut it."

"Why don't you do it right now?" suggested Jack.

So we did. We tried that, and a version of "Good Hearted Woman," and when we got through, Jack went to RCA and said, "This is what he should be doing." That real simple bass, and the harmonica, and me on the guitar with my thumb. Brer Rabbit's hiding place.

Allen Reynolds also wrote "Dreaming My Dreams" with Bob McDill; when I heard that song, it became the inspiration for the album. I sang it in one take. That's all we had, and all we needed.

*I hope that I find what I'm reaching for*
*The way that is in my mind. . . .*
*Someday I'll get over you*
*I'll live to see it all through*
*But I'll always miss*
*Dreaming my dreams with you.*

"Waymore's Blues" was a little earthier, born in the back seat of a limousine in Memphis. Curtis Buck was with me, and we got to trading blues lines, Jimmie Rodgers–style: "Woke up this morning it was drizzling rain / Around the curve come a passenger train / Heard somebody yodel. . . ." It was probably a complete steal, but so much of that early blues is part of the common musical vernacular of the South, it's hard to tell who's borrowing from whom.

Country is blues. It still is. It's the same song anyway you hear it; black or white, rich or poor. We've all been that man, singing about the woman we got, the woman we want to get rid of, the woman we want to get.

Barbara used to call me Waymore, which she got from Jerry Gropp. It's a sign of affection, a lighter version of Waylon, and a macho way of looking at myself with a sense of humor. There was a time, on drugs, that I had to have the attention of every woman when I walked into a room. Even if I wouldn't have messed with them, I had to know there was a possibility. Some of "Waymore's Blues" might sound like bragging, but I did try to say everything a good ol' boy thought he could get away with, though I probably believed more of it on *Dreaming My Dreams* than I did when I cut Part II twenty years later.

Jack and I had a little misunderstanding over "Waymore's Blues," and it brought the album to a halt. Jack got to drinking, and I was high. There were a bunch of people in the control room. Jessi and Sharon were talking real loud; it sounded like a bunch of turkeys gobbling. He was trying to clear them out, talking and laughing and moving his hands, though out in the studio I couldn't hear him. I was trying to pick and sing and concentrate on the music, and it was like a circus in there.

Jack started hitting the talkback button toward the end of the take. He was driving me crazy, clicking it on and off, and finally I just put my guitar down and said, "Everybody go home, it's all over."

Jack came up and said, "Bubba, artists don't call off sessions. Producers do."

"Not this time, Jack." I was livid.

"The session's over today?" he asked.

"Yes," I said, "and tomorrow, too."

I went home and didn't say anything. About two weeks later,

Jack called and invited me and Jessi over for dinner. He and Sharon were like Tom Sawyer and Becky Thatcher; they even dressed the part. Jack was straight as a board that night. "Bubba," he finally said. "We ever going to get in there and work on that album again?"

"This is going to sound awful funny coming from me, Jack, but you have to straighten up. There ain't but room for one crazy person in there. One wild man. And that's me."

We never did get a better take on "Waymore's Blues," which is why it fades so quickly on the record. Jack was a genius, though. He knew how to talk to musicians, pulling out things they never thought they'd play, and he put everybody at ease. He let them know when they found the groove. Just by showing up, Jack's presence influenced a session. He set an atmosphere of "fuck the world, we're here to create," and if you made a mistake, he'd help you correct it, or work it into the arrangement. The same was true of his musicians. Charles Cochran was the only piano player I knew who ever told me he ought to lay out of a song because the piano didn't fit. There's not a lot of him on the final record, but his presence and knowledge was invaluable.

Jack sang a high country tenor harmony on "Let's All Help the Cowboys Sing the Blues." He wrote it about himself, and so he wouldn't stick out like a sore thumb, he tucked his voice far back. A country tenor is where a guy sings a little too high. He was straining for the upper registers. "Looking for love, beauty, and IQ"—that's Jack. Sing it, Cowboy.

*Dreaming My Dreams* is my favorite album I've ever done. Whether it was Clement experimenting, or the sense of possibility I felt settling into Tompall's upstairs studio, surrounded by friends, or my whooping yodeling on Roger Miller's "I've Been a Long Time Leaving (but I'll Be a Long Time Gone)," or Neil Diamond talking in the liner notes about the "soul itself" of the human voice, it was a special moment in time, hanging at Tompall's, being brothers.

\*     \*     \*

Hillbilly. That was the name we gave ourselves, but we weren't hillbillies. It was really a joke. People in the Tennessee hills were hillbillies. Roy Acuff was a hillbilly.

Anybody with one eye and half-sense knows I'm no hillbilly. There wasn't a hillbilly bone in my body. If we called ourselves hillbillies, it was to put people off guard, to put ourselves down and them on, to poke some fun.

We were country boys, but we weren't from back in the sticks. It's like when I used to be called the Telecaster Cowboy. I may have liked cowboys, and dressed like one, but I was a cowboy singer. There was a difference.

The difference often worked against us. Live, it seemed like country acts were regarded as hillbilly, considered too dumb to get the first-class treatment accorded other musicians in other musics. We played our circuit, which more often than not found us in out-of-the-way places for less money, and we knew it wasn't about to change. You knew which club you would be playing in which city, and what state fair you'd be going to depending on the month. Maybe you could get a regular booking in Las Vegas, but that was as big as you were going to get.

I never figured out how I could owe the booking agency money after being on the road three hundred days during the year. The most you could ever get was two thousand dollars a night, and it often cost you nearly that much to get to the show and pay for food and lodging. The routings made even less sense. During the year I worked so much, I passed through Syracuse, New York, five times in one month and never performed there once.

You'd get stiffed about twenty percent of the time. The venues wouldn't pay you, and that wouldn't stop you from getting booked there the next time you came through town. Every once in a while, to show I was in control, I'd sometimes blow the date, never show up. I'd call Richie and tell him "Everybody's on his own. I ain't going to be there," and he'd say, "I wish you would call me sometime when the promoter isn't standing right here beside me."

I'd go to Lucky Moeller and say, "Did you ever have a day you just didn't feel like showing up for work?" He was sometimes too understanding. Lucky was from the old school, where you get a well-oiled machine running and not much can jar it out of its endless cycle. You don't show up, somebody else will, and they could keep you out on the road, forever, if you liked. You got on that horse, and you couldn't get off.

Lucky was a Kentucky Derby kind of guy. He was in his element pulling his big Mark III into the back parking lot at Louisville's Freedom Hall to oversee the traditional race concert. Flanked by his son, Larry, and WINN radio's Rob Townshend, I can see him in 1968, sandwiched between Roni and Donna Stoneman; they're wearing white go-go boots and short plastic skirts, which made me wonder why Pop Stoneman always got on me for singing those "sex" songs. Pee Wee King and his Golden West Cowboys are scheduled to go on the revolving stage next, while Tammy Wynette signs autographs, and Tex Williams, Ray Price, Dal Perkins, and myself and the Waylors wait their turns. Little Johnny "Call For" Phillip Morris introduces each act.

This was Lucky's world, all plaid jackets and shiny ties, and it was changing. No longer was it good enough to do things as they'd always been done, traveling the circuit, coming back more broke than when you left. There was an entire audience out there that Lucky's down-home view of country music didn't encompass. The Nashville that Moeller Talent represented was suspicious of the future, only now it was becoming the present, which made them the past.

The spirit of Dripping Springs was taking over country music. Sales of Willie's, Kris's, and my albums were skyrocketing, and we were invading the pages of mainstream rock magazines, like *Rolling Stone*, which had discovered Willie's Austin scene. We could feel the undercurrent of media shaking the ground beneath our feet, like a distant rumbling that signals the onset of an earthquake.

Neil took advantage of this outside interest by booking a pair of shows more notable for their symbolism than their actual stage performances. To introduce me to New York, he arranged a week for me in January 1973 at Max's Kansas City, a small and intimate club (the upstairs showroom wouldn't hold more than a hundred people comfortably) on Park Avenue South that was known as the fabled home of Andy Warhol and glitter rock. They were more used to bands like the Velvet Underground and the New York Dolls; before me, the closest they had come to country was the Nitty Gritty Dirt Band.

I looked out at the audience the first night. I had never seen such spangles, guys in earrings, girls with hair teased in four different directions, a Village underground deep in the heart of the city. I remembered how strange I'd felt when I first came to New York with Buddy. I tripped going up to the stage; with a drum kit and amplifiers, we could hardly move without stepping on the front tables.

"My name is Waylon Jennings," I said before we started. "We're all from Nashville, Tennessee, and we play country music. We hope you like it. If you do, I want you to tell everybody you know how much you like it. If you don't like it, don't say anything mean about it, because if you ever come to Nashville, we'll kick your ass."

All you have to do is open the door; people will walk through if your music can't be denied. Our week-long stay at Max's was a triumph. It was a full moon when we hit that stage, and night after night the Waylors started playing on a whole new level. Richie couldn't believe it. He hadn't been back with me that long, and he could see the turnaround. During the days, I did interviews with national magazines like *Penthouse*, spreading the word about Redneck Rock or Outlaw Country, depending on their perspective, and at night I worked on getting myself laryngitis. I was still a little weak from the hepatitis.

From there, we went to the West Coast, setting up our tent meeting at the more industry-oriented Troubadour, and visiting my old crowd at the Palomino. Crossing over didn't mean that you couldn't go back and forth.

Neil's biggest move was to get me on a bill with the Grateful Dead at Kezar Stadium. With all the overhype, it was a breakthrough to play on the home field of Haight-Ashbury High, even though Janis Joplin had shown that it was a quick hitchhike between Austin and San Francisco. Musically it didn't work. Deadheads don't care if it's Jesus Christ up there. All they've come to see is the Dead. I felt older than them; when I walked out, I probably looked like that sonofabitch who'd told them if they weren't in by eleven o'clock he was going to ground them. My kids were old enough to be among that crowd.

In the end, it didn't matter how the shows went, because the word of mouth whispered like wildfire. Neil brought it all home at the Disc Jockey Convention, where he staged an "Appreciation Concert" with me, Willie, Sammi Smith, and Troy Seals. The ballroom at the Nashville Sheraton was packed to overflowing. I opened with "Lonesome, On'ry and Mean" and closed with "T for Texas," finishing at three in the morning. Three encores. Seventy-three. One for the money, two for the show, three to get ready . . .

Willie and I were in the same boat. Neil was paddling it, and as much as he had to fight for me, he had to keep Willie bailed out. I thought for a while he'd never leave Texas, but pretty soon his sense of an alternative country scene began to take hold, and Willie started becoming a genuine superstar.

He had shifted to CBS from Atlantic, where his first concept album, *Phases and Stages*, had concerned a marital breakup from the viewpoint of the wife. Willie could sympathize with that. He was a travelin' man, and he never hid the fact that he would rather be out playing than home every night. His first love was always the road. Everything else played second fiddle. He didn't mean to be a bad guy. At least, he figured, his wives got to be in the string section.

Atlantic had folded its country division in 1974, and Willie's deal with Columbia gave him complete creative control, though when he worked up his first album under the new deal, another concept album about a mysterious *Red-Headed Stranger*, they still wondered what he was up to.

Willie got the title from an old ballad by Arthur "Guitar Boogie" Smith; he'd sung it to his kids and played it on his Fort Worth radio show. The actual song was a gothic Western mystery story that told of a dark rider who rode from town to town trailing his dead lover's horse behind him. In Willie's version, guilt and sin mixed with redemption as the rider became a young preacher who had murdered his adulterous wife and was forced to wander.

The concept proved flexible, an ongoing narrative that shuffled songs like Fred Rose's "Blue Eyes Crying in the Rain," Hank Cochran's "Can I Sleep in Your Arms," Eddy Arnold's "I Couldn't Believe It Was True," Bill Collery's "Hands on the Wheel," and the gospel chestnut, "Just as I Am," to further the biblical themes of penance and passion.

*Red-Headed Stranger* was just Willie and his band, including his sister Bobbie on piano, a tribute to the cowboy virtues and vices we hoped to emulate. We were trying to put the West back in country and western. Willie practiced what he preached by recording at a small studio in Garland, Texas. The finished album only cost twenty thousand dollars and was tracked, overdubbed, and mixed in three days. That was quick even by Nashville standards.

Neil was fixing to play it to Columbia, and he thought he might have trouble selling them on the record. It was so sparse, sometimes just three or four instruments a song. He brought me along to help him explain it. We went with Jody Fisher, who worked for Neil then and works for Willie now. The meeting was up in New York with Bruce Lundvall, then a head of CBS, and we watched as he threaded the reel-to-reel tape of the finished album.

He let it play, about a song and a half. "It doesn't sound complete," he said. He thought it might be a demo. "There's some pretty good things here, but this needs to go down to Nashville and let Billy Sherrill sweeten it. Put some strings on it."

I got up, pissed. Willie and I both liked strings, but they're right only some of the time. "Neil, you manage both me and Willie, but I tell you, if you don't get that goddamn tape off that machine and get us out of here, then you won't be my manager, and I guarantee you won't be Willie's."

I turned to Bruce. I called him a tone-deaf, tin-eared sonofabitch who didn't know nothin'. "I'm in your office, and I'm leavin', but you ain't got a goddamn clue what Willie Nelson's music is about."

As I started out the door, he said, "Wait a minute, Waylon. You come back. What am I missing?"

I said, "You're missing everything. That's what seventy thousand people come to Dripping Springs Picnic to hear. It's why people will drive all the way from Colorado or Kansas to hear Willie sing. You don't know a thing about it. That album is what he is. Billy Sherrill may be great, but he ain't got a fucking thing to do with Willie Nelson. All he can do is cover him up."

We sat back down and listened. Finally, Lundvall said, "I still don't get it, but I'm going to release this album just like it is." Then I got worried if maybe Willie wanted him to sweeten it up a little bit.

A year and a half later, Bruce Lundvall walked into my office in Nashville. He gave me a gold record of *Red-Headed Stranger* and said "This is from that tin-eared, tone-deaf sonofabitch. You were right. Here's your album."

With all of this, it was Jessi who had the pop smash.

Working on her first album, with producer Ken Mansfield and myself as co-producer, Jessi cut a song called "I'm Not Lisa." It was about a girl who hears her husband call her by another woman's name. She had written it one day in about ten minutes while practicing the piano. It was just an eight-bar phrase that she put aside, and she kept coming back to it as she learned about living in my world, and me in hers.

She had no particular connection with the name Lisa, and took the name Julie from an old song of mine, but she understood that natural insecurity that comes from a woman coming into the life of a man who has been married, or had a very close relationship with another woman, and how it takes a while to believe that maybe he didn't leave his heart behind. Though it came out of her life, and our circumstances, Jessi didn't analyze it any more than she needed. She knew she had touched on a universal feeling, and though it was certainly how she felt, it wasn't just about her. It was about everyone.

One of the reasons Jessi had married me was because she always knew she'd be in music, and sometimes that takes understanding from another musician, someone who knows what the making of music means.

Still, Jessi had put her career on the back burner when we got together, trying to understand our rhythms, and be a mother to our extended family. She wrote the song then, when we were in our first Nashville apartment, amidst life's uncertainties. She had six-year-old Jennifer, her child with Duane, who had been cradled and sheltered, and I had my teenage passle, who had been through hell and back. They didn't know what to expect, after Lynne. I was happy to see Jessi was soft and gentle with them, but she also needed to get their attention, to have them respond, so she could help them.

As for Jennifer, she was a dear sweetheart. We were thick as mud. For a while, it wasn't easy. I could tell she loved me, but she felt guilty about it. We'd be playing and laughing and hugging, and all of a sudden she'd say "I hate you. I don't want to play."

Finally, I had to call Duane, her father, and tell him that I respected his friendship, but that Jennifer was so loyal to him that she believed she couldn't have feelings for both of us. "I want you to know that I will never allow anybody to say anything bad about you in front of her, and you have to tell her it's okay to love me, too." From then on, she called him Daddy Duane and me Daddy Waylon.

When I got sick, Jessi helped care for me, even learning to cook differently, knowing that her food was medicine. Nursing hadn't been part of her repertoire till now, and standing there at the stove, preparing meals so my liver could work, so I wouldn't die, she rose to the occasion.

Somewhere inside of her she knew that we belonged together. She never pushed me, or asked questions, even after we were married. I never quit doing drugs, even at home. I was still as crazy as ever.

I didn't slow down any. Jessi just kept up.

In June 1975, she kept up and up. "I'm Not Lisa" broke off her debut album and slid pop, eventually becoming the number-four record in the country. Gold. It was a magic song, something every aspiring musician dreams of, but when it actually happens, that's when the uncertainties begin. It's a strange responsibility, to live up to the hopes of the people who come up to you and act like they know you. You might never have seen them before, but there is a relationship. They're not family, not friends, not your lover, not your child; they've bought your record, and heard your song. They do know you, whoever you is.

Jessi had to figure it out. It was the first time she had the responsibilities of a solo act. She'd had a measure of success, written songs, been featured with Duane, and guested with me. Now it was her turn in the spotlight. There was a part of her that preferred to remain slightly behind the scenes, over on the left side of the stage, singing harmony on the chorus. Her giving, and forgiving, nature meant she felt uncomfortable standing in the center. She tried not to be overwhelmed by "Lisa," so she wouldn't become "I'm Not Jessi." And she wasn't; she was actually Mirriam.

Jessi was an agnostic when I met her. Maybe even an atheist. She had come to a crisis in her faith before we met, and tried all the metaphysical doors. She was not even able to open a Bible, working her way through many untraditional philosophies before reaching back to the God of her youth.

She had prayed before she went out on the stage of the Santa Monica Civic, at one of her first solo shows, and she thought her prayer was answered when she went out on stage, devoid of fear or insecurity, perfectly pure in the moment of performance. It was a feeling that lasted for the length of the show, and when she thought about it, as years passed, she decided it was simply about being free, of letting yourself go in the care of a Higher Power. The gift of faith. She lived it in her daily life, sang it every day at the piano when she turned to the psalms, and thought that some-day I would have the dogged and contrary conviction of a King David, which is why she was in turn able to help me in my jour-ney through the valley of the shadow. She instinctively under-stood that maybe the place where people try to take refuge with drugs is a false security blanketing what is hidden in their spirit. As a substitute, or a replacement, she knew drugs were a com-petitor to this rise to self-discovery. Otherwise, why would they be needed?

Don't ask me. I was too busy being a Night Walker, as Jessi called it. And being proud of her, for achieving her dream.

I never had a pop hit, at least on the Top Forty. For a while, in the early seventies, my favorite phrase was "I couldn't go pop with a mouthful of firecrackers."

People would ask me how I felt about "I'm Not Lisa" going gold. Did I mind?

Mind? Jessi was so happy, getting checks and buying presents for everybody she loves. For me, she put the down payment on our house, Southern Comfort.

But they'd continue: You've been struggling all these years, and here comes Jessi, first album, no reputation, and she has a million-selling record right out of the chute.

"Being a fuckin' legend," I'd have to say, "I don't give a shit."

\*　　\*　　\*

Jessi was up for numerous honors at the 1975 Country Music Association awards. I wasn't going to be the one to steal her thunder, knowing how much acceptance means when you're first starting out, and so I went with her, even though I couldn't tolerate the CMA.

They were suspicious of me, as well. "Waylon," they greeted me as I walked in. "You're not here to start trouble, are you?"

Who, ol' Waymore? Just because one year I'd stormed out of the awards and didn't mind telling anyone who would listen why. It was Kris Kristofferson's night; he was a shoo-in for several categories. I had been scheduled to perform "Only Daddy That'll Walk the Line." They said they were strapped for time, and they wanted me to cut the song to one verse and chorus. I said, "Why don't I just dance across the stage and grin? Maybe do one line. That'll give you a lot of time."

They told me not to get smart. Either I did it or I got out. They said, "We don't need you." I decided that was true, and I left.

The CMA were always pulling fast ones like that. They were more concerned with their television show than honoring country music. One year they tried to make Ricky Van Shelton sing a song in the wrong key. They'd already cut the track for him to put his vocal over and he said it was too high. They told him to get off the grounds when he went out to his bus. Ran him off. They like to think that they're doing it for You, the country music fan, but they're really in business for themselves.

Now they needed me again, because I was up for Best Male Vocalist, Song of the Year ("I'm a Ramblin' Man"), Album of the Year, and Entertainer of the Year. As I walked in with Jessi, scratching at my tuxedo, her telling me I should have hit them, Neil came over to me. "You won Male Vocalist," he whispered. "Jessi didn't win anything."

So much for secrecy. If nobody's supposed to know the awards before they opened the envelope, how did word get around? My heart went out to Jessi, and though my first instinct was to get the hell gone, I thought that maybe by staying I could raise some of the larger problems that faced country music, such as its close-mindedness and suspicion of change.

When it came time for Best Male Vocalist, Tanya Tucker and Tammy Wynette made a great show of opening the winner's envelope. I tried to be nice in my acceptance speech, thanking everybody for their support, though I knew that block voting and mass trading between the big companies—we'll give you two hundred votes for your artist if you give your four hundred votes to our writer—probably had more to do with it than anything else.

At least Glen Campbell, the host, was happy. "All I can say, Waylon, is it's about *damn* time." Predictably, the CMA got a few letters protesting Glen's use of profanity.

I was happier watching Charlie Rich get drunk and burn up the Entertainer of the Year award, holding a cigarette lighter to the envelope, please. They went to grab him, but when Charlie was drunk, it was best to stay out of his way. I remember riding back from a Dripping Springs Picnic in University of Texas coach Darryl Royal's golf cart, and Charlie just wailing.

Oh, yeah. John Denver won Entertainer of the Year. Now that's what I call country.

CHAPTER

8

# THIS OUTLAW SHIT

Beyond the law. Outsiders. A whip and a gun, head 'em off at the pass, and good guys don't wear black.

If you look through the scrapbook of any kid who grew up in the forties and fifties, male or female, you'll find a frayed sepia photograph of the child dressed like a cowboy, down to the spurs, six-gallon hat, six-guns drawn, looking about as tough as any six-year-old has a right to be. The great American hero, as filtered through the movies and popular lore, and now, in the hands of a ragged assortment of Hillbilly Central characters, country music.

Excuse me; make that Pop music. Capital *P*, as in platinum.

On January 12, in the bicentennial year of 1976, RCA released *Wanted: The Outlaws*. It was a compilation of mostly previously re-leased tracks, starring myself, Willie, Jessi, and Tompall. The cover was pure Old West, a yellowed reward poster with the stagecoach air of the nineteenth-century frontier, Dodge City to Tombstone.

We weren't just playing bad guys. We took our stand outside country music's rules, its set ways, locking the door on its own jail cell. We looked like tramps, Willie in overalls, me with my hair slicked back and Levis, fringe sprouting on our cheeks and chins. I'd begun growing my face fur in the early seventies, when I was down with hepatitis. I thought, hell, I'm not going anywhere. I think I'll grow a mustache. Next I moved on to the beard.

Jessi's mom came to watch out for me when I returned home from the hospital. Her name was Helen, and she thought I hung the moon. I might be a wild man, but she'd had a vision about me a long time before and knew I didn't mean Jessi any harm. Myself was another matter.

"How's my good-looking king of the road doing? Is my daughter treating you right?"

She inspected my new facial growth, scraggly and scruffy as it was. It takes me a long time to grow anything. I don't get a five o'clock shadow until two o'clock the following afternoon, and my face seems dirty for a month. I still don't have any hair on my chest; it must be the Indian in me.

"Son," said Jessi's momma, "that beard and mustache sure looks like a bunch of piss-ants going to a funeral."

"I don't believe the way she talks in front of you," said Jessi.

I had grown it just for kicks, but when I looked in the mirror, it was like I was starting to look like myself. We all were undergoing transformations. I mean, can you imagine Willie without a beard and those braids? If we took on the guise of cowboys, it was because we couldn't escape the pioneer spirit, the restlessness that forces you to keep pushing at the horizon, seeing what's over the next ridge. When I put the black hat on and walked to the stage, carrying my Telecaster, I was staking my own piece of land where the buffalo roam. Don't fuck with me, was what we were saying.

We knew we were good. We loved the energy of rock and roll, but rock had self-destructed. Country had gone syrupy, dripping honey all over its sentimentality. Progressive country? Any music had better progress or it'll get left behind.

We were loose. Nothing to prove. I never believed you could tell people you were great; you had to show them. And increasingly, on the radio, at the concerts and festivals, we were getting our chance. We could see we were gathering a new audience, with their own shape and personality. A lot of times, they weren't country music fans, but they weren't asking us to change. They liked us the way we were. Country fans, maybe because they'd known me for longer, could sometimes give us a hard time. One night in Atlanta, some guy yelled at me, "Take that damn hat off, shave that face and do 'Waltz Across Texas.'"

I said, "You come around after the show and I'll waltz you right up against the side of the wall." I liked to challenge the audience.

We were walking contradictions, and we didn't mind. We were rebels, but we didn't want to dismantle the system. We just wanted our own patch. In the South, especially, they try to live by the rules; it's the legacy of the Bible Belt. Anybody that breaks the rules is a sinner. When you come into a working system, and start trying to change it, you are regarded as the Devil.

Anybody can think whatever they want to think, but don't try to tell me how to go about my "bidness." It's hard to tell a Texan what to do. We accepted the way people were and hoped they'd accept who we were. What we talked about was real, the truth. You could depend on it.

Outlaw music.

Hazel Smith, the great Nashville media specialist, writer, ultimate fan, and publicist for Hillbilly Central, christened it when asked by a disc jockey from WCSE in Ashboro, North Carolina, what to call the renegade sound that was bubbling out of Nineteenth Avenue South. He wanted to base a show around me, Willie, Kris, Tompall, and all the others who were making a name for themselves going up against the Nashville establishment. Other stations, one in Flint, Michigan, and another in Austin aptly named KOKE, were also starting to herald the new breed of rogue hillbilly.

"Hillbilly Central" was the name of the column Hazel wrote for *Country Music* magazine. She had a bird's-eye view of all the frantic comings and goings as she sat out in the front office and directed some of the stranger traffic that started dropping by. The building was open twenty-four hours, and she'd sometimes come in to work and find people strewn about the offices, passed out next to an empty wine bottle or an open bottle of pills. Another night of "losing weight."

I'd done a song of Lee Clayton's titled "Ladies Love Outlaws," about how women don't look at a wild man and see someone hard. Like Jessi when she saw me on television, they think an Outlaw just needs somebody gentle to settle him down. Either they're not scared or they're just as wild as you are; I ran into quite a few like that.

There was a verse about Jessi and me in it—"Jessi liked Cadillacs and diamonds on her hands / Waymore had a reputation as a ladies' man," which was only partly true—but the song's larger insight was the attraction we all feel for those who move against society's grain. Bob Dylan sang "To live outside the law you must be honest" in "John Wesley Harding"; the Shangri-Las called the Leader of the Pack "good-bad, but not evil." It's a common theme, dating back to Robin Hood and forward through Jesse James to Thelma and Louise.

To us, Outlaw meant standing up for your rights, your own way of doing things. Most lawbreakers are common criminals. Bonnie and Clyde were nothing but a couple of idiots. So was Billy the Kid; you can look and tell he wasn't all there. They got attention by killing people. The ones who shot them, heroes like Wyatt Earp or Bat Masterson, weren't any better. Those lawmen didn't want to walk the same side of the street when Johnny Ringo or Clay Allison came to town. The ones that got killed were those who couldn't aim, farmers with rusty guns they used for shooting snakes, innocent bystanders.

If I had an Outlaw hero, someone to set my standard and measure my progress, it was Hank Williams. He had touched me way back in Littlefield, through the strength of his songs and the soul of his voice. I especially loved his Luke the Drifter recitations, morality tales like "Pictures from Life's Other Side" or "Too Many Parties and Too Many Pals," usually recorded the Morning After the Night Before. Everything I did in Nashville, anything *anyone* did, was measured against Hank's long, lanky shadow.

You'd hear all these stories, how he pulled a jukebox that didn't have his records on it out to the street and shot it full of holes, or ran around all night dead drunk and pilled out and still gave the greatest show you ever saw. We thought that was the way to do it. Does your wife cheat on you? Well, I heard Hank's wife did, if only in all them lonesome blues. Did Hank miss concerts? We could, too. Did Hank write great songs and read funny books and take pills and swarm?

I wanted to be like him. We all did. Even his contemporaries held Hank in awe. Faron Young brought Billie Jean, Hank's last wife, to town for the first time. She was young and beautiful, and Hank liked her immediately. He took a loaded gun and pointed it to Faron's temple, cocked it, and said, "Boy, I love that woman. Now you can either give her to me or I'm going to kill you."

Faron sat there and thought it over for a minute. "Wouldn't that be great? To be killed by Hank Williams!"

He wound up driving Hank and Billie Jean around in Hank's Cadillac, with the two of them loving it up in the back seat. All of a sudden, it got very quiet in the car. Faron thought he should say something. "Hey, Hank, that left fender got a little rattle in it."

"Shut up, boy," said Hank. "Watch the road and keep driving. I bet you wish you had one that rattled like that."

Hank loved Audrey, his "main" wife, though life between them was unbearable. The night he married Billie Jean, on stage in New Orleans, he turned around to his steel player, Don Helms, and said, "Shag, I'm gonna marry Billie Jean tonight. Audrey be up to get me tomorrow." He worshipped Audrey, he really did. They both were screwing around, and he was surely a woman hound, but I think in some of his songs, like "Your Cheating Heart," Hank was really writing about himself.

After Hank died, it became almost an unwritten law in Nashville to try and put the make on Hank's Old Lady. Audrey always liked her boyfriends to have coal-black hair. One night, when Hank Jr. was on the show, I was walking from the bus with her, and she said, "Darling, have you ever thought about dyeing your hair black?" I told her I liked it fine the way it was, thank you. I may have laid down in the back seat of the Cadillac Hank died in when Hank Jr. showed it to me, but I wasn't about to try any of his other sleeping positions.

Both Hank's ex-wives said I reminded them of Hank. Billie Jean, who later married Johnny Horton, came to town one time and wanted to meet me, so Harlan brought her over to the office. Johnny had been killed in an auto accident. She asked me, "What are you doing later when you get off?"

"Look, lady," I said, "you killed Hank Williams and you killed Johnny Horton and you stunted Faron Young's growth. So you just leave me alone." We both laughed, me a little nervously.

If we were all walking around trying to fill Hank's boots, for me, it was literally. Hank Jr. gave me a pair of Hank Sr.'s cowboy boots, and sometimes, late at night, I'd put them on and stroll around the house. They fit pretty well. I could feel his presence hovering over me. I wore them to the studio one midnight, and while we were recording, a big lightning storm blew up. It hit a tree out in the parking lot, which then fell over my brand new El Dorado. We went out to look at it, and sure enough, the tree was fully covering the car. We raised one branch, and then another, and backed the car out. There wasn't a scratch on it.

We went back to the studio and started recording again. While we were out in the room, lightning struck the building, overloading the recorder, scoring the black facing off the tape. They made me take the boots off after that.

Another night, I was upstairs in the office with my feet up on the desk. I had the boots on and I was talking about them, and about Hank. All of a sudden, the pictures on the right-hand side of the wall slid off their hooks, crashing to the floor. Everybody left in a hurry.

"Are you sure Hank done it this way?" Each time the bus would break down, or you'd get stranded, or drive five hundred miles to a gig only to find it had been cancelled, we'd compare our troubles to Hank's. We wanted to be like him, romanticizing his faults, fantasizing ourselves lying in a hotel room sick and going out to sing, racked with pain, a wild man running loose even if it meant dying in the back seat of a blue Cadillac on the way to greet the new year in Canton, Ohio. That was part of being a legend.

Driving to Hillbilly Central one morning during the *Dreaming My Dreams* sessions, I was thinking about Hank's influence and the example he'd set for us, both good and bad. I grabbed an envelope from the seat and started writing, one hand on the wheel, the other balancing pencil and paper on my knee. When I got to the studio, we immediately recorded it—me and Richie managed to turn the beat completely around—and I read it off the envelope. Two weeks later, our bus driver, Billy, came to me and asked if he could have the envelope with the original lyrics. He'd found it on my music stand. I looked at it, and I swear I couldn't read a word. It was just scribbling.

*Lord it's the same old tune, fiddle and guitar*
*Where do we take it from here?*
*Rhinestone suits and big shiny cars, Lord*
*It's been the same way for years.*
*We need a change.*
*Somebody told me, when I came to Nashville*
*Son, you finally got it made*

*Old Hank made it here, and we're all sure that you will*
*But I don't think Hank done it this way*
*I don't think Hank done it this way*
*Ten years on the road pickin' one-night stands*
*Speeding my young life away.*
*Tell me one more time just so's I understand*
*Are you sure Hank done it this way*
*Did old Hank really do it this way*
*Lord I've seen the world with a five-piece band*
*Looking at the back side of me*
*Singing my songs, one of his now and then*
*But I don't think Hank done 'em this way*
*I don't think Hank done 'em this way.*

With its relentless four-on-the-floor rhythm, phased guitars, and eerie drones, "Hank" didn't sound like a standard country record. There was no clear-cut verse and chorus, no fiddle middle break, no bridge, nothing but an endless back-and-forth seesaw between two chords. Jack mixed the guitars together so they sounded like one huge instrument, matching their equalization settings so you couldn't tell where one blended into the other.

It felt like a different music, and Outlaw was as good a description as any. We mostly thought it was funny; Tompall immediately made up Outlaw Membership certificates and handed them out to select visitors at Hillbilly Central. We did feel like we were connected, but our musics were very different from each other. The only thing bringing us together was our attitude. We needed a change.

It wasn't just us. After the 1974 CMA awards, in which Olivia Newton-John took Female Vocalist of the Year, a more traditional Association of Country Entertainers (ACE) protested Nashville's pop swing. Ernest Tubb, George Jones, and Tammy Wynette (the meeting was held at Tammy's house) were also being denied their hearing by a wider audience. For Nashville, the door still swung one way, and Music City was usually ACEd out.

We were trying to break it open from the inside. That didn't make us any more popular. They thought we were dirty, and hell, we were. You try staying up for a week straight, or rather, un-straight. Every Outlaw needs a last stand, and we liked pretend-ing we were at the Alamo. Willie was Jim Bowie; Kris, Davy Crockett; Tompall was Buddy Ebsen; and I was the goddamn can-non fodder. Open fire!

We had ourselves a handle. CB radio was big then. We could feed our white-line fever as the Silver Eagle bus crisscrossed the superhighways of America, talking to other mass transports in the same way the media found our catchphrase and ran with it. It was almost like a hook in a song. We had a hit phrase.

In magazines and newspapers, radio and television, Outlaw music became the byword for a country music underground. A movement grows because there's a need out in the wilds of soci-ety, asking for a certain type of individual, insight, or emotion. People liked what we were saying. There was a mood that was craving our message of freedom and a fresh start. It didn't matter whether we were Outlaws or not, country-rock or rockin' country. You are only what your audience thinks you are, anyway. We rep-resented New.

Helping spread the word was Chet Flippo, who wrote reams of you-are-there copy for *Rolling Stone* and other alternative rock journals, a roving reporter inside Hillbilly Central. He witnessed firsthand the backstages, the hotel lobbies, and late-night coffee shops a late-night band of "born scrappers" might frequent. On the back of *Wanted: The Outlaws*, he wrote: "Call them outlaws, call them innovators, call them revolutionaries, call them what you will. They're just some damned fine people who are also some of the most gifted songwriters and singers anywhere." Amen.

RCA was delighted. They'd tried to find a description to cate-gorize my music since the days of *Folk-Country*, and now they fi-nally had a Concept. The marketing department breathed a sigh of relief. At last: an image.

Jerry Bradley, RCA's Nashville chief, heard them down the

hall. Jessi's success, Willie's success, and my success was impossible to ignore, as was the constant stream of media attention. He decided to jump on this careening bandwagon, asking me to put together an Outlaw anthology. I had been doing package shows with Willie and Tompall under the Outlaws concept. RCA had the rights to Willie's back catalogue, Jessi and I were lawfully wed, and when Bradley suggested the idea to me, I asked for Tompall to be included.

I liked Jerry, but he drove me a little nuts. He didn't have a clue about music, though he always tried to get involved in it, usually by remote control. I'd bring him a finished song, and he'd say, you need to do this, you're going to have to change so-and-so, and I'd go back into the studio and pretend to move the faders, and he'd okay it. He never knew I didn't fix a thing.

We'd have fights so loud in his office that secretaries would be grabbing aspirin bottles and running for cover. Jessi was sitting with Wally Cochran, a promotion man, one afternoon when I was in Bradley's office. Jerry called me a liar. I lost my temper, started cussing him up and down, and tried to get him to step outside. You could hear me all over the building. Wally was picking up the phone when the argument started and he stopped midway, frozen, the receiver inches from his face, stunned and unsure whether to rush in and save his boss. Jessi just read the paper, never losing her cool.

Jerry was Owen Bradley's son, who founded one of Nashville's premier recording studios, Bradley's Barn, and ran Decca when it was the home of Webb Pierce, Ernest Tubb, Brenda Lee, and Patsy Cline. He might have had a little something to prove, coming from a different world than I did. He was in the old style, and it was hard for him to break from his background. "You ain't got nothing to say about it," I'd tell him, but he fought me every step of the way.

He was a good merchandiser, though, and *Wanted: The Outlaws* was his baby. A reporter from *The Tennessean* had once asked him if he would support this so-called "music of the future," and Jerry said that if I was selling the amount of records that Charlie Pride did, he'd be a fool not to. Sure enough, Neil did an audit and found I was already selling more records than Charlie. After that, he jumped in front of the bandwagon and started pulling.

I didn't like calling us the Outlaws, because there was already a rock band named that; my idea was "Outlaw Music." If I had to do it over, I'd argue till I almost got him convinced and his mind changed, and then I'd quit. In hindsight, it did work out pretty well.

There wasn't anything slick about the album. It was loose-limbed, and true, and that's what people were looking for. They couldn't find it in rock and they damn sure couldn't find it in country.

We were the only alternative they had.

Some of the things on *Wanted: The Outlaws* were over ten years old. I sweetened and updated some of the vocals, added harmonies, and got Willie in to sing with me on "Good Hearted Woman." He was so high when he was doing his part he was dancing a jig out in the studio. Willie's cuts came from his *Yesterday's Wine* collection, with "Me and Paul" being a tale of his road adventures with longtime drummer Paul English, who looked out for Willie. Jessi and I had done "Suspicious Minds" together back in 1970—we still perform it live in concert, a quarter of a century later—and she sang her beautiful "I'm Looking for Blue Eyes." Tompall recorded a new version of Jimmie Rodgers's "T For Texas," and we licensed him doing Shel Silverstein's "Put Another Log on the Fire" from MGM. Shel was an honorary Outlaw in our eyes.

I remixed the album at RCA's studios, on the sly, going in late at night. "Honky Tonk Heroes" seemed to fit the concept, as did Willie and I dueting on "Heaven or Hell." We never did decide which one of us was which.

As an album, our true fans had probably heard most of it before. For the newer people, who needed a sampler of Outlaw

Music to understand what all the fuss was about, it was a perfect introduction. To set the stage, the album opened with "My Heroes Have Always Been Cowboys," a new song in which I tried to link up "the cowboy ways" I'd always admired in my "high-ridin' heroes" with "modern day drifters . . . sadly in search of / One step in back of / themselves and their slow-movin' dreams." It was an oddly downbeat way to begin the album, but it seemed to sum up the frontier loneliness that often came hand in hand with our ideals of rugged individualism.

I kept thinking of Hank, passing alone, with no friends or family around him. That was one of my secret fears, to "die from the cold / In the arms of a nightmare." It may have been why we didn't mind being lumped together, though we were all unmistakably individual. There's nobody like Willie Nelson. There's nobody like Kris, or Tompall, or Billy Joe. There's really nobody like me, and I know that. There's a loneliness and a pride there, Outlaws or in-laws, under the same roof that made us a family.

All of a sudden we found ourselves besieged with some long-lost relatives. *Wanted: The Outlaws* moved into the pop charts, and by December had sold over a million copies. It was the first country album to do so. Outlaws became hip, forecasting the rise of the Urban Cowboy, and pretty soon a lot of people began showing up on the doorstep of Hillbilly Central, flashing their horseshoe belt buckles and Jack Daniels bottles and proclaiming their enemy status.

David Allen Coe was the most sincere of the bunch, though he wasn't as rough as he wanted everybody to think. Before he became the Mysterious Rhinestone Cowboy, complete with Lone Ranger mask, he had spent considerable time behind bars, depending on which story you heard, from reform school to the Ohio State Penitentiary and on to death row, for killing another inmate in self-defense. Paroled, he headed for Nashville where his songwriting skills brought him more renown than his bad-ass bragging. He had written "Will You Lay with Me (in a Field of

Stone)" for Tanya Tucker, and was on his way to penning the classic "Take This Job and Shove It" for Johnny Paycheck, who also took to waving the skull-and-crossbones Outlaw banner. "I'm one of youse now," said Johnny, calling me up. "I'm an Outlaw."

I said, "Have you been stealing antiques again?"

The first time I met David, at the Demon's Den in downtown Nashville, he took me home to see his wife and firstborn baby. We rode in his custom hearse, and he told me all the things he was fixin' to do that I wasn't doing, and why wasn't I doing them and how tough he was and how he didn't take any shit.

His mouth was getting him into trouble. Though he had once belonged to a motorcycle gang, he had gotten on the wrong side of the California Hell's Angels. He was afraid if he went to the West Coast they were going to kill him. I said, "David, all your life you wanted to play the guitar and sing and write songs and make a living. But if you want everybody to know how tough you are, sooner or later you'll blow it."

"I am tough," he growled.

"You've been in prison, David, or at least you say you have, and you know when you stroll down that aisle between the jail cells, every sonofabitch in there knows whether you're tough or not, just by the way you walk and carry yourself. If you have to tell somebody, you ain't tough enough."

David didn't know what to think. He wrote a song called "Waylon, Willie, and Me" at the same time that he started taking potshots at us in interviews, saying that Willie and Kris had sold out, that I was running around wearing white buck shoes, and none of us were really an Outlaw. He was the only Outlaw in Nashville, an ex-convict that had killed a man with a mop handle, and if he ever caught Glen Campbell, who had a hit called "Rhinestone Cowboy" years after David started driving his hearse down Broadway with his nickname emblazoned on the side, he'd know where to stuff his goddamn rhinestones.

I saw him in Fort Worth and I put my finger right up to his

chest. "You gotta knock that shit off," I told him. "I ain't never done anything to you."

"They just set us up," he protested. "You know I love you, Waylon." He showed me his bus. He'd painted it black: the grill, the bumpers, mirrors, everything. Just like my own Black Maria, with the ghost of Hank Williams inside.

I couldn't stay mad at him for long. When it came to being Outlaw, the worst thing he ever did was double-parking on Music Row. He could drive me crazy, but there was something about David that pulled at my heartstrings.

It's a miracle Tompall and I got along as long as we did.

He was a Jack Daniels boy, and by this time I had switched to cocaine. There's no room in the middle with either of them.

Richie says that he introduced me to cocaine. To get me off the pills, if you can believe that. With Dr. Snap out of the picture, prescriptions were harder to find, and there was some bad shit on the market. I wasn't going to stop, no way, so Richie gave me some cocaine. "Look, Hoss, try this." I liked it. For the next ten years, I liked it.

Life could be good at Hillbilly Central. We spent hours in the studio, Richie and I, absorbing recording techniques, layering and balancing, our producing taking shape. There was no short-age of drugs. When Tompall finally sold the building, whoever bought it tore up the carpeting and the walls. They found all kinds of dope stashed away. When you'd been up a long time, you could get paranoid and start hiding shit. A couple of days later, you'd forget where you hid it. The whole place was like a getting-high time capsule.

You never knew what you might find. For a time, I'd leave the back door of the studio at 4:00 A.M., go down the stairs past where Captain Midnight, Donnie Fritts, and Billy Swan were throwing Bowie knives at a target, and there, sleeping under them like a street person, was a girl we called Crazy Helen, who had followed me from Saint Louis. We tried to bar her from the building, but occasionally she'd slip through and lock herself in the bathroom. I didn't know what to do with her. I tried to give her money to get back home, but after two or three days, she was back. "I sent you home," I'd say to her.

"You didn't tell me to stay," she replied.

Finally, Jessi came to my rescue. I was recording one day and Helen had gotten inside. Jessi knew exactly how to handle the situation. She walked over to Helen and said, "You love Waylon, don't you?"

Helen nodded. "Well, I do too," said Jessi. "Isn't he great?" She didn't go and cuss her out or be mean to her. Soon after that, Helen stopped coming around.

For Tompall's and my friendship, success was proving much harder to deal with than adversity. We weren't overnight sensations by any means; both of us, even by Nashville standards of longevity, were veterans. We had been recording, touring the country, and writing songs for more than a decade. We knew our way around the business, and the pleasure.

Still, without a common enemy to unite us, our best-friendship quickly fell apart. We toured together some, him with a new band that featured a black drummer and guitar player from Bobby "Blue" Bland's group, but a projected Outlaw Express never made it out of the starting gate.

Johnny Cash once told me, "You never go into business with your friends." Once I moved my publishing company over to Tompall's, we were asking for trouble. Tompall didn't trust anybody. I'm probably too trusting, or at least I was then. Somebody has to give me a reason not to trust them. You have to go back to square one; until you do me wrong, I trust you. If a lot of time we judge people by the way we ourselves are, I always wondered in the back of my mind about Tompall. If he doesn't trust anybody, should anybody trust him? So we became more wary around each other. Trouble answered us.

Neil wanted to look at Tompall's books. He didn't have anything to do with my publishing, and he wanted in on that. Neil said he needed it for the IRS, but I think he was just trying to catch Tompall off guard. I went along with Neil, and Tompall took it as a personal insult.

Even Captain Midnight couldn't keep our opposite poles in balance after that. We had made a good triangle, the Big Three, running around town having a pinball. Captain tried to be the peacemaker, but it was brutal for him. He was caught in the middle. It started on an Outlaws tour in the West: California. Midnight would go and open up for us with a few jokes. If he didn't draw any gunfire, the rest of us would head out on stage. Tompall and I weren't speaking, and the Captain was getting tired mediating between the two camps.

When it finally looked to be over between Tompall and I, to the tune of $300,000 in suits and countersuits, I offered Midnight a place in my organization. He said, "I'd love to, Waylon, but Tompall has probably one friend left in the world, and I think that's me." Tompall was right on the edge, he thought, and after a while, I understood the decision he'd made. Tompall wasn't speaking to his own brothers, least of all me. He did need somebody. I wasn't him.

I'll always miss Tompall, though. We had a lot of fun, and we found a freedom together; he's a part of my life. I still think of him whenever I run into an old pinball machine like the kind we used to play. Richie had a birthday party, about five years ago, in a bar over in Franklin. They had an ancient pinball machine in the back and I hadn't seen one for years. We were playing it, getting it up there, making it move way over to the wall where if you hit it, you hit it big. I must've run up a thousand games on that sucker. I left it with the Captain to finish off.

I should call Tompall and tell him about it. Maybe I could give him a holler and we'd drop in a few quarters. I know he'll tell me it's not where he's at anymore; he's not that simple-minded. That part of his life is gone forever, and don't be calling him for things like that, he doesn't want to hear it.

I thought it might be fun, me and him to go over and play that pinball machine once. For old times' sake.

Here comes cocaine.

It's the same as pills, but it's smoother. Lasts shorter. More jolt, more expensive.

"You got any pills?" That used to be the rallying cry of the late-night set. We shared our stashes then. Two or three pills and you could be up for twelve hours, writing songs, swarming, with enough left over for the next couple of days.

Not with cocaine. Those lines vanished quicker than you could spoon them out and roll up a hundred-dollar bill. After a while, even the haves couldn't afford to share with the have-nots. It started breaking up the ol' gang of mine.

Cocaine doesn't last. I was looking for that speed jerk. I needed more to do more, and more, and with enough cash flow to keep the level in my body up so I could stay awake for seven days ("It felt like a week," joked the Captain), I couldn't be still, wobbling around, sure thinking I was having fun. And I guess I was.

I was the happiest druggie you ever saw. Laughing and cutting up all the time. None of that down garbage. I would sometimes get to draggin' before I'd crash, but all I had to do was say good-night and fall out, just like somebody clicked the television off, recharging until I was ready to go again.

Everybody told me how great I was on drugs. I didn't realize the ones that were patting me on the back were the ones I was giving drugs to. I thought I was one in a million.

If they hadn't been killing me, and killing the people around me, I'd probably still be doing them.

There was the Burger Boy, over on the left. I was at the intersection of Eighteenth Avenue South and Broadway, sitting in my car. Across the street was J.J.'s, where we spent days and nights on those pinball machines. Right there at the corner.

Can I get you to fill it up? High test. Unleaded.

# THIS OUTLAW SHIT

I was coming right down the next corner when I realized it was all over. I pulled up at this corner, and then that corner, looking this way and that way, always thinking around the next corner something's going to be happening.

It had been like that for months. Every time I'd look for something to be going on, everybody'd be gone. There was nobody around.

I saw Captain Midnight across the street. I pulled the Cadillac over to him.

"Where you going?" asked the Captain.

"I wore this goddamn town out," I said. "There ain't nobody doing this shit but me. I'm going home."

That was the night I quit roaming.

# CHAPTER

## 9

## BUSTED

It was dark in the office. I didn't bother to put the lights on. I knew the dawn would be coming soon.

I was hiding out. Doing cocaine. Trying to write. I'd sit behind my desk with two lines of lyric on the paper in front of me, sometimes for two, three hours, thinking. Another two lines, these scraped neatly in parallel white rows and chopped with a razor blade, lay in readiness on the side. I'd have an idea for a song, but my mind would be running and speeding so fast I'd forget the next phrase before I had a chance to put pen to paper. I had snorted myself into a trance.

What was I hiding from? Not from anything in particular. I had become a prisoner of who I was, the identity I'd helped to create. Maybe it's not natural for a country boy to have all that money flowing in from every which way, and people following along in its wake, coming at him, wanting a piece of his reflected glory. Maybe I felt, down deep inside, I didn't deserve it. Maybe it was the cocaine, which had taken on a life of its own.

Jessi had a picture painted of herself next to our bed at home. She'd put it by the desk in my upstairs office to remind me what I was missing. I'd think about Jessi, alone, waiting, but I couldn't hold on to the thought.

It's funny. All your life you thirst for success, to be recognized, to get that number-one record. And once you achieve it, far beyond your wildest dreams, then you find yourself running from the fame. I shrank back. Withdrew. Mostly, I had wanted to play my music in my own way. I didn't give a shit about the rest of it. I remember telling Tony Joe White once that I wished I could start all over, that winning the war wasn't proving to be as much fun as fighting the battles.

Everybody had a song for me, even if they wrote it five minutes before. I couldn't go anywhere. I couldn't hang out. I didn't like that I couldn't be one of the boys.

I wasn't the only one who had been cast adrift. Cocaine split up the whole town. At a hundred dollars a gram, I was buying it for twenty thousand dollars a pop. You can't keep everybody's habit up, and my intake was reaching fifteen hundred dollars a day. Half an ounce. Pills were one thing; people who were struggling couldn't afford cocaine. There was one guy that had scraped up enough money and bought some cocaine to impress me and Tompall. He held it out on a mirror, and Tompall—it might have been the first time he tried it—bent down to sniff it, only he blew out instead. The shit flew all over, across the table and into the carpet. The kid looked at me and Tompall so mournfully I had to give him a pocketful, or he might've killed himself.

I knew what I was doing was not normal. I knew I was a drug addict. I called myself a junkie, as a joke to make people feel comfortable around me, but I wasn't a junkie as far as shooting up. I could never use a needle, and I didn't mix drugs. I hated downers; if there's anything I did that was right, it was only going one way. Up. When you start mixing directions, that's when those spiders and snakes start coming at you.

With cocaine, they never had a chance to get in the door. I liked to snort cocaine. I would snort half a gram in one side of my nose and half a gram in the other, shotgunning it. The tops of most people's heads would have come off if they did that. I must have had the constitution of ten men.

I was having a great time. I don't say this to advocate drugs at all. I think drugs are killers; ultimately, they ruin your life and the lives of the people who love you. You could look at me and see that something wasn't right. And everybody around me was doing the same thing. I never tried to hide it.

Maybe that's why they wanted to get me. I really don't know. They could've had me a lot of times before. They knew it, and I knew it too. We rode around with our high beams on, three buses and trucks, and we might as well have had a flashing light on top of the whole convoy letting the entire world know: We do drugs. We take drugs. We'll buy all the drugs you have. We don't sell drugs, but we sure do eat 'em. It was obvious.

I don't think they wanted to bust me, at least in Nashville. Finally, on August 24, 1977, I guess they decided they had to.

Elvis had died a week and a half before. It hardly affected me any.

I didn't think, Here was somebody who died from drugs, and I'm going to die, too. I never connected the two. But I still found it hard to believe he was gone. He was like a force of nature you thought would be there forever.

I knew he was sick. Felton Jarvis had told me one time that he had some real things wrong with him, in his intestines. That's why he was gaining all that weight. Supposedly, his stomach was twice as big as anybody else's. I didn't know anything else.

We had met formally only a couple of times, mostly in Las Vegas at the tail end of the sixties. RCA invited me to see his show, and he asked me back to visit him. He knew who I was; he called me Hillbilly.

I had a wristband on my arm because I had slipped on the pavement playing Run Around the Car with one of the Kimberlys' little kids, and I had fractured it. They had given me pain pills, but the original cast had turned the wrist in such an odd way that it still hurt all the time. I was on my way to L.A. when I had the bright idea of getting a leather wristband made that would hold the arm tight and keep the elbow from moving. I cut the cast off and threw it out the window, and went into the first leather shop I saw. I've been doctoring myself all my life.

To make it look like something, I had a metal peace sign put in the middle of it. Elvis really liked that wristband; I think he wanted it. He kept admiring it—"You hillbillies sure know how to dress"—and calling attention to it, though I wound up keeping it. We talked for a while, but I didn't hang around much.

A couple of months later, I was booked for three weeks in the main room of the Landmark, and he was across at the Hilton. I was playing blackjack about two in the morning when the hotel security came and got me. They told me Elvis had heard I was downstairs and wanted me to come up. He was having a party.

That night, I saw a side of him that was really strange. He had not progressed very much from when he was eighteen; he was still like a little boy, in so many ways. All he did was play, like a kid, and sing. Hidden from the world, he cared more for touch football than his movies. When he'd talk to you, the things that really seemed to matter to him were his badges, and his Man of the Year certificates. He showed me his toys and his trophies.

One of them was Priscilla, his wife. She came up while we were talking and sat on the arm of his chair. She put her arm around him. I was sitting across the coffee table from him. They might have been fighting, but suddenly, he swung around at her and elbowed her right in the side. Hard. She looked hurt. He turned to me and gave me a crooked grin, like I would really be impressed with that.

He could be very possessive. We both had been messing around with this girl who was a hairdresser. He didn't like the idea. One night, he wanted me to come over and play canasta with him. James Burton, his guitarist and one of my hero guitar players, told me, "I know what he wants to do. He's wanting to find out whether you're screwing that girl, too."

Everyone around him had to run the gauntlet. He threw darts at one of his friend's shins, because he was mad at him. Elvis made him stand there. They talk about him giving away Cadillacs, but I imagine a Cadillac would be earned after a few months with him.

There was never any mention of drugs between us. He kept that really well hidden. Red West may have been one of the best friends he ever had, and Sonny West, because they cared about him, watched over him, trying to keep him alive and not letting people know about his habit.

A lot of people like to say he was secretly sad, but I don't believe that. If anything, I don't think he was deep enough inside. He was having fun until the last minute. He loved being Elvis, the mystique of bodyguards, and girls screaming, and being adored. Elvis may have been the most beautiful man in the world. His face was carved like a stone, chiseled out of rock; he was just that good looking, and his voice was unbelievable.

He was a phenomenon, and he arrived fully formed. From the first notes of "That's Alright Mama," as otherworldly as they were, he never improved, or even developed. He hardly changed from start to finish, and Colonel Tom Parker didn't help. I think a monkey could've managed Elvis, and maybe done a better job. Anybody that takes fifty percent of your income and then lets Elvis call the IRS and ask how much he owes them isn't doing his job. Those movies he made were just for money. Colonel Tom wanted to manage me once but said I was uncontrollable. He was probably right.

Felton, at RCA, really cared about Elvis. He had produced "Suspicious Minds," which may be the best record Elvis ever cut, and one time he called me up to see if I could help. "He likes you," Felton said to me. "Do you think you could get him interested in music again?" I told him I didn't know, and that the only way you could find out was by getting all those yes people away from him and letting him go somewhere and hang out and play music. He might get interested, because I truly believed Elvis loved to sing.

But it was too easy to get caught up in the parties, the fancy cars, and the girls. I had a little of that in me, too. It's not that I was trying to show off, but I did reward myself every once in a while. At the end of the day, though, I cared more for the guitar I was playing and the song I was writing.

Elvis had changed the world, and now he was gone. Maybe he didn't have as much impact on me as Hank Williams or George Jones or Buddy, but most of us marked time Before Elvis and After Elvis.

He did one of my songs once, "Just Because You Asked Me To," imitating my voice. After he died, RCA wanted to put out a duet album with artists who had worked with Elvis, and asked me to sing along on his finished track. I couldn't handle that.

"Call Elvis," I told them. "If it's okay with Elvis, it's okay with me."

I was going overdrive, feeling invulnerable. If I wasn't on tour, I'd be in the studio. I went to the office and would stay there. I couldn't go home, because Jessi was asleep, like normal people.

I leased the studio next door to the office, American Sound, and I would stay in it all the time, walking back and forth between the adjoining buildings, all night long. All week long. I would record constantly, until I flopped over in the corner and went to sleep.

In early August, we had gone to Muscle Shoals Studios in Alabama to lay down rhythm tracks for a Hank Williams Jr. album I was producing with Richie.

Hank Jr. has always been to me like my little brother. Even

then, I felt responsible to him in some way. When I first met him, Audrey would not let him out of her sight. He was about eighteen, and when I worked opening his shows, along with Merles like Haggard or Kilgore, she didn't trust him with anybody but me. She let him ride on my bus.

Audrey didn't want him messing with girls. Of course, she didn't know we were getting him women and bringing them back to the hotel. When he had his accident, falling off the side of a mountain, I didn't see him for a long time. He almost died, and when he came around again, I didn't recognize him. There was somebody smarting off in the corner of the dressing room one night, and when I told him he was about to get his ass thrown out, he said, "You don't know me, do you?" It was Hank Jr.

I took him with me on the road and treated him like a king. I think he was feeling a little alone in the world, then, living in his daddy's shadow. He would get out there and the crowd would start yelling for him to sing one of his daddy's songs. But I told him, "Hank, just do what you want to do. If you feel like singing one of your daddy's songs, sing it. If you don't, sing something else. Don't give 'em a chance to tell you how to perform."

Hank Jr. is one of the best blues singers in the world, and on a good night, he can make his daddy look like a sharecropper. He's his own man, and I think I helped him come to terms with that. In 1978, we turned on the microphones and recorded "The Conversation"—"We won't talk about the habits / Just the music and the man"—which helped us both take a fond look back at the Hank Sr. who rode that thin line between "crazy" and "a saint," making him still "the most wanted outlaw in the land." When we got through, it said things about his daddy he had never thought about, especially concerning the relationship between his mom and dad. They loved each other too much, Hank Sr. and Miss Audrey, and basically destroyed each other completely; but there ain't a damn thing Hank could have done to change it.

"Don't let anybody say anything bad about your momma and

daddy," I told him. Hank Jr. never said a word, but I know it sunk in.

Hank used to call me Watashi, which means "old number one" in Japanese. I called him Bocephus. Hank Jr.'s *New South* album was a testament to our friendship and was going along very well in that late summer of 1977. From Muscle Shoals, we moved the session up to Nashville and Chips Moman's American Sound for the overdubs. On Wednesday night, the twenty-fourth, Hank had just finished his vocal on a song Jessi wrote, "Storms Never Last," and I was about to add a harmony.

Two girls from my office opened the door to the control room and came in. One of them handed me a package from Neil's office, sent via World Courier, Inc.

I had an inkling what it might be. I stuck the package under my arm and walked out into the studio area, setting the package down on a music stand in front of my microphone. I opened the wrapping. Inside, I found a second package. I cracked that open and took a quick peek, long enough to assure myself that it contained packs of cocaine. I put it on the music stand and tucked my headphones back over my ears.

But instead of music coming over the phones, I heard a crowd of people. There was this voice saying "We followed a package that came in here. We're with the Federal Drug Enforcement Agency. What happened to the package the girls just delivered?"

I've harmonized many times with ol' Bocephus, and I've never heard him sing a song with lyrics like that. I knew something was up, and that it was likely my number. Gambler's instinct.

Richie was running the session. I looked into the control room and could see him staring off to the side, out of view of the double-glass window. He had his hand down on the talkback button, letting me hear everything that was going on. American Sound had a Harrison mixing board, and that was lucky, because a lot of studio communication buttons only go one way at a time. With the Harrison, you could leave it down and talk and hear everything in return.

They had the girls. One, Lorrie, my secretary, was crying. They were both probably scared to death. "There's a package here with contraband inside it," I listened to them saying, and then I realized they didn't know that I was hearing them. I grabbed the package from the music stand and threw it away behind me. I couldn't make that shot again in a million years. It slid under a baseboard by the wall, just as pretty as you please. I knew that probably wouldn't be good enough to fool them forever, but it would work for now.

They told Richie they wanted to see Waylon Jennings. "We're recording," Richie told them. "This is a closed session. Do you have a warrant?"

"Yes," answered one. "We have a warrant for Waylon Jennings's arrest." That's the way they phrased it.

I followed what was going down, but I wasn't about to let them know that. "Turn the music on," I hollered, and Richie turned to me and started running the take, just as cool and professional as he could be under the circumstances. I acted like there was nothing unusual. They were standing there. They didn't know what to do.

Richie hit play and record, the tape started turning, and I did the harmony. It was a good take, and that's the harmony we used on the record. Still, by the end of it I was a little pissed off at the way they had come barging in there. You would've thought I was Al Capone or something.

I finished the singing and came into the control room. I didn't pay them any mind. I just looked straight at Richie and said, "Play it back, and turn it up." They were still rooted there, looking uncertain; no matter what crime you commit, it must be an unwritten law that you never mess with a recording session.

The music was going ninety miles an hour, and Richie had it cranked. He turned to me like he's talking about some flat note in the second verse.

"Do you know what's going on?" he asked.

"Hell, yes, I know what's happening," I answered. They couldn't hear him or me. We're pointing at the speaker like we're gonna have to drop in the last chorus because I rushed the phrasing.

Richie said, "Well, I'm taking this one."

"You ain't taking shit," I told him. Sometimes I thought Richie would've leapt in front of a freight train for me. "Just be calm. Don't let those sumnabitches scare you." And really, if there was anyone nervous, it was the DEA agents.

The music stopped. One of them stepped up and said, "Could we speak to you just a minute?"

I nodded. He took out two warrants, one for possession of cocaine and the other for conspiracy with further intent to distribute.

I took some time looking them over. It's not everyday you get to see how a real outlaw feels. After a while I handed them back.

"I don't know." I shrugged. "You said it's possession, and I don't see any around here. Do you?"

"We know it's here," he said. We'd both seen this movie somewhere on television before.

"If it is here," I said slowly, turning over my palms, playing my part to the fullest, "finding it might be a problem."

That wasn't their only problem, as it turned out. They had been so sure of the package's final stop that they'd only gotten a search warrant for my office. They didn't have any legal right to tear apart the studio. "Unless you allow us to search here, we can't," they admitted, a little shamefacedly. "We'll have to go get another warrant; but we're not here to arrest you and we're not going to bring the press with us or anything."

That was a nice touch, but I wasn't falling for it. There were about eight of them, all dressed in business suits. I'm sure they had guns somewhere, but they weren't showing them. There were DEA agents, and local narcs. For most of them, I could tell they really didn't want to be here. Even as we stood there jawing, more and more cops came in the door. The news had gone over the police radio, and some of my friends in the sheriff's department had come down to see that nothing funny went on.

I told them that we had to ensure that everything was legal and they'd have to get a proper search warrant. In the meantime, if they didn't mind, we were going to go ahead with what we were doing. "I know you guys have got to do your job, so do your job. But so do we. We're all for that, as long as you stay in this control room. If you go out to the studio, those microphones and equipment cost millions of dollars. You have no business being out there. So until you have a search warrant, don't leave this room." Since they had no choice, they stayed put.

I was filthy with drugs. I thought if they decided to strip-search me, I'm dead anyway. I went out to where my guitar amp was and emptied my pockets. I had a bottle of pills in one, a couple of little vials of cocaine in another. I was a walking pharmacy.

I did another vocal, and Richie came out to the studio, on the excuse that he had to adjust my microphone. He made sure to turn it off before he joined me.

"Where is that shit?" he hissed.

I said, "First of all, you don't need to know."

"Where is it at?" he asked again.

"It's all right," I told him. "It just went flat in there," and I motioned with my eyes toward the baseboard, behind the vocal booth.

He moved a few baffles around and grabbed the outer package. He invented some pretext and took it away down in the basement. He got rid of it in a crawl space under the stairs, right in front of their eyes.

Then Richie came back for the package containing the coke. They would've followed us to the bathroom; they were starting to get suspicious about all the movement. We needed a diversion. George Lappe, who had introduced us to Neil, came in the studio about this time, ranting and raving. He worked for us, and I started chewing his ass out, telling him "George, goddamnit, settle down." Everybody was watching me give him the business, shouting back and forth across the room. As I held their attention, Richie snuck into the toilet and gave it a good flush.

When he heard that water going down, the DEA guy flinched. "Waylon, where is that shit?"

I said, "If it was ever here, it's gone now." And he knew it.

Richie came out grinning, drying his hands off.

They never did find anything, but sometimes people just see what they're programmed to see. When I returned to the studio the next morning, there, plain as the sun, was one of those cocaine vials lying right next to my stool.

It was touch-and-go for about three or four days. They had found a couple of plastic bags in a trash can to the left of the toilet, which had a cocaine "presence." I was clean. Still, the next morning they took me downtown to be fingerprinted at the federal marshal's office. "Damn, I hate this," said the marshal as he was rolling my fingers through the ink.

I said, "Shit, well don't do it."

They arrested me for possession and conspiracy. Any time they'd ask me about the drugs I'd say, "Where I come from, possession means 'got it,' and you ain't got it."

I didn't have it, either. I was so mad, because I knew what had happened. The whole thing could have been avoided. It all started because Neil had been out of the country getting a quickie divorce. In fact, I've always believed that it was his soon-to-be ex-wife who tipped the DEA that there were drugs being shipped.

Before he left, Neil was supposed to take care of a personal matter for me. I had met this girl who had brain cancer, and I had bought her a trip to Jamaica with a friend of hers. She had never been anywhere. Neil was supposed to set it up, but in his rush to get out of the country he hadn't gotten to it, and he'd entrusted it to his assistant. It was almost time for the girls to get on the plane, and nothing had been done. I called his assistant and let him have it, both barrels.

To make me happy, this assistant sent me a "package." It was a peacemaking thing, because I usually got my drugs from California. I didn't take off-the-street stuff. The path led from Colombia to L.A. to me, usually delivered personally. But in this case, he had sent it via air courier.

When it didn't come the next day, he called me wondering if I'd gotten a package from him. He still didn't let on what it was. He wanted it to be a surprise. Neither one of us knew it had lain in the delivery office overnight unopened, and suspicious, they'd called in the DEA to see it. The Feds took some of the cocaine out and shipped it on, then called to say it would arrive at so-and-so time. But they slipped up when the girls brought it over to the studio instead of my office; they didn't have a search warrant for the studio.

Still, it didn't matter. They had showed their hand, and they couldn't back down now. Nor could I. When you see yourself spread across the front pages—"Waylon Jennings Arrested for Possession of Cocaine, Facing Up to Fifteen Years"—it gets to you a little bit. I was feeling hunted, like an animal. I wouldn't go home. I checked into a hotel, and they parked agents in the rooms on either side of me.

It was a media feeding frenzy, like sharks smelling blood in the water. I couldn't go anywhere without a swarm of reporters clustered around me. Richie whacked one camera man with a Coke can when I was going to see my lawyer, and got himself charged with assault and battery. He was a hotheaded little fart. We always accused him of picking on people he had to leap up to hit. He wasn't afraid of anything.

There was still no evidence. As wild-in-the-streets as I'd been, they couldn't dig up any additional dirt on me. Hal Hardin was the federal district attorney who was given the job of prosecuting me, and he called all my friends in, trying to scare them. Finally he had to admit he couldn't get anybody to say anything bad about me. I was glad to hear that. No one knew much of anything.

Neil thought we should get any possible witnesses ready for the lawyers. "Leave those people alone," I told him. They had already given immunity to one of the girls who picked up the package, even though she had no idea what she was carrying. "They don't know one damn thing."

I told everyone who might be summoned, "If they get you in that room, asking a bunch of questions, tell them the truth if you know the answer. Don't try to save me. I'm going to be all right. But if they catch you in a lie, I won't be fine, because they're going to say to me that they've got you for perjury. If I don't come clean, they're going to put you in jail. And that's when I'm going to have to tell anything I know.

"Just don't lie. Don't speculate. If they ask you a question, and you do know what the answer is, tell them, because they probably know you know. If you don't know, you're in no trouble at all."

I found out right there that if you're ever in a situation where they try to scare you, you're dead if you show fear. But if you don't fade under their pressure, you scare them. It helps to be a good card player. I saw that. They got nervous, and I was never nervous. There's only two things they can do, I thought: put me in jail or leave me alone.

The longer it took for them to find the evidence, the more popular I became. In the black bars over on Jefferson Street they'd be watching the news on television, and when the announcer would say "Waylon Jennings arrested . . . and they still have not found any cocaine," they'd all whoop and holler and go crazy. I was becoming a folk hero. Everywhere I went, to my lawyer's office, to have a cup of coffee across the street, television cameras and reporters would be chasing me. Chet Atkins once told me that I was getting so much free publicity that he thought about committing a crime himself.

After four or five days of this, they still hadn't found any cocaine. Finally, at one station, the newscaster turned the whole question around. "You know," he said, "we haven't ever thought about one thing. What if Waylon's innocent?" And I was, until proven guilty. The case and subsequent brouhaha would continue for months, and wind up costing me about a hundred thousand dollars in legal fees, but from then on I knew the charges wouldn't stick.

Jay Goldberg orchestrated my defense. He's one of the greatest lawyers in the world, and when he got into his legal mode, he was an artist. He worked with Robert Kennedy when the Justice Department went after the Teamsters, and has represented everyone from Donald Trump to names that had best be left unsaid. He came down on his own when he heard I was arrested, and showed up for the preliminary hearing. He practically stunned the courtroom when he walked in; the prosecutors knew they didn't have a chance against him.

I even wrote a song about the bust. "Don't You Think This Outlaw Bit's Done Got Out of Hand" talked about a "New York posse" that came down "protecting you from me. . . . Was it singing through my nose that got me busted by the man?" Jay almost jumped out of a building when he first heard the song. "You can't put that out," he said. "All that is is a confession." It was the first hit confession, that's for sure.

The thing about it was that people knew I wouldn't sell drugs. I might have been hooked on them, but the only way I could "distribute" them was by offering a spoon to some of my good-time buddies, of which I had more than a few. Hal Hardin had to finally admit that "He does drugs, but he's not a criminal."

I even had a preacher send me the word: "Waylon, just because you're a drug addict don't mean you can't go to heaven."

It was getting caught that made me mad. It brought on a paranoia of getting trapped with my pants down again. I knew they were tapping my phones; I knew when they had people following me. I had "friends" alerting me to what was happening. I'd get a call and the voice would say "C'mon, let's go for a ride," and when we'd get in the car they'd tell me who was checking my phone, and on what line. I had a couple of ex-FBI guys periodically inspect my home and office. After a while, finding out a lot of nothing, they just let me alone.

\*　　\*　　\*

One thing the bust didn't do was slow down my drug use. I thought that I could handle it and not let it handle me. But sometimes you can get very insulated and isolated in this business. There were weeks I would not get off the tour bus except to take a shower in the hotel. It was my safe haven. Pretty soon you begin to think you're above society's rules, and subconsciously you're not one of "them." It's a form of ivory tower.

All that mattered to me was having a good stash. If I got down to a quarter of an ounce, I'd start freaking. I'd hide little security bundles in briefcases around the house, only to come on them years later. With the pills, I was always chasing the high amphetamines gave me during the first six months. I lost it somewhere along the way, that feeling. And then along came cocaine, and it's the same thing, only smoother. And more often.

I kept a constant level of drugs inside me. I'd do a two- or three-inch line every twenty minutes or so; more than that sometimes. I always made sure to ground it up right, so it wouldn't eat holes in my nose, but I inhaled it with such force I'd bypass my sinuses. It just went right down in my lungs. I'd put it in a straw and sniff it so hard it would shoot straight back into my brain.

Maybe speeding like that was a way I could keep up with all my ideas. I needed a lot of energy to match my own inner momentum. Once I got in the studio it was hard for me to stop chasing my tail. Sometimes I'd work so long and so hard that I'd be hearing things. Once I decided to produce, engineer, mix, and master my own album. I was so deep into it, four or five days with hardly a break, that at one point I thought I was hearing a bass from another track. I was cussing and pulling faders up and down and looking for that little devil, and finally I found it wasn't on there at all. I looked around and there was nobody but me who was hearing it. Whoops.

The only time I felt in tune with myself was playing on stage. That was my norm, under the hot lights and with the band loud and full in back of me. Nobody knew how I did it some nights. I'd be on the bus, and they'd be trying to get me to wash my face before I went on. I'd be hyperventilating and it didn't look like I was going to make it. Then I'd get my hat on and grab my guitar, walk out there, and everything would settle down. It was like the pulsing in my blood duplicated the rush of performance adrenaline.

I was on the loose. I didn't know what I intended to do; I didn't intend to do anything, which is exactly what it amounted to. I knew I was going to die if I kept it up, burning the candle at both ends and the middle for a week and more, week after month after year. I thought, well, I'll die, but that'll be all right. The last thing I cared about was that it was wrecking my health, or that it was illegal. I'd heard about experiments with rats and cocaine. They'd put food in one corner and cocaine in the other, and the rats would eat that cocaine until they died.

I was chasing the high, but I never could catch it. I'd be recording and I'd tell the band and engineers that I'd be back in a minute. Everybody would be waiting and I wouldn't show up until the next day. I'd go out driving, park the car somewhere, and forget where I left it. I lost four or five cars that way. I'd order a dozen cheeseburgers, take a snort, and pass out for two days. I guess there's a little bit of Elvis in all of us.

The first time I knew I had a problem was in the back of a limousine going from the hotel to the gig. Richie was riding with me. I had only been doing cocaine for a couple of years, but he looked at me with the concern of someone who had spent a dozen lifetimes on the road bearing witness to my every mood swing and sway.

"You've got to get back and lighten up," he said simply. "You're really into it too hard." That's all he wrote. It kind of pissed me off, but I did slow down.

For a week or two I didn't do anything. He knew how to trick me into it. He'd tell me, "You'll notice that if you're off for a couple of weeks you can get that good high again." I was all for that.

Now if I could only figure out where I put my Cadillac.

\* \* \*

A couple of weeks after the bust, the CMA released its nominations for the year. Despite the fact that I refused to participate in the proceedings, claiming that artists shouldn't compete with each other, they went ahead and put me up in six categories, including Entertainer of the Year, Male Vocalist, Vocal Duo (with Willie), and Album of the Year (for *Wanted: The Outlaws*).

If anything, it proved that maybe the CMA needed me more than they thought.

The CMA wouldn't agree to withdraw my name. Willie and I decided not to attend. I told him, "I didn't go when they weren't giving me awards, and I'm not going when they do."

Willie said he wouldn't either, unless they changed the dress code to where nobody wears a tuxedo. The next thing I know, he's running up and down the aisles, dressed in his Sunday best. All the while, they were making jokes about me. Jerry Reed said I'd rather park cars at Opryland than come inside. Tennessee Ernie Ford added some pretty rough things about people who didn't support their industry.

I believed then, and I do now, that the best way you pay tribute to the music you love is by doing good work within it. Not by picking up a goddamn bowling trophy.

Still, there wasn't much doubt, CMA or no, that we were Duo of the Year. Waylon and Willie. Willie and Waylon. And we had "Luckenbach, Texas" to prove it.

*Let's go to Luckenbach, Texas*
*With Waylon and Willie and the boys*
*This successful life we're living's*
*Got us feuding like the Hatfields and McCoys*

Chips Moman had co-written the song, and when he showed it to me, he used the right approach: "I got a song here and you can't do it because your name's in it." I knew it was a hit song, even though I didn't like it, and still don't. It reminded me too much of "Good Time Charlie's Got the Blues," and it had a laid-back rhythm I kept wanting to rush. I've never been to Luckenbach. Neither had Chips or his co-writer, Bobby Emmons.

An hour's drive west of Austin, Luckenbach was mostly owned by one Hondo Crouch, who bought it because he wanted to keep the local honky-tonk post office open. Its population was in the single digits, which matched the song's chart position throughout the spring of 1977, including *número uno* on the country charts for six weeks, and even heading into the Top Thirty of the pop charts. Jerry Jeff Walker had recorded his *Viva Terlingua* in Luckenbach, which had put it on the country map, a simple symbol of goin' home. Every state has a Luckenbach; a place to get away from things.

That's why it succeeded. Our rough brotherhood, especially as we idealized ourselves, was about "the basics of love" and the finer things in an on-the-road life: "guitars that are tuned good and firm-feeling women." "Luckenbach" brought us geographically and spiritually back to Texas. The song was New Country—name checking Mickey Newbury and Jerry Jeff, Willie joining in on the final chorus to salute our twin W's—and Old, with Hank Sr.'s "pain songs" our soundtrack as we rolled along the highway to a life that sidestepped our success, and made us more human.

It was making our own myth, only in a way that touched people who were themselves caught keeping up with the joneses, whether drug-induced or materially possessed. Certainly success was causing a family feud within the Outlaws; I still wasn't talking to Tompall. Even after we settled the lawsuit, we stayed apart. I called him to say that though we'd hurt each other, and would probably never be friends again, I didn't want him to think that I hated him. You can't carry those feelings around with you. That's a bigger burden than the original conflict. Tompall wouldn't listen. I think he thought I was trying to get something out of him.

Through it all, Willie and Waylon stayed Waylon and Willie. One RCA executive kept mixing up the two. When he came to Nashville, a bean counter that had worked his way up the corporate ladder, I called him on it. "I heard that you thought Willie and Waylon were one person."

"Ah," he laughed. "But I know better now."

"All us hillbillies look alike," I told him. "So what you need to do, when you don't know their names, is just call 'em Hoss."

"Oh, Horse?"

I said, "No, not horse. It's Hoss."

"Hass?"

No, Hoss, and perhaps you better not come down here no more. I first heard the term from Ferlin Husky when I was real young. It's a sign of respect, an affectionate nickname that means somebody who's great at what they do. A thoroughbred, or a champion. A trusted friend.

That kind of describes Willie, though he'll be the first to admit that he actually enjoys getting me in trouble. "It keeps Waylon alert," he likes to say. "He could sit over there and get old and weak. I keep him young by sending him problems."

If that was the case, I'd be a babe in arms now. I write a lot of songs about Willie, because I have never thoroughly understood him. He's like a cartoon to me. I'll be the first to his door when he's in trouble, but he could screw up a two-car funeral. He's so smart, but he never learns a thing from anything that happens to him.

Sometimes I think he likes courting disaster. When he pulled his car off the road recently and took a nap, only to wake up being arrested for pot possession, I thought he was the only person in the world who could get busted for "sleeping under the influence."

But if I'm there for him, he's there for me. On the night after they booked me for the cocaine they couldn't find, Willie was appearing at Nashville's Municipal Auditorium. I joined him on stage and the crowd gave us a standing ovation. I went up to the mike and said "I didn't do it." The cheers got louder.

We made some good records together. There were more than a couple Waylon and Willie albums, and I've got the belt buckle to prove it. We celebrated the first one by heading up to New York to the Rainbow Room high atop Rockefeller Center for a gold-record party. I had been partying the night before at a Super Bowl victory bash with the Dallas Cowboys, where we'd wound up singing Elvis Presley songs till the wee hours.

Willie and I flew up to New York the next morning. I wasn't in the best shape to do a bunch of interviews. We had started at ten in the morning and kept going till eight that night. They promised me dinner, and we were sitting off in a corner of the Rainbow Grill. I was trying to sweet talk/put the make on Jane Pauley from the *Today* show; singer Tracy Nelson was sitting on Willie's lap. I thought she was his daughter, and I was trying to talk him out of screwing her.

I had my long coat on, and it was draped over a heater, so I was sweating even more than my usual overheating. There was no food, and flashbulbs were constantly going off in my face. I pulled out a switchblade comb and the photographers all jostled forward like I was going to stab someone. I wanted to throw Joe Galante out the window, though he was one of the only executives that was ever straight with me at RCA. Even the sight of the Empire State Building didn't phase me. It was so lit up, and I was so lit up, it looked like a cathouse.

"Mammas Don't Let Your Babies Grow Up to Be Cowboys" was mine and Willie's tip of the cowboy hat to our mustang values. That there was no other country that could have birthed this country music was proven in mid-1978, when the Outlaw clan was invited to the White House by President Jimmy Carter. Willie and his wife Connie went, along with Jessi, my son Buddy, and a few Waylors. I didn't go. I had been in a room down the hall, doing a snort of cocaine with a local football hero. I had told Willie to call me, but he acted like he couldn't find me. Maybe he thought I was too screwed up. When he got to the White House, Willie talked with the President about "Amazing Grace," which wasn't so amazing at that.

There's some friends you can be away from for a year, and then you get together and it's as if you pick up the conversation right where you left off. You've never been apart.

And Willie is a part of me.

I kept withdrawing, spending more time at my upstairs office, never going anywhere. I knew, as far as the drugs were concerned, when I wasn't fit to be seen, and I kept getting farther and farther into my own world.

They say cocaine is a social drug, but it was the opposite with me. I went within myself more, except of course for calling up my friends late at night, waking them up and wanting to talk.

I was so addicted, I would get up in the middle of a sound sleep and go to the bathroom at three o'clock in the morning to do a toot. I was hooked as much on the taste of cocaine, the sting in my nose and throat when I would snort it, as the high. I'd stay up for a little while, smoke a cigarette, and get back in bed.

The more I hid, the more records I sold, and the bigger the shows got. Neil liked the fact that I was playing hard to get. "Waylon's crazy," he'd tell promoters. "You better give him some money or he'll blow up your building." I wouldn't talk to the press at all, and when I did, I asked for editorial rights.

*People* magazine had pissed me off one time. They had hounded me to do an article on Jessi and I, and finally I said okay. Her mother had just died, and her heart was broken. They took pictures of her and me, talking about us like we were a couple of hillbillies, and called her mom a Holy Roller. At the end of it, they said that Jessi wanted me to get a vasectomy, and I said no, in my "male chauvinist" way, because I might want to have kids someday by another woman. I never trusted the press again.

It lost me a cover of *Rolling Stone*. Chet Flippo had written the article, but when I asked for prior approval, they didn't give it. I don't blame them now, and had I known what *Rolling Stone* stood for, I might have relented. But once I draw a line in the sand, nobody crosses over. Sorry. They weren't going to get me no more.

Paranoia was an occupational hazard. I knew they were watching me, and I was watching everyone around me. I installed closed-circuit television cameras in the halls so I could see who was coming and going. I had a private outside entrance and a buzzer to open the door from upstairs. I stationed my band manager, John Ullrich, at the window with a pair of binoculars to track a car circling the block looking for a parking place. I was mostly fooling, but I only laughed every other time. "Chief," he'd say after a night on sentry duty, unshaven, black rubber from the binoculars around his eyes like a raccoon. "There's a Volkswagen that's been going around this block all night long, and it's changed license plates four times."

I'd found out the hard way you could go to prison for cocaine. You couldn't be roaming around with a big bunch of it on your body. Carry pills in your pocket and they wouldn't even know what they were; you didn't have to re-up your high every half hour or face crashing. That didn't mean I couldn't do some very stupid things. One time I went all the way to Bucksnort, Tennessee, about thirty-five miles outside of Nashville, and I gave a check for some cocaine. I was so messed up, I didn't even know where I was at when I was out there.

Only my closest friends were allowed in the inner sanctum. I'd sit with other drug guys and do drugs together. I usually furnished them. We'd talk and listen to tapes. I found some songs on demos that were so bad you couldn't even tell there was a tune; or I'd string together songs from different records and make up a tape of my favorite stuff. Tapes of tapes of tapes.

Jessi would come up and spend time with me, staying in the office, not doing anything much. I wrote a song called "Gemini Twins" with her in the room once, and I got into that drifting-off space thing. I wouldn't let her talk for about three or four hours, because I couldn't get the last two lines right. She just sat there. What a dear heart.

We played games, poker and backgammon and bumper pool and board baseball and spades. We would go from the office right to the bus and keep playing the entire way to the show. Richie remembers we started a game of spades in Nashville and then set out for Fort Worth, dealing cards all the while. When we got to Texas, after about twelve hours, we stayed in the bus another three or four hours snorting and spading. His hand was so gripped up from clenching the cards that he had to soak it in hot water, because he didn't think he'd be able to hold the stick for the show.

Gambling. It was a way to pass the time, to keep your nerves on edge as you moved through those long blank spaces between towns, the twenty-two hours a day spent in limbo waiting for two hours of show to begin.

When we invented Farkle, a dice game with its own inner rhythm, our gambling moved into high gear. Those pots would get pretty damn big; you could lose a lot of money. We liked to bet; we'd lay odds on the monkey screwing the football. Anything. Jerry Allison, when the Crickets toured with us, played a lot, and so did Tony Joe White. We never really kept track of who owed what. It was more for the excitement, like craps, with people standing around hollering and egging each other on.

Farkle was related to a game they play in bars to buy drinks, called Horses. Rance Wasson and Gordon Payne, a pair of my guitar players, helped me come up with it. You rolled the dice in a cup and it was scored by three of a kind. You used five dice in all, four of the normal white variety and the fifth black, with my Flying W symbol in the four position as a wild card.

Three 6s equalled 600. Three 5s equalled 500, though three 1s equalled 1000. Four of anything was still counted as a three, though if you got five of a kind, you won right there and then. The object was to build on your score and be the first to reach 2500. There were all sorts of choices you could make along the way, strategies and subrules about which dice to roll again and how to add up your point total, though if you rolled and didn't get any dice in common, you lost the points you had and were out of the game. That was called Farkling.

Up on the wall of my office is a photo of the Farkle gang. There was Richie and Jerry "Jigger" Bridges, my bass player who had joined the Waylors in November of 1978 from the Muscle Shoals studio. There was Marylou Hyatt, who ran my office. There was Lisa Lightning, Randy Bob, Judy, and Crank, which was what we called Gordon. The first time he had gone out on the road with us, the Hell's Angels had gotten him all twisted up on crank, a speed derivative. He was trying to light his cigarette with a motel key, and smelling a fire hydrant, thinking it was a flower.

Deakon Proudfoot and Boomer Baker were also in the photo, on loan to us from the Angels' Oakland chapter. They were the best security I ever had. They could slice through a crowd without touching anybody, me following along in their wake, and were as loyal as they could be, second only to their motorcycle blood-brethren.

I was playing at the Boarding House in San Francisco when I met them. Deakon came up, and the first thing he said was "Waylon, I don't know what you've heard and I don't care. I love America and I'm an American. I don't like a lot of things that are happening, but I like your music," and he sat down. From that day on, we were friends.

They appreciated the Outlaw element, and that my give-a-shitter was broke. We were alike in a lot of ways; they knew I was pretty well strung out, too. They kept trouble from happening. The word went out that you don't start fights at a Waylon Jennings concert, or it might be "ball peen hammer time." Boomer was always smiling, gold teeth and all, though nobody fucked with him because you didn't want to get on his bad side. We all contributed pieces of gold to his teeth. He was Jessi's security, and he worshipped her. They're still good friends.

Deakon was the preacher, and he could dance, despite the fact that he'd had some of his toes cut off in a motorcycle accident. He weighed almost three hundred pounds, and nobody was more nimble on his feet. When a girl rushed the stage once, aiming straight for me, he grabbed her and started waltzing her around, slowly turning and pirouetting her off to the wings.

He would've gone to the wall for me. I knew that because he allowed me to argue with him. Something would happen with the Farkle, and he'd grab half the dice and I'd grab the other and we'd stare and glare at each other. Deakon would stick his bottom lip out, like a kid. We'd call each other names. Other people that got in their face like that, the Angels would probably push it in.

He would stick like glue to me. He didn't want me to be alone. In those days, Jessi didn't travel much with me, and if you didn't watch closely, I'd be out and gone, in all these strange towns. Deakon would follow me around, and I used to keep him up for so long he'd be seeing double. When we finally got to a hotel room, he'd sit down in a chair and in two minutes he'd start snoring. He'd rattle the windows he'd snore so loud. And there was a gentle thing to him as well. He made sure that when I slept, deep and hard as I did when I was crashing, I knew where I was when I woke up. He'd shake me, and before I'd have a chance to get curious, he'd tell me the day of the week, the city we were in and at what hotel, and tell me when and where my show was and how long I had until showtime.

The last time I saw Deakon, he came by the house. He had a girl with him on his V-twin Harley, and he had his colors flying. He hadn't worn his patches on the road with me. His beard was bushy and full of gray, and we were sitting out in the back on rocking chairs, talking after dinner. "I need to figure out how to get from here to Wyoming," he said, and he took out his granny glasses and started peering closely at a map. I started laughing. I wished I had a camera handy to take a picture. "Look at you, Deakon. Ol' macho's getting old." He grrrr'ed at me like a big papa bear.

I asked them one time why they were Hell's Angels. "It's the only family I've ever known," answered Boomer. "I can depend on them." There's a lot to be said for that.

It wasn't all madness. One cold morning in 1978, I heard that Jerry Moss was leaving messages for me all over Nashville. I went and knocked on his hotel door; I had never forgotten what gentlemen he and Herb were when I needed to get out of my A&M contract.

Jerry wanted to speak to me about a concept album named *White Mansions* that Paul Kennerley, an Englishman, had written with my voice in mind. Paul had heard "That's Why the Cowboy Sings the Blues" on London radio, and it set off his imagination. The object was to tell the story of the Civil War through Southern eyes. His hero was Matthew J. Fuller, a Confederate captain, who loved Polly Ann Stafford, a belle of the local plantation. Villainy was provided by the redneck Caleb Stone.

It was a country-and-western opera, ambitious in scope and heavy with superstars. Eric Clapton and the Eagles' Bernie Leadon made appearances, John Dillon and Steve Cash (who played Caleb Stone) of the Ozark Mountain Daredevils helped construct the music, and Jessi took the role of Polly Ann. I was cast as the Drifter, heralding the South's impending doom through songs like "Dixie, Now You're Done" and "They Laid Waste to Our Land."

We flew to England on the Concorde. I wore these elephant-ear cowboy boots that Larry Mahan, an old bull rider, had given me. They were pretty sharp, except the right foot seemed tight. By the time we got to England, my toes had swelled up so much I couldn't get the boot off at all. Later, I found out that it was a half-size smaller than the other. I walked around Olympic Studios, where we recorded *White Mansions* with producer Glyn Johns, with one boot on and one boot off.

Glyn only put two or three microphones on a drum kit; he understood the art of mike placement. He introduced me to the Boss phase shifter for a guitar and guided the week or so that the sessions took. On the night we finished mixing, Glyn brought over the final album to Paul's house to listen, and we sat there as the sun came up over the British Isles, till it was time to head back to America. The only sad note was that, unknown to Jessi, her father had passed away during the last hours of making the record. She might have been singing "Story to Tell" at the moment of his passage, or "Last Dance," where she's telling her loved one good-bye and saying that she'd do anything to keep that smile alive, to have him come back and have that last dance together.

The South never had a chance in the Civil War. Toward the end, they didn't have food or machinery or people. Paul told his narrative of the War from his Englishman's perspective, which meant he didn't have to take sides. He understood the tragedy. For the South, a cause that is wrong, and built on something that shouldn't be, like slavery, can't be noble. The North was no better, burning their way through Georgia and waging a war based on economics and politics as well as human rights. All they did was win. My character worked both sides of the conflict, a troubadour, more or less, and a musician who sang songs, not necessarily good and not necessarily bad.

*White Mansions* was a lovely record, and it touched me in a deeply personal way, as a man whose house is built on a Civil War battlefield and a Southerner. Though it probably went over the heads of its intended audience, making the album was one of my most enjoyable experiences.

There was no chance that *The Dukes of Hazzard* television show would prove too smart for its target viewers. A moonshine excuse for car chases and watching Catherine Bach's ass in her trademark cut-off jeans, that long-legged good-lookin' thing, it was incredibly popular. Bo and Luke Duke's ongoing war with Mayor Boss Hogg and Sheriff Rosco P. Coltrane provided about the only plot line needed. I was the narrator, or "The Balladeer" as they called me, and though I never appeared onscreen, for six years, beginning in January 1979, I got to say things like "Happy as a pig eatin' slop" and "Meanwhile, Bo and Luke Duke, not knowing that Uncle Jessie was disguised as a door, shot his knob off." Down home. Yee-hah!

The idea for the series grew out of a movie called *The Moonrunners*, which in itself was a sequel to *Thunder Road*, the Robert

Mitchum classic about backwoods stills and corn-likker cookin'. His son, Jim, had starred in *The Moonrunners*, and Ralph Mooney and I had done the soundtrack. CBS, looking for a *Beverly Hillbillies* crossed with *Starsky & Hutch*, called to ask if I would provide the voice-overs for *The Dukes*. My disc jockey training was about to come in handy. I learned a lot about the rhythm of words, even though the writers kept writing things like "wuz" for "was," as if I wouldn't get it, and even got to bring it inside sometimes: "As welcome as a skunk at a picnic or Waylon Jennings at a CMA banquet."

They liked the way I sounded, so they asked me to write a theme: "Just two good ol' boys / Never meanin' no harm. . . . Been in trouble with the law / Since the day they were born." They thought that was good but said all it needed was something about two modern-day Robin Hoods, fighting the system. So I wrote "Fighting the system, like two modern-day Robin Hoods," and they didn't even know they wrote the damn line. It was my first million-selling single, and one of the easiest records I ever cut. Even today, every time I look out on my driveway and see General Lee, the orange Dodge Charger they gave me with the rebel stars and bars painted on its roof and a big 01 bull's-eyeing the door, it makes me laugh. Great car for eluding a sheriff.

Live, the more things got insane around us, the more focused was the playing on stage. It was a great band we had then; everybody took a verse on "The Weight" except Richie and Mooney, who didn't sing. We'd tape each night with a cassette recorder, and every evening, as the seventies went through their final spin, the whole band would sit on the bus and listen back to the show. That's how different it sounded, how much everybody enjoyed their chance to play music, night after night, and cared about what they were doing.

The band could do just about anything. It didn't matter what the tune was. It just seemed like somebody would grab a hold of it and go. Get it started in one direction, and then change direction, zigging and zagging.

Mooney was at the heart of it. He was a cult legend in his own right, a steel-guitar genius, and he was in his heyday. When I played in England and introduced the band, Mooney got a bigger hand than me. He could be cantankerous, but he had a touch on his instrument that went beyond steel decorations. If you weren't in the pocket for him when he took his ride, you would be by the time he came out the other side. If it was early in the show, and things hadn't quite found their groove yet, he had the unique ability to put it there, pumping the pedals and stroking his bar across the strings.

Mooney was a few years older than the average Waylor, but he'd put the time to good use. He'd been born in Oklahoma and caught the steel fever from listening to greats like Leon McAuliffe and Noel Boggs. Moving to California, he grew up on nonpedal steels, shifted to Sho-Bud when they began adding pedals and knee levers, and over the years had backed everybody from Wynn Stewart to Buck Owens and Merle Haggard. He was probably best known for writing Ray Price's "Crazy Arms," which he penned after Mrs. "Moon" left him in 1950, while they were living in Las Vegas and he was getting "crawling, falling down" drunk. She came back when she heard the song.

If Ralph was shy when he was sober, he could be a holy terror when he got near the bottle. He knew how much I respected him, though, and I gave him a lot of room to play around the melody. The whole band had that freedom—Richie and Jigger, Rance on rhythm and Gordon on lead, Carter and Barney Robertson—and we were tight as a drum and loose at the same time. Richie, with me almost twenty years at this point, would lean back on his drum stool like Levon Helm from The Band, and Gordon's guitar was J.J. Cale swampy. Carter had a beautiful voice, and she sang backup harmonies with me; Barney played rattler piano. The Robertsons weren't into the drugs; they tolerated the rest of us, I think.

As the seventies closed, Richie moved formally into producing me. He'd learned his lessons well, and both *What Goes Around Comes Around* and *Music Man* were bookends of my music in overdrive. Virtually identical in cover look and personnel, the two albums revolved around his resolute bass drum, while the guitars swirled, traded licks, and I rode the rhythm section like a palomino. We all knew we were skating along the edge. You couldn't look down or slow up, 'cause you might fall off. You just had to go faster. On Rodney Crowell's aptlytitled "I Ain't Living Long Like This," we burned through the am-I-baby's and the wheels-go-round like there was no tomorrow.

These Waylors could have stood on their own. In fact, whenever I disappeared from a session, Richie cut most of an album on them. But when one of the members came to me and wondered when he was going to get equal billing, I had to draw the line. "Sorry, son," I shrugged. "I'm gonna tell you something you might not realize.

"I'm all you got." I put my arm around his shoulders. "Tomorrow, if you leave, they're going to say 'Where'd he go?' And I'm gonna say, 'Well, he ain't here no more,' and they'll say 'Damn, we're going to miss him.' But they're still going to be out there, waiting for me to come around and count off the set. It don't work the other way. That may sound awful and conceited, and maybe it ain't fair, but it's true."

It was a great show production-wise, and quite a caravan. We carried our own sound and lights in a Mack truck, and there were two or three buses. There was even a separate bus for T-shirts, which were sold by another Angel traveling with us from the Oakland chapter, Rick Talbot. He had several girls that came along to help him sell them, and what have you. Rick could hoot up a storm when he set his mind to it; he was the funniest guy and could keep you in stitches. One night he was out in a freezing rain, running all around, drinking from a gallon bottle of Blue Nun. As he went to get on the bus, he missed the door and fell in the wet. A few minutes later he tried to get up, but he was frozen to the ground, still laughing away. They had to pry him loose.

The more raunchy I got, the better the crowds liked it. I didn't talk at all. I didn't say anything; I didn't have anything to say. I just came out and started playing, and when I got through I said "Bye."

Out and back in, that's the way I liked it. You form a circle with your audience. Even in my stupor, I was always in tune with their moods. I could tell you what tempo songs to do next, or how they should feel. I couldn't tell you which one, but I knew, if I was in tune, and they were tuned in to me, I could move 'em around. I could pull their chain with "Bob Wills" or "Hank" any-time. These were country music fans, even though they acted like rock and rollers. Which is why "I've Always Been Crazy" was such a big hit live. On a good night, and it seemed like they just kept getting better, I could take the crowd with me for a ride. I like to drive.

Our crew had come over from rock and roll stages. They were used to Loud. You could put a match out if you held it next to Richie's monitor mix. We were playing auditoriums, arenas, foot-ball fields. Deakon formed a production company, Charlie Magoo Productions, and booked me and Willie together at Spartan Arena in San Jose, California. Delbert McClinton and Jessi opened the show, and there were as many people backstage as there were out front. The Hell's Angels had the run of the place. I broke a tooth before I went on and did my whole show with it cracked straight up. I almost reached in there and pulled that sonofabitch out. Willie said, "If you decide to do it, be sure and tell the audience." I have never understood what that meant.

We did it on percentage, splitting the take three ways. It was the first time Willie and I had played together for a while, and we each took home $150,000, which is still the most money I ever made for one performance.

As much as we were making, though, it seemed like it was costing more and more to keep the show on the road. Even discounting the six-figure sums I was spending on cocaine, the tours were running well in the red. People were hanging out and getting paid for it. We had close to fifty bodies on our payroll, and I wasn't sure what any of them were doing. There were twenty people more than we needed on the crew. If I saw somebody twice in a week, I'd ask Richie, "Are they working for us?"

My records were selling faster than they could manufacture them. The shows were sold out. We were doing it on our own. Everybody else just tried to keep up.

Including us.

For every million dollars I was taking in, I was spending double. I was going broke when I was the hottest thing in the country.

I didn't realize it at the time, but there was a hole somewhere. The money was pouring down.

One day in the spring of 1981, my friend Bill Robinson, Richie, and I sat around at the Beverly Wilshire Hotel in L.A. looking at a pile of papers strewn about the floor. My cash flow had dried up. I owed more than two million dollars. The bank had stopped my account because I was $860,000 overdrawn.

I always thought that if you make money, money will take care of itself. Willie was a lot like that, too. We didn't want to know about the business. All of a sudden, I was broke. This Outlaw "bit" was not only gettin' out of hand. It was out of pocket.

The first country album to ship gold may have been *I've Always Been Crazy*; but I'm not stupid. It was time, once again, to stop and start over.

# CHAPTER 10

## I'M ABOUT TO SING IN MY PANTS; I'VE BEEN DRY-HUMMING ALL DAY AND I'M GONNA GET THE TUNE-ACHES

Everybody whose wife is going to have a baby, raise their hand," I asked the crowd from the stage of Cain's Ballroom in Tulsa, Oklahoma.

I raised mine.

Terry, my eldest son, was working for me, and he just about fell over. The audience cheered. I could hardly start the next song I was so happy. I had talked over the phone with Jessi before I went on for the show, and the doctor had confirmed what we had suspected. She was pregnant.

Cain's is an old western swing honky-tonk graced with pictures of Bob Wills and Spade Cooley on the wall. It's been there for decades. My blood was probably racing from the excitement; we had thought about a child of our own for so long.

That night the stage lights seemed even brighter than usual. They had me blinded. I was high. The stage was tilting; I couldn't see anything, and I was starting to fall. I looked out at the room, and focused on a long column that stretched up from the floor to the ceiling, locking it with my eyes, using it to regain my balance.

That was the night I learned about centerposts. You've got to have one, something to measure yourself against and grab hold of whenever you feel life is swinging out of control. If you don't have one, you'll fall. Musically, Hank Williams was my centerpost. It's always gone back to him, the one who did everything wrong and everything right.

As for living, I realized at that moment that my centerpost was Jessi. I was not complete when I wasn't around her.

Someone to relate to. That's part of our being, and what better relation than a child?

Jessi spiritually prepared in her heart that she would be ready when there came time to have a baby. It was part of a commitment we had made to each other, to be somebody each of us could believe in, no matter what came to pass.

The baby was planned down to the night that we conceived. We both knew we needed to, if we were going to; we heard the clock ticking. I had just passed forty, and Jessi was close enough. I think she had kept waiting for me to come out of the drugs, and when she saw I wasn't nearly ready to give it up, we both knew what the deal was. We took a chance.

That chance took us to Nashville Baptist Hospital in the early morning hours of Saturday, May 19, 1979. June Carter Cash had come down to keep us company. John was on his way. We were playing spades, laying out the cards on Jessi's stomach.

I hadn't been in the delivery room when any of my other kids were born. It wasn't done that way in West Texas. They didn't want any of those big tough cowboys to faint away watching their wives give birth.

It wasn't any different for me, though times had changed. "You need to go in there," the doctors said, but the closer the contractions came, the more I thought I could better occupy myself going out to get some cigarettes.

I looked at Jessi. You could almost feel the energy moving through her, caught in some elemental force of nature. It was like she had a whole sandstorm boiling up inside her.

"Is there any way I can talk you out of this?" I asked.

She smiled and shook her head no. We were as totally together as man and woman could be.

"I'll go with you." I put on the hospital garb and sat there with her in the delivery room, holding her hand.

An intern came in. He couldn't have been more than eighteen, and he was beside himself. "John's here," he blurted. "John wants you to know he's here."

Jessi nodded that was okay.

"Mr. Cash is outside," he repeated. "Johnny Cash is out there."

Jessi rolled her what-happened-to blue eyes. She said, "Would somebody give this boy a quarter so he can go call somebody who gives a shit, 'cause I'm trying to have a baby here."

Men can never really relate to being pregnant, giving birth. All I could do was listen to the heartbeat and feel the kick. The baby was attached to her body by the cord, part of her being as well as the child it was becoming. The room took on a rhythm of its own. All those heartbeats.

We didn't know what the baby would be, boy or girl; we weren't sure till the last minute. There had been a little red-headed boy that Jessi saw in church. He was all over everything, pure boy spirit, and just the cutest kid. His real name was Shooter.

They put the baby on Jessi's stomach, right where the ace of spades had been dealt not ten hours earlier. He was hollering.

Jessi looked over at him. She was glistening. I felt light-headed. "We got us a Shooter," she declared, as Waylon Albright Jennings promptly peed all over the nurses.

"Do you want to go bankrupt?"

Bill Robinson stood up, shrugged his shoulders, and spread his hands. Richie looked forlorn. There wasn't much any of us could do. The figures didn't lie. I was swimming in red ink and about to go down for the third time.

"You're broke," he said, laying it on the bottom line for me. "Everything you've got is in hock: your buildings, your home. The bank has closed your accounts. You've spent your advances."

The worst thing was that I had been giving it away. So much money was flowing through my office that I never bothered to count it. And after a while, nobody else did either, except to take out their share. There were a lot of shares.

We had seventeen people in the Nashville office alone. There was a road manager, a band manager, a publicist, a secretary, a booking agent, a receptionist, gofers, and personal assistants all around. The assistants had assistants, and everyone was "on staff." Marylou Hyatt, who came into my organization in April of 1977, answering a want ad for a "Booking Agent Assistant," told me one time that I had someone who opened the door and another who closed it.

On the road, we put the *tour* in entourage. It was controlled chaos. There were separate crews for the lights and sound, production managers, roadies for the musical equipment, and trucks and buses to haul the caravan from town to town. We were pulling huge audiences—11,000 in Minneapolis, 14,000 in Colorado's Red Rocks—and the fact that we had a constant cast of characters gave a certain stability to the crap-shoot conditions we'd find awaiting us at each gig.

Of course, I didn't know what was out there, because I never got off the bus. Take a shower up in the hotel and then come back downstairs. Wait for the show. Killing time.

I'd see Bill Robinson backstage on my way from the bus to the microphone, standing in the wings by the curtains, when I'd work on the West Coast. He was tall and gainly, with a shock of black hair. He never said anything to me, and after a couple of times, I began to recognize him. Finally, I walked over one night and said, "What do you do? Have you got a job?" Maybe I'd hired him already.

Leather and Lace.

Live at Max's Kansas City, 1973. (*courtesy Bob Gruen/Star File*)

The Outlaws go gold: Tompall Glaser, me, Jessi, Willie, Chet, and RCA execs Jerry Bradley and Harry Jenkins.

A week without sleep and I'm having a good ol' time . . . I think.

Waylon and Willie . . .

. . . and Willie and
Waylon . . .

. . . and Jessi and Willon and Waylie.

America has been good to me and Johnny Cash.

Muhammad Ali at Shooter's christening, 1979.

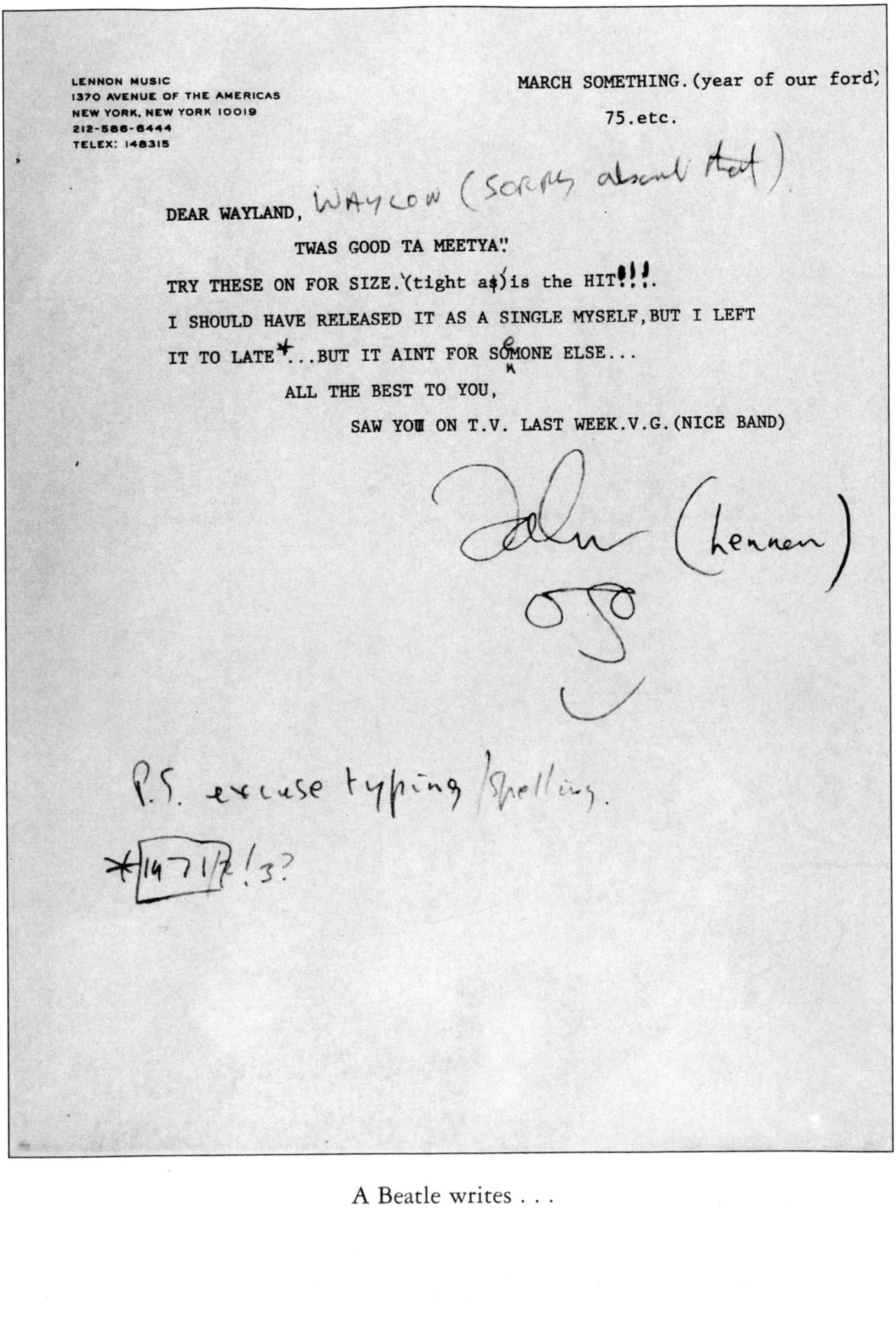

LENNON MUSIC
1370 AVENUE OF THE AMERICAS
NEW YORK, NEW YORK 10019
212-586-6444
TELEX: 148315

MARCH SOMETHING. (year of our ford)

75. etc.

DEAR WAYLAND, WAYLON (SORRY about that).

      TWAS GOOD TA MEETYA".

TRY THESE ON FOR SIZE. (tight as) is the HIT!!!.

I SHOULD HAVE RELEASED IT AS A SINGLE MYSELF, BUT I LEFT

IT TO LATE *...BUT IT AINT FOR SOMONE ELSE...

      ALL THE BEST TO YOU,

          SAW YOU ON T.V. LAST WEEK. V.G. (NICE BAND)

*John* (Lennon)

P.S. excuse typing/spelling.

* 14 7 1/2 !3?

A Beatle writes . . .

Meeting President Carter, with Shooter a babe-in-arms.

Now Bill, about that tax cut . . . (*courtesy Skipper Gerstel*)

The CEO of Waylon G-D Jennings Productions.
(*courtesy Beth Gwinn*)

Robert Redford gives me and Willie acting lessons for *Electric Horseman*.
(*courtesy Jimmy Ellis,* The Tennessean)

Hank Williams Jr. and I trade licks in April of 1987. (*courtesy Jerry Floyd*)

On the *Hee-Haw* set with Minnie Pearl and Roy Clark.

"Happy Birthday to me . . ."

Neil Diamond has always been a special friend.

I feel privileged to be in these gentlemen's company: Bill Monroe, Porter Wagoner, Carl Smith, and Little Jimmy Dickens.

The Highwaymen in the studio with producer Chips Moman, 1989.

Christmas with Shooter. He's all of eight years old. (*courtesy Beth Gwinn*)

The Jennings Clan, post-me: (*l. to r.*) Terry, Josh, Debra, Taylor, Julie, Buddy, Kathy, Tomi Lynne, Jennifer, B.J., Josie, Deana, Shooter, Jessi. Not pictured are Johnny, Whey, and Ricky. (*courtesy Billy Mitchell*)

My bride on our silver anniversary. (*courtesy Billy Mitchell*)

No, he just liked my music, and as a theatrical movie agent with offices on Rodeo Drive, he was here as a fan. Bill became one of the brightest spots in my life. He represented Jim Garner, and as I got to know him, I was able to confide in him about the growing financial mess in which I was finding myself.

Richie had spoken with him as well. I had put Richie in charge of overseeing my business, in the same way that I'd produced records with him. I'd get it started and split, leaving him to clean up the loose ends. Only now, those loose ends were unraveling quickly, and out on the road with me, being my drummer, he just couldn't be in two places at once. Richie would come off a series of dates, cross-eyed from touring, and there would be five pages of decisions to be made. I looked to him to make sure it was working, but even though he had the responsibility, he couldn't have a clue about what was happening.

That fall it had come to a screeching halt. Payroll was due, and the banks had stopped what wasn't left of our money. I tried to get ahold of Neil and he had disappeared. Don't ask me where.

He had been supposed to get the money from somewhere. Don't ask me where.

I was supposed to have been one of the top-earning entertainers of the seventies, and the money had vanished. Don't ask me where.

Where, where, where. It was like I had woken up from a long sleep on the bus, between towns, and for a second you look around and don't know where you are. Removed. And when you do realize, a sense of stepping outside yourself, seeing the whole map of where you've been and where you might be heading, then you really wake up and realize you're there. Shit's Creek.

Richie sent Neil a telegram: "We're up to our ass in alligators. Where the hell are you?" There was no answer.

It was Bill who told me how much trouble I was in. There was a lot of income, but it was being shuffled around with little sense of direction or organization. Publishing money was loaning itself to road expenses, which were being financed by advances on record royalties. No one was watching the store. Bills would pile up unopened; fan-club mail lay stacked in boxes. There were sixteen bank accounts. Nobody knew what was going on, or was taking the time to add up one and one and see if it equalled two.

Creditors were beginning to send threatening letters. I owed a quarter of a million dollars to Lear Jet alone. My American Express bill was the budget of a small state. I was giving the money away, literally. Salaries were overblown, padded out with rent-a-cars and party floors in hotels. A lot of it was buying friendship and approval, and a lot of it was people taking advantage. I got the leftovers.

During this time, an ex-IRS auditor came in and went through my finances. He didn't look too happy when he finished unbalancing the books. "There's people you can put in jail for a long time," he said. "They've stolen a lot of money from you. There's people right beside them who were not involved, but because they were there, they look involved. They'll have to go too."

I knew what he was saying, but that had never been my intention. "All I want to know is what happened," I said. "I'm not prosecuting anybody."

How could I? The main one that was involved was me. Because I didn't care. They'd come to me with a problem, and I'd say, "Don't ask me; go see somebody else." Figure it out on your own. And after a while, no matter who they are, if they work for you or love you or respect you, they say if he don't give a damn, why the hell should I?

Neil had to go. I had a huge legal bill, rolled along for two years, with nothing to show for it. It had gotten to the point where, rather than deal with me through Neil, people would rather not deal with me. He had fostered an enemy-camp mentality with RCA, creating a Waylon that didn't exist, enhancing the illusion that he was the only one who could keep me in line. Even when I sent a letter to RCA telling them that Neil no longer represented me, they called his office to see if it was okay. You can't have that. I'm a loyal person, and when somebody does well by me, I tend to remember the good. Neil had helped me and Willie in the beginning, but now it was going nowhere. My damn business was screwed up.

I couldn't stand the thought of bankruptcy. There was no reason to hit bottom. I still had my drawing power. I could sing and play guitar and lead a band. I could write songs. I could work anywhere.

Hell no, I told Bill and Richie in that October of 1981. I won't go bankrupt. I have to find the hole and plug it, and then go make the money to pay this off.

I shut it down. The office on Seventeenth. The gala touring. The too-many pals.

Marylou and Terry Lawrence, who came to work for us for eight days and stayed eight years, took what was left of our business affairs and moved it into the attic of Marylou's home. We couldn't afford to keep the office running. Besides, all people were doing was knocking on our doors with papers telling me I was being sued. We needed a place to figure out what was happening.

Marylou had worked her way up through my organization. She had started in booking, overseeing the agency contracts and riders for our in-house agency, Utopia, run by George Lappe. She untangled the fan club and made sure the newsletters and 800 telephone line were kept open, advising where and when we were playing. One day, all these boxes arrived at the office. It was the papers of my music publishing company, Baron, which had been the subject of a lawsuit between Tompall and myself. Now resolved, Marylou took over the day-to-day running of Baron, which had Jessi's songs like "I'm Not Lisa" and "Storms Never Last," and hits of mine like "Are You Sure Hank Done It This Way." She understood copyright law and publishing administration, and soon she took over issuing licenses, subpublishing agreements, and general clearances.

Marylou had played bass for Keith Sykes and had grown up

around the New England folk scene. She came to Nashville managing Uncle Walt's Band—she was married to Uncle Walt—and when they split up, leaving her with a nine-month-old baby girl, she answered my booking agency's want ad.

I came into the office through the back door one day, dressed in my regulation black hat and vest and boots, with a turquoise shirt and a leather trench coat that reached to my ankles. I was buzzing. As I walked down the hall, I could feel her eyes on me. "What are you looking at?" I asked. She had just started working for us and I hadn't noticed her before.

"You," she said. "I've never seen you up close."

"You like what you see?" She said yeah. "Good." I nodded and headed on my way.

Marylou used to hear me up in the office, singing "Slippin' and Slidin' " in open D tuning, and make my hunger runs for a dozen Krystal cheeseburgers and a couple of bags of fries. Sometimes, by the time she got back, I'd be asleep.

Marylou wasn't used to the open cocaine use up in the office, and the stash-sharing cliques that went along with it. For a time she felt like an outsider. Then one day she put a tiny bit of Coffeemate on her nose and walked around. She said they treated her differently from then on.

After I got busted, and the girl who was my right hand left, Marylou became my personal assistant. No one could be more loyal or show greater courage than she did then, especially after I gathered everyone in the organization and told them what was happening. "It's going to stop right here," I said. "You people know me, and know yourself, and I don't think you have to be told whether you have a job or not. Some of you can come back, and some I don't want back.

"If you feel you've done right by me, and if you feel like we're close, see me later and ask for your job. You'll probably get it. Otherwise, forget it."

Everything stopped for a sixty-day period. People started quitting left and right. One musician let me know that he wanted his money in cash before the show, or he wouldn't play guitar. "I don't work too well under pressure," I said, and he knew he wasn't welcome on my stage.

Marylou and Terry sorted out the financial ledgers in her attic. It took about three weeks of nonstop adding and subtracting to find a way to make it right. When Marylou protested that she wasn't a bookkeeper, I told her all I wanted was common sense. If nobody could get paid for a while, I said I would make sure her rent was taken care of, and she would have money for food. But there wasn't to be one check written until we had gotten control of the situation.

I owed more than two and a half million dollars; almost eighty percent of those creditors could have been paid with five thousand dollars, the bills that had been let go were so small. Some of them only amounted to fifteen or twenty dollars apiece.

Everyone knew that we were fixing to go through hard times. Marylou contacted all the creditors and set up payment schedules. She gave me the option of working off the debt within a year, or one that would take two years. I decided to go for the year plan and immediately left for Las Vegas, where I could make two hundred and fifty thousand in a week. I was determined not to let this one beat me.

The newly trimmed version of the Waylon Jennings traveling carnival, featuring the Crickets and Tony Joe White, hit the road. Slowly, show by show and month by month, I put money aside for the debt. While many people left, key members of the band, like Jigger and Mooney, stayed; Carter was pregnant, and she went off with Barney. Most people I'd fired stayed fired.

Among those who left, much to my sadness, was Richie. There was never any question of my trust in him, or his faith in me; he was simply burned out, in more ways than one.

He'd gotten in trouble again, for drugs, leaving some cocaine in his room in Washington, D.C., on the night we played for President Carter. One of his friends had committed suicide that day, and he wasn't thinking too clearly. He used to keep his stash in his saddlebag, and it fell over on the couch. The maid discovered it and turned it in. There was a pill bottle with his name on it next to the cocaine. How'd you like to be a cop with a confession like that?

While he was on probation, he had a fiery accident while priming a carburetor. He had to get skin grafts on his arms and was in the hospital about seven weeks. We both thought it was time he had a rest; in the long run, we knew it was over for the both of us. He didn't quit, and I didn't fire him. Richie just didn't come back. We had run it through the wall. I couldn't go, and he could, so he did. We're still close. He could still be with me today and he knows it. Richie named his daughter after me, I named my son after him, and I'm godfather to his son. Still, after twenty years and not a cross word between us, there was nothing left to do but split up.

We kept out on the road during 1982, playing state fairs and honky-tonks and anywhere that would have us. It was a vicious schedule, but we knew we had to work so many dates in order to meet the payment plans. Finally, a week before Thanksgiving, Marylou gathered the books and moved back into the office on Seventeenth. It had taken the year to straighten things out, but everyone had been paid back.

I was lucky. Sometimes you're in debt so far that you never have a chance to come out of it. I learned a lot of lessons, and was helped by the fact that I could still work. Most country artists have been broke at some time in their careers; I wasn't any different. You're out on the road, packing places and people are screaming, and you surely think everything's okay. It's hard for an artist to remain creative and still keep on top of the business. If you get too concerned with assets and liabilities, when are you going to write songs? Still, if you learn your lessons in the right place of your life, you might profit by them.

Willie, are you listening?

The Widow's Walk is a four-sided rooftop balcony perched atop an old Southern house. In the Civil War, wives would go up there and wait, watching to catch a first glimpse of the soldiers coming back from the front, their man hopefully returning from battle.

For nearly fifteen years, Jessi had kept that vigil.

Jessi's was a forgiving heart. She had to have that sense of destiny working itself out, of time bringing even the most lost to their senses, to live with me. It was past the point of husband and wife. She wasn't just trying to keep a marriage together. She was trying to keep me alive.

The only normal thing about me was my home. I'd come in, hair plastered to my forehead, dripping wet from sweat, never without a cigarette, having been up for days, and she'd be tricking me into going to sleep. She'd rub my feet and I'd pass out on the living room couch. Sometimes I'd sleep for ten minutes, sometimes for two days.

She never gave up. She didn't try to tell me what to do, but she didn't need to. I knew how I felt at home. I resented the orderliness, the normalcy. I felt unclean, like I shouldn't set on any of the furniture. I might get it dirty. Like I knew I was wrong.

Part of it was self-destruction. Maybe you feel a little guilty for having things other people don't have—more than you need. You don't have to come from humble beginnings to understand that. Everywhere you look, some got and some don't. I knew as hard as I'd worked, fate had been on my side. That's gambling: a little bit of card-counting and the luck of the draw.

Jessi looked on our home as a sanctuary. Nobody could bother me there. I wouldn't bring my druggie buddies to the house. On the bus, it was the opposite story. Anybody could get in there; some never got out.

I wasn't home that much, anyway. I was working most of the time, or at least thought I was working. I spent hours and hours and days and nights in the studio. I'd get an idea and keep chasing it. I'd think it was a smash. Most of the time I'd have to do it over the next week. I couldn't trust my instincts. Richie and Jigger saved a lot of tracks for me, just by holding the music down, to stop it from flying off the track. I would have great ideas, but I just didn't know how to implement them, how to get them across, because I was too high. Later on I could come back and take that idea and make it work.

Sometimes, from the drugs, you'd get to hearing things in the studio. Richie was always chasing little buzzes and hisses, and I'd be out there, waiting for something to happen. I didn't want to lose the feel of the song because of some high-frequency noise nobody could hear. I never knew a record not to be a hit because of some dirt on the guitar track.

One night at American Sound we were working on a song, but the board kept breaking down. They kept telling me to wait a minute, and wait another minute. Finally, I muttered, "Goddammit, y'all hurry up. I'm about to sing in my pants. I've been dry-humming all day and I'm gonna get the tune-aches." Did I say that?

Jessi knew better than to give me ultimatums. She always wanted me to get off drugs because I wanted to do it, not because she told me I had to. Someday, she thought, but she never told me outright to quit them. It was hard for her to wait, and she knew in her spirit that the time was going to come. Through her faith, she had a vision that I would get clean in about eight years, which means she started asking for my deliverance somewhere in 1976. "Lord," her prayer used to go, "watch over ol' Waylon 'cause he's so dumb."

We talked about it sometimes, but I could sidestep any conversation and avoid the subject whenever it got too close for comfort, outmaneuvering her. One thing I can always say is that even in the worst of my drug usage, I was never mean to Jessi. There never was a time that I didn't love her and that she didn't know it. But I wouldn't allow her to talk about drugs. If she did, I would tell her off real quick and go about my business.

She kept poking vitamins down me. I really didn't believe I would live past forty-five. It was a romantic thing. We called it the Hank Williams Syndrome. Along with roaring on Hank's road to ruin, you were expected to die young.

It was ironic. Rather than give me strength, the drugs made me vulnerable. People could have anything they wanted out of me. I would try to buy their approval, playing the clown to get them to like me. I enjoyed my reputation as a wild man, and I would joke about being a junkie and crazy. All I was doing was saying, I'm not really crazy. I'm wrong. Just like Jerry Gropp was still whispering the word in my ear.

Nobody made me feel worse than Shooter. Our little Waylon Albright was the joy of our lives, as you might expect. I would sing to him and he'd just look at me; his momma would sing and he'd start crying. I loved to rib Jessi that he looked more like me than her, but really, he was our love child, the symbol of our togetherness, from the moment we brought his baby bed into the house.

He was a sensitive little guy, and he knew something wasn't right with me. Shooter's attention span was much longer than mine. He'd be around me for a minute and he'd have to leave, because I was scattered. I think I made him uneasy. I was all screwed up, trying to hold him, feeling like he was so little in my big arms.

I thought I could keep my drug use hidden around the house, but one day, when he was about three, he came in the room and found one of my straws. He picked it up and started sniffing on it. I didn't think he'd ever seen me do that, and it threw me.

There's a gap in there. There's a lot I don't remember. Both George Jones and I say that a lot, and maybe that's a good thing. We were both out there chasing our tails for a reason, to understand how far out we could spin and still find our way back. You have to test your limits, whether they're physical, mental, or artistic. That we did; the only problem is some of it happened so fast it was over before we could start recalling it.

I don't regret cocaine. What's the use? It was part of the times we lived in, the songs we sang, and the drugs we took. Who knows where one left off and the other started? We were having a fine ol' time, and as long as we didn't slip over the edge, grasping at air as we slid down the slope, toppling over the precipice, well, that was the dues we paid. The only thing was that it was hard to stop once you got your drug or alcohol momentum. Some never do; and that's when you're not around to write your autobiography.

I knew how to live it up. I wouldn't trade a moment of those wild times, and I still crack up whenever I think of just how manic we could be. One half-time, we found ourselves in the locker room of the Oakland Raiders, who were down six-nothing to Kansas City. I had gotten to know quarterback Ken "Snake" Stabler and defensive tackle John Matuszak. Matuszak was a crazy man. I weigh two hundred pounds and he could pick me up over his head. With one hand.

The pressure in the locker room was unbelievable. Coach John Madden came through the room, took a bottle of Maalox, and drank it straight down. Over on another bench, a guy was throwing up. Fred Biletnikoff, the great receiver, was walking around like a zombie. He didn't want to lose his concentration. I didn't envy those guys; in that world, you're only as good as your last play.

I was down there with Deakon and a couple of friends. We got to tooting the Raiders up. We were in two stalls in the bathroom, and we kept hearing "I'm a big man, pass that over here." We handed it back and forth until pretty soon it was all gone. Oakland went back out on the field and won 54–6. They gave Terry the game ball. Later that night, Deakon and Matuszak started eyeing each other up. They were fixin' to try one another. If that had happened, I would've stepped away a couple of hundred yards. Luckily, they got to talking and settling down.

Not me.

I rocked and rolled and country and westerned. Nobody could have had more fun. I've always believed it's your life, and you can do whatever you want with it. If, that is, you live in a cave like a hermit. But when it affects other people's lives, when you destroy their lives along with yours, you have no right to make them suffer. None.

It got to where my music started to show the strain. I was

doing bad records. Missing shows due to laryngitis. Not picking up the guitar unless I was getting paid. Not caring.

I was feeling bad. I couldn't get my breath. I was losing weight suddenly. I'd get dizzy spells at high altitudes. I'd be driving and have to pull over and get out of the car. We'd be in Lake Tahoe, or Aspen, and I'd turn to Jessi and grab hold of her arm, gripping her tight, leaning on her. We still couldn't talk about it.

Robert Duvall had asked me to produce an album. He's a good singer, but I had to tell him I couldn't do it. "I'm too far in on drugs," I told him. "I'm going to have to pull up and pull back. I can't even cut my own records."

Jessi herself felt drained and depleted. She'd been my rock for so long, and she was at the end of her waiting. In her gift of faith, she felt she had been tempered by her Lord, or she wouldn't have been able to pull back and have the patience to see us through. She had inquired about treatment centers and clinics, and talked to John Cash about how he'd wrestled with his demons. I knew I was in trouble, and my friends and family had me cornered, but Jessi understood that I wasn't the type of guy to bag and throw in the trunk of a car and get committed. If you tried to make me be something, I was too stubbornly defiant. Strength or weakness, this heel-digging probably caused me as much unnecessary trouble as it has kept me from compromising my music.

She saw that the spirit was willing, but my flesh was weak, and getting weaker. Still, spirit can beat flesh, just like paper covers rock, or match burns paper. Resolve only flows one way. At least I was heading in the right direction.

I'm not going to quit. I'm just going to stop.
I never said I'd quit. I'm not going to get off.
I'm just going to stop.
This time. This is the time. I wasn't even aware my heart had made a hard decision until I said it aloud.

My body felt like a sewing machine. Always going. I had the frenzies. Every bone and every joint ached.

"Even unknowing," as Jessi put it, I had crossed the boundary between my past and future. I thought I would take off the month of April, clean up for thirty days, get my health back and my feet on the ground, and enjoy some of that looking-for-a-feeling when I got back. I told Jessi I'd always be a drug addict, and do cocaine, and that this was just temporary. To slow it down.

I leased a house in Arizona with the help of my friend Bob Sikora, who was still running clubs like Mr. Lucky's in Phoenix and owned a string of Bobby McGee's restaurants. It was out in the desert, and I've always respected the spiritual purity of that stark land. Jessi's dad had lived about eighty miles as the crow flies southeast from Phoenix, down below Superior, around Rey copper mine. It was wilderness. He built a cabin along the Gila River, and in the morning you could get up and see prints in the sand, where mountain lions, rattlesnakes, and wild boar had been.

I'd go out there to taper off drugs, and it seemed to help. The desert would soothe me; I could exist without stimulants for weeks at a time, drawing on the desert's silent company. Jessi's dad built race cars in the twenties, and he had constructed auxiliary motors that ran the electricity and water, along with other gadgets. He'd tinker with them, mining his claims for molybdenum and copper, sure he was going to make a fortune. We knew he already had. In his own way, he was a genius. He had found a piece of the world that he belonged in.

You had better respect the desert, because the desert leaves it up to you. It's not going to help. There's nobody you can pay to find your answer and bring it to you. You can't set back and wait on it. The desert is going to leave you totally alone, to see if you can find the strength within yourself to survive. There are no distractions. You can't outfox the desert. You'll die trying.

The house was on the desert's edge, in Paradise Valley up by Tatum Boulevard. Though I didn't know it, we didn't yet have a place to go to when we left Nashville for Phoenix. The hideaway we had originally wanted had fallen through, and Bob Sikora literally talked this woman out of her home. By the time we got there, it had been stocked with groceries and was ready for us. When Jessi went into the kitchen, she opened the pantry where the dishes were kept and saw a set of china that she hadn't seen since she was a small child and her mother had collected them from local gas stations as premiums. She couldn't believe it, and she took it as a sign, a way of telling her that this was where we were supposed to be.

On the night of March 31, 1984, I did all the cocaine I could and left twenty thousand dollars worth on the bus. I didn't think I could handle withdrawal without an escape hatch, though it must've been frightening for Jessi to know the drugs were sitting out there, just waiting for me to have a moment of weakness. I parked the bus in the circular driveway and prepared myself to wait it out. A doctor would come in and give me vitamin shots, but otherwise I knew I was on my own.

My body reacted as if somebody had pulled out the plug. I had sudden convulsions. It was like I was caught in a revolution, with snipers on the rooftops and battles being waged on every corner. My nerves were in a constant grind of readiness, waiting, every cell about to explode with anticipation, for some relief that just wouldn't come. My bones hurt. I didn't sleep. I'd wake up at all hours of the night with toxins pouring out of my body. I got sick; it was the first common cold I'd had in years, as my body flushed out the cocaine residues.

I'd sit out on the swing in the front yard, watching the sun come up. I'd still be there when the stars began to shine. As my mind started to clear, I got to seeing the look on Jessi's face. It was hopeless and helpless. She was so sad, watching me vacillate between life and death, unable to do more than watch me go through it. I realized then what I was doing to her, that it wasn't just me who was under the influence of cocaine, and then I looked around at everybody around me who cared anything about me, and basically, that same look was on their faces.

For two or three weeks, I learned how to feel my emotions again. When you're normal, you can give as well as receive; on drugs, it all goes inward and never gets let out. I woke up one morning, toward the end, and Jessi was sitting there, by the end of the bed. I had only been asleep ten minutes. "Jessi, my spirit's dying, and there's nothing I can do about it."

There wasn't anything she could do but wait, pray in her fashion, and let me know that she was holding fast, right by my side. I couldn't have done it without Jessi. She is the most giving person I've ever met, and anytime I felt like I just couldn't stand withdrawing further, she let me know, by her gentle presence, what would be waiting for me on life's other shore.

There was a grand piano in the house, and she sang from a big *Reader's Digest* book of old songs that was on the music stand. We went for short walks. I clung close to her. She knew I needed somebody to be my partner. Shooter played in the front yard, and I watched him as I sat in the swing, knowing he was my greatest inspiration. Back at the house, Maureen, our "administrator" at *Southern Comfort*, practiced her art of ritualistic feeding, serving my favorite meals, sometimes six or seven a day, topping them off with peach milkshakes and little prizes for each milestone passed. I must've gained twenty-five pounds.

After about three weeks, I got to where I could sit for a time and feel my mind clearing out. I realized, that's the end of it. I waited another day to make sure about what I was thinking, though I still felt I had only "stopped." That was my key word.

I was in the car with Jessi one afternoon, watching the desert scenery go by, and I turned to her and asked if so-and-so knew "that I quit." She stared at me. I realized what had just come out of my mouth. I didn't believe that I had said that.

"Did you hear me?" I asked her, though I was really directing the question at myself.

It had come from deep within, and we both understood it was absolutely true. I wasn't ever going to do drugs again, as amazing as that sounded. I had painted myself into a corner, and when I give my word, I don't break it.

A month after entering my own halfway house, I walked out the door, slightly shaky, but feeling strong, at least physically. I was anxious to see what life was going to be like, though I didn't dwell on the mental hurdles that were sure to come. I sniffed the fresh desert air, crisp in the morning, feeling it rush into my nose and lungs where once drugs had lived and breathed. I felt washed out.

Back on the bus, there was still that twenty thousand dollars worth of cocaine waiting for me. The last temptation. I didn't want to deal with it, and I wasn't about to pass along my troubles to somebody else. I was worried that we might have a wreck and it would be found, or about the consequences if they decided to try and bust me, not knowing I'd quit.

I went in the back, unearthed the briefcase with the coke, and took it to the front of the bus. I handed it to Jessi. "You, of all people, deserve to do with this whatever you want."

She went to the bathroom, poured it in the bowl, and hollered, "Hallelujah!" She was the happiest girl in the world. And I was the happiest boy.

I had to learn how to walk into a room.

I didn't know what I was supposed to be like, who I was supposed to be like, or what was expected of me.

What I did know was that all I had to do was pick up the cocaine and the straw, and I'd get my old self back.

I would have night sweats about drugs, getting mad at myself while I slept because I usually took it in my dreams. I hated the way I looked, because once I started gaining weight, I couldn't stop. I thought I was nothing without cocaine.

For a long time, it was like I'd lost somebody close to me. I was in mourning, pining away. The best way I can explain it is there's a guy over there. He's another person. You can do anything you want to because you can blame it on him. He's a good-time Charlie, and a lot of fun. You really like him, because he's your escape from every damn problem you got in the whole world. And when you quit drugs, he dies. Lay out a line, and he's alive again.

That's why you have to stay away from him. Change playmates and playgrounds. It's like the crabs they sell on street corners in

Mexico. If you watch, they're just milling around, with nothing to keep them in the pan but a lip about an inch high. Until you see one try to get out and another pull him back. Your drug friends don't want you to quit.

It had nothing to do with how well I knew them. I called everybody and said, "If you're going to be around me, you can't do drugs." That was it. If they had to do drugs, they would have to find somewhere else to do them. It worked the other way, too. When I quit drugs, the guy who sold them to me stopped dealing. He may have been an angel in disguise, because I could always rely on him to get me cocaine that was pure and hadn't been stepped on. He kicked the habit, and I got him a job. He and his family are doing great now.

I got out right before crack, for which I've always been thankful. I'd put cocaine on the end of cigarettes and smoked it, but my only experience with freebasing made me know it wasn't for me.

A lawyer friend came to a show one time, about three or four years before I quit, and said he had found the most wonderful high on earth. He set up the pipe and we smoked the crack. Within a minute I had a feeling come over me that if I jumped out a window, it would be fine. I could fly. Or if somebody made me mad enough, I could kill them and it would be okay.

I got out of the chair and sat in the corner. I had enough presence of mind to know that I was in trouble, that I was not in control anymore. I hated that. While I sat there, waiting for the drug to wear off, I had the worst thoughts I ever had in my life, hateful and spiteful and mean. I wanted to bust everybody's head in the room.

There was something unholy about it. When the lawyer came up and asked how I liked it, I told him he better get his ass away from crack. It was poison, pure and simple.

Later on, when Richard Pryor had burned himself freebasing, I remembered that experience. We had known each other for a while, and our mutual friend, Jennifer Lee, had called me with the news. She was distraught, and I was trying to think of something comforting to tell her. Finally, I said, "Look, they're going

to have to do a lot of skin grafting. If they need extra skin, I'll donate some."

It wasn't until I got off the phone that Basil MacDavid turned
to me and said, "What do you think they're going to do? Call him
Spot?"

I was lucky that my drug use only went so far. I knew a beautiful little girl once, and after talking with her for a while, she ex-
cused herself and disappeared into the next room. When she
didn't return I went looking for her. She was sitting at the
kitchen table with a needle in her arm. She had just shot up, and
the look on that perfect face was so sickening, I couldn't bear to
be in the same room. I left. I could never handle that.

Every once in a while, to this day, I'll run into one of my hidden stashes, a vial tucked in the corner of an old suitcase or an
inch of cocaine buried in the bottom of a boot bag. Even now, my
first instinct is to pick up a straw and snort it. The temptation
doesn't go away.

When it comes, I don't try to ignore it or get mad at myself for
thinking it. I'll say, "Man, it would be great to get high just
once." I move across the room. "Damn, I wish I had some cocaine." Jessi's heard me say it any number of times. She knows
what I'm doing. It's on my mind, and I'm spitting it out instead
of holding it deep inside, where the craving might have a chance
to take root. It lasts thirty seconds. Then I go on with my life.

I was sitting with Shooter in a restaurant booth. He was on the
inside, and he got his coloring book out. He was all of five years old.

He put his left arm through my right, and we sat there for
about an hour while he colored. Shooter hadn't ever done that before. I'd never been able to sit so still for so long with him.

I wasn't about to move my arm.

CHAPTER

11

# WILL THE WOLF SURVIVE?

It wasn't over. Not by a long shot.

It took me eight years to find my way back from drugs, to rediscover the creative tension in my music, the sweet spot balanced between rhythm and melody where the song generates its own momentum and all you can do is express it.

Eight years, to be able to write a song. Eight years, to be on stage and not feel like I was boring people sick. Eight years, to figure out who I was again. To get over it.

Eight long years. That's not to say the work I did during that time didn't have any value. I made some good, decent records and always sang from the heart. I hit better notes now that I wasn't plagued by "laryngitis." I played on the beat, instead of ahead of it. Probably only I noticed that instead of pushing myself, I was being pulled along by my own legend and the skills I'd learned in a lifetime of performing.

Jimmy Bowen did as much for me as anybody, because he knew

what I was going through. I had spent two decades on RCA and gone from being the new kid on the block to a grizzled war vet with a raft of ribbons and medals. My discography needed a book to keep straight, and I'd outlasted most executive regimes, an array of studios, and a whole generation of pressing plants.

Sometimes history works against you. Carrying the burden of my past into each new release, it seemed like I wasn't hearing anything new. Neither was RCA, and they'd been accustomed to larger-than-life success. When my records started selling more steadily, and less explosively, taking their time in the marketplace, they weren't willing to look at me the same as they might a newer artist. We had peaked.

The song "America" was my farewell anthem for RCA. I had found the original version on a Sammy Johns album in 1975 when he hit with "Chevy Van." You couldn't find the melody in it, though I loved what the words said. It was the time of the U.S. Olympics in 1984. I've always thought that Ronald Reagan didn't do everything right, but he did give some pride back to the country; we were apologizing for being great. I got inspired by that Olympics and wanted to write a patriotic song.

Everything I had was too corny and didn't sound right. Then I remembered that song from nine years before. It wasn't just flag waving. It was talking about the ideals we had fought for and the blunders committed in their name, and the honor that lay behind our national character. In the decade since it had been written, we had "let them come home" from Vietnam, where it had once been "You should let 'em come home." I always thought those who went to Canada got a really bad rap. I'd have sent my boy there, too, instead of that uncalled-for place.

"They're all black and white and yellow too / and the Red man is right, to expect a little from you / A promise and then follow through." I found the song again and listened to it with a decade's distance. I changed the melody, and Jigger produced it. I even made a video to go with it, a forerunner of the way music would be watched as well as listened to from then on.

When my contract came up for renewal in July of 1985, I didn't resign with RCA. It was no longer a delivery of masters in their eyes. The contract had words like "mutual consent," which translated into more partnership, less money. We were just too familiar with each other. I passed on it.

Promises work both ways. If I'd thought RCA would have revved their engines in return for having some say-so in my records, I might never have headed off to non-Nipper pastures. But I knew it was time to try something fresh. I didn't have the strength to do it on my own, and if I was going to work with someone, I wanted to have faith in where we were heading and know it would be a clean start.

And sober. It was a new me, and I was learning to live with him. Bowen, at MCA, offered me the chance to take another run at it. I signed with him in September. Jimmy never gave anyone creative control or artistic freedom. When the lawyers started talking, they said he wouldn't do it, and I wasn't going to sign without it. Everyone broke the negotiations off.

Bowen finally asked one day how the contracts with Waylon were going, and they said, well, it's not going to happen. He said, "Are you kidding? Give him what he wants. He'll just take it anyway."

That's when I knew he was my man. And I gave him all the freedom he wanted. Him and Don Was are two of the most fun, and trusting, producers I know. And the most trustworthy. You can let them have the reins and rely on where they'll take you.

I always want control. I want it in writing. And then I'll give it to who I damn please.

Jimmy Bowen and I traveled back in time together just about as far as we could go. His Rhythm Orchids, who he shared with Buddy Knox, had come out of Dumas, Texas, about two hundred miles north of Lubbock, in 1956. Jimmy was a disc jockey on K-triple-D up there, and played bass for the Orchids. They'd recorded "Party Doll" at Norman Petty's studio, and released it on their own Jewel label. It became a West Texas hit, and

Roulette picked it up for national release. The night before they were to get on a plane and go up to New York, I booked them in Littlefield. We had a battle of the bands, my band against their band, and that's the first time I saw Jimmy. The next thing I knew he was in the Top Ten with "I'm Sticking with You" while Buddy Knox was riding next to him with "Party Doll." They were stars before Buddy Holly, and certainly inspired the Crickets to make the trek to Clovis.

On the tour after Buddy had been killed, we were up in Minneapolis and I saw a guy come through the door with the most beautiful woman on his arm. I had never seen anything that clean and "purty." It was Jimmy, and he looked like a matinee idol; he had a tie on and everything.

He approached country music with the same sense of sharp-creased style, learning everything there was to know about it, sitting behind the mixing board like it was the cockpit of a 747. By the time he got to Hillbilly Central, ah, Glaser Sound Studios, working with Hank Williams Jr., Mel Tillis, Jimmie "Honeycomb" Rodgers, and the Glasers themselves, he had some of the smartest ears in the business. Jimmy wasn't a welcome sight in Nashville for a long time, but he helped turn that town into a great recording center. They would've stayed in the Stone Age of music if not for Bowen. He said, we're going to cut records that compare with what we hear on rock and pop stations, using the latest technology. He knew that if you're going to be in the business end of music, you've got to compete, and he expected a dollar's worth of work out of everybody. A lot of people didn't like Jimmy, but most were jealous of him.

After I signed with MCA, we gave it our best shot, through a couple of albums. I tried to keep an open mind about Jimmy's way of doing things, and for his part, he let me try anything I wanted to. He was very devoted to me and wanted me to succeed. The thing was, he knew I couldn't do it right then. He knew I was off balance.

*Will the Wolf Survive?* A good question, and not a ready answer.

It was the first time in years I'd recorded without my band, except for Jerry Bridges holding down the bass. I didn't play guitar on the sessions; I was "the vocalist." Nor did I write any of the songs. Jimmy picked most of them, and he had a good ear, from the Los Lobos title song to Steve Earle's "The Devil's Right Hand." We recorded digitally in Nashville, at Sound Stage; it was a new age of technology, proclaimed on the album's front, though the record was still released on analog vinyl.

Compared with some of my earlier works, it might not have fit people's expectations of me. That was the point. Bowen kept talking about the "new Waylon Jennings," who was off the drugs, who had a new outlook on life. He wanted to get away from "what I had done," which was the heavy undercurrent of rhythm and the bad-ass vocal style. Put on a late-seventies track like "Clyde," and you could hear the bottom foot thumping away, voice up close and in your face, growling out the lyrics. I had already done that, and he hoped I could stretch out. I hadn't progressed any, which was a little bit of laziness on my part.

I look back now and see what he was talking about. He would work with me until the morning came helping me find it. If I wasn't happy, he'd stay there through the next day. Jimmy would never walk on me, and I appreciated that. But I had lost the thread. I was trying to sound like what I thought he wanted me to sound like instead of me. I'd think, What the hell, I sang that good, and in the end, I was imitating myself, trying too hard to satisfy people who thought I had ruined my music by straightening up. Bowen knew that.

It was all down to me. Jimmy tried his level best, making my recording sessions like an event. Everything was in place—a great studio and players, excellent songs, people who cared—but I couldn't rise to the occasion.

On *Will the Wolf Survive?* and its follow-up, *Hangin' Tough*, it was like I was off in a corner of a separate room, clouded by delay, distanced. I wasn't leading the band. I was trying to get my feet back on the ground, and that took as much concentration as singing. Though I was off drugs, I was still smoking heavily, and my voice showed the wear and tear.

You lose all confidence when you come off drugs. It may have been artificial energy, but when I was high, I wasn't afraid to try things. I'd get to where I couldn't be still, on top of the beat, just weavin' and rockin', and I would come up with some of the most outrageous ideas. I was uninhibited.

When I stopped playing rhythm guitar on my tracks, even though I'm not a great guitar player, it was like I had suddenly started to worry whether I was good enough to be part of my own sound. If you stop believing in yourself, your songs stop caring about you as well. I didn't realize at the time that the thing that had made me my own man was my inner confidence, the faith and courage that allows you to get up before a group of strangers and articulate their hopes and fears. To take the guitar out of my hands was like trying to sing without opening my mouth. I couldn't make the tempo mine, or the words more than sentiment.

The feel. Sometimes you can't see or hear it, but you always know when it's there. Or not.

"Cash," I said. I didn't mean Johnny.

They had asked me how I was going to pay for the gold Cadillac. It had a wheel in the running board and was long-nosed, stretched like a limousine. I had been looking for a Fleetwood. This was a Seville, one of only five made. I couldn't resist. I had told the dealer in Scottsdale, Arizona, that I was going to come back for the car, and here, on this Saturday morning, there was a crowd of people waiting to see the transaction.

Jessi stood next to me. I reached in the top of her brassiere and pulled out a few hundreds. Then I pulled out a few more. I kept reaching and pulling until I paid the whole forty-five thousand dollars. Every now and then I'd pinch her and she'd squeal. The guy was so flustered, he had to keep writing up the order again and again.

It was a childhood dream. I had gotten to relive what I saw Jaybird Johnson do, back in Littlefield. When I was a kid, one of my first jobs was at the local Cadillac showroom. One evening, as I was sweeping up, Jaybird came in, fresh from selling bootleg whiskey at the Dew Drop Inn across the tracks. He was with his wife, and he sat in a few of the Cadillacs until he found one that was to his taste.

"Do you like it, honey?" he asked her. She nodded yes.

"Well, pay the man," he declared, and she started reaching in her brassiere and pulling out tens and twenties. Jaybird's Cadillac cost about two or three thousand dollars, but that was a lot in those days.

When Jessi's chest returned to normal, we took the Cadillac for a spin. I knew it was expensive, but I had just kicked drugs and didn't mind taking it out of one nose and putting it in another. As I pulled out of the parking lot, I turned on the radio and one of my own songs, "I May Be Used (But Baby I Ain't Used Up)," was playing. We drove down the road, Jessi and I and Shooter.

"It's an omen, Dad," said Shooter.

I had gone home.

First and foremost in my life was Jessi. For us, the healing came quickly. There was a bond between our two selves from the moment I left drugs. Those holes that are empty in a relationship, because you're married to something else, were filled.

Jessi lives in the gray area; with me it's either all right or all wrong. She'll look for the other side, the opposing viewpoint, and then balance them with where she thinks she ought to be. When I'm mad, I don't want to hear the other side. She's a peacemaker, and she's proved she can survive better than me. She's the strongest person I've ever met in my life, because she does not care about herself. It's not first with her, and after looking for every way in the world to make me look right, she doesn't hesitate to tell me when I'm wrong. She's not afraid of me.

She made me not afraid of me, as well. She knew that the little things I was confronting were not as big as I was making them out to be, and yet that didn't make them any smaller. I could see my own facial expressions, and those around me, in a mirror that made me aware of the nakedness of being on stage before the world. The drugs obscured a lot, but they also masked my creativity and stopped me from drawing on what could provide my greatest strength. Jessi had faith that I would keep on recovering, walking through each day one at a time. I hadn't lost my art; she knew I'd just misplaced it. She never stopped believing in me. Jessi even wrote a song once in the early seventies, "Darling Darling It's Yours," after RCA had given me their Golden Boot award as a consolation prize, which she thought was like "throwing crumbs to a king." For her, I wrote "You Deserve the Stars in My Crown."

In her eyes, I was a paradox like King David, always questioning, arguing, trying to resolve the contradictions between this life and the next, whatever they might be. David the musician and singer of psalms, having it out with David the military and secular leader, a give-and-taking between Heaven and earth. I couldn't help it. Even with old Hallowed-be-thy-Name, I couldn't accept anything for granted. I needed to find out for myself.

If I believed in reincarnation, I'd have to say that Jessi is on her last time around, just like my dad. You can hear it in the purity of her voice, the playing of her piano, the way she writes songs that don't rhyme but say everything that needs to be said. She lives her faith.

I never did things halfway. When I quit drugs, that was it, but I probably doubled or tripled my cigarette smoking. I always had one clenched between my teeth, dangling from my mouth, lighting the next. It was a standard prop on my album covers. I'd be craving something, and the nearest thing I'd grab was a cigarette. I couldn't go more than ten minutes without one. I smoked up to seven packs a day.

My diet wasn't any better. I was a big eater. My favorite breakfast was sausage, gravy, and biscuits. Cheese eggs and jelly.

Scrambled egg sandwiches. Three fried eggs with sausage or bacon. When I moved on to lunch, I'd eat three or four ham-and-grilled-cheese sandwiches, piling on the lettuce and tomatoes, jalapeños and onions. Dinner would be a roast with potatoes and carrots cooking in with the gravy. Before I went to sleep, I'd grab a few scrambled egg sandwiches and down a glass of milk. For a snack, I'd refry a dozen doughnuts in butter.

That's how you join the Zipper Club.

I was playing at the Crazy Horse. It's a joint in Orange County run by the nicest man that's ever been in the nightclub business, Fred Reiser. I was booked to play two shows there, and the night before, as I was fixing to lay down, I coughed. Both my arms, not just one, started hurting like I couldn't believe. It wasn't like the frozen shoulders that I'd had on and off for the last eighteen months, a tendinitis that I thought I'd cured by getting a more flexible guitar strap.

Jessi rubbed my arms till they stopped hurting, but the next morning, when I went down to breakfast, the pressure had moved to my lungs. I felt like I had water in there, and my arm had started hurting again. I went out for a walk. It was lucky I made it back, come to think of it.

The pain subsided when I returned to the bus. We changed hotels to be nearer the Crazy Horse, and had brunch. After we ate, the ache started again, really bad. I went upstairs and lay down. It wouldn't quit. I took a hot shower; then I lay down and started breathing really hard, just to get air in my lungs. I fell asleep, till about three o'clock, until Bill Robinson came to the door with Jessi telling me they thought I needed to let the doctor check me.

"I feel wonderful," I protested. "There's not a thing wrong. That's over with. There's no need. Whatever it was, I don't know, but I'm fine and don't have anything hurting."

We went down to dinner. The first show was at seven o'clock. I ordered chicken fried steak with gravy; and they had a thing called corn chowder that I loved. I took one bite of that, and one bite of chicken fried steak, and the pain hit me hard again. I said, "I'm going to have to go and sit outside and get some air."

I went and got on the bus. I was hurting bad. I sat down. My chest and neck felt tight. I lit a cigarette and took a big inhale. It hurt so much I threw the cigarettes across the bus and lay down on the couch.

Jessi and Fred came out. "You don't look good. Why don't we get you checked?" I shook my head. I knew I'd be all right in a minute. Sure.

The best they could talk me into was a cardiologist's intern. He told me he wasn't a doctor yet, but it didn't take a specialist to see that this had to do with the heart. I couldn't keep saying no; it hurt too bad.

They gave me nitroglycerin, and sure enough, it made the pain stop. I could breathe again. We went over to the emergency room and a doctor who looked like Larry Gatlin read my blood pressure. Larry and I have butted heads quite a few times, and Jessi wasn't sure he was the right medic for me.

"You're in the process of having a heart attack," he said. "You haven't had one, and you're not having one yet." He gave me a pill. Later on, I found out that the one pill cost eight thousand dollars. I wondered, if I hadn't had insurance and money, if I was off the street, would he have given me that wonder drug?

Bill came into the examining room with me. We had bet twenty dollars on a Dallas Cowboys–San Francisco 49er's game, and to show you what kind of friend he was, as they were strapping the electrocardiogram onto me, he asked me to wait a minute. "I've been watching that game," he said. "It looks like San Francisco is going to win. Why don't you get somebody to hold that twenty bucks, because you never know how these things are going to turn out." It hurt to laugh so hard.

The nurses chatted among themselves while they took my vital signs. They were talking about a gang shooting that had happened the night before. They'd brought the guy into the operating room and were working on him, and the rival gang came in and shot him some more on the surgical table. I felt like I was in good hands.

The doctors tried angioplasty, where they try to open the blockages in your arteries like a plumber opens a blocked sewage line, but I was the 1 in 4 it doesn't take on. I relied on a stash of nitro pills and waited for the next symptom to show. After one particularly bad night, in the fall of 1988, I got ready to do a Johnny Cash benefit on the other side of Knoxville from Nashville, in Bristol, Tennessee. Sharp as a pistol.

Jessi was on the phone with the doctor, but as he was advising me to "come in," I was saying "I'll see him when I get back." We started out of town, but about twenty miles away, we had to turn around. Again, I wasn't having a heart attack. I was about to have it.

The truth was, I needed a bypass. Four of them, as it turned out; quadruple. I asked for time to think about it—I was over-booked as usual—but I could see myself in Podunk, Arkansas, with some damn veterinarian standing over me saying "I ain't never done this before. You going to help us, Waylon? Hold this scalpel, and give us those knives when we need 'em."

I was on the road all the time. I was scheduled to go to Europe in a few months. I didn't want to be away from home and have something happen.

One thing was for sure. It was the last I would see of banana pudding. Joyce Holland, the wife of Johnny Cash's drummer, W.S., made up a big batch. I ate all of it I could, and the next morning, I checked into Baptist Hospital.

Every time I've been in a hospital, I wake up and there's John Cash. I think he must make a habit of sitting by my bedside. One holiday season, I opened my eyes at home on the couch and he was there, dressed like the spirit of Christmas future. He spooked me. I was pretty messed up. "What're you doing here?" I grumbled.

"I like to visit my friends on Christmas Day," he said in that canyon-river voice.

I fell back to sleep and woke up again. He was still there. "Ain't you got any other friends?" I asked.

I had watched John's ups and downs with drugs over the years. He had never told me to straighten myself out, or got preachy, though for a time he had to stay away from me for his own good. When I'd come out of the desert in 1984, he had talked to me nearly every day, telephoning if he couldn't come in person. We encouraged each other, though we were careful not to make any claims or act like counselors from a treatment center. We were both savvy to the ways of the world and knew the best thing was probably to stick close together, reinforcing our bond. When John was clean and sober six months, Jessi threw a celebration for him. June and John did the same for me when I turned my half year.

At the party, June wrote a song for me and sang it. So did John, and a bunch of other people. He told me later that it was the greatest night of his life, because his best friend was in wonderful shape. "We can look each other in the eye," he said, "and we ain't hiding anything."

We both had always known when the other was lying, denying, and concealing the drugs from each other. Now here we were, laughing and singing, having fun and everybody witnessing it. Not scared of anything or anybody.

When you have people around you that love you, like him or Jessi, it really gives you courage. Nobody could have done it for me. Nobody could have done it for him. We did it together.

Now we were about to have another shared experience. "I'm fine," I told John as the anesthesia started to wear off. "But you don't look so good yourself."

Sure enough, they had a doctor check him over, and before you could say "shot a man in Reno," they put him in the room next to mine. He had to have an emergency bypass, too.

I'd quit smoking. John hadn't, and they were trying to clear his lungs before they operated. He had to wait a few days, and all the while he kept asking "How ya doing?" and I'd say "Couldn't be better."

The fact was that I had seldom felt worse. I was allergic to morphine, though it took them a while to figure that out. Lying in the recovery room, I couldn't get my breath. The oxygen they were feeding me seemed hot. They tried changing the tanks. Jessi was looking at me, and my eyes were wild, because I didn't know what was happening.

They finally diagnosed the problem and put me on Tylenol 2. That was all. It figured; after all my drug use, I had to be allergic to morphine. If I coughed, it felt like a herd of horses had stamped across my chest. I had told the doctors before not to get me strung out on anything, because I didn't want to repeat my addiction problems. They took me at my word.

I couldn't tell John because I thought he'd run off if he knew how bad I was hurting. When they finally operated on him, I went in and told him I was sorry about lying to him.

"Eat your heart out," he laughed. "I ain't allergic to nothing." He could have all the morphine he wanted.

You can find humor in everything. I couldn't believe that after cutting your chest practically in half, they got you up to walk on the second day. Two male nurses came in to get me ready for my stroll. The first thing they did was sit me up and set me right on my nuts. I'm too macho to have one of those boys reach in there and pull my balls out, so I'm stretching and straining to pick myself up, trying to maneuver them around, when this female nurse comes in with a syringe for me. It was about a foot long.

Her name was Chloe and she was beautiful. "Okay, Mr. Cowboy singer," she said. "You're going to get up and walk now, or I'm going to stick this right in you."

"I don't need you, Chloe," I groaned. I did, though, as I got shakily to my feet.

I had no wheels. I was weak and drained. Jessi would walk by my bed, and each day I would try to pinch her on the butt. I'd keep missing, but on the fourth day I knew I was getting stronger because I grabbed her.

Being in a hospital is a great leveler. "I'll tell you what the equalizer is," I said to John one day when we were sitting around.

"What do you mean?" he asked me.

"The thing which makes you one with every human being in the world. When they get you up to walk you, you can hardly stand up, and they put that little gown on you. You're about halfway down the hall, and you feel the draft from behind. You know you ain't got no back, and you got no shorts on, and people are looking at your ass.

"That superstar shit goes right out the window."

I was more depressed that Christmas than I'd ever been. I was missing cigarettes, a habit I'd nourished since my days out in the Littlefield clubhouse. Right to this day, if I'm dealing cards, I'll stick my hand in my shirt pocket, searching for a smoke. Even when I play solitaire. My cousin Wendell had told me that there were only five days of actual nicotine withdrawal to worry about; "chewin' the rugs," as he called it. After that, you just had to stop reaching for them.

My hitting-bottom ran deeper, though. I couldn't see any future, even though I'd been granted a fresh start. I think your mind believes that you die when they stop your heart to perform the bypass. It can't understand the fact that life can be interrupted. As the brain deals with that, reconnecting its damaged roadways, you try to realize what it means to be brought back from the dead. My daddy died when he was fifty-three, and now I had the chance to outlive him that he never got. My own mortality weighed heavily upon me.

I must've been in that mood right before the operation. I wasn't sure about how much time I had left. I was feeling bad all the time. That's the thing when you're having heart problems; you deteriorate very slowly. Those veins don't stop up overnight. You begin wondering if you ever felt good.

*A Man Called Hoss* was an album that grew out of an idea I had for a one-man show, a monologue to myself about where I'd been, singing my story. Divided into chapters, each illustrated by a song, I told my self-tale, from prologued birth to the last chapter, "The Beginning." My "Living Proof," as I called it in chapter 7.

I worked on the concept with songwriter Roger Murrah. I had done two or three of his songs, including "Where Corn Don't Grow," and I liked the sparse way he approached things. To the point. Chorus and bridges are fine, but sometimes they're crutches to get you through the story. I was always cautious about overwriting. A song is like a circle, and to return it to where it begins is the storyteller's art. A round trip. "Bringing it home" I always called it.

Somebody talked me into doing a narration between the cuts, and I've regretted that part of the album, though it remains one of my favorite records. If you have to tell somebody the story as you're singing it, you don't have faith in the power of the songs, and the songs didn't need any extra help. "Rough and Rowdy Days" related the fable of John and myself as well as I could tell it, sitting across a kitchen table, and I always wanted to write a song with four lines in it that lasted six minutes like "Where Do We Go from Here."

We tried it out as a one-man show in California, and also at Duke University. It was just me singing to tracks, and telling stories, and enlivening these songs as we went along. It was fun to do. Bowen called it an audio-biography.

Autobiography. It's like a travelogue. You think, "I've been somewhere," and you want to tell people about it. Maybe they'll see some of themselves along the journey, but most of all, you tell your story to get it straight, at least in your own mind. To figure out what you've done right, and where you've gone astray, and why maybe the wrong things turned out to be needed for the right things to happen.

You look back over these events, pieces of time, characters and question marks, each funny and sad, light and dark in their own way. The last chapter should always point forward. That's the moment you have left to do something even better. A sequel.

"Storms Never Last" was a song of Jessi's that seemed to open the way to the future. She had found the phrase while waiting in a doctor's office and, watching what I was going through, had written it as a personal song to me. She was going to throw it away, but I had her change "Waylon" to "Baby." She recorded it first, and then later I did a version of it in 1980, on my *Music Man* album. The words seemed to mean more and more across the years as we faced down each crisis, a wave of doubt looming large and getting smaller and finally disappearing as we passed over and through it. We became ever closer to one another, her anchor to my ship at sea.

> *You followed me down so many roads, baby*
> *I picked wildflowers*
> *Sung you soft sad songs*
> *And every road we took*
> *God knows our search was for the truth*
> *And the cloud brewing now won't be the last*
> *Storms never last, do they, Jessi?*
> *Bad times all pass with the wind*
> *Your hand and mine stills the thunder*
> *You make the sun want to shine*

Shooter was the cornerstone between us. He's not what you might expect from a kid of mine. He likes industrial rock groups like Nine Inch Nails and Ministry and has turned me on to Enigma and Metallica. He says he doesn't care for country music, but he learned drums from Richie Albright and plays congas with me on summer tour. He's got a room full of computers and programs his own video games, a post-modern child of the future as much as I'm a pre-primitive father.

I can't help it. I wouldn't want to help it. I've always been crazy about kids. If there's a crowd of adults and a kid, I'll go straight for the kid, every time. Sometimes I feel like the Pied Piper. My dad was a big tease when it came to children, and maybe it's a little bit of my daddy, or my own sense of being a daddy, that helps me to instantly get down on their level. After a few minutes they think they're just as big and tough as ol' Waylon. I can argue with them, play their games, and they're never afraid of me.

It'll be funny. Sometimes I scare grown-ups half to death. One night in Austin, I came out of the Armadillo and it was dark. A couple walked up and asked me for a photo. He was shaking, and she was trembling. They had a little girl with them, and I looked at her, trying to think of a way to make them feel comfortable. "Are you afraid of me?" I asked, and she answered me with a little grin and shook her head no. Then she came over and gave me a hug. That's always been my barometer with myself. You can't fool children.

Kids love to tell me what to do. One of my favorite little friends is my goddaughter Haley Hyatt, Marylou's child. She'd ask me if I was tired and if my back was sore. When I said yes, she'd take one finger and rub a corner of my shoulder. "Does that feel good?" she'd ask. "Is that helping you?" I had to admit it did. Then she'd say, "I'm kind of like your mother, aren't I?"

"You sure are, honey," I'd agree.

Then she'd stick that finger right in my face and start shaking it. "Okay, then you better straighten up," she'd scold, giving me all kinds of what-for. Jigger's daughter, Jessica, is another one who spends most of our time together telling me she knows what's best, and I better do what she says and why she's the boss.

I got Haley back when she had chicken pox. She hated having those spots on her face, and finally I told her to gather a few of those pox when they fell off and put them into an envelope and send them to President Carter 'cause he'd just raised my taxes. She turned to her mother. "Way-a-lon is sometimes so silly."

Playing music helps keep you childlike. The first thing a kid will react to is a song. From the time they're born, we put little jingle bells over the top of their cribs and sing to them. Shooter used to go to sleep to my music; he called them "Daddy tapes." Later, he played my records. He couldn't read the labels, but he recognized the Flying W when he saw it. I'd ask him, "Shooter, do you know any songs?" He'd play "Are You Sure Hank Done It This Way" over and over until it had skips and scratches. Then he'd sing "Are you sure Hank / Are you sure Hank / Are you sure Hank . . . ," just like the record.

I never wanted him to go to school. In my mind, when you put the little book into his hands and sent him into the building, it was all over. He might never come back. I wanted to have him tutored, and on his first day, after he'd put his little arms around my neck, I stayed outside and waited under a nearby tree. If he'd walked out of that school, we both knew he'd never have to go back, but he stayed, and when he graduated years later, I stood under that same tree and thought about how much he'd grown, and me with him.

I used to wear my cowboy hat wherever I went. One day we were going out to a toy store, and he took the hat and said "Let's leave that in here so people won't bother you." Nobody did.

He's got more than one vote in our family. It may jump up and bite me in the rear end one day, but I've always told him, if I say no to you, you have a right to ask why. If I don't have a good enough answer, then I'll try to see it his way. The best thing I can give him is my ears and my attention. A lot of times, especially with my other kids, I haven't followed that through. I blew it in so many ways with them, back when I wasn't much more than a kid myself. Harlan Howard says that he thinks artists and musicians should wait until they're in their late thirties before settling down and starting a family. Before then, you're much too focused on your career, hanging out with your cronies, staying up late plunking guitars. All those things that don't make you a good husband and father. I was trying to become a success and in some ways I was very selfish. With Shooter, when he asks, "Dad, can I see you for a minute," I make sure there's nothing that's going to stand in the way of our talking.

He never mentioned my time on drugs; later, he would relate it to when "Daddy used to cuss." Not that my language has ever been pure. Still, I figured I would have to tell him someday, if only because he might hear it from somebody else first. Other kids can be really cruel in their innocence and honesty. I knew it had to come from me.

"Shooter," I started. "Remember when you talked about when Daddy used to cuss." He was hooking up an electronic gadget.

"There was a reason. I still cuss, but that time there was something else involved."

"What?" he asked, deftly despatching a squad of alien hellfighters.

"I was on drugs."

"Oh, you mean you drink beer?"

"No, I did cocaine." He furrowed his brow, because he'd heard of it. "I was on drugs for twenty-one years, and I haven't been on them for a long time. Somebody's going to tell you someday and I just want you to know that I told you first. It's not anything I'm proud of, and there's nothing I can change about it, but it was a real scattered, bad time for me in there."

The next day the school called and said they were going to have a discussion about drugs and wanted to be aware of just how much I had let Shooter know about my past. They didn't want to say anything that might make him wonder about me.

Instinct. When I get the feeling I should do something, I do it. Right away. I go by my animal senses. One time, a woman "stalker" started following me around, writing me letters, going to my hometown, talking to my mother and the newspapers. She thought she was the Queen of Sheba. I was Solomon, typecast again. One morning, I got up with the kids and told them never to leave school with anybody but Richie, our housekeeper Maureen, or Jessi. That afternoon she tried to kidnap two of them.

Jessi and Maureen liked to work up to things, and they were a little concerned about Shooter's reaction to the news. The day after I told Shooter about the drugs, he was in the living room playing quietly. Maureen came in and said, "Shooter, are you okay?"

He said yeah. "Is there anything bothering you?" asked Maureen.

"Nope."

"Did anything Dad say yesterday about drugs and things bother you?"

He perked up. "About him kicking coke? Nah."

I had another confession for him that I had to face, about leaving school in the middle of the tenth grade. I always felt that one of the worst things I ever did was not finish my education. I could blame it on myself, but I always thought that you can't go to a child with a paddle in your hand and expect him to learn through fear.

Governor and Martha Wilkerson of Kentucky had gotten to be my friends and they wanted me to do a benefit. I didn't even ask them what it was about. It was a black-tie type of thing, and as I went off, after my last song before the encore, I asked one of the guys who worked for me what the benefit was for. He told me it was for Martha's Army, a program designed to encourage high school dropouts to get their General Equivalency Diploma.

I went back out and talked to the crowd. "I really believe in learning," I said. "Now I've got a pretty good job, but I have never walked into an office where I didn't feel a bit intimidated because I knew on the other side of that door there was somebody who was educated. And I'm not."

When I left the stage, Martha was on me like a duck on a junebug. "You're going to get your GED," she said. And I said I would.

I was always telling Shooter how important school was; now I was honor bound to prove it to him. It gave me a chance to really show him what it meant to me, and in a way, what he meant to me.

"My mind is thirty years from learning mode," I said to him one day after they sent me the books and tapes to study. My best thing is to have somebody work with me. "You've got to help me."

He was studying fractions at the time. I hadn't thought of fractions ever, except how to divide the door at a show or Hank Williams singing "If you love me half as much as I love you." So we sat down and worked together. He would be my teacher. Sometimes I'd be doing good, and he'd be so proud, and other times he watched me struggle. He made up questions to ask me and gave me tests. We learned together, and he was thrilled to be able to teach his dad something.

By the time I took the equivalency test, I was as ready as I was going to be. I worked on it all one day, and after eight hours, I got up and was more exhausted than I could ever remember. It wore my brain out and made me believe that anyone who understands algebra should go to a treatment center.

Still, I passed the exam, and I got my diploma. Littlefield High School sent me a ring, class of '89, which I'm proud to wear on my right hand every single day, and means I'll be attending my twenty-fifth reunion in the year 2014. If my third-grade teacher could only see me now.

MCA was in turmoil, and they had me for two more albums. I didn't want to be in the middle of that. Bowen and I had scored one number-one country record with "Rose in Paradise," and our work together had been a positive thing, but the upheavals at the company seemed insurmountable. That's when I called Jimmy and asked him for a favor. To let me go.

"There's only two things in my life," he said to me. "One of them's love, and the other is business. And you ain't never been business."

In November of 1989, I moved over to CBS, where Epic said

they would give me what I wanted: creative freedom and no "control compositions," which in effect penalizes you for writing your own material as an artist. Bob Montgomery was my producer, a good songman whom I'd known peripherally in Lubbock when he was the middle-man in Buddy, Bob, and Larry.

"I'm not intimidated by you" was Bob's favorite line to me. It was the most I got out of him. I heard that phrase so many times I began to wonder why he was being so defensive. He was really hot to team me up with Willie. "I want Willie involved in this," he said almost the first day we were in the studio.

"Oh no, you don't," I told him. "Not in Nashville. Willie don't give a shit about this. He'll bring some songs he likes to do, but he's not into that other stuff. He could care less about the arrangements. Think of him as Sinatra. He likes to come in and sing and leave."

He kept on about Willie, and so did I. "The minute Willie gets here he's gonna get on that bus, and here comes some of his old smoking and drinking buddies and they're going to have a good time out there. They're all songwriters, and Willie looks around and sees that they could be doing a bit better and maybe he should go off a bridge for them, and the next thing you know here is Willie coming around a corner and there'll be somebody behind him wailing and Willie will say 'He wrote this song and we're going to do it.' It'll be a dumb fuckin' song, and we're stuck with it. Don't put Willie through that and don't put me through that. If he wants to be here, he'll be here. Willie's got a big heart, and if a guy starts crying in the right tune, he'll do it."

Bob eventually got his way by doing the Waylon and Willie *Clean Shirt* album, which Epic thought had too many Mexican horns. They didn't do too much with my first album for them, *The Eagle*, either, despite "Wrong" finding its rightful spot on the charts. Jerry Gropp must have smiled down from left-hand Heaven.

One of the reasons I had originally gone with Epic was the presence of Marge Hunt. I'd known her since she was sixteen, and we had been friends for years. I thought she was one of the people in the A&R department who would be on my side. I reunited with Richie for the album that would become *Too Dumb for New York City*, looking to find the key to the sound we had created together in the seventies. Richie figured it started with my guitar playing, and convinced me that Br'er Rabbit's Hiding Place, the rhythmic thumb I use for strumming, should come out from undercover. Suddenly, while I was in the studio, a young guy named Doug Johnson started dropping by. I didn't know it, but he was the new head of A&R.

He told me how much he loved my work, and I was one of his inspirations. Then he started calling Richie with suggestions. When Richie told him, well, we're not finished with it yet, they changed into demands.

One night Reggie Young was in the studio, and Johnson stopped by. "I hear an Eric Clapton guitar on that," he said.

"Why don't you put it on?" I said, sitting him down in the seat behind the mixing board and pointing him at Reggie. He sat there. I looked over his shoulder. The air could be cut with a knife. I didn't move until he did.

The album was beautiful, he kept assuring me, only he wanted us to keep cutting sides. Change a verse and a chorus. Remix and remaster. I said, that's bordering on fucking with me. By the time *Too Dumb* came out, in 1992, we were both pissed off. Epic sat on the record, big-time.

Don Was had wanted to do a record with me. When I talked to the Epic A&R department, they wanted to give me a budget of only $150,000, just about what a new act gets. At this point, my old friend Marge Hunt said, "He ain't worth it."

If you can get a guy under forty years old or Waylon Jennings, you take the guy under forty. That's what they were telling me. Oh, yeah: Young Country. I had been Young Country once myself, and maybe Ernest Tubb and Carl Smith and Roy Acuff had felt me nipping at their heels. But I didn't do it at their expense.

I tried to follow in their tradition and comprehend the depth and meaning of what they were singing about. The experience.

You always need new blood. I look and listen to Travis Tritt and Leroy Parnell and Beth Nielsen Chapman and Mark Chestnutt, and I see country's next generation starting to grow. There ain't no hats-and-thighs there; just intelligent artists, searching for their dreams and singing yours.

Country is the only music I know that seems to have no age boundaries. You look out at the audience, whether it's a boot-heel saloon or state fair, and there's everything from babies to grandparents, with a lot of wild folk in between. They appreciate that you don't have to be of any one generation to know love, loss, fireworks and playing-with-fire, and that we all need to share a good time now and again.

Videos mean you have to be good-looking these days. I don't know how Ernest Tubb or Hank Locklin would fare on the small screen; they weren't what you would call pretty. Still, every new generation picks up a little from what's going on around them. George Jones and I may have chosen country, while Jerry Lee Lewis, Brenda Lee, and Johnny Cash immigrated to these fair shores; but the presence of rock and roll in our music was undeniable. Television only enhanced the glitter of Porter Wagoner, not to mention Crook and Chase.

I didn't mind a bunch of new mavericks on the scene. But Epic was telling me my time was over with. People don't want to hear you sing. Radio don't want to play you no more.

One day I went up to their office. They asked me to call up radio stations and influence them to play my record. They put me in a room, gave me a cup of coffee, handed me a couple of pages of phone numbers, and walked out. I sat there. There were cutouts of everybody but me around. Marylou placed a couple of calls for me. At one, the program director wasn't there; at another, they put her on hold.

I thought, boy, there was a time when I wouldn't do this. Then

I thought again. What did I mean, there was a time? I ain't doing it now. I told Marylou, "Let's get in the car."

You gotta know when it's time to leave. Don't look back.

I wasn't planning to record anymore. I knew I could play live for as long as I wanted; my shows still sold out, and I was doing more than a hundred dates a year. I couldn't possibly perform all my songs in a night anyway.

I didn't have to write any songs, so of course I got extraordinarily prolific. The only difference was these "poems"—they hadn't been set to music yet—were all from the perspective of a five-year-old boy.

I had started to watch *Sesame Street* because of Shooter. I missed it the first time around, because my first kids had graduated elementary television about the era of Captain Kangaroo. I love the way the show talks to children, and the pains that are taken to not mislead children, and to teach them at the same time. The music is clever as well, and when I appeared on the show to sing "Wrong," it kind of fit naturally.

I'm proud to say that I'm a personal friend of Big Bird. Whenever I appear in the New England area, Carroll Spiney and his wife, Debbie, come visit the show. Nobody believes he's Big Bird, or Oscar the Grouch, until he opens his mouth. I've seen little kids rooted to the spot when they realize he's the soul of *Sesame Street*.

Carroll and Debbie live in an old house that is just like a fairyland. A model train runs around the rafters, and toys are spread everywhere. He is transformed when he puts on the yellow Big Bird costume, all eight feet tall, his hand up in the air making the movements of the mouth and eyes, and the other moving around as the Bird's wing. There's a television set monitor inside the chest, so Carroll can see what's happening outside, though he has to do everything backward. He's the only Big Bird that's ever been.

He also is the voice of Oscar the Grouch. If both he and Big

Bird are onscreen, Debbie's back there moving Oscar. He takes great pains to make sure children don't see him with the top of his Big Bird outfit off. He knows imagination is built on illusion, and Big Bird isn't anything more than a Big Kid himself.

I played a turkey farmer in the movie *Follow That Bird.* They dressed me up in overalls and a plaid shirt, put a red bandanna in my pocket and a straw hat on my head. I hate to ruin your Thanksgiving dinner, but those gobblers are nasty creatures. I smelled like turkey for weeks.

We were sitting in the cab of a truck for one scene. I hadn't stopped smoking yet, and Carroll hadn't smoked for ten years, but sitting next to me in the small truck cab, between takes, surrounded by tobacco haze, he began thinking it wouldn't be such a bad idea.

We were covered in flies, up north of Toronto. A square cloud in the sky passed overhead, spitting lightning. It was hot. Carroll had set the top half of his costume outside the truck. We were sitting there. Suddenly, we smelled something burning. I looked over and Big Bird was going up in flames! I had set him on fire. That's a good way to get yourself strung up by an angry mob of four-year-olds.

I was thinking a lot about children, watching Shooter move toward his teens. I had written a story, with Shooter's help, about a racehorse that didn't grow. He was a miniature pony, who reminded me of when Shooter had been the shortest kid in his class. He'd worried about it, fretted on it, until one day he came home and said, "Dad, I'm not the littlest kid in my class anymore. There's this girl from Texas that just moved here."

The horse in the story, nicknamed Useless, was the runt of the litter and the pride of the farm. He was so mischievous that it was thought they were going to sell him to a traveling circus, but a lightning storm allowed Useless to become a hero, rescuing the bigger horses from the barn when a fire erupted. "The Little Horse That Didn't Grow" had saved the day.

I wrote a song, "(Some Things Come in) Small Packages," to

go along with it. Then I wrote a poem called "Dirt," remembering how I used to put some dirt in my grandpa's snuff, and how it was the best toy of all. And then I wrote "A Bad Day," which was inspired by a five-year-old friend of mine named Charlie, who lives in Tulsa and reminded me of my grandson Josh, who's always getting into scrapes; and "When I Get Big," "I'm Little," and "Cowboy Movies," where my Saturday afternoon matinee idols were seen through the eyes of a Nickelodeon and Muppet fan.

I never liked children's records; I always thought they talked down to kids. But these poems were different. I was seeing life through the eyes of a five-year-old boy, and that five-year-old boy was me. I wanted kids to know that everything they're going through, the little missteps they get in trouble over, I got in trouble for that, too. That's okay. That's part of growing up.

I was getting back my sense of wonder. Going back to the dreaming days of lying back on the grass, looking up into the sky, "off to see the world / If I could only fly."

Shooter read the poems and said, "Dad, they look like songs to me." I started arranging them into verses and choruses. Jessi added her encouragement. Epic had just started a children's label, but they wanted a cast of superstars to do the singing. That wasn't what I had in mind. I remembered when I had sung "Mommas Don't Let Your Babies Grow Up to Be Cowboys" and "The Tennessee Waltz" at Shooter's school; there had been a children's chorus backing me up. They'd be the only superstars on any children's record I envisioned.

Someone at Epic played it for Shelley Duvall, the actress, who passed the word along to Lou Adler, who used to produce the Mamas and the Papas. He had just had a little girl, which made him more than susceptible to the charms of children, and had started an offshoot label called Ode 2 Kids. He said, "You've got me in your pocket if you want it." I loved his enthusiasm.

At the same time, Clifford "Barney" Robertson called me after many years. He and his wife Carter had been Waylors ten years before, and the last time they'd seen me I was a crazed man. They had started a family, and phoned to say hello. What had he been doing?

"You're not going to believe this, but I produce children's records," said Barney.

Well, I had something he wouldn't believe, either. I asked him to produce these songs, and we decided to use only country instruments. Sonny Curtis came along for the acoustic ride. From my Waylors band, steel guitarist Robby Turner, drummer Jeff Hale, and Jigger pretended they were back in the sandbox. Even Oscar the Grouch grumbled a little bit from inside his trash can.

*Cowboys, Sisters, Rascals and Dirt* wasn't a grown man singing children's songs. I thought it was a big rascal singing about little rascals, and when I got to my own little rascal, well, "Shooter, you are a friend of mine. . . . Your life makes my life worthwhile."

It was like coming face to face with a younger version of myself, walking down a street in Littlefield, bare feet meeting tooled cowboy boots. Both of us couldn't know what the future would bring, so it was free to lead anywhere, to anything.

Possibility. Hope. The excitement of the moment of creation. All I knew for sure was that songs and ideas were starting to pour out of me, sometimes so fast I couldn't write one down before the next one started growing. I'd found my way back to me, at last.

CHAPTER

12

# THE TROJAN HOSS

And then there's the road.

For any migrating performer, travel takes on a life all its own. The shows become stopovers; the highway is where you spend most of your time. In transit. In transition.

You enter a strange space when you get on the bus. You're not home, and you're not there yet. You're on the way.

Mostly, you're living in the present. Day to day. All you're really concerned with is getting to the show, wherever it might be. Everything else is looking around at your surroundings, taking stock of where you've been, where you might be headed, cruise-controlling the speedometer. You have a lot of time to think about what you're doing, and yet you're doing it.

It's a traveling universe, your own private world that consists of whoever is on the road with you, the jokes you share, the camaraderie and idle chatter and tall tales and slices of life you encounter; and then leave. The Flying W.

Having a bus helps, because it's like your traveling home. You can eat on it, sleep on it, and like I did for a while, never get off it except to play. It's filled up with everyone who was ever in your band, hopped on after a show and stayed for a few more towns, became family or friends, or joined the crew, who might be the motleyist bunch of them all, and really sees to it that we all get from one place to another. Ready to move on.

On. That's as good a description as any. When I'm home at *Southern Comfort*, outskirting Nashville, I'm most definitely off, sitting in my big chair with a remote control and a glass of iced tea by my side waiting for the boxing matches to start. Dinner at five? You got a deal.

But when I step on board Shooter IV, even if we have a day off to play golf and kick back along the way, I'm *on*, tapping into the energy of whirlwind touring, five cities in seven days, eleven cities in two weeks, twenty-five cities in two months, one hundred cities in a year. It gets in your blood.

If you do it for thirty years, it becomes your natural rhythm. You might get off the road and feel tired, beat, needing to sleep in your own bed. All you want to do is lay down and rest. Once you get rested, you get restless. Then you're back out there again.

Jessi says we don't play music for a living. We bounce for a living. The real rhythm of the road is up and down, jostling and knocking your body around as you navigate the speed bumps. You can get dingy. Silly. It's really not natural to stay on a damn bus, all day and all night, going from one place to another. Everyone tries to grab some sleep, but you can't, at least not more than an hour or two at a snatch. Cradled in your bunk, drapes drawn, no light, you wake and think it must be morning. It never is.

When you first start out, you think you have it made. You're young and ready for anything. You shake your head at those unfortunate people who have regular jobs, go home every night, eat supper, fall asleep, and start the same old ritual the next morning when the alarm goes off. The further along you get, the more you realize that maybe they have the best setup of all.

It works in reverse, too. They look at you sailing down the highway and think that must be wonderful. It's glamorous, no doubt about that, unless you take into consideration how you itch around the edges because you haven't had time to wash, and are bone tired from lack of deep sleep, and haven't eaten anything more than a ham sandwich from a backstage deli tray.

Yeah, we've got the video player and the stereo system, the microwave and games galore. We can stop at any truck stop and fill up on the hamburgers, T-shirts, and souvenir postcards that are the stock in trade of Roadside America. We know that the next destination is a show where we'll play our music and people will let us know how much they appreciate our coming by to visit them.

But when you've traveled three hundred miles on a bus . . . well, you've traveled three hundred miles on a bus.

Shut the door and let's get rolling.


We've got a full house this trip. Every band member that's ever played with me is along for the ride, scattered around the inside of a bus that looks like every bus I ever owned, from the Black Maria through a succession of metallic Eagles to my latest Prevost. This is the Quitter's Party to end all parties, where we sit around and remember those moments where we lived, breathed, and played music together. Being a band.

The bass players are sitting over in the corner, talking about whether to go five-string. There's Jigger, and Duke Goff, and my brother Tommy, and Sherman Hayes, and Kevin Hogan and Sonny Ray and even Paul Foster. The guitarists take up the whole back of the bus. Gropp is leading the pack, which is fitting for someone who worked for me five different times. Gary Scruggs shoots the breeze with Billy Ray Reynolds, while Rance and Gordon play a little Farkle. There's Jigger, again! He moved over to the six-of-strings section a couple of years ago, and he ain't left since.

The drummers are grouped around the kitchen table, beating

out calypso rhythms. Richie's over there, Jack Huffman and Jeff Hale. The steel section mostly consists of Mooney, Fred Newall, and Robby Turner trading licks; Robby's mom Berniece and dad Doyle were in Hank's original Drifting Cowboys, and when he was twelve, he took guitar lessons from legend Jimmy Bryant. Mooney's telling Robby how he wrote his hit song, "Psycho Falanges." Robby is tying keyboardist Fred Lawrence's shoes together. They'll have so many knots he'll have to cut 'em off. Sometimes I'd hate to have to travel on the band bus. They're crazy over there!

Right now, though, they're all over visiting me. I'm like Ulysses, and Troy is about to fall.

I always wanted a band. I need guys I can depend on, to be my cast of characters, and since I never use a set list, whatever gang that winds up playing with me has to watch what I'm doing, otherwise I win the game of Stump the Band. There's only one time I'm the honcho, and that's when we're up on the stage. I don't want to be any big boss the rest of the time. I never cared for that star-sideman mentality.

I like looking around and seeing Jigger step on one of his pedals and ride into a solo. I had a blast when Robby would do his Elvis or Liberace imitation (hint: they were one and the same). I used to love when Richie would step on the beat in back of me and I'd turn around, and he'd be sticking out his plate with the two upper false teeth on his tongue, waggling it, laughing while he whacked out the 4/4.

The Waylors are the only constant I have on the road. We are like an Indian tribe; once you join, you're always a member. That's what the Quitter's Party is about. No matter how you got on board the bus, or the circumstances under which you left, it's a way to get together with your fellow road warriors and swap war stories. We're a very select bunch. When Cheryl Ladd asked me on her television special how you get to become a Waylor, I told her it was easy. "Walk around and say 'Hi chief.'"

Road life is harder than it looks, once the initial romance wears off. The only thing that'll get you through the hard times is a sense of humor. You make a lot of stupid jokes on the road, and most of them sound pretty suspect if you tell 'em in mixed company a few weeks later. We never know where road humor comes from, or where it goes when we get off the bus. But at the time it starts you laughing, finding a good punch line will get you through a lot of bad patches. We broke down one time, and Duke Goff crossed the road and put one of those orange cones on his head and called himself Captain Diesel. Pretty soon we had a whole cartoon going, with Diesel, whose real name was Cecil, and a sidekick named Rusty Reflector. His archenemy was Dirty Old Lowshoulders, and there was Ramp Woman, his gal, who worked in a truck stop. Had a little dog named Bringawrench.

Yeah, it seemed funnier at the time. But it made the hours we sat by the side of the road go fast, and we got to the show.

That's all the goal you need on the road. When do we go on? How much farther till we get there? Sometimes it's as much of a challenge to arrive at the gig as it is playing well. With bizarre weather conditions, missed connections, and garbled directions, it's lucky anybody gets anywhere at all. They used to book us eight hundred miles apart. We'd run on the stage, run off the stage, take off in time to get ready during the last sixty miles of the trip to jump back on the stage, and then do it again.

Sometimes you literally go around in circles. We were seven miles from Philadelphia when we stopped at a diner to eat. The Lyle brothers were traveling with me, and when Richie started feeling tired, Gene Lyle took over driving. We were playing poker in the back. About four hours later, he yawned, stretched, and said, "Somebody's going to have to spell me." I looked outside, and there was a sign that said "Philadelphia: 15 miles."

Flying adds a whole dimension of derring-do, and one I'm not sure I enjoy. I don't feel in control in the air. The hardest time I had going anywhere, I was in Dallas, and we were playing in Longview, over by the Louisiana border. I saw I couldn't make it by land, so I chartered this little twin-engine airplane. We got in it, took off, and all of a sudden the lights went out. We landed at another airport and switched to a Cessna single-engine. I wasn't happy to be there. I remembered Buddy. I was a little out of it, and I made sure to tell the pilots before going to sleep up in the air that if I woke up and this airplane was going down, I was going to whip their asses all the way to the ground.

We ran out of gas and had to land in Athens. My grandmother's mother was buried there. They had about three lights on their runway. It's sixty miles from Longview. It's already nine forty-five, and we're supposed to start at nine.

A cop gets a work release inmate to drive me to the show. Ninety miles an hour. We get there, and the promoter says, "You missed it. You're not going to get paid." Thanks, pal.

Most of the time we did make it. Duke had never flown before and we had a festival to play in Riverside, California, up in the hills. There was so much traffic we couldn't drive. After a turbulent flight from Dallas, we hopped on a two-engine plane in L.A. and started flying through the canyons to Palm Springs. Duke was pale as a sheet, holding on with white knuckles. It was a bumpy flight, and every time we'd hit an air pocket, his eyes would cross.

I asked him what was wrong. "I've never flown before," he moaned.

I almost didn't have the heart to tell him that we were fixin' to get on a helicopter next. When that took off, he put his one hand on the seat, his other on the roof, and didn't move the whole time.

My rule now is three hundred miles between shows, a couple more if you're not playing the night before. It doesn't make traveling through a New England spring snowstorm, or an Oklahoma thunderstorm, or a South Dakota hailstorm any easier. At least, though, you have a fighting chance.

The one thing the road doesn't need is prima donnas. Nobody is catered to, and that goes from the lowest member of my crew to me. We all have a function to fulfill, and it's a challenge to make sure the shows run right. The one thing that I hate to hear is "It's not my job." If it needs doing, it should be done. People look at and applaud the musicians, but somewhere, off to the side of the stage, there's a guy who has outsmarted the room, set up the equipment and made sure it worked, inspired the band to play their instruments without worrying why they can't hear them, saw that they're well-lit so a mood can be created and sustained, tuned a guitar and soldered a patch chord, setting up and breaking down from early morning to late, late at night.

I'll turn around and give them a thumbs-up after the first few songs, just to let the crew know I appreciate them. You can almost hear them breathe a sigh of relief.

It's close quarters, no doubt about that. There's only so much privacy you can maintain, and whenever a small bunch of people are rubbing right up against one another, you can bet that sometimes emotions will snap out of hand. You get mad quick, and friends quicker. Everybody takes a turn being the butt of the day's humor. You'll get on somebody and ride his ass, and he better laugh, too, because if he don't, it's going to be three days more of ragging.

Sometimes you go crazy. There's a motel in Fresno that still has a flood line up the side of its adobe wall because we put Blue Cheer in the water fountain. In Ohio, I stuck a duck from room service behind the heater grill; this was in the summer. I never went back the next winter to see how it smelled. John Cash once cut off the legs of all the furniture in the room and then called the bellhop, acting like nothing was the matter.

In 1979, for my forty-second birthday, the remaining members of the Crickets, Joe B and J.I., presented me with a special gift: the motorcycle that Buddy Holly had bought on his way back to Lubbock in May 1958.

It's always been one of my favorite Buddy stories. You can see him and the Crickets getting off the plane in Dallas. They had been touring incessantly since early January, from a World Hit Parade tour that took them as far as Australia, to an English jaunt and then back to America with Alan Freed and the Big Beat. Returning home after four nonstop months, they must have been elated at the heights they'd ascended, and badly in need of blowing off a little steam.

They loved Marlon Brando in *The Wild One*, and when they got to Dallas as a connection to Lubbock, they decided on the spur of the moment to buy motorcycles and drive back home on them. They took a cab into the city and walked into a Harley-Davidson shop. They had their eyes set on a trio of 74-inchers, but the proprietor didn't think they had any money and treated them like a bunch of bums. "Hell, you boys couldn't even begin to handle the payments on that."

They then went over to Miller's Motorcycles, which specialized in English bikes. There, Joe B. and J.I. bought a Triumph each, a TR6 and Thunderbird, respectively, while Buddy picked out a maroon and black Ariel Cyclone, with a high compression 650cc Huntmaster engine. They paid cash, bought matching Levi jackets and peaked caps with wings on them, and rode home through a thunderstorm. For that moment in time, they were on top of the world.

· Buddy's dad had kept the Ariel until 1970, when he sold it to someone in Austin. J.I. and Joe B. found it, had it shipped up to northern Texas, where on my birthday, I walked into my hotel room after the show and saw it sitting there.

What else could I do? I swung my leg over it, stomped on the kickstarter, and it burst into roaring life. First kick. It was midnight, and it sounded twice as loud bouncing off the walls of that hotel room. I knew Buddy wouldn't mind.

On another birthday, they got me but good. We were in Salem, Oregon, and as usual, toward the end of the show, I started "Suspicious Minds," at which point Jessi is supposed to walk in from the side of the stage singing it to me with a hand-held microphone.

That night, my road manager, David Trask, slipped on Jessi's suede dress, her blouse, a wig, and a scarf and put a roll of paper towel in his hand. I heard Jessi's voice from the wings, but out comes this *thing* sashaying toward me. I almost swallowed my guitar pick.

David was with me almost eleven years, and I can never forget the first time he worked on my stage. He had come to Nashville knocking on doors, and Randy Fletcher, our production manager, took a liking to him. He asked him if he could tune guitars. David figured all you needed to do was line up the strings on a strobe tuner. That night we had a concert at the Houston Livestock and Rodeo Show. I never did a soundcheck, and they have a custom of driving you around the arena, waving at the crowd, before depositing you on stage. I walked up to my guitar proudly, slung it over my shoulder, and hit a chord. It was in tune all right, except the strings were all an octave low.

David hid behind the amp line while I blamed it on Hank Sr.'s ghost. It was such a full-blown mistake that I had to forgive him, but I told Randy to find him something else to do. About that time, in 1981, I had gathered everyone together and told them that I was fixing to cut the payroll and scale everything back. Randy said David was honest, and he stayed on to collect the money and settle the shows.

I didn't trust too many people at the time. Especially promoters. I wanted my money in cash. Not certified checks. Not cashier's checks. Not checks in the mail. Cash. Half as a deposit, and the rest the night of the show.

After five or six shows a week, that would add up to a lot of greenbacks. Sometimes David would come off the road with a couple of hundred thousand bucks. We had a safe on the bus, but that didn't rest David's mind any. Sometimes he'd stuff all the money in a pillowcase and sleep with it.

You could bet he'd sometimes get paranoid. On another birthday, in Rockford, Illinois, a fan gave me a big mylar balloon. We brought it on the bus and left it there, while the party traveled up to Minneapolis. About two o'clock in the morning, my stomach felt upset and I called David looking for Rolaids. "There's some on the bus," he said. "I'll get them for you."

He went out to the bus, pushed aside the back curtain, flipped the lights on, took the Rolaids out from the drawer. Checked the safe where the tour money was stashed. Switched off the lights. That mylar balloon had followed him down the aisle, and as he turned to go, he stared it right in the face. We heard the scream up on the second floor of the hotel.

I'll tell you how honest David Trask is. Once, in the course of organizing our finances, we audited four years of on-the-road expenses, down to show percentages and gas receipts. In the end, we owed him a dollar.


We were pulling out of Fort Smith, Arkansas, when the posse surrounded us. Cops everywhere, lights flashing. They pulled out our driver and held him at gunpoint while they checked identification and vehicle numbers.

I don't know why they noticed us. I mean, isn't a bus painted all black, down to the grill and bumpers, just another interstate vehicle? It turned out a convenience store had been robbed a few miles back, and we fit their description.

When the Black Maria pulled up by the stage door of the theater, people knew who had arrived. Me, too. It was the first real bus I'd ever owned, a Bluebird. Before that we'd had a succession of limousines and station wagons, beat-up motorhomes and pickup trucks. Now we were going to travel in style; all of us, band and crew and me, on one bus. We looked ominous.

Hank Sr. rode that bus with us. We'd glance up from our stupors and card playing and he'd be sitting in the front passenger seat, hat and all. Or we'd be going down a smooth road and hear a clatter from the back. It wasn't that we were haunted; we were proud to have his guiding spirit riding shotgun.

Over in the driver's seat was Harley Pinkerman. He had a little bit of the dandy in him, like Porter Wagoner, with a fine silver pompadour all puffed up, and he even dressed like him. The rest of us might straggle out of the bus like bums, but Harley would have on his zipper Beatle boots and a finely decorated jacket. When we'd stop at a biscuit-and-gravy place to have breakfast, they'd ignore me and go straight for him. "I know y'ins somebody," they'd say. "Y'ins from the Opry." They thought he was the star.

I think Harley drove on the road just to play high-stakes poker. He tells people that he won my bus in a game once, but there's no way in his life he could beat me. He did seem to clean up on Bobby Bare, though. One time, there was fifteen thousand dollars in the pot, all riding on one hand. Bare and Johnny Darrell had dropped out, and it was down to me and Harley. Every time he would raise me, I'd say, "Harley, better think of the wife and kids."

We were playing jokers wild. He had three aces showing, and had the good-looking hand, but I had a joker showing, and an ace, three, four, and five in the hole. Mine was a straight flush. Sometimes you think your eyes are burning through the cards, you're looking at them so hard, making sure you ain't made a mistake. But he's raising me, and I know all he can have is three aces. I've got his other ace. The only other thing he can have is a full house; you need four of a kind to beat a straight flush.

"Goddammit, Harley, I'm telling you I got you beat. You knock it off. Quit raising me." Everytime I said that, he'd pop in another thousand. The pot was close to twenty grand. Finally, I had to say, "I'm going to call you. I could own you, but I'm going to call you."

He turned over his full house and I turned over my straight flush. He ate the fuckin' cards. Chewed 'em right up.

Later, his daughter Kathy married my son Buddy. When we have a grandchild together, it'll go to show that blood is thicker than gasoline.

The Black Maria was a gas-burner, and Harley drove it until I needed to go diesel. Gasoline engines aren't set up for high mileages. You needed something to last a million miles. After I put a diesel in it, I gave it to Rick to use for the concessions. When I decided to sell the Black Maria for good, every rock and roller tried to buy it. I wound up giving it to a local black church in Nashville, and they still keep it going. That must take some powerful praying.

You got to love your bus. For a time, I never left it. The generator ran for eight straight years; we never turned it off. We'd just wear them out and get another. When my RCA contract came through in the mid-seventies, I ordered one of the last Silver Eagles made in Belgium. It's a legendary bus in country-music circles for good reason, all torsion-bar suspension and featherbed ride. They upped the luxury standard for country performers considerably when they became popular in the seventies, just about the time that the interstate system started taking over from the four-lane blacktops. Ninety thousand dollars was what they cost then, and I'll never forget when they called me from the airport to say "Your Eagle has landed." I went out to look at it and there sat a bus with a seat in it. No tires. I guess all you had to do was flap its wings and it would take you to Duluth.

After three or four years, we stepped up to a Golden Eagle. When Richie sold it to John Hartford, we bought our first Prevost, which we called Shooter I. They're the Cadillacs of tour buses, shifting by computer chip instead of by hand, and they're made up in Canada. We're up to Shooter IV now, and to celebrate, we've gone to a forty-five-foot length instead of the usual forty. That extra not-quite two yards will come in handy over the next hundred thousand miles, and works out to about an inch every 1666.66 miles. Cheap at twice the price.

"Play 'Japikta'!" yells some guy out in the audience. I don't know what he's talking about. We do one song and then another.

"Play 'Japikta'!" he hollers again. I never take requests, but I'm curious to understand what he's asking for. After the third time he shouts it out, and figuring he ain't going to stop, I say, "Man, we don't know that song."

"Oh, yes you do," comes the response. "You played it last night."

I turn back to the band. "You guys know that song?" They shake their heads no.

I'm about to go on with the show, when the guy lets fly with "Play 'Japikta'!" Okay, I think, Mr. Wise-ass. You sing the song. Which he does: "Japikta fine time to leave me, Lucille. . . ."

Well, I'll be a suck-egg mule.

There's always the threat of violence when you get up on stage. You don't know when trouble will come your way or how you'll deal with it.

I recorded a Harlan song for *Nashville Rebel* called "Green River," but I never liked it. Even when people yelled from the audience for it, I wouldn't play it. "That's a terrible song," I'd say, half-kidding. "I don't do that no more."

One night, I must've embarrassed a guy who called it out. I was starting back to the dressing room when he came at me, all fire in the eyes. He turned me around with one hand on my shoulder and said, "I just wanted to hear 'Green River' and you smarted off at me. How'd you like me to slap some of that smartness out of you."

I was staring at his belt buckle. He was big; he looked like he'd fight a circle saw. I knew I was in trouble. My adrenaline started flowing. You're only as fast as your fear carries you, and when you come down to it, there's only a thin line between cowards and heroes. Sometimes being one is smarter than going down as another. "Look," I said to him, "I have had one hundred and seventy-five fights in my life, and I've lost every one of them. You'd do well not to fuck with me because I'm bound to win one someday." He started laughing, and so did I, and we became friends after that.

Sometimes the endings weren't as happy. Over the holiday week that Jessi first came to Phoenix to visit me, we were playing at J.D.'s. It was traditional for us to celebrate our homecoming right before or after Christmas, and we had just finished our show for the night. The place had cleared, it was about one-thirty, and I was getting ready to head for the front door.

"Chief!" yelled Jimmy Gray, who played bass for me at the time. "Don't come out here. There's a man with a gun!"

I had my black limousine parked by the entrance. Ben Dorsey was driving it. Ben Dorsey. I couldn't leave the band. Sure enough, a man was standing there waving a pistol, and he poked it toward me.

I thought I could talk to him. He wasn't listening. He told me to get Ben out of the car. Ben just sat behind the wheel, frozen. He had all the doors locked and wouldn't let anybody in. The guy pointed his gun at my head. "You tell him to open the door or I'll blow your brains out."

I said, "Ben, maybe you might open the door." Ben didn't move. "Ben, get your ass out of there!" He moved even less.

Finally the guy waved us back into the bar. I'd seen him hanging around after the show, over in the corner, in an area where people usually didn't sit. J.D.'s served food there during the weekend afterhours, but this was midweek and it was closed. We walked all the way back to the stage area. It seemed like we covered miles. One time I started turning around and he pushed me a little bit. I could feel my anger rising. "Wait a minute," I said, and he aimed the gun toward me. I thought, that ain't gonna work.

When I get in a panic situation, time slows down for me. I can get scared as bad as anybody in certain situations, but I've always been able to calm down and try to figure a way out. We turned toward the dressing room. It was constructed of nothing more than Sheetrock; you could put your hand through it, a door in the drywall, and that was it. I stared at the guy with the gun. He looked high, and scared, and that made us even more frightened.

"What the hell do you want?" I asked him.

"I want your money" was his reply.

"I haven't got any money."

"You mean you're going to die for nothing?" he said. That's when I knew that if somebody made a wrong move, this sonofabitch would kill them.

I smiled at him. I didn't even mean it; I couldn't think of anything else to do. He regarded me quizzically, confused, uncertain, and lowered the gun. As he did, I spun into the dressing room, slamming and throwing the bolt shut on the door. He didn't know what was in the room, or that he could just pop up against the wall and bust it down.

"Your ass is mud now," I hollered over the partition. "I'm going out the side door here and get the cops. They're going to be all over this place in two minutes." Of course, there was no side door. I was trapped.

The guy grabbed Jimmy Gray, throwing him to the floor and holding the gun to his head. I couldn't see what was happening, but I could tell Jimmy's voice wasn't normal. "Chief . . ." he called.

"Is that you, Jimmy?"

"Uh, yeah. . . . Chief, you can come out now. He's gone."

Jimmy Gray's brother, Paul, had been killed in Atlanta about six months before. He had been slated to come out on the road with us and had been shot after a party. "Jimmy, it looks like it's going to wind up like your little brother, isn't it?"

"Yeah," he choked back. "It's all right. Open the door!" Which told me the guy was still out there, telling Jimmy what to say.

"I know you haven't left, you bastard. I gave you a chance. Now I'm leaving." I slammed the couch down like I was shutting a door. He fired at the dressing room. The bullet went through the wall.

In the meantime, Richie had left early with a girl. He had stopped to get something to eat, and found the keys to the band's station wagon in his pocket, so he headed back to the club. He saw the limousine in the front of the club, with Ben locked inside, not moving, and didn't think anything of it. Ben was like a statue. All he was missing was the pigeon shit.

Richie walked into the bar. The door was open. An old man was over in the corner downstairs, mopping. Upstairs, the long bar stretched along the right. He saw a cluster of people down at the other end. Richie had just smoked a "doobie," and his heart started pounding when he saw the guy with the gun.

He ducked down behind the bar and slithered along its length. He ran into James D. Jr., holding a pistol, crouched behind the Lone Star tap. When he got to the other end, he looked around the corner and saw Jimmy lying on the floor, with the gun to his head. Their eyes met. Jimmy looked terrified. Richie pulled back in disbelief.

While I distracted him slamming the door, Richie ran for the exit. The guy saw him and took off after him. We all piled out. I grabbed James Jr.'s gun and fired a shot at the top of the door. There were sirens in the distance. James Jr. slammed the front door, locking him outside. The guy raced back and forth, caged, and then took off for the rear fence. Cops spilled out of their cars. There was gunfire, and he fell, sprawled in the parking lot, paralyzed. Later, they searched his car and found a pair of baby shoes in the back. That hurt me worse than if he'd shot me.

Ben got out of the car when the newspapers started coming around. I was standing there, trying to get my composure back and figure out what had happened, and Ben comes over. "Tell 'em, Chief, tell 'em."

"Tell 'em what?"

"Tell 'em how I jumped in front of you and saved your life." He turned to the reporters. "I did. The guy was fixin' to shoot him, and I was going to take the bullet."

Ben is The Road, and everybody who's ever "road" a highway has a Ben Dorsey story. He worked for me then. He works for Willie now. Sometimes people come up to Ben and think he's Willie and take pictures of him. They don't know it, but they've gotten a souvenir snapshot of one of the most exasperating and lovable characters who ever wore a backstage pass.

He's what used to be called a band boy. A valet and driver. Over the years, Ben brushed the clothes and steered the wheel for the likes of Hank Thompson, Faron Young, Ray Price, Denver

Pyle, and even John Wayne. He'd learned the tricks of the trade, and if you were hungry at four in the morning, Ben could go out in the quietest town and bring you back a six-course chicken dinner. Whenever we thought something was impossible, we'd think, "Well, Ben Dorsey could've done it!"

That didn't mean you didn't have to watch him all the time. He was a little squirrely, with a million excuses on why he wasn't where he should be when, and talking these tall tales driving down the freeway eighty miles an hour. I'd tell him to watch the road, and he'd say, "I am watching the road—through the rearview mirror!"

Once, in Vegas, these two women took a fancy to Ben. We were playing at the Nugget, and he walked in, one on each arm, though it looked like they were holding him up. He was even skinnier than usual. I told him if they ran him any more ragged, he'd be nothin' but head and ass. "You know what, Chief," he said. "They've got me down in that motel room, and all they let me have is buttermilk and oysters."

Good Doctor Ben Dorsey, he called himself. He'd follow me around, eleven steps behind. Once I stopped short and he ran right into me. He was great to wind up. When Willie's wife threw the ashtray at the Wagon Wheel and hit Ben, Faron Young came over and told him he was going to call a lawyer. "We're going to get you a lot of money," he said.

Ben, with a bandage on his head, goes to Faron's office the next day. He sits there while Faron's lawyer makes a phone call. "Mr. Dorsey will settle for nothing less than a million dollars. This man will never be the same."

Ben sat in eager anticipation. The lawyer shouted into the phone. "What do you mean? He's wounded and hurt. We will not take nine hundred thousand dollars!" He slammed the receiver into the cradle.

Ben was shocked. "You should'a took it. You should'a took it!"

The next day the lawyer called again. "We've considered your nine-hundred-thousand-dollar offer and . . . you're not going to give that much? Five hundred thousand dollars?" Ben is flinging his arms about, shaking his head.

"Take it, goddammit!" He's screaming.

The lawyer says no. "Mr. Dorsey is not used to being treated this way. We'd rather sue." Ben slumped in the chair.

The offer was down to ten thousand dollars after a couple of days. Ben was in turmoil. The phone call is made. "You're offering us nothing!" Ben hears. "And you're going to sue us?" Ben buried his face in his hands, going "Oh, no, no, no . . ."

I see him these days whenever Willie and I tour together. And sometimes, during the course of the evening, whenever Ben starts helping out too much, introducing me to his wife, Mary, for the fourth time, or handing me a sheaf of business cards that people have slipped to him for some scheme or another, I'll shoot Willie a glance. "Ben?" he'll say.

"Ben," I'll say. And that's all we need to say.

It's a lot quieter for me on the road these days. It wasn't always that way. I'd never trade a moment of the memories I've stored up, but I wouldn't want to go back and live it again. Hell, I was lucky enough to live through it the first time around.

I've had my share of "Rainy Day Women." Most of them have pretty wonderful lives now, without me. There's no need of messing that up. Traveling from town to town to town, especially in my early years, I craved companionship. You never see a "rainy day woman" when things are good. You run into her when there's a problem, and stay with her until you lose your problems in her arms.

I did very little damage. When you're in the public eye, there's always women who want to sleep with you because of who you are, but I never worried about what they were thinking. I only cared about what they were doing. I would run from one to another in hotels, and a lot of them probably never even knew I was there.

Like Richie. Sometimes he needed help with his girls. They

used to call him Short Stroke. I'd go step on his back when he was in the sack, and the girl would say thank you.

One of the funniest things that ever happened to me was when I was younger and on the road in L.A. with a certain well-known female country artist. No names, please. We were mostly friends, but one night she was alone, and I was alone, and we started circling each other. We finally wound up in a room, talking. One thing led to another and then another until we had climbed between the sheets. We were both a little embarrassed, dropping the "em." "I ain't never done this before," she told me.

"Well, you ain't never done it yet," I said, as I climbed out of bed and headed for the door. We laughed about that for a lot of years after.

I've always respected women. Not to brag, but I've had most races, creeds, and livestock. A lot of performers, if they go to bed with a woman on the road, they think of her as a slut. As a person and a man, what does that make them then? Lowlife or high living, you give as good as you get, and I don't think women's sex lives have a thing to do with the kinds of human beings they are. I learned that from knowing Sue Brewer, who was one of the most gracious people that ever walked the face of the earth, and loved being with men. The way she put it, "The worst I ever had was wonderful."

It's far more touching to me to look out at the audience and see a little girl who is finding in my music the key to her life's trials. When I was playing at J.D.'s, there was a woman named Topper who came every night. All she did was sit at a table and cry at some of the songs, because her heart had been broken. The music helped her express her feelings. There was nothing between us, and wasn't going to be. We never needed to take advantage of that friendship.

Looking down at some sweet young thing in a pair of tight jeans and a half-undone blouse screaming in the front row, things haven't changed much. Without wiggling my ass, I still know how to push her buttons. All it takes is a look.

"Sit down," I'll tell her when she's at her wildest. "I've got boots older than you."

We played for President Carter at Freedom Hall on the night he tried to rescue the hostages from Iran. He couldn't make the show, but the First Lady, Rosalynn, came out, and we walked down the receiving line of U.S. Senators before we went on.

The Secret Service was a little nervous about Deakon and Boomer. They kept coming up to us and asking politely how we were doing; we knew they had metal detectors. "Why don't you ask them if they've got any guns, and put that detector away?" I asked. They didn't look amused.

It was a fun show, though I can't imagine what they would have thought if they looked in the back of the maintenance tent and saw the crew chopping out lines of cocaine for whoever needed a quick pick-me-up.

I liked Carter a lot, and I got a lot of flack for ignoring him that one time. I didn't do it on purpose, though he worried that I didn't like him. He had asked Buddy, "Where's your dad? Is something wrong?" and Buddy could only shrug and say "He's just not here."

Later when Shooter was about a year and a half old, Jimmy and Rosalynn invited us for lunch. They sent a car, and sat Shooter, bottle and all, in the President's seat in the Cabinet Room. She was smart and savvy, and I thought Jimmy Carter was probably too good a man for the job.

We went back to the White House when President Reagan was in office. Shooter was studying about the government in school, and I made some calls to see what we might visit in Washington, D.C. We got all the way to the Oval Office. It was a different me than the last time I had been a presidential invitee; I was clean, for one.

Maybe because I was so late for so many years, I've become very punctual. If I say I'm going to knock on your door at quarter to one, you'll hear me knocking at twelve forty-four and fifty-nine seconds. I don't like to keep people waiting, and I don't like it when people keep me waiting. It's a waste of time for both of us.

When we arrived, Reagan was out in the garden with the Israeli prime minister. We were supposed to meet at eleven. Shooter knew how I was. I will leave.

Shooter had on a suit and tie, and shoes that were too small. His feet were hurting. He said, "Dad, Ronald Reagan told us we could go in there at eleven o'clock. It's eleven o' five now. Are we staying or leaving?" The Secret Service guys cracked up.

The party's over. Time to head out of here.

Hey, it's been good to meet-and-greet you, too. I ain't been up in this neck of the woods for a while. I think we'll be back in the summer, or this fall. Or maybe next week. Sometimes I don't know if we're coming or going. I have to look at the itinerary.

Let me know how you're making out, and if there's anything I can do to help. Say hi to your wife/cousin/momma/best friend/ bandmatebusinesspartnerbrother-in-law for me.

We've got a long way to travel tonight. They say the road is closed before the state line so we might have to go the long way around. Mississippi floods have washed out some of the bridges from Milwaukee. There's construction west. A six-vehicle pileup outside of town. Speed traps. Traffic.

Thanks for stopping by. Be seeing you.

Where do we go to from here?

CHAPTER

13

# THE FOUR HORSEMEN

Inside the vocal booth. Ocean Way Studios, Hollywood:

*"You look like the guy who picked up the check for the Last Supper."*

*"One more mistake, and out you go."*

*"Willie tuned me out so long ago, he can't hear what I'm saying. Look, he's pretending to listen to us."*

*"Everybody turned everybody off."*

*"Want to do that one all over again?"*

*"I'll do it all over you."*

*"I don't give a shit. When you figure out I really don't give a shit, the world will be better for you."*

*"Could you move it over a little bit, so I don't have to stare at your ass?"*

*"We're gonna make a hillbilly out of you yet."*

*"Kris, tell them to kiss my ass."*

*"I may look like I wasn't paying attention but I am."*

*"You gotta put your headphones on, or should I kick you when you're supposed to come in?"*

*"Aren't you glad you're you?"*

*"Make it up if you want to."*

*"I'd like to do it in another key."*

*"I'd like to slow it down."*

*"I got behind and never caught up."*

*"This song is getting slaughtered in here; everybody's got a different idea."*

*"There went my one shot for the record."*

*"You're the one starting it out there, Cochise."*

*"I'm not singing the line before so it's never me."*

*"I'll be there to help you when you need it."*

*"I ain't got a word in edgewise for twenty minutes."*

*" 'Been waiting'—is that Been Dorsey waiting?"*

*"Every time I think . . . fortunately, I don't do that often."*

*"John, we'll get back there in the repeat, godammit."*

*"The truth may set you free. These days you know the truth and the truth will leave you."*

*"I couldn't find my ass with a bull fiddle."*

*"I've played everything but an extension cord."*

*"Are you going to wear the same T-shirt all week?"*

*"I guess it's true people get to look like their pets."*

*"You hear the one about the dog named Sir Francis Bacon? It was a strange name for a dog, but it was a strange dog. He screwed pigs."*

*"I don't like anything I can't pronounce. I hate France."*

*"What do you mean, Waylon? They've got fine wine, beautiful women, and five hundred kinds of cheese."*

*"So's Fort Worth."*

There's the four of us standing there, grouped around microphones. The Highwaymen. John, Kris, Willie, and me.

I don't think there are any other four people like us. If we added one more, or replaced another, it would never work. Nobody else was considered when the idea for a group first starting growing. There was never a fifth wheel.

John says that we came together because we all have a life commitment to the music. We know the same songs, but we sing them from different perspectives. We can blend the early country of the Carter Family with Texas swing, southern gospel, and rockabilly, and each of us feels comfortable singing real slices of life. There's not one of us who hasn't come face to face with his own mortality, and many's the time we've gone through our struggles and survivals together. There's a blues song that talks about the "key to the highway." That's our friendship, unlocking any door that stands between us, and it keeps four very different individuals together.

It ain't easy. We love each other, but give-and-take can still get shaky, at least until we lean back and start playing the music. All of us are used to having our way and doing things our own way. Maybe we should be called the Highwaysmen. If anything, though, our troubles erupt when we worry too much about upstaging the other guys, getting in their way.

When we first took the Highwaymen out live, it looked like four shy rednecks trying to be nice to each other. It almost ruined it. That didn't work, for us and the audience, and it was really bothering me, how different we were on stage than when we were sitting around in the dressing room. We had just come back from Australia, and were set to play a week at the Mirage in Las Vegas. After the opening night, I was fixin' to quit. I talked to John about it and he was feeling the same way. "I get a little nervous," he said. "I don't want to look like I'm trying to steal your thunder."

That was it. We were boring each other and the audience. It may be hard to think of Johnny Cash as intimidated, but that's the way we were. You can't have four big guys tiptoeing around each other on stage. Nobody has a good time.

So we decided to help each other out, whether each of us

thought we needed it or not. Don't ask. Just do it, and don't worry what the other one thinks. Make fun of each other, cut up, poke some much-needed fun. Willie would be singing "Crazy," and I'd run up to the microphone and add "Stupid . . ." They may have seemed little things, but they were enough to make us loosen up and not take ourselves so danged serious. By the end of the week, with Willie dancing across the stage and John and Kris singing harmony neck-and-neck, we had the wildest show, and it made us a group.

John had brought our four personalities together initially, in Montreaux, Switzerland, in 1984. Every year, he had a television Christmas special, and that holiday season he wanted us all to come over. We were interviewed one afternoon when we had arrived in Europe. A nervous journalist came in and asked, "Why Switzerland? Why would you do a Christmas special in Switzerland?"

He stuck the microphone over in front of me. I said, " 'Cause that's where the baby Jesus was born," and he dutifully wrote that down.

Actually, it was the Highwaymen who had the immaculate conception. We got along "handsomely," as John put it. We started trading songs in the hotel after we worked on the special, and someone said, like they always do, we ought to cut an album. Man, this is forever.

Usually everyone goes their separate ways after that, but the idea took hold. Chips Moman had come over to Switzerland to do sound, and when he came back to Nashville, he was working with Willie and John, recording a duet to finish out John's album. I stumbled in to visit, and a little later, Kris came by.

We remembered a Jimmy Webb song called "Highwayman" that we had all liked in Switzerland, and since we were in the same place at the same time, we did a track on it. Then another, and another. The album was underway without us even knowing it. It was the first of three we've done under the collective name of the Highwaymen.

There used to be another group called the Highwaymen, who were best known for the folk tune "Michael Row the Boat Ashore," and they sued us over the name. They had long since retired, but we did a charity show with them opening and squared it away. *Highwayman* came out in 1985, containing things like "Desperadoes Waiting for a Train" and Johnny's "Big River," which he wrote after listening to delta-influenced blues singers like Robert Johnson and Pink Anderson. We toured, learning how to unwind with each other, and returned to the studio in early 1990 for *Highwayman 2*. As an album, it could have used a little more time spent on it. We ran in and out too quick, and we didn't have that one great song. It's hard to find material that goes over with four people, each with strong let-it-all-hang-out opinions.

Our last album, *The Road Goes on Forever*, came out in spring of 1995, and I think it's our best, so far. Three's the charm. It was produced by Don Was, who has worked with me, Willie, and Kris individually, and is one of the nicest, most unassuming guys you'd ever want to meet. Don't let him fool you, though. He orchestrates his sessions with the skill of a master conductor, and the week we spent as the Highwaymen in Ocean Way, choosing songs, working up arrangements, dodging film crews, and getting the tracks down, required some complex juggling. Through it all, Don was at his ease, moving everything forward, keeping everybody loose and alert, and letting nothing phase him.

He had helped me a lot when I returned to RCA's fold at the end of 1993. They had put out a double-CD box set of my career there, *Only Daddy That'll Walk the Line,* and seeing my work as a whole, and the respect with which I was accorded, I started listening when they asked me to newly record again. Vice president Thom Schuyler understood what my music was about, and that's all I've ever asked.

I went into the studio with Don in January of 1994 to cut the songs that would go to make up *Waymore's Blues (Part II)*. We clicked from the start of the first take, which was the title cut.

Before we began, I had told Don and the band, which included drummer Kenny Aronoff, guitarist Mark Goldenberg, keyboardist Benmont Tench, and steel player Robby Turner, to forget about everything they had ever heard me do. "I want you to play what you feel in these songs. I'll take care of the Waylon Jennings part."

Don himself played stand-up bass, with his shoes off, no less. "Don," I said. "I'm country, but I'm not that country!"

For his part, Don was looking at what he called my essence; he wanted to create an instrumental texture, a pad of colors, rather than have the usual trading of licks. He didn't want to lose me in a sea of arrangement. He called it impressionistic, like a painting, and when we heard "Waymore's Blues Part II" come over the speakers, I understood what he was getting at. It had been twenty years since I had cut "Part I," and you could hear the many changes I'd been through as the atmospheres swirled. I was still saying the things that every macho you-don't-mess-around-with-me guy might say, but I probably didn't feel the need to live up to them as much now.

There were things like "Wild Ones," where I remembered the times when me, Willie, and Jessi had come to town and how we had shaken Nashville's hierarchy up in our fight to keep the music honest. There was "Endangered Species," which I wrote with Tony Joe White, acknowledging some simple virtues that were maybe in danger of becoming extinct. There were more like me at one time, the song was saying, and though "a man in love is what I want to be," it was also talking about the way you carry yourself, and how where once the song and the performance of the song was the thing, now videos have shifted the emphasis to looks and showmanship. Sometimes the visuals take the romance and fantasy away from the hearing, and "that's what makes me / An endangered species."

"Old Timer" was very dear to my heart, a poignant tale about an old mountain man from Jackson Hole, Wyoming, who loved a woman from Saint Paul. She came to visit her brother, and they met each other in the wilds. He could never tell her he loved her; he was too "tough" for that, but he cleaned up and bought some fresh clothes and thought about the new feelings coursing through his body. "I don't know about love," he mused as he trudged through the deep snow to see her, "but I was quite taken in by it all." In the end, she went back home, and though he acted like it wasn't any big deal, he asked to be buried up high in the hills, where "I bet on a clear day you can see all the way to Saint Paul." I was proud to tell that story.

And I was proud of the album, because it felt like I was back in command of myself, sure of my creativity, knowing I was reaching for something I hadn't done before, and finding it. You can feel very alone in the studio. It's just you, the microphone, and your guitar. If you have a friend in the control room, and a band you trust, that's when the magic happens.

We're all fans of each other, and that's what makes watching the Highwaymen such a treat. For us, most of all. Sometimes I'll be just sitting back and enjoying the show when it's my turn to come in. We're our own appreciative audience.

With the best seat in the house, we get to see each other as we really are, and how we react to the fame that surrounds us. Me and Kris think John and Willie are like Truman and MacArthur sometimes. They won't admit it, but there's a little bit of competition between them. Willie might be late getting to the stage, and John will say, "Where's Willie? I'm going back to my dressing room." Both of them enjoy their star power. When John went to the Eastern bloc countries, they called him "Your Majesty," and he liked that, until he found out it was a guy from the KGB. We try not to take it too seriously, though.

Most of us spent so much time wandering in the wilderness on our way up the ladder that we were able to adjust gradually to our renown. I always felt that was the best way to do it, to struggle and build a following. If it happens overnight, it's likely to leave in the next morning.

Legend. Superstar. Entertainer. To me, that five-pointed badge is there hanging on your dressing room door. When I come to work, I pick it up, and after I'm done with the show, I leave it hanging there for whenever I return, or the next artist to use.

You are whatever the audience thinks you are, whatever they care to call you while you're in the spotlight. You owe them a good performance. More than that? The rest of the time you're a human being, and that's all you are. If you get past that, if you think that you're more special than your talent and your luck, then it comes back to haunt you.

In the Highwaymen, none of us are too big to be picked on, to have their ribs poked and tickled. I never cut anybody any slack. If I tease you, that means I love you. If I don't say a word, better watch out: I don't want you around.

I love to get on Willie about his headband or his guitar playing. There's no way he could get that busted-up guitar of his in tune, so that's why I tell him he uses such wobbly vibrato. He's trying to keep those strings from banging into each other.

We all wind up taking different roles in the Highwaymen. John is bigger than life. His presence makes us larger, and his compassion keeps opening us outward; yet there's a dark menacing side, something that he has no control over, and that gives us an element of danger and unpredictability. Sometimes he looks like he comes from a different historical era. He could've been Jesse James, or the Apostle Paul. It was Paul who said, "Woe be unto me if I don't preach the gospel." He knew that if you share what is buried deep within your heart, then what is buried deep in your heart saves you; if you don't bring it out, then what's hidden within your heart will kill you. John Cash walks that line.

If he's Paul, Willie must be Saint Peter. He floats freely, founding his church on whatever rock he cares to perch on. It's tough to get him to make a decision, because he never plays favorites. He used to bring the whole show to a standstill with "Angels Flew Too Close to the Ground," but to him it was just another song. He's not there for the money, nor has he ever forgotten where he came from. I still think Willie will wind up back in the honky-tonks. We were down in Texas not too long ago, and he had worked all day and night, until two o'clock in the morning, on his sixtieth birthday special. His daughter was playing at a local club, and he went down there after and played for hours, the club jammed and him jamming. That's where he's the happiest.

Kris taught us how to write great poetry. Politically, he swings us to the left; and I'd hate to think what would happen to him if Leonard Peltier was guilty. He wants everybody to have a fair shot, even if they're wrong. He's great for getting things simple, and to the point, and he's probably the only theatrical performer among us, a true actor in every sense of the word. Kris is probably the most enthusiastic about the music. Willie's not enthusiastic, but he probably needs the music more than any of us. John loves the music, pure and simple. When we were rehearsing for a tour, John came in and wanted to do "Ghost Riders in the Sky." We had already learned some twenty tunes, and nobody wanted to add another one. Except Willie. He'd be happy to learn it. We found out why on opening night. Only Willie set up a music stand off to the side of him and played along. Wish I'd thought of that.

We don't spend too much time worrying about if it's got four parts. If it does, great, and a song like "It Is What It Is" off the third album lets us pass the song around like a hot potato. Part of the fun is guessing who sings where; others rely on the ensemble effect. We're making so much noise, it doesn't matter that one's starting on a verse while the other is ending up a chorus.

Don had his hands full in the recording, because we all are stylists, and we got that way by sounding like nobody else. It's tough to get us singing in harmony. Kris and I are probably the closest in voice; I can phrase with Willie better, since I've been doing it for so long. I know where he's going, even if I can't figure out why.

They depend on me to do the worrying, to advise them on the business, to watch out for all of them. I don't mind, unless it makes me responsible for more than I can handle. Which usually brings me to Jack Clement. Sure enough, the Highwaymen were playing the Fort Worth Livestock Show, preparing to go to Europe, and I started fretting about how the stage might sound in a strange continent, and how someone speaking a foreign language, who doesn't know who we are, or what we sound like, could ground us. Thinking about who might help us out, I remembered someone who had worked with all of us at one time or another, that "good friend of mine," Jack Clement.

It seemed like a reasonable idea to bring Jack along to watch over the board. After the first night, however, he called Willie in the morning. "Come on down to my room, Will," he said with that lilting melody in his voice. "You've got to do something about your rhythm. You start in last week and wind up next week. You're not on the beat. You've got to sing on the beat."

"Fuck you, Jack," retorted Willie, and then came back to me chuckling, and said, "I've always wanted to say fuck you to somebody whose real name is Jack."

Then he stopped laughing. "What's with him?" he wondered. I told Willie not to worry and went to Jack and asked him to knock it off.

Jack was only getting warmed up. He had more suggestions. Why does the band have to make all that noise before the curtain rises? I said, heck, that's part of a show. He said, "Why don't you put a table on the stage? Then you guys could play cards while one of you was singing."

I said, "Jack, I want you to listen to me. The soundman you're working with can't speak English. He needs you, and we don't. Consider the front of the stage out as your domain and leave the rest to us. And especially, stay away from Willie. I'm one of the few people who can tease him about his singing. As far as rhythm, that's his style, the back-phrasing and everything. He spent years figuring out how to do that."

It went along pretty well until Jack tried out the local schnapps. He got in the elevator with Willie and a bunch of other people and said, "You're really fucking 'Good Hearted Woman' up. You're doing it twice as fast as you're supposed to."

It's tough to light Willie's fuse, but he was on the phone with me in seconds. "He's driving me crazy," he yelled. I wanted to sing "Stupid." Willie wouldn't slow down. "I want him out of here." Then he stopped short. "Do I do 'Good Hearted Woman' too fast?"

I said yeah, but Jack wasn't the one to tell him.

It was my job to break the news. I took John with me. "Willie don't want you here," I said. "I told you not to bother him."

"I didn't mean no harm," said Jack, a little sheepish and hung over. And he didn't.

Kris came by a few minutes later and John told him what had happened. "Oh, no," said Kris. He was on his way to smoke a joint with Willie before we went on.

"Wait a minute," I said. "Why don't you smoke two joints? When you get about halfway down on that second one, lean over and say, 'Maybe you were a little hasty about Jack?'"

Sure enough, Willie comes back, eyes twinkling, and half-smiling. "Aw," he said. "Let's give Jack another chance. I'm sure he meant well."

That night, Jack was behind the mixing desk, choreographing the show in his mind, slapping the echo and twiddling the eq. Doing his dance.

Even stars have stars. I'll be the first one who starts leaving when they begin talking about legends. I'm not comfortable with that. But that doesn't mean I don't have legends of my own that can turn my knees to jelly and my mouth into a silly grin.

Ernest Tubb always called me Son, which meant he liked me. He took me on his bus one time and chewed me out for smoking. He was always trying to quit himself, and died from emphysema because of it. In later years, he took to chewing gum, though it didn't help.

I sang on an album of his once, though he wasn't there. They had his voice on the tape, and at the part where I was supposed to come in, he'd say "Aw, sing it, Waylon." I melted. I got so taken listening to him say my name that I forgot to open my mouth. It made me feel just like that kid in the back room of Grandpa's cafe, squeaking along to the jukebox and holding my broomstick for dear life.

Ernest was my hero; he wasn't my role model. He drank pretty good, and probably had his faults, but I don't think entertainers are cut out to be role models. I have a hard enough time being a role model for my child; your kid shouldn't have to look up to me. They should be looking up at you, their parents. Don't put the responsibility on me, though I would never do anything mean or dishonorable in front of a kid. I have a respect for their young minds and open honesty.

A hero is when you feel honored to be in their presence, to have crossed their path. When Hazel Smith brought Bill Monroe over to the *Honky Tonk Heroes* sessions as a surprise, I tried to be calm, but I felt my hands sweating, and I was shaking. My daddy had Bill Monroe's picture on the wall at home. In our house, it was the flag, the Bible, and Bill Monroe. Sometimes Bill Monroe was first.

I think of that whenever I'm asked for an autograph, on my way out of a restaurant or backstage at a show. If you sign one, you have to sign them all; sometimes, there's just too many people to do the line justice, to get your picture taken for the bragging rights, to snap a souvenir of your dream date with Waylon. But people like to know they stood on the same patch of ground as you, and maybe the last chorus of that song was for them.

You get it back, seeing yourself in other people's eyes. Tompall and I had set up a booth at Fan Fair one year, the annual Nashville meet-and-greet for the country hardcore, with a pinball machine and Us. It would've been better if we just played and jawed, and people watched us as if we were in J.J.'s, but instead we decided to sign autographs.

A little blind girl walked up to me. "Is it really you?" she asked.

I said, "Yes, it's me."

"Can I touch you?" And she reached up and took hold of my hands. She held them tight. Then, she put her fingers up to my face, tracing its outline. Her own face was showing me every feeling she was having, the realization and the wonder and the joy combined.

From her blind eyes, she saw me. Tears came sliding down her cheeks, and mine.

Sometimes meeting your ideals is a little sad. I was having a party in Atlanta at the Albert Pick Motel when I found out Jimmy Reed, the great "Baby What You Want Me to Do" bluesman, was in town. I sent a car for him and he came over. Johnny Cash had given me a twelve-string dobro guitar, and one of the strings had broken. Jimmy looked at it and said, "I don't believe I've ever seen an eleven-string guitar before."

It was a wild party, with strippers on one side of the room and guitar pulls on the other, but I never got up from sitting in front of him, watching him play that dobro, all night. He would get to playing, and he would squeal when it started sounding good. At one point, he looked at a horseshoe ring on my finger that George Jones had given me, with a big diamond in the middle. "That's a pretty ring." He sighed. "I used to have one like that." He held out his hand to me, and there was a gold-plated ring with the setting gone. "Old Jimmy, he ain't doing so good no more."

That about killed me. I thought, here I am, a cocky little guy, and here's this great man, and they've robbed him of everything. I'm sure he was a pain in the ass sometimes, and stayed drunk a lot, but he was Jimmy Reed, who sang about the "Bright Lights, Big City" and "Big Boss Man," and he deserved better. He had been kicked out of his hotel and had another week to go in Atlanta, so I got him a room at the Albert Pick for the remainder of his stay. At least I was able to do something for him.

That's the difference between the white and black blues. Black musicians go to the source, dead on, right to the heart of it, maybe because they have to fight even harder to make themselves heard.

All you had to do was listen to Miles Davis's voice to know how much he had screamed in his life for the right to blow his horn. He'd rasped his throat in a hospital, blowing it out trying to get loose from drugs. It was like he had no vocal cords left.

"Who's the whitey?" he asked when Neil, his manager, brought me over to his house. He wouldn't look at me for a while. "You know that new roadie you hired for me," he said to Reshen. "He called me a motherfucker." Then he glanced over in my direction and added, "I don't mind being called a motherfucker, but when he said it, it had an Irish accent and too many r's." We laughed, and I knew he had accepted me.

Sometimes guys whose talent you've admired from afar become your close friends. John Cash was like that, and every once in a while I would step outside our relationship and be a little in awe of him. The same is true of George Jones. He has more complexes than anybody I ever met—"I can't sing that low," he'll tell me, even though both of us know just how low we can go, given the wrong opportunity—and to talk with him, you'd never think that here is one of the greatest country singers alive. But he is.

Singing *is* George. He tries to live, breathe, and eat the song while he's singing it, and he's told me that, especially when he's in the studio, his mind goes completely blank but for the focus of the story and the melody in his throat. He imagines the man, or woman, he's singing about and how they might be reacting to every word.

On the other hand, he doesn't pay a lot of attention to the world around him. When he played Sacramento, California, recently, some of his band went up to Donner Pass to see where those pioneers got stranded in a nineteenth-century snowstorm and started eating one another. When they got back to the hotel,

George wanted to know where they'd been. They told him they'd been to see where the Donner Party had turned cannibal.

"Wouldn't you know I'd miss something like that," said George. "I've been on the road so long, I ain't seen a newspaper in two weeks!"

Nobody could match my state of mindlessness like George when we were in our glory days. We both enjoyed our success and got a little overwhelmed by it. In George's case, it was alcohol that was his demon of choice, one beer leading to another, and not helped by the fact that the only places you play when you're starting out are honky-tonks, bars, and lounges. There are more George Jones stories than he could possibly forget, almost as many as Hank Williams, and he likes to claim that his memory is "blurry." I'm always happy to help him remember some of his more cantankerous moments. Like the evening he came over to visit, on a spree, and started flailing about in my living room, yelling at Mary Mann, Shooter's grand-godmother. When it looked as if he might go to sleep, I had the bright idea of giving him a big glass of whiskey to help him nod off. Wrong.

He started tearing everything up. I ran into the room and he threw a metal-framed picture at my head. It just missed me; if it had landed half a foot to the right, it would have knocked me cold for a week. I tried to get him to calm down, but he kicked at me. Finally I had to sit on him. He even played possum on me once, which shows you how he got his nickname, pretending he was choking. When I let go and said "George, y'all right?" he hit me in the face.

I didn't know how much longer this could go on. I was on drugs myself at the time, and after about thirty minutes, I began to get tired. Cocaine doesn't last that long. Jerry Gropp was with me, and he tried to hold down George's feet. George kicked him in the thumb and broke it. It seemed like he was getting stronger, or I was getting weaker. I had no choice but to tie him up, lift him up on the couch, and try to see he was comfortable. I never felt so bad in my life, thinking, Here's the greatest country singer that ever lived, and I'm tying his ass up.

"Now you be still," I told him. "I'm going to call your manager to come pick you up."

George sneered at me. "I'll get you, you Conway Twitty–actin' sonofabitch," he said.

I couldn't hold back a laugh. "What do you mean by that? You hit me in the face and kick me in the nuts, you cuss the ladies in the house, you break my guitar player's thumb, and now you call me a Conway Twitty–actin' sonofabitch? I'm the one who's gonna do the gettin'.'"

When he went in for his heart bypass a while ago, his wife, Nancy, called me in Vicksburg, Mississippi. "George isn't going to stay in the hospital unless he talks to you."

I went in to visit him. I told him what to expect and that there was nothing he could do but lie back and wait for it to be over. Remembering Bill Robinson's little joke with me, I couldn't resist asking him what he intended to do with his DeLorean, with the batwing doors and six hundred miles on it. "You might write down on a piece of paper that you want me to have it." I could hear him swearing and hollering at me down the hall.

After the operation, he wouldn't go to physical therapy without me. They wanted him to walk on a treadmill, ride a bicycle, and do some stretches. He said, "I ain't doing it unless you do too."

"I don't need to do that. There's nothing to it. It's like spitting over a log."

He leaned over to me. "I'm depending on you not to let them make me do something that'll make me look silly."

I said, "George, after all you've been through, there ain't a thing these doctors in here could do that'd make you look any sillier than what you've done to yourself."

George and I met back when I was a disc jockey at KLLL. I asked him if he liked bluegrass music and he said, "Hell, no." We'd run into each other now and again, though I don't think he knew I sang until we met up at Sue Brewer's a few years later in Nashville. But I'd heard his records, both as a country artist who scored with "Why Baby Why" and some of the more rockabilly-type things he was cutting for Starday's H. W. "Pappy" Dailey, out of Houston. Like me, George could've probably gone rock if he chose to, but having spent a lot of time watching Hank Thompson and Bob Wills through the windows of his local honky-tonk, and listening to the Opry on Saturday nights, he decided he didn't really like rock and roll. One time, though, I heard him on the *Louisiana Hayride*. Elvis was taking it away from everybody, and George got pissed. He came on before Elvis and did Little Richard's "Long Tall Sally" in that growl voice and just wiped him out.

From the mid-fifties through the seventies, George rode the whirlwind of country music. He had dozens of hits, recorded with and married Tammy Wynette, and led a life that sounded like an entire country jukebox all rolled into one. By the end of the 1970s, he had bottomed out from drinking and slid into bankruptcy. Sound familiar?

It may have been the blind leading the blind, as George puts it, but John Cash and I came to his rescue. We didn't ask if we could help. We just did, helping George keep his home, cars, and buses. We tried to keep it a secret, but he found out through the bank. I know he'd do the same for me, if I needed it.

His talent is raw, natural, and I don't think he knows why he's such a great singer. He just is. It's not something he's developed. He never seemed to progress or lose it; like Elvis or Willie or Jerry Lee Lewis, the first time you heard him, he was just as good as he is now.

The best thing we ever cut together was a record of "Night Life" that we did on one of his albums for Billy Sherrill. I'm singing so high you wouldn't believe it's me. On another all-night session, we sat on two stools, facing each other across a Plexiglas baffle and filled up four reels of tape. We were both gone, and I don't think we ever finished a song. One of us would start laughing, or we'd take turns passing out. Jigger just sat there holding his bass, watching these two pitiful people chasing each other's tail.

Everyone imitates George these days, and yet he can't get played on the radio. That's true for a lot of us from an older generation. It used to worry me, but once you accept that it's not going to change the way you sing a song, and it's not going to stop people from coming out to see you play—in fact, maybe they come out and see you play because they *can't* hear you on the radio—then you say it's radio's loss. George has been making records for forty years. At one time he was on four different labels. They couldn't burn him out with a torch. He's still here.

Connie Smith and I practically came to town at the same time. She arrived in Nashville in June 1964, signed by Chet to RCA after Bill Anderson discovered her at a talent show in Elkhart, Indiana. From the time she was five, Connie always wanted to be a country singer on the Opry. Her first song, "Once a Day," hit number one on the charts, and a year after she arrived in Nashville, she was asked to become a member of the Opry.

She's a "feel" performer. Even when she went into the studio, she didn't overly learn her songs; she'd know part of them and fill in the gaps as she went along, and was usually just as surprised at what came out of her voice as everyone else.

I had met Connie on the package shows organized by RCA, and kept in touch when she left secular music for a while to follow her faith and raise her family in the seventies. A few years ago she was going through a divorce, and I called her one morning, just wanting to check up and see how she was doing. She told me things were rough, and shared some of her troubles. Jessi makes a good pot of coffee, I let her know, and I was on my way to come bring her over to the house.

I beeped the horn at her front door. She had just gotten out of the shower and had her hair up. I was waiting in the car in my pajamas and cowboy boots. I thought, wouldn't it be funny if we got in a wreck. We'd hit the tabloids for sure.

From then on, Connie has been part of our family's inner circle. You can always find her and Jessi singing at the piano, and when we went to Israel in 1993, she accompanied us. It's an amazing country, even if you take the religion out of it. If you think of our history as lengthy, stretching over a couple of centuries, here's a piece of land that people have been fighting over for thousands of years. It kind of puts you in your place.

I saw something there that proves to me how much life doesn't stand still. We were up in Galilee, at Peter's house, and came back through Jericho. As we started the return to Jerusalem, the four of us crammed into a van, I looked out over the desert. There was the brightest little pin of light I'd ever seen. I asked the Palestinian who was driving us what it was, and he said he didn't know.

As we got nearer, it grew brighter. I began looking for three camels on the horizon, bearing gifts. Finally, I saw that it shone from a Bedouin tent, stark against the wilderness. They're nomads, and they've been moving back and forth since the beginning of time. It was quiet, and the night had turned cold and clear. At first I thought the light might be a campfire. Then I took a closer look, and saw it was the glow of a television.

Nothing stays the same. In Calgary, Canada, an old cowboy came into our hotel and started talking to me about these two prize bulls he had on his ranch. One was named Willie and the other Waylon. He had on a sheepskin coat, a big cowboy hat, his Levis stuffed into his boots, and a mustache stained and dripping with snuff. While we were talking, I heard a high-pitched sound. It was his beeper going off.

I thought, don't that beat all.

I feel the same way about some of the younger guys, and girls, in country music. You can smell the change in the wind, whipping up the tumbleweeds. There's surely a new generation out there, and it's ready for its turn in the follow spot. I don't intend to be old and in the way, or let anybody run me off. Sometimes, it's only natural we're going to tussle over the same turf. Country music is a lot like Israel; everybody wants to build a church on its holy shrines. Still, I like to think that we're all talking about the same spirit, the one that makes us want to pick and sing, and all the fussing and fighting over who gets played on the radio or headlines the state fairs don't amount to much more than a range war.

We need new blood. I once suggested to promoters that they have special nights where they let in kids under fifteen free, to bring them into the country-music fold. They need their heroes, just like I needed mine.

The best of the new performers remember where they came from, who opened the doors they step their line dance through, and don't try to figure they invented a pair of tight jeans and a guitar. Marty Stuart loves the old Opry tradition, and I saw just how much one night when he and I were sitting around singing with George Jones. George coughed, spit a wad of phlegm into a handkerchief, and cleared his throat.

"There's people in this world who would kill to do that with their voice," I joked to Marty.

"If I thought it would make me sing like him," answered Marty without missing a beat, "I'd swallow it."

Sometimes it seems like Marty is everywhere. He'll jump in and start playing even before he's asked. "You're the musician from hell," I once told him, but you can see he's having more fun than anyone in the world. Connie says that watching Marty and Travis Tritt run around together is a little like catching a glimpse of me and John in the old days. They feed off each other and go a little further than they would if they were by themselves. If Marty's around, and he sees Travis, he's going to be a little more Marty, and vice versa. Two is better than one, and both of them will push the other a little harder.

Travis is about my favorite new singer. What a talent, and a writer. He hones his songs, cares about them, and he knows how to work that rock-and-roll hoofbeat so it turns into a stampede. For me, he's a cross between Hank Williams and Ray Charles, and when I hear him sing "Old Outlaws Like Us," I know he's one of the brightest hopes of country music today.

Of course, the next generation better not believe everything they hear. At this point, I've been accused of all manner of carousing. Mostly, it's something that I might have done, or would have done, or couldn't even imagine doing. Pretty soon it's etched into stone. If I led the life that people think I did, I'd be a hundred and fifty years old and weigh about forty pounds.

There's enough wild nights to go around, though, and I do enjoy letting the newer cow-punkers on the block know about the rigorous standards of roaring they're expected to uphold. Joe Galante from RCA once called and said, "Clint Black really likes you. Can we go to lunch and you can tell him some old Waylon and Willie stories?"

We met up with his manager, Bill Ham, and I started recounting. I told him of all the phones I used to destroy, dialing a number, putting it to my ear, and walking off. He listened to tales of Hillbilly Central and Dripping Springs, and Joe would keep encouraging me, saying "Tell this story, Waylon, tell that one."

After I got through talking, Clint pushed back from the table. "I can let you know one thing I've gotta do," he said. "I've got to get rid of this goody-two-shoes reputation I've got."

Both Bill and Joe looked at him in horror. "No, no! We just wanted you to hear the stories!"

You never do know where the stones you throw will land. One time, I was at an awards show, and I heard a voice behind me saying "Mr. Jennings, you're like a god to me." I turned around and it was Billy Ray Cyrus, offering his hand for me to shake. All I could think of was, if I'm your god, what does your devil look like?

\*     \*     \*

The thing is, we're in this together, the old, the new, the one-hit wonders and the lifetime achievers, the writers and the session pickers and the guy who sells the T-shirts. The folks that come to the shows, and the ones that stay at home and watch it on TNN. Those who remember Hank Williams, and those who came on board about the time of Mark Chestnutt, who named his baby boy after me.

In the spring of 1995, I hosted eight shows of a series for the Nashville Network, called *The Legends of Country Music*. One program featured Jessi and I sitting around with June and John, swapping reminiscences and interrelations. Another found me alongside Bill Monroe, Little Jimmy Dickens, Porter Wagoner, and Carl Smith alternating verses of "The Great Speckled Bird." Beth Nielsen Chapman, Lyle Lovett, Bobby Bare, Guy Clark, Billy Joe Shaver, and Rodney Crowell came to visit. George Jones cancelled the night before. Kris stopped by, and the father-daughter bluegrass gospel of Jerry and Tammy Sullivan closed each show. We had a tribute to Roger Miller with Chet and Willie, Mary Miller and Roger's kids. Travis Tritt, Leroy Parnell, Danny Dawson, and Kimmie Rhodes represented country future, while a host of young cowboys joined me for "All of My Sisters Are Girls," and an equal number of cowgirls backed up Jessi on "All of My Brothers Are Boys." Country future's future.

My friends. This town is big enough for the all of us.

CHAPTER

14

# I DO BELIEVE

When people ask me who I admire most in the world, I always have the same answer: Muhammad Ali.

I thought he was too smart-ass for his own good when I first heard of him, but after I realized what he was doing, he left-hooked me quick. I guessed he had seen Gorgeous George, the wrestler, and how people loved to hate him as he paraded around the ring with his blonde curls and mincing walk, before he pile-drived his opponent into the mat. Muhammad talked about himself with a grand sense of humor, but it helped that he was probably the most gracefully flamboyant boxer of our lifetime.

I enjoyed watching him fight, and respected him because he stood up for what he believed. When they drafted him, all he had to do was join the army and keep his mouth shut. They probably would've let him fight exhibitions and live in a fancy barracks, but he was one of the first to say that the Vietcong had never done anything to him. They'd never called him a nigger. He said no, rejecting the draft because of his religious beliefs, and lost the heavyweight championship belt. Muhammad gave up what he loved most, what he had worked for all his life, because he didn't believe in the war. For four years, the only fighting he did was to stay out of prison.

He brought such class to boxing, and even after they overturned his conviction, Ali was never bitter about the fact that the government had robbed him of his peak years. Later, I found out what a kind and generous man he was. Watching him in the ring, he'd have his opponent helpless and then start yelling at the referee to stop the fight. He didn't want to hurt anybody, killer instinct or no.

Kris brought me back to Muhammad's dressing room the night he won the belt back from Leon Spinks. Before the fight, he was the most calm man you ever saw, sitting on his trainer's table, waiting, sure it was a done deal. When I left, he simply said "Waylon," and gave me a big hug.

We had lunch in L.A. a few months later, and after Shooter was born, I called him and told him we were having a christening. "We'd love to have you," and sure enough, he showed up and flopped down on the couch. "I'm here to integrate this joint," he said with a smile. Then he cast his eye over to Deakon. "And I'm lookin' for a heavyweight to fight tonight." It was the only time I've ever seen Deakon say "not me."

I had just bought the bus we called Shooter I. It wasn't even furnished yet; I don't know if it had license tags. Muhammad asked me for the keys, drove to Louisville to see his momma, and then brought it back. He could have kept it for all I cared. He means that much to me, and the world.

"I had a terrible dream, Jessi."

We were up at Big Cedar Lodge, deep in the Ozarks south of Branson, Missouri. It was the Christmas holidays of 1994, and for the first time we had our entire clan with us, all the kids together at last. Even in the best of families, it's hard to get siblings to see eye to eye with each other, or their parents; and given the rough times I'd been through in the past, we'd hardly had the best of families.

This was our reunion, in more ways than one.

"Jessi," I said. "I don't know what to make of this dream. You were smiling and everything, but whenever I'd ask you to get married, or wonder whether you'd do it again, you'd say no."

"Well, honey, don't you worry about that," she said, giving me a little hug. "I'd marry you a thousand times."

"Okay," I replied, a little chirpily. "How about today?"

"Aw, isn't that sweet." She didn't get it.

"I said, let's get married today." Slowly it dawned on her that I was serious. And I was.

I'd planned it for weeks. For our first marriage, it wasn't the most solemn of occasions. I was strung out, and she was laughing her way through it. After twenty-five years, I thought it was time for me to tell her again, in front of the whole family, how much I loved her.

I picked out a wedding dress and they fitted it long distance. I called John and Jeanie Morris, and Debbie, at Big Cedar, and they took care of arranging the details. The funniest part was listening to Jessi on the phone, making dozens of plans for the weekend, arranging lunches and outdoor events, and them just nodding and going along with whatever she said, knowing something completely different was going to happen.

The reunion was meaningful for me on a lot of levels. I wanted to get all of my children together; it felt, somehow, a time that we should make peace and have a healing. Some of my kids have had a tough time, partially because of me and as much in spite of me. At this point, no one needs to put the blame on anyone else. If I wasn't there for them when they missed me, then I tried too hard to make up for it, and maybe that wasn't right either. Climbing on the bus to drive from Nashville to Branson, we put all of that in the past. Where it belongs.

Connie Smith came, and Will Campbell arrived to perform the

ceremony. Will has united in marriage everyone in my band at least once, and three of my kids. "What if Jessi says no when you ask her?" he joked. "Does this mean you've been living in sin all these years?"

We hid them in their rooms until the moment arrived. The dress fit Jessi perfectly; she looked like a sixteen-year-old in it. And when Will got up and said "What the Lord has joined together, man would do well not to piddle with," I felt we had come full circle.

Will Campbell is a bootleg preacher. You can find him on Saturday night at Gass's, near Mount Juliet in Tennessee, sitting in with the band and having a nip if he feels like it. He's my "guru."

He represents the soul of the South, to me, and he's one of the only people who I care what they think about my doings. He was raised a Southern Baptist, in Mississippi, which is about as Southern Baptist as you can get. When he graduated from Yale Divinity School in 1952, he took a pastorate in a small North Louisiana town. His major interest was social issues, and he was pro-union and pro–racial equality, two topics that didn't go over too well with some white churchgoers in his 1950s parish. When he spent his Sunday sermons talking about organizing the local mill, and dwelling more than he should on "The Negro Question," as it was called then, he didn't last long. That's how he became a bootleg preacher. It just means he does it wherever he can, and to whoever cares to listen.

The one thing I respect Will most for is that he believes his job is to leave the door open; it's you who has to walk through. One time, when I was worried about John, I went to Will and asked him what I should do. I knew in my heart that something had to be done, but I also figured that the last thing anybody needs is some righteous ex-addict telling him to get off drugs. He also knew that in my frustration, I was starting to get angry at John.

"Damned if I know, Waylon," he replied. "I can't see as we've ever been able to straighten anybody out that didn't want to do it for themselves."

Then Will told me the story of a poor black woman, standing by the graveside of the white woman who had employed her. She'd been treated badly, yelled at and abused over many years, and though the woman wondered if her employer "knew that I loved her," she finally couldn't take it anymore; she left the grave, mad. That night, as she lay there half-asleep, Jesus came to the foot of her bed. He said to her, "If you just love people that are easy to love, that ain't no love at all. It's not hard to love somebody if they're good to you. Yet if you love one, you've got to love them all."

Will himself understands the practice of what he preaches. While involved in the civil rights struggle, he had a dear friend, Jonathan Daniel, shot by a redneck deputy down in Alabama. Will went to the friend's bedside and was with him till he died, slow and painfully. Then he went directly to the courthouse, where the deputy was in jail, and ministered to him. That, in my personal church, is a preacher.

He considered race relations, and improving race relations in the South, as his calling, and Will was very active in the civil rights movement, more as an observer, he'll say, since there were no white leaders. They were some who thought they were, but for Will, that was a black movement, black-led, black-organized. There were certain things he could do, however, as a white man, that a black person could not do, including relating to a lot of hard-nosed people on the other side, including some in the Ku Klux Klan.

He knew Dr. Martin Luther King very well, and was the only white person present at the formation of the Southern Christian Leadership Conference in Atlanta. For Will, that was "not quite as romantic and heroic as it might sound." It was his "job." His religious tradition came out of the sixteenth century, where the Baptists' view of the separation of church and state meant they would not go to war or condone the death penalty, and that human beings were born free and created to be free.

I saw this in him the first time I watched Will perform the marriage service. Johnny Darrell was the groom, and Will started out by saying "There's a passage in the Scriptures which says that you 'render unto Caesar's what is Caesar's.'" He asked the newly Mr. and Mrs. Darrell for their wedding license, signed it, and tossed it aside somewhat contemptuously.

"As far as the state of Tennessee is concerned," he said, "you're married. That's all that piece of paper is, a legal contract, and like any legal contract, it doesn't entitle you to very much. It doesn't teach you how to love one another, and it certainly doesn't grant you happiness. The only thing it gives you is the right to sue each other."

I cracked up when he said that, and listened harder when he added, "Marriage is about love, compassion, commitment, and caring. It has nothing to do with legality."

Will lives out by rural Mount Juliet and does his writing in a small log shack about a ten-minute walk through the fields from his house. I go out there sometimes when I need to be centered, when the questioning that I always do is calling for answers. We'll sit out in the sculpture garden, where he takes metal junk he picks up from his property and welds it together to form found objects of art, and we'll talk about this and that.

You're not supposed to question things in most religions. The church gives you the answer; God talks through them, and not to you. I can't accept that. My whole nature is one of asking why, and who made me that way? Why would He put us on Earth and give us the ability to reason right from wrong, and then tell us to call him about everything we do?

I think people are put on this Earth to make their life count. That is the payback. To be judged by their accomplishments, and not sitting and shaking and shivering in a front-row pew. When my child does something good, whose chest swells the biggest?

That's my credit, in the achievements, not him praising me and telling me how great I am.

God has duties, too. He brought us here, and He should see to it that we have enough to eat. That we shouldn't suffer, or war over who gets into the uptown section of Heaven. Religion is a personal, individual thing, and everybody that reads their version of a Bible gets a different interpretation. There's twenty-eight thousand different faiths, and you can't tell me that only one of them is right.

The same is true with music. When I came to Nashville, I wanted the bottom, the insistent kick drum. I brought it into my songs, and they said, "You can't use that rock-and-roll beat. It's not country." I said, bullshit, there ain't nothing rock and roll about it. It's just a beat. We have beats in all music.

That sort of thou-shalt-not thinking leads to a tribal mentality, dividing and separating and turning brother against brother. If you don't belong with us, if you won't join our exclusive sect, then you're an infidel and you'll burn in hell. That's what the church says. Ignorance is no excuse, they'll threaten you, despite the billions who have never heard of the Bible, or the entire populations that are being killed at this moment over how they worship and pay tribute to their faith. If that's a way to honor God, then I need to wonder why. All the hair-splitting, the baggage and the trappings, of how many angels can sit on the point of a needle and sex is nasty nasty nasty, what's it worth?

Those were the question marks that turned me against the Church of Christ, what I rebelled against as a young child looking for reassurance. There was no room for grace; it was all hellfire and brimstone. I'd gone through enough hell on my knees pickin' cotton, and living in poverty, without going to church and reliving the despair, or putting it off to the next world. I wanted to hear a message of hope, of respect for other human beings and all of humanity. Human kind.

Religion should be liberating, like music. It should be about deliverance, not worship. Freedom.

Will came out on the road with me a few years ago. I gave him a job, but I never told him what it was. Mostly I liked having him around. After a few days of wondering why he was along, he started cooking for us on the bus. Late at night, we'd talk.

We were going from Greensboro to Tampa when Will turned to me and asked, "Waylon, wha'chu believe?" That's how he said it; a Southern expression. *Chu*. It's almost a greeting, or a serious question, depending on the context.

"Yeah," I replied, way down in my throat.

If you're going from Greensboro to Tampa on a "stagecoach," you know a conversation need not be rushed. We were quiet for a long time. Finally, Will said, " 'Yeah?' What's that supposed to mean?"

"Uh-huh," I answered. The conversation ran aground.

Will thought about that exchange, reflecting on the state of my cast-iron soul, and all he knew of me, and the next day he told me it was one of the most profound affirmations of faith he'd ever heard in his life.

*Yeah.*

*Uh-huh.*

I didn't understand it that well myself. All I was telling him was that I was a believer, whatever that was. There wasn't much else to say. That I could say.

Over the next fifteen years I thought about the question he'd asked me.

What is believing? I knew it wasn't like those television preachers, with their thousand-dollar suits and trimmed mustaches and gold chains, saying you could be saved depending on how much money you donate to their theme park. And I understood that there were things we couldn't understand, that we had to take on faith, like the love I feel for Jessi, the bond a father feels for his child, or the spirit of music as it touches Heaven.

*In my own way I'm a believer*
*In my own way, right or wrong*

## I DO BELIEVE

*I don't talk too much about it*
*It's something I keep working on*
*I don't have much to build on*
*Just a faith that's never been that strong*

I started writing the song in 1993, trying to be as plain with the words as I could. Sometimes poetry obscures the meaning of what it's trying to say, and I didn't want to confuse myself. I kept thinking of when Will was invited to speak at a congregation on the border of Harlem, in New York. I don't know if it was a black church or a white church, but when they asked how they could do something to benefit the community, he looked around at the sumptuous furnishings and fine decorations, and shrugged his shoulders. "You people wanted me to come and talk to you about how you might break down some of the barriers between you and those living across the street. Maybe if you sold this building and spread the proceeds around a little bit, that might help a lot." They didn't invite him back; he didn't tell them what they wanted to hear.

*There's a man there in that building*
*He's a holy man they say*
*He keeps talking about tomorrow*
*While I keep struggling with today*
*He preaches hell and fire and brimstone*
*And heaven seems so far away*

It's not the religion. Being born, it's between you and God. That's the one-on-one. For me, your contribution to the world is what you'll be judged on, come judgment day. It's something from deep inside of you. Help one another along, and try not to intentionally hurt anybody. We're here for each other. God loved David's singing, his harp playing, and maybe, just maybe, He was amused by David's dogged determination to find his own place in the world. That may be one man's interpretation, but at least it's mine.

*I believe in a higher power*
*One that loves us one and all*
*Not someone to solve my problems*
*Or to catch me when I fall*
*He gave us all a mind to think with*
*And to know what's right or wrong*
*He is that inner spirit*
*That keeps us strong.*

When I finished the song, and before the Highwaymen recorded it, I showed it to Will.

"That'll preach," he said.

Yeah. Uh-huh.

At this point, I've given up everything but oxygen. I'm still on drugs, taking handfuls of pills, only this time they're for my heart and my blood sugar and my well-being.

I'd be lying if I said I didn't miss my wild days. "Sometimes when I hear the wind, I wish I was crazy again." I sent that song of Bob McDill's to John Cash once when he had gone straight and I was still messed up. We wound up recording it as a duet, which seems fitting. It can get rough, keeping to the straight and narrow, especially when I'm trying everything I can do to live. My hands hurt, and even though they've operated on them, they can still get so numb I can't even feel the guitar. I get dizzy spells; lightheadedness. Maybe it's riding the bus. Some of these things might have been affecting me when I was on drugs, and I just didn't know it. I liked to get above the pain. Go out in a blaze of glory.

I do know that my new direction is for the better. I have a stable, easy life; everybody around me tries to take care of me. I may have to watch what I eat, but Maureen cooks meals that are as healthy as they taste good, Jessi pumps vitamins down me and makes sure I take my medicine, and Shooter tells me what White Zombie is up to on the Internet.

I haven't slowed down. I'm not sure I even know what the words would mean. I keep thinking about leaving the road, but I never do. It's a cycle. Even after the bypass, when I was ready to quit, I went out once and got that instant feedback and appreciation, with people shouting, girls dancing, and folks putting babies on their shoulders, and was back for good.

I've always got a song I'm working on in my hip pocket, or an idea that might need coming to fruition. You're never really done with your work in a lifetime, though sometimes other people are able to carry it on for you. The other day I went over to Emerald Studios in Nashville and cut a track of Buddy Holly's "Learning the Game," with Mark Knopfler of Dire Straits. It's one of the simplest songs Buddy ever wrote, and I saw him record it on a tape recorder in his living room, right before we left on the final tour. I don't think it was finished. It's only one verse and a chorus, but the way Mark stretched it out, it seemed complete and realized.

Music passes along. Buddy taught me things about what he was doing, and I picked out certain elements and made them my own. The same with Ernest Tubb or Carl Smith or Hank Williams. You never hear a piece of music the way the artist intended. You're hearing it through your ears, and your own imagination. Somewhere, a kid in a bedroom is listening to one of my records, and maybe he's picking up on a chord progression, or a vocal inflection that catches his fancy, and he tries to learn it. He gets it almost right. In that "almost" is where you can find his personality, his creativity, his style. Hers, for that matter. Ours.

All we need is the willpower and determination to see our vision through. Clayton Turner is a friend of mine who is a graphic artist. He's also a quadriplegic, and he draws by gripping a pencil in his mouth and painstakingly stroking each line just so. His pictures are large, and when he gets up as far as he can reach, he has to turn the picture over and work on it upside down.

If art is the answer, what's the question?

One of the strangest gigs I ever played was on a tour with the World Wrestling Federation. The idea was that I would open up the night's mayhem, though they left it up to me whether I wanted to go two falls out of three with Hulk Hogan. At one arena, the stage was set up behind the chairs, which were bolted to the floor facing the ring. For the entire show, the audience had to watch us twisted in their seats, craning their necks and contorting their bodies.

Needless to say, we cancelled the rest of those venues. I thought about that what-are-we-doing-here again last year, when I scheduled a series of acoustic shows: "unplugged," as they like to call them these days, and thought it might be an interesting change of pace.

It's a good idea, on paper. I enjoy singing my songs accompanied only by an acoustic guitar. It's how I initially write them, and the intimacy of the setting allows you to hear each nuance, syllable against syllable, emphasizing interpretation. I've always had fun taking a song and changing it to fit my mood, shaping it as the spirit moves me.

In a honky-tonk, though, you ain't got a chance. Cowboys are whooping and hollering, half drunk and the other half drunker, shouting out for their favorite songs and having a good ol' time on a Saturday night.

I'm playing with just an acoustic, with Jigger on another acoustic and Fred Newall on dobro, and you can't hear anything. It's packed to the rafters. There's a constant hubbub in the room, and I'm trying to sing louder. They're shouting out for "Honky Tonk Heroes" and "Hank" and I'm getting mad.

Mad at these fine people who are excited as hell, happy to see me, giving me some of the hard-earned money they've worked for, and wanting me to be the guy that most of them have followed for decades.

I'm sitting up there on a stool trying to be everything but what I was when I started. The thing that brought me to town, and made me what I am today, and I'm trying to pretend that it doesn't exist. They want me to be ornery, like the song says.

That honky-tonk would have been set alight with a band. I didn't have anything with which to fight back the noise. I didn't even have my hat.

Black, creased Texas-style, with a silver belt around the crown. The hat.

It's not so much a piece of wearing apparel as it is an attitude. If I realized how much the hat made me appear differently when Shooter asked me to take it off when we went to the toy stores, I also underestimated what it did for me when I walked on a stage. More important, what it meant to those folks out there, who put on their own hats when they leave the house to go honky-tonkin', and who shout out "1962 at [so-and-so]" and "Remember Silver City!" They're letting me know they've been with me the whole time.

I never want my fans to use the words "used to be" when they come around to see my show. I don't owe them a change; I owe them myself, being me, whoever they think I am. They're the only judge and jury I feel responsible to, and I have enough respect for their good sense to know that they won't steer me wrong. They won't change my music, because that's the basis for my trust in them. They like that I went up against and beat the system, and was an Outlaw before the movement ever got a name. They want me to be a hardass sonofabitch if you get me mad; and they want to know that I'll never be mad at them.

Every so often, I find myself caught up in being the New Waylon. Change is important, even essential, and it's one way an artist can stay ahead of the new-is-better obsession that we get on CNN every day. But you have to think about what you're changing, and who you're confusing, and whether booking shows in symphony

halls, leaving my black hat at home to gather dust alongside Andrew Jackson's hickory walking stick, is going to prove good or
bad in the long run. I always liked turning the St. James Theatre
on Broadway into a honky-tonk; I wouldn't want to turn a honky-
tonk into the St. James Theatre.

Sitting alone with an acoustic guitar on that stage, thinking I
was starting to become something other than me, I had to laugh
at myself. Another grand awakening. Even after all these years,
you still have to watch where you find your motivations, and you
have to keep on remembering to be who you are.

People may tell me that I look better without my hat. Looks
aren't everything, unless you're looking at you through me, and
paid to get in, in which case, you better like what you see. A hat
isn't just something you wear on your head. It's your halo.

I get up early in the morning. Jessi calls me a "springer." My
eyes open and I'm awake, ideas that have been circulating around
my subconscious coming to life, and I have to do something
about them.

While the house is still asleep, I walk downstairs and out the
back door. Tinkerbell, our large long-haired cat with the pushed-
in face, accompanies me outside.

It's the end of March. Spring comes early to Nashville, and the
trees are already budding. Out in back of the house is a small
room that has a couple of guitars and a karaoke cassette machine
that I use for recording my songs as I think of them. Mostly,
though, all I have is a piece of paper and a pencil.

I think I get the most satisfaction out of writing a good song.
I'm in no hurry. Sometimes I'll carry an idea around with me for
a year, not knowing what I'm trying to say, chewing on a line here
and there, sure that the song itself will tell me what it means as
it grows in my mind. Songs don't lie.

You can ride on that high for days, the idea emerging from the
music you hear deep within. You may have to strain to listen for
it, pulling it toward your consciousness like a distant radio sta-

tion through the static, trying not to get impatient and make it something more predictable when you can't tune it in as well as you want. I close my eyes and let it fill my heart.

Playing the music inside you. That's what a musician is.

What I am.

# EPILOGUE

*T*here's *a lot of going back, coming back.*

*Labor Day in Littlefield, and everybody is out for the annual Denim festival, held under a miles-long Texas blue sky with the heat shimmering waves in the distance.*

*The bus pulls up alongside the Lion's Club Youth Center for a Shipley family reunion. Momma ushers me through the whirl of family, second cousins and nieces and nephews and even Uncle Elvis, who I used to buy those cigarettes for. In the hall where I first played on stage with my brother Tommy, singing Hank Snow songs and scared to death, I stand in the room and watch the new crop of kids play out their games on that same stage, chasing each other around in circles, starting their growing up.*

*My own growing has taken me a stone's throw over to the Ag Community Center field along Hall Avenue, where, later tonight, surrounded by a sea of lawn chairs and fire-breathing bar-b-q cook-off tanks, myself*

379

*and Jessi, Tommy, and John and June Cash will take the stage. Like I said: Family.*

*Momma moves on and off the bus, introducing me to people I haven't seen in years and years. She's Momma, and she has a right to be proud today. We've come a long way from the outskirts of Littlefield. There's a constant parade of blood and not-so-bloody relatives, friends I can barely remember, and faces that seem oddly familiar, carved by time's experience and the wisdom that comes with life's living. Kind of like my own reflection, when I look in the mirror.*

*I've been doing that a lot the past couple of years, working on this book. Sometimes it's like trying to walk in my own footsteps. When I played a show recently at the Surf Ballroom in Clear Lake, the first time I'd been back since that fateful night in 1959, making my peace with the spot where I last saw Buddy sitting, hot dog in hand, laughing, the me then mingled with the me now until I couldn't tell where one started and the other left off. Probably there's no clear line, which is how your story becomes told.*

*The truth is, I've had it luckier than most. I'm comfortable with who I am, and I know my own limits, even though some of them I had to learn the hard way. I ain't got a thing to be bitter about.*

*Maybe I purposely set it up that way, so I wouldn't get disappointed. I didn't have any goals. I think that's a dangerous thing, if you take aim and achieve it. Once you get to your destination, it's over. Done did everything that needs done. I didn't want to be king of the world. Things just kept popping up. What did I have the right to expect? Anything past the cotton patch was free, gratis.*

*I never thought it would last. Not for so many years. You know where I'm good? Coming down the other side. I've been real good at that, because I always knew it was there.*

*Every once in a while I get a longing look toward town, at the me I used to be. I'd like to get crazy but I know I can't do that again. I gave my word to Jessi and Shooter, and myself. No more.*

*Will Campbell says if you love somebody just because they're good, well, that's not love. I don't know if I'm right or wrong, but I do what's*

*right for me. I didn't have much of a choice. There's always going to be a
yahoo like me over here, that can't get it. That's got to do it his own way.*

*Live and learn. Die and forget it all.*

*"I'm looking for my youth," I tell the press conference over at the Cres-
cent Motel, "but she's gone."*

*Actually, though it's a good line and gets a laugh, it's not exactly true.
She's here. Momma sits on the stage, right on the drum riser, clapping her
hands and watching her family. Tommy comes on; it's his first time playing Littlefield, oddly enough, and he's excited. "I'm going to stand here
and beller, and I hope you like what you hear," he tells the crowd, and
when he sings a song about "Those Three Brothers of Mine," he calls me
and Momma and Bo and James D. up on the stage for a family portrait.
Somewhere above, I know my dad is watching, feeling Texas-proud.*

*It's an Event, for sure. John strides out to sing with me, and I think
of the curve at Bula, where his big voice is probably carrying right now,
and how his song has carried in my life for over forty years. Jessi moves
behind the white piano for her set, and when she gets to our duet on "Deep
in the West," I hold her hand and harmonize with her, looking out over
the town, caught in the setting sun with the infinite Lone Star night
waiting in the wings, and remember when Heaven seemed so far away.*

*In the morning, I'll take a walk through Lubbock and pay my respects
at the statue they built for Buddy. Then I'll say my good-byes and get
back on the bus, heading toward tomorrow.*

# WAYLON JENNINGS AND JESSI COLTER: A SELECTED DISCOGRAPHY

The following is a chronological overview of the recorded works of Waylon Jennings and Jessi Colter. For a complete listing, John L. Smith has spent many years compiling a thorough book-length discography—published by Greenwood Press of Westport, Connecticut, and London—that includes session dates, recording studios and musicians, all available alternate versions and releases, chart positions, and the ephemeral minutiae of a lifetime lived in song. Our appreciations to John for his attention to detail and investigative zeal, and his invaluable dedication to the matrix number of preserved sound.

Song titles are listed in italics, while albums—both records and compact discs—are in boldface. Approximate release dates are given; as most of Waylon's singles were concurrently released on albums, we have not included separate singles, except for the early, pre-album years. Repackagings are not covered, except where a "Greatest Hits" might prove an introduction to Waylon's body—and mind and soul—of work, and an essential soundtrack to this autobiography.

BRUNSWICK BR 9-55130 *Jole Blon* / *When Sin Stops* (3-59)
Waylon's first release, recorded Sept. 10, 1958, at Norman Petty's studios in Clovis, New Mexico, produced by Buddy Holly.
TREND 102 *Another Blue Day* / *Never Again* (1961)

TREND 106 *My Baby Walks All Over Me / The Stage* (4-63)
A&M 722 *Love Denied / Rave On* (4-64)
A&M 739 *Four Strong Winds / Just to Satisfy You* (8-64)
A&M 753 *Sing the Girls a Song Bill / The Race Is On* (10-64)

SOUND LTD 1001 **Waylon Jennings at JD's** (12-64)

| Side 1 | Side 2 |
|--------|--------|
| *Crying* | *Dream Baby* |
| *Sally Was a Good Old Girl* | *It's So Easy* |
| *Burning Memories* | *Lorena* (Paul Foster) |
| *Big Mamou* | *Love's Gonna Live Here* |
| *Money* (Jerry Gropp) | *Abilene* (Paul Foster) |
| *Don't Think Twice* | *White Lightning* |

A&M 762 *I Don't Believe You / The Real House of the Rising Sun* (1965)
The A&M masters were eventually collected onto an album released in March 1970, entitled **Don't Think Twice**. (See separate listing.)

RCA LPM/S-3523 **Folk-Country** (3-66)

| Side 1 | Side 2 |
|--------|--------|
| *Another Bridge to Burn* | *Just for You* |
| *Stop the World* | *Now Everybody Knows* |
| *Cindy of New Orleans* | *That's the Chance I'll Have to Take* |
| *Look into My Teardrops* | *What Makes a Man Wander* |
| *Down Came the World* | *I'm a Man of Constant Sorrow* |
| *I Don't Mind* | *What's Left of Me* |

RCA LPM/S-3620 **Leavin' Town** (10-66)

| Side 1 | Side 2 |
|--------|--------|
| *Leavin' Town* | *You're Gonna Wonder About Me* |
| *Time to Bum Again* | *(That's What You Get) for Lovin' Me* |
| *If You Really Want Me to I'll Go* | *Anita, You're Dreaming* |
| *Baby, Don't Be Looking in My Mind* | *Doesn't Anybody Know My Name* |
| *But That's Alright* | *Falling for You* |
| *Time Will Tell the Story* | *I Wonder Just Where I Went Wrong* |

RCA LPM/S-3736 **Nashville Rebel** (12-66)

| Side 1 | Side 2 |
|--------|--------|
| *Silver Ribbons* | *Norwegian Wood* |
| *Nashville Bum* | *Hoodlum* (instr.) |
| *Green River* | *Spanish Penthouse* (instr.) |

## SELECTED DISCOGRAPHY

| | |
|---|---|
| *Nashville Rebel* | *Lang's Theme* (instr.) |
| *I'm a Long Way from Home* | *Rush Street Blues* (instr.) |
| *Tennessee* | *Lang's Mansion* (instr.) |

The soundtrack album from the American International film starring Waylon. *Norwegian Wood* was not used in the film.

### RCA LPM/S-3660 **Waylon Sings Ol' Harlan** (3-67)

| Side 1 | Side 2 |
|---|---|
| *She Called Me Baby* | *Beautiful Annabel Lee* |
| *Sunset and Vine* | *Heartaches by the Number* |
| *Woman, Let Me Sing You a Song* | *Tiger by the Tail* |
| *The Everglades* | *Heartaches for a Dime* |
| *She's Gone, Gone, Gone* | *Foolin' 'Round* |
| *Busted* | *In This Very Same Room* |

### RCA LPM/S-3825 **Love of the Common People** (8-67)

| Side 1 | Side 2 |
|---|---|
| *Money Cannot Make the Man* | *Ruby, Don't Take Your Love to Town* |
| *Young Widow Brown* | *The Road* |
| *You've Got to Hide Your Love Away* | *If the Shoe Fits* |
| | *Don't Waste Your Time* |
| *Love of the Common People* | *Taos, New Mexico* |
| *I Tremble for You* | *Two Streaks of Steel* |
| *Destiny's Child* | |

### RCA CAL/S-2183 **The One and Only** (11-67)

| Side 1 | Side 2 |
|---|---|
| *Yes, Virginia* | *Born to Love You* |
| *Dream Baby* | *Down Came the World* |
| *You Beat All I Ever Saw* | *The Dark Side of Fame* |
| *She Loves Me* | *John's Back in Town* |
| *It's All Over Now* | *Listen, They're Playing My Song* |

### RCA LPM/S-3918 **Hangin' On** (2-68)

| Side 1 | Side 2 |
|---|---|
| *Hangin' On* | *Gentle on My Mind* |
| *Julie* | *Right Before My Eyes* |
| *The Crowd* | *Lock, Stock and Teardrops* |
| *Let Me Talk to You* | *I Fall in Love So Easily* |
| *Woman, Don't You Ever Laugh at Me* | *Looking at a Heart That Needs a Home* |
| *The Chokin' Kind* | *How Long Have You Been There* |

RCA LPM/S-4023 **Only the Greatest** (7-68)

Side 1

*Only Daddy That'll Walk the Line*
*California Sunshine*
*Weakness in a Man*
*Sorrow (Breaks a Good Man*
   *Down)*
*Christina*
*Such a Waste of Love*

Side 2

*Walk on Out of My Mind*
*Kentucky Woman*
*Long Gone*
*You'll Think of Me*
*Wave Goodbye to Me*
*Too Far Gone*

RCA LSP-4085 **Jewels** (12-68)

Side 1

*New York City, R.F.D.*
*Today I Started Loving You Again*
*Folsom Prison Blues*
*If You Were Mine to Lose*
*See You Around (on Your Way*
   *Down)*
*Six Strings Away*

Side 2

*Yours Love*
*How Much Rain Can One Man Stand*
*Mental Revenge*
*I'm Doing This for You*
*You Love the Ground I Walk On*
*My Ramona*

RCA LSP-4137 **Just to Satisfy You** (3-69)

Side 1

*Lonely Weekends*
*Sing the Blues to Daddy*
   *(w/Bobby Bare)*
*Change My Mind*
*Farewell Party*
*Rings of Gold* (w/Anita Carter)
*Alone*

Side 2

*Just to Satisfy You*
*I Lost Me*
*I've Been Needing Someone Like You*
*For the Kids*
*I Got You* (w/Anita Carter)
*Straighten My Mind*

RCA LSP-4180 **Country-Folk** (w/The Kimberlys) (8-69)

Side 1

*MacArthur Park*
*These New Changing Times*
*Come Stay with Me*
*Cindy, Oh Cindy*
*Games People Play*

Side 2

*Mary Ann Regrets*
*Let Me Tell You My Mind*
*Drivin' Nails in the Wall*
*Long Way Back Home*
*But You Know I Love You*
*A World of Our Own*

RCA LSP-4260 **Waylon** (1-70)

Side 1

*Brown Eyed Handsome Man*

Side 2

*Yellow Haired Woman*

## SELECTED DISCOGRAPHY

| | |
|---|---|
| *Just Across the Way* | *Where Love Has Died* |
| *Don't Play the Game* | *All of Me Belongs to You* |
| *Shutting Out the Light* | (w/Anita Carter) |
| *I May Never Pass This Way Again* | *Yes, Virginia* |
| *The Thirty Third of August* | *This Time Tomorrow (I'll Be Gone)* |

*Yes, Virginia* is a different version than used on **The One and Only.**

### A&M SP-4238 **Don't Think Twice** (3-70)

| Side 1 | Side 2 |
|---|---|
| *Don't Think Twice, It's Alright* | *Just to Satisfy You* |
| *River Boy* | *Kisses Sweeter than Wine* |
| *Twelfth of Never* | *Unchained Melody* |
| *The Race Is On* | *I Don't Believe You* |
| *Stepping Stone* | *Four Strong Winds* |
| *The Real House of the Rising Sun* | |

### RCA LSP-4333 **A Country Star Is Born** (Jessi Colter) (5-70)

| Side 1 | Side 2 |
|---|---|
| *Too Many Rivers* | *If She's Where You Like Living* |
| *Cry Softly* | *Healing Hands of Time* |
| *I Ain't the One* | *That's the Chance I'll Have to Take* |
| *It's Not Easy* | *Don't Let Him Go* |
| *He Called Me Baby* | *It's All Over Now* |
| *Why You Been Gone So Long* | |

Waylon produced this album with Chet Atkins and Danny Davis, and appears on guitar and vocal harmony throughout.

### RCA LSP-4341 **The Best of Waylon Jennings** (6-70)

| Side 1 | Side 2 |
|---|---|
| *The Days of Sand and Shovels* | *Only Daddy That'll Walk the Line* |
| *MacArthur Park* | *Just to Satisfy You* |
| (w/The Kimberlys) | *I Got You* (w/Anita Carter) |
| *Delia's Gone* | *Something's Wrong in California* |
| *Walk On Out of My Mind* | *Ruby, Don't Take Your Love to Town* |
| *Anita, You're Dreaming* | |

### UNITED ARTISTS UAS-5213 **Ned Kelly** (7-70)

The soundtrack album for the film about the famous Australian outlaw starring Mick Jagger. Waylon does *Ned Kelly, Shadow of the Gallows, Ranchin' in the Evenin', Blame It on the Kellys,* and *Pleasures of a Sunday Afternoon.*

RCA LSP-4418 **Singer of Sad Songs** (11-70)

| Side 1 | Side 2 |
| --- | --- |
| *Singer of Sad Songs* | *Honky Tonk Woman* |
| *Sick and Tired* | *She Comes Running* |
| *Time Between Bottles of Wine* | *If I Were a Carpenter* |
| *Must You Throw Dirt in My Face* | *Donna on My Mind* |
| *No Regrets* | *Rock, Salt and Nails* |
| *Ragged but Right* | (w/Lee Hazlewood) |

RCA LSP-4487 **The Taker / Tulsa** (2-71)

| Side 1 | Side 2 |
| --- | --- |
| *The Taker* | *Tulsa* |
| *You'll Look for Me* | *Casey's Last Ride* |
| *Mississippi Woman* | *A Legend in My Time* |
| *Lovin' Her Was Easier* | *Sunday Morning Coming Down* |
| *Six White Horses* | *Grey Eyes You Know* |

RCA LSP-4567 **Cedartown, Georgia** (8-71)

| Side 1 | Side 2 |
| --- | --- |
| *Cedartown, Georgia* | *Bridge Over Troubled Waters* |
| *Big D* | (w/Jessi) |
| *The House Song* | *It's All Over Now* |
| *Tomorrow Night in Baltimore* | *I'm Gonna Leave* |
| *Pickin' White Gold* | *I've Got Eyes for You* |
| | *Let Me Stay Awhile* |

*It's All Over Now* is different than the master used on **The One and Only**.

RCA LSP-4647 **Good Hearted Woman** (2-72)

| Side 1 | Side 2 |
| --- | --- |
| *Good Hearted Woman* | *Do No Good Woman* |
| *The Same Old Lover Man* | *Unsatisfied* |
| *One of My Bad Habits* | *I Knew You'd Be Leaving* |
| *Willie and Laura Mae Jones* | *Sweet Dream Woman* |
| *It Should Be Easier Now* | *To Beat the Devil* |

RCA LSP-4751 **Ladies Love Outlaws** (9-72)

| Side 1 | Side 2 |
| --- | --- |
| *Ladies Love Outlaws* | *Delta Dawn* |
| *Never Been to Spain* | *Frisco Depot* |
| *Sure Didn't Take Him Long* | *Thanks* |
| *Crazy Arms* | *I Think It's Time She Learned* |
| *Revelation* | *Under Your Spell Again* (w/Jessi) |

## SELECTED DISCOGRAPHY

### RCA LSP-4854 **Lonesome, On'ry and Mean** (3-73)

| Side 1 | Side 2 |
|---|---|
| *Lonesome, On'ry and Mean* | *You Can Have Her* |
| *Freedom to Stay* | *Pretend I Never Happened* |
| *Lay It Down* | *San Francisco Mabel Joy* |
| *Gone to Denver* | *Sandy Sends Her Best* |
| *Good Time Charlie's Got the Blues* | *Me and Bobby McGee* |

### RCA APL1-0240 **Honky Tonk Heroes** (7-73)

| Side 1 | Side 2 |
|---|---|
| *Honky Tonk Heroes* | *You Ask Me To* |
| *Old Five and Dimers* | *Ride Me Down Easy* |
| *Willie the Wandering Gypsy* | *Ain't No God in Mexico* |
| *Low Down Freedom* | *Black Rose* |
| *Omaha* | *We Had It All* |

### RCA APL1-0539 **This Time** (4-74)

| Side 1 | Side 2 |
|---|---|
| *This Time* | *It's Not Supposed to Be That Way* |
| *Louisiana Woman* | *Slow Movin' Outlaw* |
| *Pick Up the Tempo* | *Mona* |
| *Slow Rollin' Low* | *Walkin'* |
| *Heaven or Hell* (w/Willie) | *If You Could Touch Her at All* |

### RCA APL1-0734 **The Ramblin' Man** (9-74)

| Side 1 | Side 2 |
|---|---|
| *I'm a Ramblin' Man* | *The Hunger* |
| *Rainy Day Woman* | *I Can't Keep My Hands Off of You* |
| *Cloudy Days* | *Memories of You and I* |
| *Midnight Rider* | *It'll Be Her* |
| *Oklahoma Sunshine* | *Amanda* |

### RCA APL1-1062 **Dreaming My Dreams** (6-75)

| Side 1 | Side 2 |
|---|---|
| *Are You Sure Hank Done It This Way* | *Let's All Help the Cowboys Sing* |
| *Waymore's Blues* | *the Blues* |
| *I Recall a Gypsy Queen* | *The Door Is Always Open* |
| *High Time (You Quit Your* | *She's Looking Good* |
| *Lowdown Ways)* | *Dreaming My Dreams* |
| *I've Been a Long Time Leaving* | *Bob Wills Is Still the King* (live) |

*Let's All Help the Cowboys Sing the Blues* is a different version than on the single release PB-10142.

CAPITOL ST-11363 **I'm Jessi Colter** (1975)

| Side 1 | Side 2 |
|---|---|
| *Is There Anyway (You'd Stay Forever)* | *I'm Not Lisa* |
| *I Hear a Song* | *For the First Time* |
| *Come On In* | *Who Walks Through Your* |
| *You Ain't Never Been Loved (Like I'm* | *Memory (Billie Jo)* |
| *Gonna Love You)* | *What's Happened to Blue Eyes* |
| *Love's the Only Chain* | *Storms Never Last* |

Waylon produced this album with Ken Mansfield playing guitar and providing vocal harmony.

RCA APL1-1321 **Wanted: The Outlaws** (1-76)

| Side 1 | Side 2 |
|---|---|
| *My Heroes Have Always Been Cowboys* | *Good Hearted Woman* |
| *Honky Tonk Heroes* | *(w/Willie)* |
| *I'm Looking for Blue Eyes* (Jessi) | *Heaven or Hell* (w/Willie) |
| *You Mean to Say* (Jessi) | *Me and Paul* (Willie) |
| *Suspicious Minds* (w/Jessi) | *Yesterday's Wine* (Willie) |
| | *T for Texas* (Tompall) |
| | *Put Another Log on the Fire* (Tompall) |

*Honky Tonk Heroes* is different from the cut first used on the **Honky Tonk Heroes** album.

RCA APL1-1520 **Mackintosh and T.J.** (3-76)

| Side 1 | Side 2 |
|---|---|
| *All Around Cowboy* | *Shopping* (instr.) |
| *Back in the Saddle Again* (instr.) | *(Stay All Night) Stay a Little* |
| *Ride Me Down Easy* | *Longer* (Willie) |
| *Gardenia Waltz* | *Crazy Arms* (instr.) |
| (instr. w/Johnny Gimble) | *All Around Cowboy* |
| *Bob Wills Is Still the King* | |

This is the soundtrack from the motion picture starring Roy Rogers. The cuts of *Ride Me Down Easy* and *Bob Wills Is Still the King* are different than previously released.

RCA APL1-1816 **Are You Ready for the Country?** (6-76)

| Side 1 | Side 2 |
|---|---|
| *Are You Ready for the Country* | *MacArthur Park (Revisited)* |
| *Them Old Love Songs* | *I'll Go Back to Her* |
| *So Good Woman* | *A Couple More Years* |
| *Jack a Diamonds* | *Old Friend* |
| *Can't You See* | *Precious Memories* |

**RCA APL1-1108 Waylon—Live** (12-76)

| Side 1 | Side 2 |
|---|---|
| *T for Texas* | *Pick Up the Tempo* |
| *Rainy Day Woman* | *Good Hearted Woman* |
| *Me and Paul* | *House of the Rising Sun* |
| *The Last Letter* | *Me and Bobby McGee* |
| *I'm a Ramblin' Man* | *This Time* |
| *Bob Wills Is Still the King* | |

Though originally planned as a two-record set, only a single album was released. The additional tracks were to be *Lovin' Her Was Easier, Look into My Teardrops, Lonesome, On'ry and Mean, Freedom to Stay, Big Ball in Cowtown, The Taker, Mississippi Woman, Mona, Never Been to Spain,* and *Are You Sure Hank Done It This Way.*

**CAPITOL ST-11477 Jessi** (1976)

| Side 1 | Side 2 |
|---|---|
| *The Hand That Rocks the Cradle* | *Without You* |
| *One Woman Man* | *Darlin' It's You* |
| *It's Morning (and I Still Love You)* | *Would You Walk with Me (to* |
| *Rounder* | *the Lilies)* |
| *Here I Am* | *I See Your Face (in the Morning's* |
| | *Window)* |

Waylon produced this album with Ken Mansfield, and added guitar and background vocals.

**CAPITOL ST-11543 Diamonds in the Rough** (Jessi) (1976)

| Side 1 | Side 2 |
|---|---|
| *Diamond in the Rough* | *Oh Will (Who Made It Rain Last* |
| *Get Back* | *Night)* |
| *Would You Leave Me Now* | *I Thought I Heard You Calling My* |
| *Hey Jude* | *Name* |
| | *Ain't No Way* |
| | *You Hung the Moon (Didn't You* |
| | *Waylon)* |
| | *A Woman's Heart (Is a Handy Place* |
| | *to Be)* |
| | *Oh Will* (reprise) |

Waylon produced this album with Ken Mansfield playing guitar and singing background vocals.

### RCA APL1-2317 Ol' Waylon (4-77)

| Side 1 | Side 2 |
|---|---|
| *Luckenbach, Texas* (w/Willie) | *Medley of Elvis Hits:* |
| *If You See Me Getting Smaller* | *That's All Right* |
| *Lucille* | *My Baby Left Me* |
| *Sweet Caroline* | *Till I Gain Control Again* |
| *I Think I'm Gonna Kill Myself* | *Brand New Goodbye Song* |
| *Belle of the Ball* | *Satin Sheets* |
| | *This Is Getting Funny* |

### CAPITOL ST-11583 Mirriam (Jessi) (1977)

| Side 1 | Side 2 |
|---|---|
| *For Mama* | *There Ain't No Rain* |
| *Put Your Arms Around Me* | *God, I Love You* |
| *I Belong to Him* | *Let It Go* |
| *God, If I Could Only Write* | *Master, Master* |
| *Your Love Song* | *New Wine* |
| *Consider Me* | |

### RCA AFL1-2686 Waylon and Willie (1-78)

| Side 1 | Side 2 |
|---|---|
| *Mammas Don't Let Your Babies* | *I Can Get Off on You* |
| *Grow Up to Be Cowboys* | *Don't Cuss the Fiddle* |
| *The Year 2003 Minus 25* | *Gold Dust Woman* |
| *Pick Up the Tempo* | *A Couple More Years* (Willie) |
| *If You Could Touch Her at All* | *The Wurlitzer Prize* |
| (Willie) | |
| *Lookin' for a Feelin'* | |
| *It's Not Supposed to Be That Way* | |
| (Willie) | |

A limited number of this album was pressed in gold vinyl.

### CBS KC-35313 I Would Like to See You Again (Johnny Cash) (7-78)
Waylon/Cash duet on *There Ain't No Good Chain Gang* and *I Wish I Was Crazy Again.*

### CBS KC-35314 Bare (Bobby Bare) (1978)
Waylon sings a verse of *Greasy Grit Gravy.*

### CBS KC-35319 Bold and New (Earl Scruggs Revue) (1978)
Waylon sings on *The Cabin.*

# SELECTED DISCOGRAPHY

A&M SP-6004 **White Mansions** (1978)

A Civil War concept album with Waylon singing *Dixie, Hold On; The Union Mare and the Confederate Grey; The Southland's Bleeding; They Laid Waste to Our Land;* and *Dixie, Now You're Done.*

RCA AFL1-2979 **I've Always Been Crazy** (9-78)

| Side 1 | Side 2 |
|---|---|
| *I've Always Been Crazy* | *Medley of Buddy Holly Hits:* |
| *Don't You Think This Outlaw Bit's* | *Well All Right* |
| *Done Got Out of Hand* | *It's So Easy* |
| *Billy* | *Maybe Baby* |
| *A Long Time Ago* | *Peggy Sue* |
| *As the Billy World Turns* | *I Walk the Line* |
| | *Tonight the Bottle Let Me Down* |
| | *Girl I Can Tell (You're Trying to* |
| | *Work It Out)* |
| | *Whistlers and Jugglers* |

CAPITOL ST-11863 **That's the Way the Cowboy Rocks and Rolls** (Jessi) (1978)

| Side 1 | Side 2 |
|---|---|
| *Roll On* | *Hold Back the Tears* |
| *Black Haired Boy* | *Maybe You Should Have Been* |
| *I Was Kinda Crazy Then* | *Listening* |
| *That's the Way the Cowboy Rocks* | *Don't You Think I Feel It Too* |
| *and Rolls* | *Love Me Back to Sleep* |
| *My Cowboy's Last Ride* | *My Goodness* |

Waylon, adding guitars and vocals, produced this album with Richie Albright.

FIRST GENERATION FGLP-0002 **Ernest Tubb—The Legend and the Legacy** (5-79)

Waylon duets with Tubb on *You Nearly Loose Your Mind* and *When the World Has Turned You Down.*

RCA AHL1-3493 **What Goes Around Comes Around** (11-79)

| Side 1 | Side 2 |
|---|---|
| *I Ain't Living Long Like This* | *Ivory Tower* |
| *What Goes Around* | *Out Among the Stars* |
| *Another Man's Fool* | *Come with Me* |
| *I Got the Train Sittin' Waitin'* | *If You See Her* |
| *It's the World's Gone Crazy (Cotillion)* | *Old Love, New Eyes* |

EPIC E-35544 **George Jones: My Very Special Guests** (11-79)
Waylon/Jones duet on *Night Life.*

LONE STAR L-4605 **Still Fighting Mental Health** (Don Bowman) (1979)
Waylon appears with Willie and Bowman on *Willon and Waylie, East Virginia Blues,* and *Hot Blooded Woman.*

RCA AHL1-3602 **Music Man** (5-80)

| Side 1 | Side 2 |
|---|---|
| *Clyde* | *Sweet Music Man* |
| *It's Alright* | *Storms Never Last* (w/Jessi) |
| *Theme from Dukes of Hazzard* | *He Went to Paris* |
| *Nashville Wimmin* | *What About You* |
| *Do It Again* | *Waltz Across Texas* |

CAPITOL ST-12185 **Ridin' Shotgun** (Jessi) (1981)

| Side 1 | Side 2 |
|---|---|
| *Ridin' Shotgun (Honkin')* | *Ain't Makin' No Headlines (Here* |
| *Holdin' On* | *Without You)* |
| *Nobody Else Like You* | *Jennifer (Fly My Baby)* |
| *Somewhere Along the Way* | *Hard Times and Sno-Cone* |
| *Wings of My Victory* | *A Fallen Star* |
| | *Ridin' Shotgun (Tonkin')* |

Waylon produced this album with Randy Scruggs and provides guitar and background vocals.

RCA AAL1-3931 **Leather and Lace** (1-82)

| Side 1 | Side 2 |
|---|---|
| *You Never Can Tell (C'est La Vie)* | *I Believe You Can* (w/Jessi) |
| (w/Jessi) | *What's Happened to Blue Eyes* |
| *Rainy Seasons* (w/Jessi) | *Storms Never Last* (w/Jessi) |
| *I'll Be Alright* | *I Ain't the One* (w/Jessi) |
| *Wild Side of Life / It Wasn't God Who* | *You're Not the Same Sweet Baby* |
| *Made Honky Tonk Angels* (w/Jessi) | |
| *Pastels and Harmony* | |

RCA PD1-6344 **The Pursuit of D.B. Cooper** (1-82)
A soundtrack album from the motion picture, Waylon does two versions of *Shine*—one straight, one bluegrass style—and duets with Jessi on *You Were Never There.*

## SELECTED DISCOGRAPHY

**RCA AHL1-4247 Black on Black** (2-82)

Side 1
*Women Do Know How to Carry On*
*Honky Tonk Blues*
*Just to Satisfy You* (w/Willie)
*We Made It as Lovers*
*Shine*

Side 2
*Folsom Prison Blues*
*Gonna Write a Letter*
*May I Borrow Some Sugar from*
  *You*
*Song for the Life*
*Get Naked with Me*

**RCA AHL1-4455 WWII** (10-82)

Side 1
*Mr. Shuck and Jive* (w/Willie)
*Roman Candles*
*(Sittin' On) The Dock of the Bay*
  (w/Willie)
*The Year Clayton Delaney Died*
  (w/Willie)
*Lady in the Harbor*
*May I Borrow Some Sugar from You*

Side 2
*Last Cowboy Song*
*Heroes* (w/Willie)
*The Teddy Bear Song*
*Write Your Own Songs* (w/Willie)
*The Old Mother's Locket Trick*

**CBS FC-37951 Always on My Mind** (Willie Nelson) (1982)
Waylon guests on *A Whiter Shade of Pale.*

**RCA AHL1-4673 It's Only Rock and Roll** (3-83)

Side 1
*It's Only Rock and Roll*
*Living Legends (A Dying Breed)*
*Breakin' Down*
*Let Her Do the Walking*
*Mental Revenge*

Side 2
*Lucille (You Won't Do Your*
  *Daddy's Will)*
*Angel Eyes (Angel Eyes)*
*No Middle Ground*
*Love's Legalities*
*Medley of Hits:*
  *I'm a Ramblin' Man*
  *This Time*
  *Don't You Think This Outlaw Bit's*
    *Done Got Out of Hand*
  *Clyde*
  *Good Hearted Woman*
  *Ladies Love Outlaws*
  *Luckenbach, Texas*
  *I've Always Been Crazy*

CBS FC-38562 **Take It to the Limit** (w/Willie) (4-83)

Waylon/Willie duet on *No Love at All, Why Baby Why, Take It to the Limit, Black Jack County Chain,* and *Old Friends.*

RCA AHL1-4826 **Waylon and Company** (9-83)

| Side 1 | Side 2 |
|---|---|
| *Hold On, I'm Comin'* (w/Jerry Reed) | *I May Be Used (But Baby I Ain't Used Up)* |
| *Leave Them Boys Alone* (w/Hank Williams Jr., Ernest Tubb) | *Sight for Sore Eyes* (w/Jessi) |
| *Spanish Johnny* (w/Emmylou Harris) | *I'll Find It Where I Can* (w/James Garner) |
| *Just to Satisfy You* (w/Willie) | *The Conversation* (w/Hank Williams Jr.) |
| *So You Want to Be a Cowboy Singer* (w/Tony Joe White) | *Mason Dixon Line* (w/Mel Tillis) |

MCA-5435 **Bill Monroe and Friends** (12-83)

Waylon and Monroe duet on *With Body and Soul.*

RCA AHL1-5017 **Never Could Toe the Mark** (6-84)

| Side 1 | Side 2 |
|---|---|
| *Never Could Toe the Mark* | *Sittin' Me Up* |
| *Talk Good Boogie* | *The Gemini Song* |
| *People Up in Texas* | *Where Would I Be (Without You)* |
| *Sparkling Brown Eyes* | *Whatever Gets You Through the Night* |
| *If She'll Leave Her Mama* | *The Entertainer* |

TRIAD TELP-1001 **Rock and Roll Lullaby** (Jessi) (6-84)

| Side 1 | Side 2 |
|---|---|
| *Rock and Roll Lullaby* | *I'm Going by Daybreak* |
| *Wild and Blue* | *Partners After All* |
| *Stormy Weather* | *Easy Street* |
| *I Want to Be with You* | *I Can't Stop Loving You* |
| *I Forgot More Than You'll Ever Know* | *Tiger* |

Waylon: guitar, background vocals.

CBS FC-40056 **Highwayman** (5-85)

Waylon appears on *Highwayman, The Last Cowboy Song, Big River, Desperadoes Waiting for a Train, Welfare Line* (all w/Cash, Willie, Kris Kristofferson), and *Against the Wind* (w/Cash, Willie).

## SELECTED DISCOGRAPHY

### RCA AHL1-5428 **Turn the Page** (7-85)

| Side 1 | Side 2 |
|---|---|
| *The Devil's on the Loose* | *Rhiannon* |
| *You Showed Me Somethin' About Lovin' (I Never Knew Was)* | *Drinking and Dreaming* |
| | *As Far as the Eye Can See* |
| *Good Morning John* | *Turn the Page* |
| *The Broken Promise Land* | *Those Kind of Memories* |
| *Don't Bring It Around Anymore* | |

### RCA CBL1-5475 **Follow That Bird** (7-85)

The soundtrack album for the Warner Brothers film starring the Sesame Street characters, Waylon has a part in the movie and sings *Ain't No Road Too Long* with Big Bird, The Count, Grover, Cookie Monster, Gordon, and Olivia.

### RCA AHL1-7184 **Sweet Mother Texas** (2-86)

| Side 1 | Side 2 |
|---|---|
| *I'm on Fire* | *Be Careful Who You Love* (w/Cash) |
| *Me and Them Brothers of Mine* | *Sweet Mother Texas* |
| *I Take My Comfort in You* | *Living Legend* |
| *Looking for Suzanne* | *Hanging On* |

### MCA-5688 **Will the Wolf Survive?** (3-86)

| Side 1 | Side 2 |
|---|---|
| *Will the Wolf Survive* | *What You'll Do When I'm Gone* |
| *They Ain't Got 'Em All* | *Suddenly Single* |
| *Working Without a Net* | *The Shadow of Your Distant Friend* |
| *Where Does Love Go* | *I've Got Me a Woman* |
| *That Dog Won't Hunt* | *The Devil's Right Hand* |

### CBS FC-40347 **Heroes** (w/Johnny Cash) (5-86)

| Side 1 | Side 2 |
|---|---|
| *Folks Out on the Road* | *Even Cowgirls Get the Blues* |
| *I'm Never Gonna Roam Again* | *Love Is the Way* |
| *American by Birth* | *Ballad of Forty Dollars* |
| *Field of Diamonds* | *I Will Always Love You (in My Own Crazy Way)* |
| *Heroes* | *One Too Many Mornings* |

### MCA 5911 **Hangin' Tough** (1-87)

| Side 1 | Side 2 |
|---|---|
| *Baker Street* | *Fallin' Out* |
| *I Can't Help the Way I Don't Feel About You* | *Deep in the West* |
| | *Between Fathers and Sons* |

*Rose in Paradise*
*Crying Don't Even Come Close*
*Chevy Van*

*The Crown Prince*
*Defying Gravity (Executioner's Song)*

### MCA 42038 **A Man Called Hoss** (10-87)

Side 1
*"Prologue"*
*"Chapter One . . . Childhood"*
*Littlefield*
*"Chapter Two . . . Texas"*
*You'll Never Take the Texas Out*
*of Me*
*"Chapter Three . . . First Love"*
*You Went Out with Rock 'n' Roll*
*"Chapter Four . . . Lost Love"*
*A Love Song (I Can't Sing Anymore)*
*"Chapter Five . . . Nashville"*
*If Ole Hank Could Only See Me Now*

Side 2
*"Chapter Six . . . Crazies"*
*Rough and Rowdy Days*
*"Chapter Seven . . . Drugs"*
*I'm Living Proof (There's Life*
*After You)*
*"Chapter Eight . . . Jessi"*
*You Deserve the Stars in My Crown*
*"Chapter Nine . . . Reflections"*
*Turn It All Around*
*"Chapter Ten . . . The Beginning"*
*Where Do We Go from Here*

### MCA 42222 **Full Circle** (10-88)

Side 1
*Trouble Man*
*Grapes on the View*
*Which Way Do I Go (Now That I'm*
*Gone)*
*Yoyos, Bozos, Bimbos and Heroes*
*It Goes with the Territory*

Side 2
*How Much Is It Worth to Live in L.A.*
*Hey Willie*
*You Put the Soul in the Song*
*G.I. Joe*
*Woman I Hate It*

### CBS C-45240 **Highwayman 2** (w/Cash, Willie, and Kris) (2-90)

*Silver Stallion*
*Born and Raised in Black and White*
*Two Stories Wide*
*We're All in Your Corner*
*Tonight*
*American Remains*

*Anthem '84*
*Angels Love Bad Men*
*Songs That Make a Difference*
*Living Legends*
*Texas* (Willie)

### EPIC EK-46104 **The Eagle** (6-90)

*Workin' Cheap*
*What Bothers Me Most*
*The Eagle*
*Her Man*
*Wrong*

*Where Corn Don't Grow*
*Reno and Me*
*Too Close to Call*
*Waking Up with You*
*Old Church Hymns*

## SELECTED DISCOGRAPHY

**EPIC EK-47462 Clean Shirt** (6-91)

*If I Can Find a Clean Shirt*
*I Could Write a Book About You*
*Old Age and Treachery*
*Two Old Sidewinders*
*Tryin' to Outrun the Wind*

*The Good Ol' Nights*
*Guitars That Won't Stay in Tune*
*Makin's of a Song*
*Put Me on a Train Back to Texas*
*Rocks from Rolling Stones*

**EPIC EK-48982 Too Dumb for New York City Too Ugly for L.A.** (8-92)

*Just Talkin'*
*Silent Partners*
*Didn't We Shine*
*Too Dumb for New York City*
*Armed and Dangerous*

*Heartaches Older Than You*
*Hank Williams Syndrome*
*A Lot of Good*
*I've Got My Faults*
*Smokey on Your Front Door*

**WJ 1001 Ol' Waylon Sings Ol' Hank** (1992)

Side 1
*Jambalaya*
*Half as Much*
*I'm So Lonesome I Could Cry*
*Blues Come Around*
*Why Should We Try Anymore*
*Be Careful of Stones That You Throw*

Side 2
*I Won't Be Home No More*
*Mansion on the Hill*
*Hey Good Lookin'*
*Cold Cold Heart*
*Honky Tonkin'*

Available in cassette only.

**ODE 2 KIDS RCE-74041-70602 Cowboys, Sisters, Rascals and Dirt** (5-93)

*I'm Little*
*I Just Can't Wait*
*When I Get Big*
*All of My Sisters Are Girls*
*A Bad Day*
*Dirt*

*Cowboy Movies*
*If I Could Only Fly*
*Useless*
*Small Packages*
*Shooter's Theme*

**RCA 66299-2 Only Daddy That'll Walk the Line—The RCA Years** (1993)

Disc 1
*Stop the World (and Let Me Off)*
*Nashville Bum*
*Nashville Rebel*
*Green River*
*Love of the Common People*
*Walk on Out of My Mind*
*Only Daddy That'll Walk the Line*
*Just to Satisfy You*

Disc 2
*Amanda*
*Rainy Day Woman*
*Are You Sure Hank Done It This Way*
*Dreaming My Dreams with You*
*Waymore's Blues*
*"T" for Texas*
*Bob Wills Is Still the King*
*Are You Ready for the Country*

*Willie and Laura Mae Jones*
*Six White Horses*
*The Taker*
*Lovin' Her Was Easier*
*Good Hearted Woman*
*Black Rose*
*Lonesome, On'ry and Mean*
*Honky Tonk Heroes*
*You Asked Me To*
*It's Not Supposed to Be That Way*
*This Time*
*I'm a Ramblin' Man*

*Jack of Diamonds*
*Luckenbach, Texas*
*Don't You Think This Outlaw Bit's Done Got Out of Hand*
*The Conversation*
*I Ain't Living Long Like This*
*Clyde*
*Dukes of Hazzard*
*Storms Never Last*
*Shine*
*Lucille (You Won't Do Your Daddy's Will)*
*Never Could Toe the Mark*
*Looking for Suzanne*

Currently the best available retrospective on Waylon's RCA career.

## RCA RMJ66409-2 **Waymore's Blues (Part II)** (9-94)

*Endangered Species*
*Waymore's Blues (Part II)*
*This Train (Russell's Song)*
*Wild Ones*
*No Good for Me*

*Old Timer (The Song)*
*Up in Arkansas*
*Nobody Knows*
*Come Back and See Me*
*You Don't Mess Around with Me*

## LIBERTY C2-28091 **The Road Goes on Forever** (The Highwaymen) (4-95)

*The Devil's Right Hand*
*It Is What It Is*
*Waiting for a Long Time*
*Everyone Gets a Little Crazy Now*
*The End of Understanding* (Willie)
*I Do Believe* (Waylon)

*Live Forever*
*The Road Goes on Forever*
*True Love Travels on a Gravel Road*
*Death and Hell* (Cash)
*Here Comes the Rainbow Again* (Kris)

## JUSTICE 2101-2 **Right for the Time** (5-96)

*Waymore's Blues (Part III)*
*Cactus Texas*
*The Most Sensible Thing*
*The Boxer*
*Hittin' the Bottle Again*
*Wastin' Time*
*Kissing You Goodbye*

*Carnival Song*
*Out of Jail*
*Lines*
*Deep in the West*
*Right for the Time*
*Living Legends (Part II)*

# ACKNOWLEDGMENTS

No man speaks with his own voice only. Many friends and family shared their reminiscences, anecdotes, and camaraderie, providing an invaluable point of view. Sometimes I might have remembered it a whole different way, and that's what makes this an auto-biography. Like I said, I like to drive.

Among those who lent their time and memories were Chet Atkins, Jack Clement, Captain Midnight, Richie Albright, Sonny Curtis, Johnny and Jo Western, Billy Jo Shaver, Hazel Smith, Dion, Bobby Bare, David Trask, Connie Smith, Jerry Moss, Don Was, June Cash, George Jones, Jerry "Jigger" Bridges, Harlan Howard, Ben Dorsey, cousin Wendell Whitfield, Aunt Frieda Dyer, brothers Tommy and James D., Littlefield's own Jimmy Stewart, and Will Campbell.

I would especially like to thank the Highwaymen:

John—bigger than life.

Willie—sings out of rhythm, lives out of rhythm.

Kris—pure inspiration.

Literary agent *provocateur* Tony Secunda saw that it was time for me to tell my tale and didn't let up till the book he'd hoped for was on its way. That he's not here to see it published is a part of every life's story, and we miss him; that it's here at all is testament to his vision, tenacity, and madcap spirit. He made it right. Mary-lou Hyatt balanced him on the left, especially as the project got underway, and Mel Parker, our editor, carried the ball over the goal line. Their encouragement was essential and appreciated.

For names, dates, facts, and faces I might never have gotten right, the enthusiasm and written works of the following authors and record collectors helped our research: Paul Hemphill, John Goldrosen, Dave Laing, Peter Guralnick, Michael Bane, R. Serge Denisoff, Chet Flippo, Bob Allen, Charlie All-Ears, Irwin Stambler and Grelun Landon, Robert Shelton, Dennis Farland and Don Larson, and Tom Clark. Back issues of *Hoedown, Country Rhythms, K-TUF Country, Country Music Review, Country Music, Billboard, Cashbox,* and the *Lamb County News-Leader* proved evocative of their time, as did the hours spent at the Lincoln Center Library of Performing Arts and the archives of the Country Music Hall of Fame.

Above and beyond the call-of-duty bronze stars to Nikki Mitchell, Leigh Grinder and the office gang, Schatzi, and Frankie. Battlefield medals to Jigger and the Waylors, past and present.

Special thanks to The Family:

Mom for making me possible.

Maureen Rafferty, who keeps my own personal Camelot (Southern Comfort) together and teaches the world what will and won't do for me.

Lenny, Stephanie, and Annalea for becoming honorary members.

My children for my grandchildren: Terry (Whey, Johnny, and Josh), Julie (Taylor), Buddy (Maybe later), Tomi (five grand dogs), Jennifer (B.J.), Deana (Ricky, Josie), and Shooter (Tinkerbell, our cat).

And all love and honor to Jessi. I do believe she has a direct line to God, which don't put me in too bad a position.

*W.J.*
*Nashville*
*Spring 1996*

P.S. Thanks to Waylon for giving his story to his sons and daughters and always remaining my hero.

*Little Miss Jessi Colter*
*(Waylon's Last Wife)*

# PERMISSIONS

# INDEX